THE US WAR AGAINST ISIS

THE US WAR AGAINST ISIS

How America and its Allies Defeated the Caliphate

Aaron Stein

I.B. TAURIS
LONDON • NEW YORK • OXFORD • NEW DELHI • SYDNEY

I.B. TAURIS
Bloomsbury Publishing Plc
50 Bedford Square, London, WC1B 3DP, UK
1385 Broadway, New York, NY 10018, USA
29 Earlsfort Terrace, Dublin 2, Ireland

BLOOMSBURY, I.B. TAURIS and the I.B. Tauris logo
are trademarks of Bloomsbury Publishing Plc

First published in Great Britain 2022

Cover design by Dani Leigh Design
Cover image © DELIL SOULEIMAN/Getty Images

A catalogue record for this book is available from the British Library.

A catalog record for this book is available from the Library of Congress.

ISBN: HB: 978-0-7556-3480-4
         PB: 978-0-7556-3479-8
         ePDF: 978-0-7556-3481-1
         eBook: 978-0-7556-3482-8

Early and Medieval Islamic World

Typeset by Integra Software Services Pvt. Ltd.
Printed and bound in Great Britain

To find out more about our authors and books visit www.bloomsbury.com
and sign up for our newsletters.

CONTENTS

INTRODUCTION: A VERY AMERICAN WAR

Two American F-15E Strike Eagles, a tennis court-sized two-seat fighter jet capable of delivering ordnance on a precise set of coordinates, often would set up in a continuous thirty to forty degree 1.5 G turn around the city of Raqqa in the Syrian Arab Republic. The cinder block buildings below, built haphazardly in a series of belts around a small and dense old city, was the home to the Islamic State (ISIS), and its network of poorly trained, but tenacious, militia members, many of whom had traveled from countries around the world to join the notional caliphate. ISIS stunned the world in 2014 after it leveraged state collapse in Syria and a long-standing network in Iraq to defeat its jihadist cousin, Al-Qaeda in Syria, then dubbed the Nusra Front. The Islamic State rampaged through western and northern Iraq to take control over a swathe of territory roughly the size of Great Britain, forcing a global response to defeat the group. The war against ISIS was always meant to be small and focused. But its repercussions have been considerable and far reaching, including helping to cause a serious rupture in Turkish-Western relations and indirectly contributing to Russia's return to the Middle East.

This book explains the war against Islamic State in Syria from the point of view of the men and women who fought it and the diplomats who sought to manage it. The prosecution of any war is complicated and fraught, with choices having to be made about how best to fight against an elusive enemy committed to withstanding the use of force. The American war in Syria was no different and its prosecution enmeshed the United States in a truly modern conflict, where US men and women fought the war from all around the world, connecting with a partner force that leveraged air power and Special Operations Forces (SOF) to wage a traditional ground campaign untraditionally. The story of war against Islamic State is one of trade offs about how to keep the American presence limited, albeit while trying to manage a recalcitrant Turkey, and ensuring that tensions with Russia did not escalate. This story is captured in this book, perhaps for the first time in print.

The Islamic State was a problem that many in the United States military were acutely aware of, as the group began to grow in strength in early 2014. The group's rapid takeover of much of Iraq catalyzed civilian leaders to contemplate armed intervention, but only if that intervention was kept limited and narrowly focused and aimed at ousting the group from territory it controlled. Internet-savvy and armed with weapons stolen from the Bashar al-Assad regime's vast stockpiles and the American-equipped Iraqi military, the group imposed upon its subjects a draconian set of laws and restrictions, enforced with the threat of death, filmed in gruesome detail for videos to be distributed in mass online. The group's establishment of a notional proto-state attracted thousands of foreigners, many of whom flew to the Republic of Turkey and then crossed the lawless border.[1] As the United States grappled with the broader humanitarian crisis of the Syrian civil war between 2011 and 2014, it was the threat of transnational terrorism that prompted American overt military action and underpinned the authorities used to legally sanction military action. For much of the war, the United States sought to limit its involvement, choosing to refrain from the commitment of ground troops in favor of clandestine support for anti-regime militias based in contested parts of northern and southern Syria, with logistical links mostly based in neighboring Turkey.

The war against ISIS was fought in a very American way. The military resources were cutting edge, but also small in number. The forces on the ground were, too, highly trained and specialized, but also thinly spread and kept to a minimum, and joined only on the ground by America's closest allies, the UK and France. The result, once the United States chose to get involved, was never in doubt. But, even in victory, the costs of war remain considerable. The American relationship with Turkey, a member of the North Atlantic Treaty Organization (NATO), is in tatters, and these small numbers of elite forces were ultimately forced from the border by a Turkish invasion, aimed at defeating America's Syrian Kurdish partner force that bore the brunt of the fighting against ISIS.[2]

Beyond the results of the ground war, the fact is that Western action in Syria contributed to Russian intervention. A clandestine, intelligence-led arming program in Syria's northwest, aimed solely at forcing Assad to capitulate and negotiate, prompted backlash from the Russian Federation and Moscow's military's direct intervention in support of its ally in Damascus.[3] The Syrian Kurds, whose fighting prowess and logistical network enabled the Western war against ISIS, were momentarily empowered, but have succumbed to a Turkish invasion at odds with American and European wishes. The Turkish invasion, however, has prompted Russian counter-measures, which oddly enough may signal a deepening Turkish-Russian relationship that further drove a wedge between Turkey and its traditional transatlantic allies. As for ISIS, it remains a loose insurgency with access to coercive rents and able to operate in sparsely populated and poorly policed Syrian villages and towns, the probability of Islamic State's ability to reorganize and regroup to carry out attacks is high, following the collapse of American-backed security structures, and the return of the Syrian regime to territory that United States had pledged to defend from external attack. An attack, as it would turn out, came from Turkey, and not from Russia, the regime, or Iran.

The story of the war against the Islamic State is often told through the group's own structures and ideology, beginning with the group's emergence from the insurgency in Iraq, to its ideological development in US-run prisons, and then its consolidation of authority in Syria and Iraq after state collapse. The American military and diplomatic side of the story has not been told, including why the

United States and its allies intervened in the way that they did, and how domestic politics and legal authorities shaped American military action, and how US actors negotiated with the Turks and Russians. A careful reading of Western action is necessary because the war was revolutionary in its prosecution, but still entailed messy politics to manage.

The United States and its allies chose to fight the group with as little of a ground footprint as possible. This approach, dubbed "by, with, and through" for the military's reliance on local actors to bear the brunt of combat, aided by precision fires and airpower on call, is a model of intervention the United States and the West more broadly will consider again in the future. This book will focus on the politics of the war, beginning with how the hesitancy to nation-build shaped how the war would be fought, guided the legal authorities that underpinned the use of force in Syria, and explain, in great detail, how the United States and its allies fought ISIS with a Kurdish militia that has prompted Turkish outreach to Russia.

The American intervention in Syria was executed in phases, focused first on cutting off the group from its logistical hubs in Turkey and ending the trans-border foreign fighter flow. Following the seizing of territory along the Turkish-Syrian border, the coalition began its march down the Euphrates River, accompanied by a push from northeastern Syria, through small towns and villages, toward the city of Raqqa. The battle plan was to assault Raqqa and ISIS-occupied Mosul in Iraq simultaneously. However, American tensions with Turkey and a reluctant and belated host of elements of the counter-ISIS coalition slowed the implementation of the plan to equip the Syrian Kurds for a close-quartered fight in a dense urban environment. The city-hopping assault hugged the Euphrates River and snaked along the main highway, both of which passed through and around Raqqa.

This march brought the United States and its allies into close proximity to Russian air and ground forces, raising the stakes of what was intended to be a small counterterrorism operation, and informing US and allied policymakers about the future of Russian operations in contested spaces in the region. As the United States fought ISIS, Russia sought to use it's military to force American political concessions and to facilitate Russia's crossing to eastern bank of the Euphrates River. These unreported and tensely fought aerial battles played at over the skies of the Middle Euphrates River Valley, a sparsely populated place that assumed considerable geo-strategic importance for the world's two competing powers, and nearly resulted in missile launch to down one another's jets on more than one occasion. The contest for supremacy in this part of Syria ended momentarily in America's favor, but also underscored key lessons for future Western security planners. After years of neglect, Russia now intends to play an overt and forceful diplomatic and military role in the Middle East, which will require a sober and coherent policy approach in the years to come to adequately address.[4]

This new reality includes a new geopolitical constant, wherein the West should assume a Russian willingness to use force to secure their own interests beyond their borders and in an expeditionary way that defied assumptions about Moscow's military capabilities. It also has revealed that Russia's military is more formidable than the West had assumed before Moscow's intervention on behalf of Syria, and that Russia has adopted tactics that obfuscated and complicated a coherent Western response to its use of military force.[5] Russia has also managed to capitalize on the war's negative impact on Turkish-American relations, narrowly, and Ankara's ties to Europe and NATO more broadly. The result has been Moscow's rapprochement with Turkey, following a period of intense rivalry for supremacy in Syria that Russia won, and then culminated in Ankara's acquiescence to Russian supremacy, leading to the purchase of Russian-made weapons.

From the outset of the war against the Islamic State, Turkey resisted giving support to the American battle plan. Ankara's concerns are easy to understand: The American war plan was dependent on its partner force, the Syrian Democratic Forces (SDF), to execute. The SDF is held together by a tightly knit central leadership core comprising Kurdish fighters linked to the Kurdistan Workers' Party (PKK). The PKK is a Marxist group that was founded in Turkey in the late 1970s and gained popularity because it paired its leftist, pro-Kurdish agenda with violent acts against the Turkish state.[6] The group's leader, Abdullah Ocalan, fled to Syria just before the 1980 military coup in Turkey. Once inside the country, Ocalan leveraged his position to build-out training camps in the Lebanese Republic's Becca Valley to train recruits from Turkey, Syria, Iraq, and Islamic Republic of Iran, to conduct guerrilla warfare in southeastern Turkey. The PKK-led insurgency in Turkey grew in the 1980s and has continued ever since, undermining the country's stability and forcing a significant recalibration of Turkish security policy away from defense against a potential invader to internal defense against a restive element of the population. The Turkish government, along with the United States and the European Union, has listed the PKK as a terrorist group.

Despite current tensions in their relationship, the United States and Turkey also have a long history of working together to combat the PKK. The most notable point of collaboration came after Turkish threats forced Hafez al Assad to cease his support for the PKK, forcing Ocalan to flee in 1998, and then in his capture in 1999.[7] Following his imprisonment in Turkey, the PKK rebranded its affiliates, including in Syria, where the Democratic Union Party (PYD) and its associated militia, the Peoples' Protection Units (YPG for male units and YPJ for female units), were founded. For Ankara and Damascus, Syria's decision to cease support for the PKK created the political space for the two sides to tighten relations. In 1998, Turkey and Syria signed the Adana Agreement, which created a framework to pressure the PKK in northeastern Syria. In the years that followed, particularly with the rise to power of Turkey's Justice and Development Party (AKP), under control of the current president Recep Tayyip Erdogan, and current Syrian leader, Bashar al Assad, Syrian-Turkish relations deepened. With the PKK isolated in Iraq and the Syrian regime's repression of Kurds in the northeast, Ankara and Damascus had removed the main impediment to closer relations: Syrian regime's support for transnational, Kurdish terrorism.

As part of a broader effort to deepen Turkish relations with its neighbors, and to carve out a regional foreign policy more independent of the United States, the two sides signed a free trade agreement in 2004 and lifted visa restrictions in 2009. These twin agreements connected more deeply Turkey's Gaziantep with Syria's Aleppo, the two cities that would later form a key logistics supply route for the supply of material of fighters and weapons for the insurgency—and indirectly contributed to the serious downturn in bilateral trust with the United States. Just months before the civil war in Syria began, up to 40,000 Syrians would travel the 75 miles to shopping malls in Gaziantep to purchase luxury goods.[8] As Syrian security deteriorated in 2011, Ankara sought to leverage this good will with Bashar al Assad to its advantage, and to convince the Syrian leader to make political reforms. These efforts failed and under pressure from the United States, Turkey joined the growing numbers of countries calling for Assad to step aside. By December 2011, Damascus severed the link with Turkey, ending much of the cross-border trade, turning the bustling border city into the main jumping off point for the resupply of armed rebels, and the final major waystation on the transnational migration route Islamic State and Al-Qaeda sympathizers moved through to join these groups as they fought the Syrian regime and each other in the multisided civil war.

The roots of the downward spiral of Turkish-American relations are interlinked with the collapse of Turkey's greatest strategic prize in the post–Cold War world: the global isolation of the PKK and the bottling up of Turkey's internal Kurdish-led insurgency in the relatively isolated and underdeveloped border areas with Iraq and Iran. The collapse of Syrian state authority allowed for the PYD to assume control of areas the regime had to vacate, as it grappled with the collapse of security in the western half of the country. The Kurdish issue for Turkey grew more acute after the United States intervened.

The American military intervention, from its inception, was designed to limit US involvement and thrust responsibility for the ground offensive to SOF. The ISIS war began rather abruptly and, like any bureaucracy, the military had to stand up to a task force, based in Iraq, linked to the Combined Air Operations Center (CAOC) in Qatar, MacDill Air Force base in Tampa, Florida, and tethered to a small contingent of special operators sent to Syria in October 2015.[9] American SOF and their British and French cousins are no strangers to operations in the Middle East. For many, the demands of the war in Iraq had demanded constant rotations, alongside deployments to Islamic Republic of Afghanistan, Libya, Mali, and elsewhere. The war in Syria, however, would be different. As an outgrowth of the odd nature of the war's prosecution and rapid start, the fight against the Islamic State in Syria was SOF-led, with the first elements going into the country part of Joint Special Operations Command (JSOC), followed by US Army Special Forces. In both cases, these two groups had deep links to two Iraqi Kurdish parties, the Kurdistan Democratic Party (KDP), led by the Massoud Barzani and his sons, and the Patriotic Union of Kurdistan (PUK), then under control of Jalal Talabani and his sons. The American relationship with the PUK Peshmerga, the Kurdish militia in Iraqi Kurdistan, in particular, would prove fortuitous as the United States planned its opening moves against the Islamic State because they provided the introduction to the leader of the YPG in Syria, Mazlum Abdi, which enabled the partnership that defeated the Islamic State, and allowed for US troops to work remotely with the SDF from eastern Iraq.[10]

In parallel, the US military launched, in coordination with Turkey a Train and Equip (T/E) program to bring vetted Syrians to Turkey, where they would receive US training to secure the border areas from Islamic State. The military results were poor, with the US- and Turkey-backed groups unable to take and hold relatively sparsely held terrain, settling into a frustrating game of territorial ping-pong. Faced with these frustrating outcomes, the United States authorized a cross-river, SDF-led assault on Manbij, a small Syrian town that assumed considerable geopolitical significance as the war continued. This decision violated a Turkish red-line, creating the impetus for independent Turkish military operations in Syria, culminating in the October 2019 invasion of northeastern Syria that upended dicey diplomatic efforts to manage Turkish security concerns, and then forced a hasty American and European withdrawal from the border.

The American-led efforts in Syria had an unintended outcome: Faced with a broader concern about the Syrian regime's ability to ultimately win the war against the insurgency, Russian president Vladimir Putin authorized the deployment of Russian forces to bolster the Syrian regime. Russia's intervention in the war has had a tremendous impact on the course of the conflict, but remains understudied. Moscow had watched the war unfold since 2011, until the regime's struggles forced Bashar to appeal for direct help. This appeal came in the summer of 2015, where he acknowledged manpower deficits and the negative toll the war had taken on the Syrian Arab Army and his inability to sustain offensive combat operations to take back territory that was lost to the insurgency.[11] At this point, the CIA program in the northwest had grown more potent, particularly after two extremist groups, the Al-Qaeda-linked faction, then calling itself Hayat Tahrir al Sham and its erstwhile frienemy, Ahrar al Sham, a Syrian group that had jihadist elements but sought to situate their group's ideology within the milieu of the Syrian uprising, agreed to cooperate in a joint offensive to take control of Idlib. This group, dubbed Jaysh al Fateh, took control of Idlib. The offensive was entirely bittersweet because it included US-backed groups outfitted with TOW anti-tank missiles fighting in tandem with extremist elements, and together they did weaken the regime. However, it came with a cost. Syria's Al-Qaeda affiliate took control of vacated territory, forever poisoning the revolution, further complicating the American response, and creating an untenable situation for all the external parties to the civil war—perhaps with the exception of Turkey.

Russia's response to the regime's crisis was to intervene more forcefully.[12] In September 2015, the Russian Air Force deployed to Khmeimim Air Base, beginning what would become a definitive offensive that wiped out nascent US-Turkish cooperation along the border and knocked Ankara out of the clandestine war against Bashar. Russian air operations were more robust than US officials had expected and, as Moscow deepened its involvement in the conflict, its ability to generate combat sorties surprised American and European policymakers. Using a ruthless campaign of bombing, backed by special operators on the ground to advise and assist the haphazard and decrepit Syrian army, Moscow turned its military attention to the US- and Turkey-backed groups active in Syria's northwest.

As Russia began its bombing campaign in September 2015, it first sought to attack groups that had taken safe haven along the Turkish-Syrian border. For much of the war, Ankara had been patrolling the border with F-16 jets, harassing any Syrian jet that threatened a small, 5-kilometer or so deep zone along certain border pockets. Moscow ended that safe haven. But in so doing, violated Turkish airspace on a handful of occasions. On November 24, 2015, the Turkish government had finally had enough and authorized the Air Force to fire on any aircraft that violated Turkish airspace.[13]

The Turkish downing of a Russian Su-24 bomber changed the trajectory of the war for Ankara. Rather than be deterred from further operations, Moscow increased the scope of its bombing along the narrow highway connecting Turkey via Azaz to Aleppo. This bombing complicated Turkish flight operations in Syria, as part of the US-led anti-ISIS coalition, to help provide air support for a push from what US officials had dubbed the Marea line. This axis was to have served as the jumping off point for the Turkish-American operation. Instead, it came under Russian assault. Turkey was forced to cease flying over Syria for fear of being shot down.[14] The collapse of the US-Turkish effort to close the Manbij pocket has had serious and deleterious effects on the transatlantic relationship. However, it did not come for lack of trying to work around Turkey's Kurdish issue. Instead, it stemmed from broader, political and military challenges inherent to the Syrian civil war and the risk-averse Turkish and American political elite in charge of this phase of the war. Moscow also played a role, surprising Ankara and Washington with the Kremlin's appetite for risk.

The end of the US-Turkish relationship in Syria has its roots in factors as prosaic as geography and regional familiarity. As the Islamic State rampaged throughout northern Iraq, it was the plight of a vulnerable and geographically isolated minority, the Yazidis, as well as the Islamic State's advance to the outskirts of Erbil, the Iraqi Kurdistan region's capital city, that forced America's hand. As vulnerable Yazidis fled from a smattering of villages south of Mt. Sinjar, the ISIS assault began at dawn and was met with little resistance. The village's protectors, KDP Peshmerga, fled, retreating toward their strongholds inside Barzani-dominated territory to the east. The vulnerable population fled north, making their way in convoys up a snaking road to the top of Mt. Sinjar. In June, as the first Special Forces members made their way to Baghdad, the situation in the area was deteriorating.

In early August 2014, President Obama authorized the first airstrikes against the Islamic State to break the siege on the mountain. These strikes came just days before American Marines, SOF, and British Special Air Service (SAS) landed to survey the situation and plan for the counteroffensive.[15] The first aircrafts in were carrying aid, not bombs, and flew as part of an Anglo coalition, led by the United States with contributions from the United Kingdom and Australia. These large cargo planes were escorted by US Air Force and Navy fighter aircraft. With the cargo planes so susceptible to ground fire, the pilots flew low and fast, and could not remain over the mountain for more than fifteen minutes.[16]

The first bombs to drop on the Islamic State were fired from an unmanned aerial vehicle, as the group approached a key bridge that if crossed would have allowed Islamic State to threaten Erbil, the capital city of Kurdistan region. The American outreach to the YPG began around this time, beginning with Talabani's PUK introducing the United States to the YPG.[17] The PUK and US Special Forces fought together closely during the 2003 invasion of Iraq. American Special Forces were also embedded with the Peshmerga between 1991 and 1996 before an intra-Iraqi Kurdish civil war prompted a US withdrawal from northern Iraq and the deployment of Special Forces before the 2003 invasion of Iraq began. The US Special Forces–PUK attack began on the morning of March 28, 2003, and ended the day of the invasion on March 30. The PUK and the United States would be asked to harass Iraqi armored divisions during the invasion, culminating in the assault and occupation of Kirkuk.

The YPG began to plan to rescue Yazidis and managed to carve out a road, flanked by ISIS to the south, to drive Yazidis west to Syria. From there, those who managed to escape would cross back into Iraq and placed in internally displaced persons camps in Duhok. The rapid ISIS advance was eventually beaten back and its momentum slowed. The ISIS mobilization gave the nascent US coalition an opportunity to locate and target ISIS as they amassed on roads leading to the city. The airstrikes began as ISIS assaulted and conquered much of the city, bottling up the Syrian Kurds in a small section along the Turkish-Syrian border. The battle for Kobane marked a turning point for the United States in the nascent war against ISIS. It also spilled over to Turkey, sparking an intra-Kurdish battle, pitting Islamist, ISIS-supporting Kurds against leftist, PKK-supporting Kurds.

In both cases, the growing ISIS threat and the rise of a YPG-led resistance challenged Turkish policy considerably. Ankara, wary of giving direct support to the group, sought to bind the YPG to the Arab-majority opposition it supported, based primarily inside Turkey, and active in the country's northwest. This policy coincided with a political decision to engage in peace talk with the PKK's imprisoned leader, Abdullah Ocalan. These talks faltered, as Islamic State in Turkey unleashed a wave of bombings that destabilized Turkish cities and, eventually, was one of many factors that contributed to the end of the Turkish government's peace talks with the PKK. The result was a return to violence inside Turkey and the start of a months-long Turkish military campaign to reclaim city centers lost to a PKK-affiliated youth militia.

The Turkish military operations in Turkey's southeast began in December 2015 and have continued ever since. These operations have also expanded to include the invasion of northern Aleppo, which was under ISIS control, and then Afrin, a YPG-held enclave. Ankara has also been conducting counterterrorism raids in northern Iraq, all as part of an effort it has deemed a "war on terror." This war stemmed from a re-calculation of Turkish interests vis-a-vis Syria in 2016, after the Russian Air Force used firepower and coercive diplomacy to sever the Turkish supply line to opposition-held Aleppo. Following the loss of the city to regime forces in December 2016, Turkey pivoted from a policy of overthrowing the Assad regime, premised on uncomfortable cooperation with the United States, to one of outright hostility toward Washington because of its cooperation with the SDF. The Turkish calculus, from this moment on, focused on breaking the US-Kurdish partnership in Syria. This decision culminated in the October 2019 Turkish invasion of northeastern Syria, which did just that. In a chaotic few weeks, Ankara managed to force the United States from territory along the Turkish-Syrian border, only for the regime and Russia to fill the vacuum.

It was not always this way. The United States, along with Britain and France, had found a winning military formula for war in Syria. The battle for Raqqa was the culmination of the American war effort in Syria that began with the introduction of Special Forces in 2015, continued after the Kurds took back Kobane. Despite Turkish resistance, the war against Islamic State proceeded as intended and reached the gates of Raqqa by June 2017.

On the city's outskirts, American SOF were working from a small targeting vehicle, and embedded with elements of the SDF, a Kurdish-led militia that has spearheaded the American-led war against Islamic State. In squat, cinder block buildings, shielded from overhead surveillance, Islamic State militants punched small holes in walls and positioned sharpshooters overlooking the narrow Raqqa streets. The sound of gunfire echoed off the buildings, occasionally masking the persistent buzz of American-operated armed drones, flying orbits below their manned aircraft cousins in a stack of aircraft capable of delivering precise bombs anywhere they would be needed. The real-time imagery was fed to a small, indistinct American truck capable of monitoring the real-time feeds of the tens of aircrafts flying in the area.[18] This was brought to bear overwhelming American and allied firepower, delivered on target to enable the local ground offensives.

The war against Islamic State was depending on two uniquely American mechanisms of war: airpower and SOF, working alongside allied forces, the UK and France on the ground, and other mostly Western states in the air, and how these three elements could be brought to bear to fight a non-state actor. The result has been a clear victory for the United States and its coalition partners. ISIS has been territorially defeated, its ranks decimated, with few coalition member losses. The ground forces that did the brunt of the dying, the Syrian Kurds, however, remained politically isolated. After years of fighting alongside the West, transatlantic interests with Ankara and overarching concerns about "losing Turkey" limited how far the United States and its allies were willing to go to include the SDF in broader political talks.

In the war's aftermath, and the hasty Western withdrawal, it has become clear that the United States and its allies had a plan for battle, but refused to make the concessions necessary to secure victory. The reasons for this are easy to understand: To secure the peace, Washington and Europe would have to compromise with Russia. And for political leaders, faced with Putin's revanchism, beginning with his invasion of Ukraine in 2014, followed by his commitment of forces in Syria in 2015, and then his interference in the US election in 2016, few if any in Washington and Brussels were interested in compromise. The thought of working to compromise with Moscow was, of course, unpalatable and politically uncomfortable for much of the West. And yet, it was Turkey's outreach to Russia helped to facilitate its core goal of breaking the Western resolve to remain in Syria and to put pressure on the Syrian Kurds.

The war has proved the military prowess of the West. But it has exposed deep political failing, endemic to wars of choice. Throughout the conflict, American diplomats engaged extensively with their counterparts in Ankara, but rarely achieved anything substantive with the Turks and relations soured. The same is true of diplomatic outreach to Moscow, which has not directly opposed the US war effort against Islamic State, but has resisted Western efforts to end the conflict in ways that would see Bashar al Assad sidelined. This dual-headed stalemate persists, as does the US presence in northeastern Syria, which remains intact even after former president Donald Trump sought to withdraw troops on multiple occasions.

The broader lesson from Operation Inherent Resolve (OIR) is that the war has been devalued in the eyes of many American politicians, as the country seeks to focus more on planning for great power conflict. OIR may be the last of the post-9/11 wars, focused on a non-state actor and the main focus of US national security decision-making. A rare bipartisan and transatlantic consensus has emerged, following America's disastrous invasion of Iraq, and the inability to secure peace in Afghanistan. The war in Syria has demonstrated that, when needed, the United States and its allies can defeat an entrenched terror group with relative ease, and without shedding Western blood. It also underscores how difficult it is to create militias, but how militias that share the West's interests can enable warfare by proxy. However, it has also shown that no war is cost free, and as the Syrian civil conflict continues, the political repercussions—ranging from the deterioration of relations with Turkey to Russia's return to the Middle East—will endure and are intertwined with the decision to intervene in Syria in the first place.

This book explains how this came to be, and how the war was fought, and what this means for the future of Western security policy, how the Americans ended up partnering with the Kurds and how Ankara eventually chose to diverge from its traditional allies and invade US-held territory in Syria. This story is about US technological overmatch, which allowed for military planners to watch battlefields in Syria from all over the world, and talk directly to the pilots and operators fighting—and how that hindered air operations and irritated operators and pilots. It is also about the challenges of managing divergent national interests and how a shared antipathy for Islamic State cannot overcome broader disagreement about both Turkey and Russia's vision for the future of the Middle East and the threats that emanate from the region. As part of this story, this book explores how countries reacted to American decision-making and how the geopolitical dynamics that contributed to Russia's intervention in the war. This Russian decision brought the two world powers face-to-face in aerial and ground clashes along the Euphrates River. The Syrian war has been small and, for the West, relatively casualty free. This war featured great powers and innovative tactics. This book tells the diplomatic and military history from the point of view of the men and women who fought on the frontlines with the SDF.

Chapter 1

THE ORIGINS OF US POLICY: A SUPERPOWER AND THE KURDS

Abu Musab al-Zarqawi was not your typical emir. But he managed to oversee the establishment of a terrorist organization that terrorized Iraq and, eventually, managed to take control over its second largest city. President Barack Obama had sought to end the self-declared Global War on Terror (GWOT), declaring in May 2013 that the United States was at a "crossroads" and must "define the nature and scope of this struggle" against terrorism. This definition, Obama would later indicate, would be defined "not as a boundless 'global war on terror,' but rather as a series of persistent, targeted efforts to dismantle specific networks of violent extremists that threaten America."[1] After 487 days, on September 22, 2014, Obama authorized the first airstrikes against the Islamic State, launching an air and ground campaign that has continued ever since. The United States was choosing to enter a complicated multisided war in Syria and Iraq to once again combat terrorism.[2]

As early as 2012, the heirs to Zarqawi's ideological struggle were busy embedding themselves within the Syrian opposition to Bashar al-Assad, the authoritarian president who assumed power after his father, Hafez, died of a heart attack in the capital, Damascus.[3] The gangly and angular ophthalmologist was not his father's first choice to take power, but assumed the position by default after his older brother, Bassel al-Assad, was killed in a car crash near the Damascus airport.[4] The Assad regime had, throughout the Cold War, carved out a niche for itself as a useful Soviet client, taking advantage of Moscow's weapons exports to build up a large military to counter its neighbor Israel.

The Assad regime is a minoritarian government, wherein Syria's Allawis have gained considerable political and military power since Hafez took power in 1970. The power of the state rests on its dynastic politics, the state's provision of jobs to the citizenry, and the security services, tasked with defending the country from external and internal threats. This basic social contract is in tension with liberal democracy and has hindered Syria's political and economic development. In the late 1980s and extending into the early 1990s, the private sector became more important for the regime, raising a broader question about how to simultaneously deepen economic reliance on companies without creating a pathway for their political empowerment. This created a two-tier system of large, politically connected enterprises that were able to take advantage of economics reforms, and a larger cadre of small- and medium-sized businesses that lacked the type of access to the regime to make life easier for them. This status quo prevailed up until Hafez's death. Upon taking power in 2000, Bashar accelerated efforts to privatize the Syrian economy, as part of a broader effort to undo his father's centrally planned system, in favor of an economy wedded to neoliberal economic theory.[5] Cast as a reformer, Bashar also sought to use Syrian foreign policy as a national asset.

The Al-Qaeda-planned attacks on September 11, 2001, complicated relations with Washington, resulting in a series of contradictory outcomes and policies. Despite antagonistic relations with the United States, Syria was a destination for Al-Qaeda members the United States or other countries captured and then sent for questioning in secret prisons around the world.[6] The regime was also a key ally to many members of President George W. Bush's "Axis of Evil," including Iran and North Korea.[7] Bashar's relationship with the third Axis member, Saddam Hussein's Iraq, was more complicated and adversarial. Both countries adopted the Ba'athist political ideology, the pan-Arab and anti-colonial ideology that permeated Arab polities in the 1940s, and under which Saddam Hussein and Hafez al-Assad molded to fit their authoritarian impulses. The two countries had overlapping, anti-Israeli interests and fought together (albeit disjointedly) during the 1973 Arab-Israeli war. However, relations never fully matured and, by 1979, had soured when Saddam Hussein toppled then Iraqi president Ahmed Hassan al-Bakr, who had been spearheading talks with his counterparts in Damascus on a political union.

In the same year the tensions in Iran had boiled over, and street protests toppled the American-friendly Shah Reza Pahlavi, transforming monarchical Iran into an Islamic Republic, bound to a system of clerical rule guided by Ayatollah Ruhollah Khomeini. The Syrian-Iranian relationship grew thereafter, built on relationship of mutual interest, linked to the adoption of anti-Israel security policy and support for regional terrorist groups. At the outset of the Iran–Iraq war, Damascus sided with Tehran, agreeing to supply its new ally with weapons and materials throughout the war. Syrian relations with Iran has hindered its relationship with Washington, and also created opportunities for both Hafez and Bashar to use the promise of peace with Jerusalem to engage with Washington in open-ended talks about a potential settlement. Following the US invasion of Iraq in March 2003, Bashar pursued this dual-tracked approach in relations with Washington. On the one hand, Damascus served as a node in the Central Intelligence Agency (CIA)-run rendition program. And yet, on the other, Syria served as they key overland route for foreign jihadists to transit to Iraq during the US occupation.

Zarqawi oversaw these ratlines, building out an organization that would after his death declare a caliphate in Iraq and, again, in Syria. Zarqawi's pathway to Syria began in Kandahar, Afghanistan, where fourteen jihadist groups took advantage of the safe haven the country's leadership, the Taliban, had granted them.[8] Al-Qaeda was one of the fourteen groups. Al-Qaeda was established in 1988 toward the end of the Soviet occupation, with the intent of training elite jihadists to attack Arab governments. Bin Laden's outlook changed sometime thereafter, and by 1996 he had settled on a controversial strategy of attacking the so-called far enemy—the United States—as a means to force Washington to end its support for the region's governments. Absent this protection, Bin Laden argued, his forces would be able to topple regional governments and create an Islamic State. This decision prompted a wave of terrorist attacks against the United States and Europe, culminating in the attacks on September 11, 2001.

Zarqawi had an entirely different approach to terrorism, but filled a recruiting need for Al-Qaeda. In 1998, the group had weak ties to the Levantine countries and faced a rival recruiter, Abu Mus'ab al-Suri, a Syrian who had a long history of fighting for jihadist causes. According Brian Fishman, Suri was a "polyglot ... who worked on and off again with Al Qaeda, and was a veteran of the seminal Jihadi uprising against Hafez al-Assad in the 1970s and 1980s," but who eventually grew to become one of Bin Laden's biggest critics for his focus on attacking Western targets.[9] Born into poverty in Zarqa, Jordan, Zarqawi transitioned from being a troubled teen, interested in drugs and accused of sexual assault to the brutal leader of a series of terrorist groups, based in Iraq and oftentimes working at cross purposes with Bin Laden's guidance on how to prosecute jihad. However, his links to the Levant gave Al-Qaeda an entry point to the region, increasing recruits from the area to join the group.[10]

The jihadist world changed overnight on September 11, 2001. The Al-Qaeda attacks killed thousands of Americans, but the intra-jihadist warnings about the danger of the American response proved prescient. Just days after civilian airliners plowed into the World Trade Center buildings in New York, and a second plane hit the Pentagon, the United States began its military response. Operation Enduring Freedom, the name given to the American invasion of Afghanistan, began with the insertion of small teams from the CIA, followed by elements from Joint Special Operations Command, backed by overwhelming air power.[11] The American war against the Taliban was brief and effective and the war dispersed the jihadist groups that had enjoyed safe haven in Afghanistan.

Zarqawi fled Afghanistan from Kandahar, after narrowly missing being killed in a US airstrike, and fled to Pakistan before traveling to Iran. He ultimately made his way to northern Iraq, where he was welcomed by a Kurdish-majority jihadist group, Ansar al Islam (AAI). The group had a small training camp in the mountainous border with Iran, in Iraq's autonomous Kurdish zone. After taking refuge with AAI, Zarqawi would travel in the Levant, activating a network of men to recruit from and who he could smuggle into Iraq after Saddam Hussein was toppled. His Kurdish hosts, in March 2003, were the first target in the American war against Saddam Hussein, and led by American Special Forces, dubbed Task Force Viking.

The United States has the world's most advanced military, outfitted with weapons designed to defeat the Soviet Union, and operated by men and women now trained to fight in the Iraqi desert. As the United States plotted its war against Saddam Hussein, one of the first Special Forces teams chose a different means to infiltrate the country: A Jeep Grand Cherokee and a beat up red pick-up truck with tinted windows and a lowered suspension.[12] The 10th Special Forces Group is assigned to European Command's (EUCOM) area of responsibility, but after the 9/11 attacks they spent most of their time in the Middle East.

In 2003, 10th Group's historical focus on European defense had taken a backseat to the demands of GWOT. "10th Group was regionally aligned against Europe, with a rich tradition of deterring the Soviets through irregular means, the demands of Afghanistan and Iraq forced the Group to shift focus almost entirely in the mid-2000s," according to a current 10th Group member. "I was given Arabic as my language, since most of the work being done at the time was in Iraq, and not Europe."[13]

The US Special Operations community has a long history of working with the Iraqi Kurds, dating back to the First Gulf War in 1990–91, and then the follow-on imposition of a no-fly-zone (NFZ) following that conflict and before the American-led invasion. In 2003, the CIA and a Special Forces Pilot Team, whose job was to prepare to wage unconventional warfare, had holed up at a house near Sulaymaniyah, Iraq.[14] Iraqi Kurdistan is controlled by two family-run patronage networks, each with its own militia, that together are called the Peshmerga. This has given Westerners a misleading picture of their unity, which has scarcely ever existed, and the two families are often in tension. The Barzani clan controlling Erbil out to Duhok and down to the outskirts of Mosul heads the Kurdistan Democratic Party (KDP). The Talabani family controls the eastern swathe of the territory, with control over Sulaymaniyah and the outskirts of oil-rich Kirkuk, and is in charge of the Patriotic Union of Kurdistan (PUK) and its associated Peshmerga.

The US military had carved out a relationship with these two factions after the 1991 Gulf War, with 10th Group maintaining a presence in Zakho, near the border with Turkey and in KDP territory, and via constant interaction with the PUK.[15] This partnership was born out of tragedy. As the United States ousted the Iraqis from Kuwait, then president George H.W. Bush encouraged the Kurds to rise up against the Iraqi leadership. However, after violence erupted, the United States stood aside as Saddam Hussein used helicopter gun ships and amassed artillery to beat back the offensive after the PUK had briefly sided control of Kirkuk.[16] The military onslaught prompted a mass exodus of Kurdish civilians from urban areas to the mountainous border region with Turkey, creating a secondary refugee crisis that Ankara had to contend with. The dire humanitarian situation prompted coalition intervention to impose an NFZ over northern and southern Iraq.

The NFZ over Iraqi Kurdistan was initially part of Operation Provide Comfort, a military mission that began in 1991, and then transitioned to Operation Northern Watch, enforced by a composite wing of US Air Force aircraft. At the outset of the NFZ, the Iraqis did try and test it on a handful of occasions, leading to a series of F-15C shoot downs of Iraqi air force jets. By 1994, "the No Fly Zone the north was like the gentleman's NFZ. We only enforced it during the day, when the Turks would allow us, and only for a couple hours a day," according to Col. (R) Mike "Starbaby" Pietrucha, who deployed to Turkey on multiple occasions to enforce the NFZ during the 1990s.[17]

The safety this NFZ provided enabled the two major families in Kurdistan to focus on their own power struggle. By 1996, tensions had boiled over, and the KDP and PUK-affiliated Peshmerga began to fight one another in a civil conflict. The PUK managed to gain the upper hand, prompting Massoud Barzani, the patriarch of the Barzani clan and the de facto leader of Iraqi Kurdistan, to invite Saddam

Hussein's army to quell the PUK. Jalal Talabani, for his part, had sought help from neighboring Iran, placing the United States in a rather difficult situation.

For the American men on the ground, the Kurdish civil war forced the withdrawal of the forces deployed in 1991, as part of operation Provide Comfort, the name given to the mission to defend the Iraqi Kurds from aerial attack. "There was always some degree of emotional scar within 10th group about the Kurds," according to a retired Special Forces member. "The 10th Group guys, they used to always talk about the Provide Comfort era and how they pulled out of the Zakho house in 1996. In 2003, there was an excitement about making it right with the Kurds for what happened after 1991. We tell guys not to go native, but it is hard not to fall for the Kurds."[18]

These linkages to both the KDP and PUK were an important factor in shaping how the United States planned to intervene in the country after the 9/11 attacks. During the build-up for the invasion, the Bush administration sought to make a definitive linkage between Saddam Hussein and Al-Qaeda. The intent was to demonstrate that Saddam Hussein was harboring and supporting the terrorist group, ensuring that the Iraqi dictator would qualify for preventative military action. Just one day after the 9/11 attacks, President George W. Bush sought to reassure the American public that "the search is underway for those who are behind these evil acts" and warned that "we will make no distinction between the terrorists who committed these acts and those who harbor them."[19] This shift in policy signaled the American shift to preventive war and the decision to use military force to deny safe haven to terrorist groups to disrupt external plotting.

As the United States prepared for war against Iraq in 2002, the job of selling it to the American people and to wary allies was left to then Secretary of State Colin Powell. In the speech, Colin Powell warned of a "sinister nexus between Iraq and the al Qaeda terrorist network, a nexus that combines classic terrorist organizations and modern methods of murder. Iraq today harbors a deadly terrorist network headed by Abu Musab Zarqawi, an associate and collaborator of Osama bin Laden and his al Qaeda lieutenants."[20] The first challenge for the United States was augmenting the number of forces in northern Iraq to prepare for the invasion. As the initial teams were moving into northern Iraq, the United States and Turkey remained at odds over the looming invasion, and whether Ankara would allow an invasion from its territory.

The United States and the Turkish Republic have been allies since 1952, when Turkey formally joined the North Atlantic Treaty Organization (NATO). The two countries shared overlapping views of the Soviet Union and worked together to deter Russian aggression along Turkey's borders. After the end of the Cold War, Turkey's interests began to change, as a generation of new leaders began to consider deepening relations with Turkey's neighbors in the Middle East, Central Asia, and Eastern Europe. Turkey's domestic security situation deteriorated, following the rise of a secular-minded and Marxist-inspired insurgent groups dubbed the Kurdistan Workers' Party, or PKK.

Kurdish politics in Turkey have historically been repressed. Kurdish political factions, in turn, have gravitated toward leftist political platforms, focused on egalitarianism and a tearing down of social hierarchies that stratify society. The PKK's ideological founder and most revered figure, Abdullah Ocalan, was born in Sanliurfa, an ethnically mixed city at the edge of Turkey's Kurdish-majority southeast. Growing up poor, Ocalan moved to Turkey's capital city, Ankara, in 1966, where he was soon swept up in the growing leftist counterculture politics dominant at the time.[21] After he was arrested in 1972, Ocalan gravitated toward radical leftist politics, leaving prison with a passion to help instigate a political revolution. By 1973, he was advocating for armed struggle to liberate the Kurds and to overturn what he deemed an oppressive state system, in favor of truly independent Kurdish state.[22] Unlike many of his peers at the time, Ocalan gravitated toward the use of violence to enable his vision for an independent Kurdish state, rather than focus on endless philosophical debates about whether the Kurdish people had reached a level of enlightenment to be true socialists. This call-to-action, according to Aliza Marcus, galvanized elements of Turkey's Kurdish population and allowed for Ocalan to attract a larger number of followers.

The first PKK attack against the state did not take place until August 1984 in Semdinli and Eruh. Ocalan planned these attacks from Syria, where he had fled to in July 1979, after increased violence in Turkey and fears of a coup prompted him to seek out a safe haven across the border.[23] From training camps in Syrian-controlled Lebanon, the PKK trained cadres of fighters, who would then infiltrate into Turkey. These fighters would rely on support from local villages, many of which the state would later target to try and starve the PKK of support. The PKK's strength ebbed and flowed between the 1980s and 1990s, commiserate to the intensity of the Turkish military's efforts to eradicate the group. However, these efforts were often brutal, including the forced depopulation of Kurdish villages,[24] a cycle that engendered considerable backlash amongst this part of the population, and which helped to feed the latest round of fighting that began in 2014 and has continued for over a half-a-decade in parallel to the war against Islamic State.

The Turkish focus on its own internal insurgency shaped its thinking about regional stability. Throughout the 1990s, Ankara and Damascus clashed over the PKK, and Hafez's support for Ocalan's activities inside his country. This changed in 1996. The surge in PKK attacks in the 1990s prompted a shift in Turkish thinking about how to deal with its Syrian neighbor, beginning with the issuing of a memorandum stating flatly that Syrian support for the PKK was an act of aggression and that Turkish action against the group would fall under Article 51 of the UN Charter's provision for self-defense.[25] Shortly thereafter, Turkey and Israel signed a defense cooperation agreement, a short-lived effort to deepen cooperation between the two countries across a multitude of domains, ranging from intelligence sharing to defense industrial cooperation.[26] These twin Turkish actions were the first two opening moves in a broader, military-focused effort to coerce Hafez to end his support for the PKK. By October 1998, Ankara had escalated to making direct threats for armed conflict. Under the guise of a NATO exercise along the border, Turkey increased the number of troops along the border and sharpened its warnings. Syria responded by sending its own troops to the border and moving SCUD ballistic missiles closer to Turkey.

However, by October, Hafez signaled his willingness to compromise, sending word through an Iranian intermediary that Damascus had begun to crack down on PKK networks. Turkish coercion eventually led Hafez to expel Ocalan from Damascus, ending the Syrian-PKK entente that had flourished for close to two decades. Ocalan's escape first led him to Italy, where he holed up for a few weeks, before he traveled to Russia, and then on to Greece. From Greece, he fled to Nairobi, Kenya, where he took refuge inside the Greek consulate. Throughout this journey, the CIA was monitoring his communications and whereabouts by tracking his mobile phone, passing this information to Turkey. As it would turn out, the United States had a sizable presence in the country because it was investigating the simultaneous Al-Qaeda bombing of the American embassies in Kenya and Tanzania.[27] At his final destination, the CIA duped Ocalan, who had wanted to fly to the Netherlands to seek a hearing at the International Court of Justice (ICJ), to leave the Greek consulate building he was staying in and head to the airport. A Kenyan security official picked him up and delivered him to a Turkish commando team that had flown in shortly before. After his capture, Ocalan softened his revolutionary demands, ushering in a new era for the PKK and its vision for a future Kurdish state that would manifest itself in Syria, after the war with ISIS began in 2014.

The successful coercion of Damascus in 1998 resulted in the signing of the Adana Agreement, which obligated Damascus to deny the PKK safe haven. The agreement included a series of provisions Egypt played a role in shepherding this agreement, as did Iran and the United States. The intent was to tamp down tensions and prevent conflict, which was possible throughout this period. The Adana Agreement had a series of provisions that enabled Turkish officials to embed with their Syrian counterparts and included four unpublished annexes.[28] The final annex allowed for the Turkish military to invade up to 5 kilometers into Syria if Damascus had failed to uphold its obligations.

This arrangement coincided with the American decision to officially designate the PKK as a terrorist group,[29] a watershed moment for Ankara, and putting place mechanisms that the two sides would use after the 2003 invasion of Iraq to share intelligence. Throughout the 1990s, Turkish human rights abuses had undermined their relations with the United States and Brussels, hindering Ankara's import of weapons from foreign suppliers. In retrospect, this was the high point for the Turkish-led fight against the PKK. By 1999, Damascus had been cowered, Ankara had captured Ocalan with American assistance, and the spate of Kurdish attacks had decreased due to sustained Turkish military pressure. It would not last.

Fighting with the Kurds: The Origins of the Bilateral Relationship with Washington

The American special forces in Iraqi Kurdistan could not pronounce Sulaymaniyah, the PUK-held city where the initial special forces teams were deployed to prepare for the invasion. The 3rd Special Forces Group dubbed the city "Ass West" and was waiting in Romania for the order to fly to the airfield and a second, dubbed Bashir, near Erbil.[30] The American overflight and the US request to use bases in Turkey for the ground invasion of Iraq was the most pressing foreign policy issue for the recently elected Justice and Development Party (AKP). The AKP swept into power in 2002, largely because its major competitors performed so poorly, and Turkish voters were eager for a change in political leadership after suffering through a recent economic downturn.

The Turkish Republic's electoral system is designed to disenfranchise small political parties to prevent Kurdish political parties from entering parliament. The threshold to enter parliament is 10 percent, a much higher barrier-to-entry than most democracies in Europe. In the 2002 national election, the AKP only won 34.3 percent of the vote, but because only the Republican People's Party (CHP) cleared the 10 percent threshold, the AKP received an absolute majority of the seats in the assembly. This ceded the power and responsibility for the decision to allow American combat troops in Turkey to invade Iraq to the party.[31] As the United States prepped for war, the AKP failed to rally its entire parliamentary caucus to support the invasion; denying on March 3, 2003, the US military the permission needed to invade Iraqi Kurdistan from Turkey.

The March vote in Turkey was a month behind the schedule the Special Forces teams tasked with operations in the north had planned for. After losing access to Turkey, the best staging base for the first flight into Iraq was in Romania, which changed the infiltration from simply driving across the border to a complicated series of flights, dubbed Operation Ugly Baby. This name was chosen because the flight and operation was so risky and ugly that only a mother could love it. The insertion of US Special Forces into Iraq began with the movement of six MC-130 aircraft flying first to Jordan, before taking off again for the flight to Iraq. The six aircraft were 20,000 pounds above the normal limit and had to fly low and fast to avoid detection from Iraqi surface-to-air missile radars, but which then exposed them to lethal ground fire. "The aircraft were shot to shit," and one aircraft had to divert to Turkey, according to Giaconia.[32] The other five aircraft did manage to land, which made the ingress operation "the longest low level infiltration since World War II."[33] The battle that ensued a few nights later was dubbed Operation Viking Hammer, an unconventional warfare campaign to tie up Iraqi forces in the north and to take Kirkuk and Mosul and to eliminate the threat of insurgent attack from the rear, led by an antecedent to the Islamic State, AAI.

Flying low over the horizon at about the same speed as a commercial civilian passenger jet, seventy Tomahawk Land Attack Cruise Missiles (TLAMs) struck targets in the mountains east of Halabja, just inside the border with Iran. The Tomahawk is a near-perfect weapon, perfected over its decades of service to strike with great accuracy. In this case, the TLAM flew where it was supposed to, but the fighters of AAI had prepared a worthy defense, setting in motion the first ground battle during the invasion of Iraq. The fighting ended with AAI elements fleeing across the border with Iran. The United States would soon topple the Iraqi government, but after declaring "mission accomplished" soon found itself enmeshed in an insurgency the Americans failed to understand, at first, and then struggled to squelch once recognizing the problem, and in constant squabbles with Ankara over the emergence of a stronger Kurdish entity in Iraq's north.

The American-led battle in the north was a precursor for the challenges that awaited the United States during the later fight against Islamic State. The initial campaign faced extreme resistance from Ankara and, following the successful end of combat operations, the United States and its NATO ally continued to squabble about Kurdish territorial control in a frail and neighboring state. The United States military, writing from Baghdad in 2003, went as far as to suggest "Turkish [Special Forces] have worn U.S. Army uniforms when ambushing PKK units, apparently to try to provoke PKK attacks on Coalition Forces [CF]" and that "Turkish regular forces have pointed guns at CF, including following CF vehicles with their tank tubes."[34] Turkey's goals, simply put, were to put pressure on the United States to attack the PKK, which the United States was never willing to do to the level Ankara had demanded. These tensions foreshadowed what would come later, as the United States prepared for war against Islamic State.

The insurgency, however, was the far more pressing of the issues the United States had to grapple with. Despite the early successes against AAI, Zarqawi soon emerged as the critical figure in organizing the Sunni-majority insurgency, then overseeing a group dubbed Tawhid wal-Jihad.[35] In his first act of terror, Zarqawi sent militants, Thamir Mubarak and Nidal Arabiyat, to bomb the Jordanian Embassy in Baghdad, killing seventeen. Twelve days later, he was linked to the bombing of the United Nations office in Baghdad, which killed twenty-two. By 2004, the mercurial former convict declared allegiance to Osama Bin Laden, despite both men sharing widely different visions about how best to achieve the same goal: the declaration of an Islamic State. For Zarqawi, the pathway toward this shared goal began with extreme and violent sectarianism, rooted in the killing of Shia.[36] This approach was at odds with Bin Laden, but as he was holed up in a compound in Pakistan, his direct sway over the day-to-day operations of the Iraqi insurgency was limited to infrequent letters sent to Zarqawi and others by many couriers. After declaring allegiance, Zarqawi's groups morphed into what the United States dubbed Al-Qaeda in Iraq (AQI). AQI was, in fact, more brand oriented, and dubbed itself Islamic State Iraq, the precursor to its current incarnation, Islamic State.

Throughout 2005, the US military desperately sought to quell intra-ethnic violence in Iraq. As Zarqawi increased his attacks on Iraqi Shia, US military officials had concluded in December 2005 that the AQI insurgency had failed to "foment sectarian violence. Terrorists attempts to provoke Shi'a have failed."[37] This assessment was unfortunate and overly optimistic. Sixty miles north of Baghdad in Samarra, a Sunni-majority city that is home to the Askariyah shrine, one of the four holiest sites for Shia Muslims. The shrine has a spectacular golden dome and the burial location of Shia Islam's tenth and eleventh imams. Just after midnight seven members of AQI subdued the local guards and placed explosives in mosque's dome. At 7:00 a.m. that same morning, they blew the roof, an act that prompted Shia militia reprisals and hastened the simmering sectarian civil war.[38] The United States, by this point, was facing two competing insurgent movements, and was caught in between AQI-instigated ethnic violence and the counter moves by Shia militias eager to provide security for their own people.

The United States never solved the challenges the Iraqi insurgency posed, but did alter its own military strategy, surging additional forces to Iraq to provide stability and reinstitute long-learned lesson about adopting a strategy to mitigate societal support for an insurgency. This effort was primarily focused on undermining local support for Zarqawi through the co-option of Sunni-majority tribal elements that had previously supported its sectarian kin. This process was later dubbed the "awakening" and has been mythologized as a panacea for many failings before and after the US-led invasion, despite the gains made proving to not be sustainable or replicable elsewhere the United States had deployed.[39]

"During my '06-'07 tour we were up north near Baiji, a predominantly Sunni AOR [area of responsibility]. Toward the end we did the Awakening and all that crap," one US soldier recounts. "That one was weird. There were dudes in ski masks wearing PT glow belts that we had to turn in so that they could get issued to the guys who had been blowing us up for the previous year."[40] PT glow belts refer to the ubiquitous reflective adornment soldiers in Iraq and Afghanistan were required to wear at all time to ensure that motorists could see soldiers at all times of the day, a rather absurd footnote to the American missions in Iraq.[41] Regardless of the attire these reconciled militants were issued, the outcome is undeniable. The number of attacks in AQI strongholds declined, as the number of US troops in these areas increased, and tribal elements maintained their fragile partnership with the US military.

During this time period, the United States began a concerted hunt for Zarqawi, with the intent of killing or capturing the man who was wreaking havoc across the country. By 2006, the hunt for Zarqawi had eclipsed efforts to track down Bin Laden. In April, a US analyst watching the same set of buildings from overhead for weeks finally found what he was looking for. A convoy of cars arrived, prompting a raid that led to the intelligence needed to crack Zarqawi's inner circle.[42] By May, the United States and Great Britain had identified Zarqawi's spiritual advisor and, after locating him, followed him to a house in Balad, just a few miles from where the headquarters of US commander tasked to hunt him was located and then authorized an air strike to kill him.

The killing of Zarqawi touched off a leadership succession inside the group, leading to the elevation of Abu Omar al Baghdadi, whose real name was Ibrahim ibn Awwad al-Badri al-Samarrai, as his successor. He was killed in 2010, giving way to Abu Bakr al Baghdadi, the leader that led the group to its financial, political, and military peak, before the territorial proto-state ISIS established was destroyed in both Iraq and Syria by American, European, Iraqi, and Syrian-Arab and Kurdish forces in 2019. He ruled until he too was killed by US forces in Syria.

The GWOT and America's failings in Iraq and Afghanistan, coupled with the mythologized story of success in tamping down the Sunni insurgency in Iraq, have had an outsized impact on how the most recent war against Islamic State has been judged. Looking back, the antecedents for the successes and challenges Washington faced as it went to war in 2014 were salient as far back as 2003. Yet, the hangover from the unsatisfactory outcomes of the GWOT, coupled with the unlikely political success of Barack Obama, eroded congressional willingness to vote on the use of military force abroad. Absent this oversight, an American president has used this authority to launch small wars, turning to SOF to help solve hard security challenges, without having to suffer from much scrutiny from a war-weary public. These men and women, when paired with American and European air power, can do tremendous things. These outcomes have reinforced the cycle of executive dependence on a small sliver of the armed forces to fight its small wars, a necessity after the failings of the larger conflicts in Iraq and Afghanistan.

As the United States and Europe prepared for war against Islamic State, it had to grapple with polities wary of conflict, a national security elite committed to putting the wars of choice in the Middle East in the rear view mirror, while a group threatened to topple the American-allied government in Iraq, and whose allure was attracting thousands of foreigners to cross on open border with Turkey and fight for an Emirate that if allowed to flourish could lead to a spate of terrorist attacks abroad.

Chapter 2

STATE COLLAPSE AND THE ROAD TO WAR: POLITICS AND WAR PLANNING

The United States was never truly prepared to sanction the overt use of military force against the Syrian regime. To do so, President Obama would have needed support from Congress, which was wary of voting in favor of a resolution to authorize the use of force in September 2013. Instead, the war against Bashar al-Assad was kept in the shadows and overseen by the CIA. This program began slowly in 2013, ramped up, and by 2015 was leading to direct battle field successes. The US Department of Defense (DoD), in contrast, lacked the authority needed to strike regime targets. The rise of the Islamic State, in a way, solved the debate about how the United States would intervene. The group's historic links to Al-Qaeda allowed for the US government to rely on counterterrorism authorities to use military force, a process that needs Congress to vote to sanction the use of force.

The American war began in Syria and Iraq, as they usually do, with lawyers and able men and women of the DoD examining what they are legally allowed to do, and then trying to present a series of options to senior leaders, who then would distill further to present to the president and senior civilians leaders for consideration. The major factor for war planning against the Syrian regime was that Congressional approval would be needed to sanction the use of force. The cost of any military action would dwarf the funding allocated for a series of counterterrorism programs, built to facilitate partnership with security services around the world to combat terrorism. The price tag for even a relatively limited program to vet and train Syrian fighters was estimated to cost $500 million, a sum that would require both new Congressional authorities and a new appropriation of cash to implement. The debate for legal authorities rarely makes it on to the front page of any major newspaper, and is rarely a core focus of think tank events designed to think up options for the United States to consider. However, at this point of the American war effort in Syria, they were necessary to take action against the Assad regime.

The Collapse of Syria: The Turkish View of the Conflict

The United States was not prepared for the collapse of the Syrian state. The revolt against Bashar al-Assad began in Deraa with a series of peaceful protests.[1] The Middle East was in a state of flux, with protests having swept Tunisia's Zine

El Abidine Ben Ali from power, forcing Egypt's Hosni Mubarak to resign, and a Western military intervention in Libya to help topple authoritarian Muammer Qaddafi. The uprisings also sparked protests in Jordan, an American ally, and had spread to Syria. The United States has had tepid relations with the Assad family, viewing the former Soviet ally as a threat to Israel for much of the Cold War, and then as an enabler of the Sunni insurgency after the 2003 invasion of Iraq, and Iran's most important Arab ally. The collapse of the Syrian state forced the Obama administration to confront a challenge it was not prepared for: the popular overthrow of successive Arab governments. The Syrian Arab Republic was not a top-tier issue for American foreign policy. The Assad regime was not a direct threat to the United States homeland, but its hostile relations with Israel and historically close ties with Russia and Iran ensured that it would remain a tertiary priority for the United States.

"I was [in Iraq] from June '06-'07. We straddled the surge," Michael Noonan, a reservist with the military transition team, 3rd Iraqi Army division in western Ninewa told the author, "There was a ratline system [of foreign fighters] coming from Syria, they would use the wadi line to the northwest of Tel Afar. The route is pretty intuitive, you just need to look at Google Earth and follow the Wadi system [from Syria into Iraq]."[2] As Bashar was running men and weapons into Iraq, elements of the American government were trying to overcome tensions with Israel that had reached a boiling point after the 2006 Israeli-Hezbollah war and broker a peace agreement between the two sides.[3] In 2008, the Turkish government stepped in and, using its increasingly close ties with Damascus, sought to reinvigorate Israeli-Syrian talks.

Ankara's diplomatic outreach came at a time when Turkish foreign policy was undergoing a pronounced shift, linked to the ruling AKP's first concerted effort to consolidate its power in Turkey's then anti-Islamist political system. Famously, Erdogan sought to court Assad during a holiday in Bodrum, the popular tourist destination on Turkey's Mediterranean coast. The two leaders met at the airport and famously spent time together in a carefully scripted meeting designed to show that the two leaders were intent on deepening political ties.[4]

Working closely with then prime minister, Recep Tayyip Erdogan, a bookish and spectacled academic, Ahmet Davutoglu, was elevated to the position of foreign minister, replacing the technocratic and economically focused Ali Babacan. This transition coincided with a much broader, internal battle in Turkey for control of the bureaucracy. This time period in recent Turkish history shaped events that would take place almost a decade in the future, beginning with the slow purge of the country's former military elite and replacement with a new generation of Turkish military officers. More broadly, the AKP had made a tactical alliance with Fethullah Gulen, an exiled Turkish cleric who had fled Turkey in 1999 for refuge in the United States. Gulen and Erdogan come from different political-Islamist movements and have little in common. However, both men were persecuted after the Turkish military, working in concert with elements of a staunchly secular judiciary, coerced the elected government, headed by the founder of Turkey's political Islamist movement, Necmettin Erbakan, to resign as prime minister in June 1997.[5]

This event in Turkish history has been dubbed the "post-modern coup" and ushered in a period of political repression that negatively impacted both Erdogan and Gulen. Erdogan was ultimately arrested for reciting a poem and sent to prison some 120 miles north of Istanbul.[6] Gulen, in contrast, fled to the United States, claiming to need urgent medical attention. These two men, one in exile and the other as prime minister and then president, reshaped Turkish society before a power struggle resulted in a failed coup in July 2016. In the interim, the AKP and the Gulen movement were working in concert. The AKP relied upon Gulenists to fill out positions within the bureaucracy, beginning the process of diluting the ingrained opposition to Erdogan and his party throughout Turkish institutions. In 2007, shortly before Davutoglu's appointment, Turkey's second largest party, sought to block the appointment of Abdhullah Gul as president, citing his Islamist background and the fact that his wife, Hayrunnisa, wore a headscarf.

The tensions over Abdullah Gul prompted the Turkish military to issue an e-memorandum on the military's website expressing displeasure and overtly threatening the government. In parallel, the Turkish constitutional court opened a case against the AKP, which could have resulted in the party's closure. These twin events did not have the intended effect. In response to this pressure, Erdogan called for snap elections in July 2007, where his party solidified its parliamentary dominance; winning 341 seats and securing 46.6 percent of the votes cast. In parallel, the AKP and its then ally, the Gulenists, began its bureaucratic counter-offensive, which resulted in a series of fraudulent charges leveled at the military framed internally and for foreign audiences as a step toward Turkish democratization.

The Ergenekon investigation started with a raid in Istanbul and was initially focused on a cadre of ultra-nationalists, including retired Land Forces Colonel Fikri Karadag, the founder of the ultranationalist Kuvayı Milliye Dernegi (National Forces Association or KMD) and Bekir Ozturk, the head of the KMD. Ergenekon refers to a mythical valley in the Atlay Mountains in Central Asia, where myth making has suggested Turkic tribes took refuge in after a series of defeats by the Chinese and other non-Turks. From this valley, the Turks eventually created the Gokturk Empire, after a mythical wolf, Astena, led them from the valley.[7] This legend has considerable resonance amongst nationalist Turks; so much so that the far right has adopted a gray wolf as a symbol for their movement. As for the investigation, Ergenekon was a broad term for the Turkish deep-state, which refers to elements within the Turkish security apparatus that carried out quasi-independent acts of violence to counteract certain political parties, with the intent of ensuring that the state remained true to a strict interpretation of the tenets of the country's founder, Mustafa Kemal Ataturk.[8]

The raids were sold to the public as a force for good and as government steps to roll up the "deep state," whose role in civilian politics had undermined Turkish democracy. The focus on elements of the Turkish military was the first salvo in a broader effort to coup-proof the state. The Balyoz case targeted the military leadership directly and was more damaging than the efforts in Ergenekon to undercut the "gray" entities that could be counted upon to support the toppling of the AKP. In 2009, the Turkish daily *Taraf* published documents delivered anonymously to the newsroom, which were reportedly blueprints for a coup. The documents purportedly recounted the conversations of 162 military personnel at a conference in Istanbul, where the accused discussed how to administer the country in the event of state collapse. The officers involved admitted to attending the conference, but insisted that the discussions were not a coup plot.

Many of the documents were obvious forgeries; however, it is not out of the question that a small number of officers were planning to overthrow the AKP. There was tension between the AKP and the military. The Ergenekon investigation was led by members of the Gulen movement, acting in concert with the AKP and Erdogan. In retrospect, this investigation represented the height of this specific Islamists, and also had deleterious effects on Turkish institutions. The purges of the national police force and the judiciary that took place between 2008 and 2011 coincided with a bolder AKP agenda, including on the execution of foreign policy. By 2011, the AKP-Gulenist relationship was under strain, leading Erdogan to begin taking steps and pressure the group to more properly entrench itself as a junior partner. This effort proved fraught and, beginning in late 2013, escalated when Gulenists leaked surreptitious recordings of Erdogan, his family, and many of his ministers engaged in large-scale graft. This fight pushed Turkey into turmoil, the final outcome of which was the failed July coup attempt.

Davutoglu is a Turkish Islamist, whose academic work grafted German philosophy on to traditional Islamist ideas about Middle Eastern politics to argue in favor of a pronounced shift in how Ankara conceptualized its place in the world. The Middle East, Davutoglu argued, had been artificially divided after the fall of the Ottoman Empire, and the once supra-national Ottoman identity had been usurped by European nationalism, giving way to a series of artificial identities that had stunted political development in the Middle East. The Western powers, he further argued, had reached agreement with the region's autocratic leaders, justifying their joint suppression of democratic movements as necessary for their own security interests. The Arab rulers, he suggested, have used an inflated threat of communism, during the Cold War, and later militant Islamism, as a means to ensure open-ended Western backing to support their authoritarian rule. This backing, then, has given autocratic rulers carte blanche to suppress their own people; and in particular, Islamist movements that better represented regional national identity and the outlooks of the people.

The AKP, therefore, had an opportunity to expand Turkish influence because the party's religious roots could "inspire" the region and their shared faith, Islam, bound Ankara tightly to its neighbors in the Arab world. The AKP's outreach to Bashar al-Assad, in this context, made little sense. Bashar is neither an Islamist, nor was he a model of Arab democratic governance. However, he was the lynchpin in a broader regional agenda Ankara was intent on pursuing. His strong, centralized government ensured that Turkey retained a security partner, committed to the Adana Agreement and ensuring that the 1998 success against the PKK would be sustained. The AKP was also intent on creating a more autonomous foreign policy, centered on expanding Turkish influence with its neighbors, independent of its traditional Western allies. To do so, the AKP reached a series of free trade agreements with its neighbors and, concurrent to that, steadfastly worked to eliminate restrictions to the free movement of people between countries. In September 2009, the AKP finalized a visa-free agreement with its counterparts in Damascus, which complemented the free trade agreement that came into force in 2007, and proposed establishing a broader "Arab Free Trade Zone" that also included Lebanon and Jordan.[9]

Relations with Syria, in particular, remained on a positive trajectory, including on hard security issues linked to the PKK and expanding the terms of the Adana Agreement to include more specific provisions on intelligence sharing in October 2010, which the AKP-dominated parliament passed in 2011. The erosion of border controls tightly connected the Turkish city of Gaziantep with Syria's Aleppo, which are only separated by 75 miles of highway, and at one point were bound together as part of the Aleppo Province during Ottoman Empire. This connection would later serve as a key artery for the illicit supply of weapons and materiel to the anti-Assad insurgency, and also as the main jumping off point for Muslims eager to join the Islamic State. In June 2010, the attraction was more prosaic: "Gaziantep is the first stop out of Syria: it's more developed and it has better shopping," Emin Berk, who was then in charge of small business dealings between Gaziantep and Aleppo, told the *Financial Times*.[10]

Between 2006 and 2009, Turkish-Syrian trade jumped from $800 million in 2006 to $2 billion, and Ankara had the intention of increasing trade to over $5 billion. At the outset of the Arab Spring, Ankara and Damascus had ample reasons to cooperate. They were benefiting financially from increased trade and, on the security side, the two governments retained an interest in maintaining pressure on the PKK. For Ankara, Assad was seen as a reformer, and the key node in the broader effort to expand Turkish influence. Davutoglu was aware of the contradiction between his embrace of Islamism and his outreach to Assad. He described Turkish-Syrian relations as akin to West Germany's *Ostpolitik*, the Cold War era term used to explain Bonn's entente with East Berlin and broader effort to retain cordial ties between East and West Germany. Ankara's version, Davtuoglu argued, would accelerate the country's broader effort to become more deeply intertwined with its Arab neighbors.

Turkey and Syria have, now, become deeply intertwined, but the days of thousands of Syrians flocking to Turkish shopping malls are over. Instead, the violence of war has forced Syrian refugees into Turkey and, beginning in late 2011, Ankara made the choice to give lethal aid to various opposition groups. Ankara's use of lethal force was not its initial preference. As the Arab Spring protests swept through the Middle East, the Turkish government adopted a country-by-country approach to the protests. In Tunisia and Egypt, the AKP supported political change and sought to carve out close relationships with Muslim Brotherhood-linked political parties. In Libya, Ankara sought to protect its historically close economic relationship with Muammer Qaddafi, and resisted giving support to its Western allies right up until the last minute, when military action was inevitable and Turkey risked being on the outside looking in of a post-Qaddafi transition. In Syria, Davutoglu was tasked with managing the crisis, with the intent of ensuring that Bashar made enough concession to the growing protest movement to end them with his regime intact.

The United States had an entirely different relationship with Damascus. By 2010, the American efforts to broker a peace agreement between Israel and Syria had failed. The United States, too, was in the process of drawing down from Iraq, while simultaneously augmenting its forces in Afghanistan. The Obama administration was focused on ending the two American-led wars in the region and managing the demands posed by the unrest in many Arab countries.

The Libya Debate: Congressional Push-Back against the Use of Force

The Arab revolts touched off a series of secondary challenges for its neighbors and Europe. This problem began to manifest in February 2011, as protests swept across Libya, and Qaddafi's use of force began to prompt people to leave for Europe.[11] In response, France and the United Kingdom began to consider military action and sought support from the United States. The Obama administration was hesitant to support military action, with then secretary of defense, Robert Gates, arguing that "a narrow no-fly-zone likely would have little effect on the movement of ground forces or in protecting innocent civilians," so any action would have to directly target the Libyan regime targets on the ground.[12] Despite Obama's reluctance to support military action, by March 2011, the United Nations Security Council had passed Resolution 1973, which authorized the establishment of an NFZ and included language that allowed "all necessary measures" to be taken to protect civilians.[13]

At the outset of the conflict, Congress warned the administration that its decision to use force without consulting congress violated the war powers act, the legislation passed in 1973 to place constraints on the president's ability to use force abroad. The Obama administration argued that "U.S. operations [in Libya] do not involve sustained fighting or active exchanges of fire with hostile forces, nor do they involve U.S. ground troops."[14] In June 2011, the situation devolved further after Democrat Rep. Dennis Kucinich and Republican Rep. Walter Jones filed a toothless lawsuit claiming the administration had violated the law. These debates did not result in any substantive congressional oversight and, by August, the issue was momentarily moot. The NATO-led air campaign had turned the tide of the conflict and, by October, Libya's oddball authoritarian had been chased from power, forced to flee, and holed up in Sirte, where a mob found him hiding in a drainage pipe, sodomized with a combat knife, and killed him after his convoy was bombed by a French aircraft.[15]

His death was not universally celebrated. The NATO-led air campaign also shifted thinking in Russia, an erstwhile American adversary amidst a major military modernization program. During the debate at the United Nations, Russia chose not to wield its veto and abstained during the vote for UNSCR 1973. At the outset of the NATO intervention, Russian foreign minister Sergey Lavrov criticized strikes on Qaddafi forces, arguing Russia "consider[s] that intervention by the coalition in what is essentially an internal civil war is not sanctioned by the U.N. Security Council resolution."[16] Moscow's criticism, according to former secretary of state Hillary Clinton, was disingenuous because she opined in her recounting of events, "[Russia] knew as well as anyone what 'all necessary measures' meant."[17] Russian irritation would matter, considerably, during the debates about Syria and shaped American thinking about the merits of intervention.

"Air-to-ground strikes, including on the convoy, have nothing to do with a no-fly zone," Russian foreign minister Sergey Lavrov stated, repeating Russia's insistence that NATO had overstepped its mandate, and argued that "the Libyan rebels violated the Geneva Conventions."[18] Moscow's angry condemnations of the air operation reflected an early view of the Arab Spring and the prevailing idea that the turmoil in the Arab world was similar to the "color revolutions" that swept Eastern Europe at the end of the Cold War. This paranoid way of thinking ascribed a Western hand to the democratic protests and assumed that radical political change would be disadvantageous for Russian economic interests. As Alexey Malashenko explains, "Countless Russian publications explained the Arab Spring in terms of conspiracy theories and the idea of a Western plot to further its own selfish interests—in particular, squeezing Russia out of the Middle East."[19] More practically, as Dimitri Trenin writes, the Libya saga closed the door on current Russian president Vladimir Putin's acquiescence to cooperation with the West—and the United States, in particular—and hardened the point of view within the Kremlin that collaboration with adversarial powers was not a viable mechanism to manage regional crises.[20]

The stage was set. The three major antagonists in Syria, on the eve of the uprising, had different national interests, differing conceptions of national interests, and would gravitate toward different actors to support. The same is true for the other actors involved; namely, the Gulf Arabs and the Islamic Republic of Iran. The antecedents of the general dysfunction amongst the supporters of the anti-Assad opposition are also rooted in the Arab Spring—and how each country's national security elite viewed the prospect of political change. The flashpoint was Egypt. Turkish foreign minister Davutoglu viewed political change in Egypt, and the Muslim Brotherhood's political strength as a net positive for Turkish national interests. In Turkish foreign policy circles, there was a consensus that Ankara and Cairo could be a new "axis" of democratic states, capable of challenging the dominant American position in the Middle East. The AKP, and Davutoglu in particular, was positing the idea that Turkey was offering an alternative vision to the Western status quo, which he argued was autocratic and required political repression. Turkey, in contrast, was on the side of the people, and championing a democracy and political justice.

The reality, of course, is that Obama administration was watching the events unfold and figuring out on the fly how to respond to monumental changes in a region most had thought was stable. However, the Turkish vision for the region differed considerably from the Gulf Arab states, led by the gerontocratic Saudi monarchs and the younger, but equally authoritarian leadership in the United Arab Emirates. The Saudis, in particular, had a hostile view of the Brotherhood and have sought to squelch the group's political ascendance in Egypt and elsewhere. The major shock for Riyadh and Abu Dhabi, as it would turn out, came when the United States endorsed political change, calling on its long-time ally, Hosni Mubarak, to step aside.[21]

Moscow was also caught off-guard. The narrative in Moscow, according to Dmitri Trenin, was first focused on fomenting the conspiracy that the United States and Europe were orchestrating the protests. That conspiracy, however, began to shift from America the omnipotent to America the incompetent, culminating in the Kremlin "watching in amazement" as Washington "pulled the plug on Mubarak," a long-time ally and key US partner.[22] Oddly, both Russia and American allies in the Persian Gulf were surprised that the United States would choose political change over a known ally, and each would determine, albeit for entirely different reasons, that political changes in the region were a net negative for their national interest. The Arab States were concerned about regime survival and blamed Washington for what they viewed as inadequate support, while Moscow viewed the outcomes of the uprisings as detrimental for Russian political and economic interests.

Both Washington and Ankara found themselves supporting the protest movements, albeit for different reasons. Turkey saw the changes as the start of a broader transition that would result in the end of the United States' dominant role in the region. Washington, in contrast, felt morally compelled to support democratic protests, believing that once the dust settled, a modicum of normalcy would return and core American interests could be maintained. These dynamics, ultimately, all manifested in Syria: Turkey sought to empower the Muslim Brotherhood and other political Islamist movements, while the Gulf States gravitated toward its own factions—and then staked out positions in opposition to Ankara. Russia sought to preserve the status quo, while Washington was caught between its natural predilection toward supporting democratic change, but being wary of getting bogged down in a military conflict it didn't want to fight.

Breaking with Assad: The Rise of a Militarized Opposition

The protests in Syria began in Deraa, a fairly large city on the border with Jordan that would later be dubbed "the cradle of the revolution." The protests began after the Syrian regime arrested fifteen teenage boys. They were caught spray painting the slogan "the people want the downfall of the regime."[23] In response, the locals protested and ignited what would become a wave of protests that would gather every Friday, and which spread throughout the country. The Syrian regime, unable to end these gatherings, began to fire into crowds to kill innocent civilians to end the gatherings. The regime did try and appear altruistic, instituting cosmetic reforms to try and appease the protesters; Bashar sacked the then prime minister and replaced the Cabinet; granted Syrian Kurds citizenship; and gave amnesty to prisoners, including releasing some from the notorious Sednaya Prison.[24] At the early stages of the protests, Samer Abboud writes that there was no single leader directing the protests, nor were there any signs of significant Islamist penetration.

The Assad regime, however, portrayed the anti-government protests as being foreign controlled and dominated by radicals, a description that Russia would later adopt after it intervened in September 2015.[25]

By June, the protests had escalated, and the regime had responded with overwhelming force. Faced with escalating violence, both Ankara and Moscow opted to pursue similar strategies. Russian foreign diplomats counseled their counterparts in Damascus to make concessions to the protesters, according to Dmitri Trenin.[26] Turkish foreign minister Davutoglu, acting at the direction of Erdogan, visited Damascus in April, where he reiterated Prime Minister Erdogan's previous insistence that Assad make reforms to appease the protesters.[27] However, by August, Turkey's patience had worn thin. Erdogan warned: "Until today, we have been very patient, wondering many times whether we can solve this, whether words translated into actions … now we have come to the last moments of our patience." In a last ditch effort, Erdogan once again dispatched Davutoglu to Damascus, warning that Assad had fifteen days to make concessions. During Davutoglu's visit, he reportedly chastised the regime for its aggressive action in Der Ezour and Hama and thought that he had reached an agreement with the regime to withdraw from these cities and release political prisoners. However, after returning to Ankara it was clear that the regime had lied to the Turks.[28]

The United States was cautious, but as the protests began Obama administration sought to pressure its allies, including Turkey, to break ties with the regime. In late August, and in parallel to similar actions with America's European allies, Obama announced that "for the sake of the Syrian people, the time has come for President Assad to step aside."[29] Inside the White House, the break with Assad touched off a more serious debate about arming the opposition. In 2012, then CIA director David H. Petraeus presented a plan to begin supporting elements of the armed opposition in Jordan. Secretary of State Hillary Clinton and former defense minister Leon Panetta, along with chairman of the Joint Chiefs of Staff, Gen. Martin E. Dempsey, backed the plan.

The most important decision-maker, President Obama, worried that covert intervention would fail to topple Bashar al-Assad and create a pathway to increase overt military involvement to finish the job. Obama, according to the *New York Times*, based his initial assumption on a series of CIA studies about the efficacy and outcomes of previous US efforts to clandestinely arm and train insurgent and opposition groups.[30] "At that time, nobody thought Assad would be overthrown instantly," the then ambassador to Syria, Robert Ford, recounted. "There was a sense in the Obama administration that a large part of the army was Sunni and unreliable, and that while the officer corps was going to stay loyal, the foot soldiers would not. It looked to us, that in a war of attrition, and more soldiers defected, eventually the Allawis would lose."[31] In retrospect, one State Department official noted this thinking was fallacy. "That was one of the basic simplistic propaganda driven errors in analysis from the beginning; this thinking that of course the Sunnis would defect. For people who really knew what was up, they understood Syria to be at least equally and probably more divided on class and urban-rural lines than just this sectarian one."[32]

At this point of the war Ankara was coming into line with the American position on Assad and had begun to deliberate how best to support the nascent opposition. In September, Turkey downgraded relations with the regime. In November 2011, Erdogan compared Assad to Hitler and warned that he could suffer the same fate as Qaddafi, saying the Libyan leader "got killed in a way that none of us desired, after using the same phrases that you use."[33] The Turkish change of policy came after the United States had broken with Damascus. "We had asked the Turks to join the Obama statement," according to Ambassador Ford, "but they had initially refused. They had warm ties with Assad up until the uprising." By this point, Ankara only had nascent ties with the opposition, but would soon emerge as the hub for the Free Syrian Army and the armed resistance.

The reaction in Moscow was different. In contrast to the thinking in Ankara and Washington, Russian analysts concluded that Assad could withstand the internal revolt if protected from external interference and reinforced with weapons and support. As Trenin notes, "It was in Syria that Putin decided to make a point that U.S. driven regime change in the Middle East had limits; that outside military intervention in Syria would not be permitted; and that world's supreme authority, in matters of war and peace, was the UN Security Council, where Russia had a veto."[34] By May 2011, the United Nations Panel of Experts, tasked with monitoring a weapons embargo placed on Syria, reported on the Turkish inspection of a plane bound for Aleppo that made a stop-over in Turkey. Upon inspection, the Turks discovered weapons and ammunition listed as "auto parts" to evade detection.[35] Russia, for its part, used its position at the United Nations to shield these early weapons transfers, foreshadowing the partnership they would establish with Iran in support of Bashar in the years that followed.

The Turkish city of Antakya, the bustling border town opposite the Bab al-Hawa border crossing with Idlib, emerged as the first hub for the armed opposition. "That place was crawling with foreign operatives," a person based in the area back at the time told the author. "I think back with a degree of amazement of how surreal it was. Idealistic young Syrians who, simply due to fluency in English, were rubbing shoulders with diplomats, military undercover operatives, seasoned humanitarian aid workers, and journalists."[36] By 2012, Gaziantep emerged as another hub for the anti-Assad armed opposition, with multiples of meetings taking place at the two shopping malls that just two years or so prior, thousands of Syrians were purchasing goods at the height of the Assad–Erdogan entente.

The mood in Ankara in 2011 was that, once the November 2012 election was in the rear view mirror, President Obama would sanction military force.[37] The Turkish government favored the creation of a safe zone across the entirety of its border, modeled on the NFZ Ankara grew to abhor over northern Iraq because it created a safe haven for the Iraqi Kurds. Ankara's push for an internationally enforced buffer zone was linked to its broader effort to cultivate an opposition government, based first in Turkey, and which would move in to the zone once it was established. The Turkish government, in contact with proponents of the nascent United States-led arming strategy, had chosen to believe that the United States would use armed force to remove Assad from power—and Ankara was prepared to help.

The illicit flow of weapons began in 2012 and included inputs from a multitude of countries that, for a brief moment, settled on a common strategy to topple the regime. The United States, at this point, was not yet covertly involved, and was debating the merits of a large covert arming program. Obama ultimately authorized American covert intervention because the actions of its ostensible allies in the conflict—Qatar, Turkey, and Saudi Arabia—were unwieldy and uncoordinated. Qatar was the most willing to flout warnings coming from the United States about the provision of one weapon in particular: shoulder-fired anti-aircraft missiles. These man-portable air defense systems, or MANPADS, could be reappropriated to shoot down civilian aircraft—a reality that American Air Force pilots would face in 2017. "The FN-6 is pretty badass. There was a delivery of Chinese FN-6 MANPADS to one Sunni extremist group, who then sold it to someone, who then sold it someone in ISIS, who then shot it at us near Der Ezour. The pilot luckily went against his training to avoid it."[38]

Despite the risks and many warnings, mobile phone videos shot in Syria showed Chinese-made FN-6 fired missiles, and eventually prompting the United States to chastise Qatar for its provision of these weapons. The Qatari weapons shipments also prompted consternation in Riyadh, Abu Dhabi, and Amman, with each government reportedly warning that Doha was being too flippant with its support for the opposition and was too comfortable with the Islamist elements of the anti-Assad opposition.[39] These tensions polarized the region in the wake of the Arab Spring, with two rival camps emerging. Turkey and Qatar emerged as the camp most willing to work with and through Islamist groups, and cut outs for the Muslim Brotherhood, in particular. Saudi Arabia and the United Arab Emirates, in contrast, sought to work through more nationalist groups. These tensions prompted each of these two blocs to back different actors in Syria, with militias acting as key proxies for each of these actors. "We became aware that the Turks were working with Jihadist elements around January 2013, and tried to get them to stop," a former senior official indicated. Ankara and Doha, along with other Gulf countries, were amenable to working with the United States, but not at the expense of their favored groups and who they had bet on to punish Assad for the civil war. This disparate approach to the opposition helped to fracture it in Syria and, over time, eroded trust between elements of the US government and Ankara. It also prompted a reluctant Barack Obama to try and assert some control of the types of weapons different groups in Syria were receiving.

In Spring 2013 Obama authorized the start of Timber Sycamore, standing up two operation centers in Jordan and Turkey to vet and send arms to the anti-Assad opposition.[40] From the outset, the United States sought to engage its allies, turning to oil-rich Saudi Arabia to provide funding for training and to provide the bulk of the weapons, while CIA did the training and oversaw dispersement. As one official recounts, "Things had been stuck, but after the chemical weapons attacks in August 2013, [Obama] felt comfortable enough to give weapons to the FSA. [The United States] had already been involved in the training, but this was when the U.S. started providing weapons."[41] The trainers for this program were culled from US SOF and the basic program would, eventually, serve as the model for the overt, DoD-led effort that would begin later in the war. By October 2014, Vice President Joe Biden, speaking at an event, suggested that there were "several thousand" people who had been vetted and linked to the program were in Syria and fighting.[42] "This program has never been truly understood," a senior official explained. "The program that shall not be named was the largest in the [CIA's] history."[43] As a second official continued, "This program did more and was intended to do more than most of the people out there realize."[44]

This program was slotted under Title 50 of the US code, which provides the statutory authority for intelligence activities, including covert action, and allowed the CIA to oversee the initial training and housed under a presidential directive to keep the intent secret.[45] The intent was to bolster the ongoing efforts to organize the Syrian opposition, which was being pulled between its different patrons in the Gulf and Turkey, and which never truly had control over the actions of the armed militias in the country. "Nobody thought the opposition was coherent," a former senior Obama official told the author. "The challenge was to try and influence their deliberations through the giving of support."[46]

Despite the challenges, the stage was set. On one side, the anti-Assad opposition had gained access to weapons, both from the United States and from its regional allies. These regional countries had their own favored proxies operating outside the rebel military structure the United States had grafted on to and these relationships reflected the ideological schisms that had emerged during the Arab Spring. Meanwhile, Bashar had carved out his own pipeline for arms, turning to his old friends, the Russian Federation and the Islamic Republic of Iran. The war, however, would soon take a turn, as a splinter group that had penetrated Syria at the outset of the uprising asserted itself and laid its claim to Syrian territory.

The other looming issue was that the opposition was beginning to radicalize and Al-Qaeda-linked elements had begun to make their way to the country to take up arms against Assad, and in support of their broader goal of establishing an Islamic Emirate. Jabhat al Nusra was formed in 2011 at the outset of the Syrian uprising and in coordination with the self-declared Emir of Islamic State Iraq, the now-deceased Abu Bakr al Baghdadi. Baghdadi was the second successor to Abu Musab al Zarqawi, who was killed in 2006. To lead operations in Syria, Baghdadi turned to Abu Muhammad al-Jolani, a veteran of the Iraq insurgency and, like Baghdadi, was incarcerated at Camp Bucca, the vast facility that many jihadist members were once housed after being captured by US forces in Iraq.[47] Jolani was the appointed Emir of Iraq's Ninewa province, a critical node in Islamic State Iraq's operation and a critical source of revenue for the group, even when it was at its nadir in 2009.[48] Jabhat al Nusra enmeshed itself within the broader anti-Assad milieu, grafting its Islamist bona fides on to the nationalist insurgency. "We saw contacts starting between Nusra and FSA—and I mean contacts, not tactical coordination—in Fall 2012," according to former ambassador Ford. "When we would raise it with the Syrian opposition, they would say we don't like them, but we are fighting a common enemy, and we need to cooperate a bit, and we don't want them to turn on us."[49]

Nusra's approach to the anti-Assad uprising was in line with the urgings of Osama Bin Laden, who before his death in Pakistan issued a series of letters to his deputies, resulting in his successor, Ayman al Zawahiri, issuing a set of "general guidelines" that sought to de-emphasize intra-Muslim violence that undermines local support for the group, as it seeks to maintain its focus on attacking the United States. Guidelines aside, the United States saw fit to designate Jabhat al Nusra a terrorist group, citing their links to AQI in December 2012.[50] Within a year, tensions between Jolani and Baghdadi escalated, and in 2013 the two sides had a dramatic falling out. The result was a schism within the Jihadist movement inside Syria, with Jabhat al Nusra formally taking up the mantle of Al-Qaeda, while Islamic State stayed true to the actions of Zarqawi. For the United States, the initial Al-Qaeda-linked presence posed a considerable policy challenge. The CIA sought to manage this problem through the vetting of fighters, but there is no doubt that American weapons provided to Syrian groups, as well as weapons that Turkey provided its own factions, made their way into Nusra's weapon stockpiles. It is also undeniable that the pairing of Islamists and CIA armed rebels, working in tandem, pushed Assad to the brink, prompting the overt deployment of Russian troops in the country late 2015.

Planning for War: Congressional Push-Back and the Rule of Law

Up until late 2013, the United States was not seriously contemplating overt military force against the Syrian regime. President Obama, wary of intervention but concerned about the illicit spread of weapons of mass destruction, warned "[The United States] cannot have a situation where chemical or biological weapons are falling into the hands of the wrong people" and "we have communicated in no uncertain terms with every player in the region that that's a red line for us and that there would be enormous consequences if we start seeing movement on the chemical weapons front or the use of chemical weapons."[51] This dual framing, linked to both the regime's use of chemical weapons and the potential that illicit actors could gain access to these weapons, framed how the Obama administration grappled with this issue and the Pentagon's contingency planning for war.

With the CIA program shunted away under Title 50 authority, initial thinking about using the military was relegated to a secondary role. This changed on August 21, 2013, following events in a besieged neighborhood just outside Damascus. In the early morning hours, a slew of 330 millimeter surface-to-surface rockets were fired into a dense urban area, carrying the nerve agent Sarin.[52] The regime attack killed 1,429 people[53], according to US intelligence, and prompted the initial plan for a series of airstrikes on Syria chemical weapons targets, conducted in coordination with the UK and France. However, by August 29, disagreement in Britain upended former prime minister David Cameron's effort to win parliamentary approval for military action, after fellow Tory Party members chose to vote with Labor against the motion.[54]

In the United States, the American populace was divided over whether or not to use military force in Syria, with an 80 percent majority of respondents believing that the White House needed Congressional approval to take such action.[55] After dispatching Secretary of State John Kerry to make an impassioned case for the use of force, Obama changed his mind about the planned air campaign and directed the White House to first seek Congressional approval before taking any military action.[56] Obama argued that he was "mindful that I'm the president of the world's oldest constitutional democracy. I've long believed that our power is rooted not just in our military might, but in our example as a government of the people, by the people and for the people." According to NBC News, the White House was "fairly confident that Congress will grant them the authority to launch a strike."[57]

This proved to be false hope. As Patrick Homan and Jeffrey Lantis write in their book *The Battle for U.S. Foreign Policy,* "The White House might have guessed congressional sentiments before the 'red line' declaration. Many lawmakers had been deeply frustrated by President Obama's decision in 2011 to intervene in Libya's civil war without seeking congressional authorization for the use of military force."[58] The prospect of American military action in Congress united a series of disparate actors, ranging from the progressive caucus, inside the Democratic Party to the libertarian and right-leaning Tea Party faction within the Republican Party, and a slew of middle-of-the-road lawmakers wary of voting in favor of a strike that the American public did not support. Faced with the likelihood of defeat, the vote was never held and the request withdrawn.

The efficacy of military action remains a subject of debate. There is a faction within the United States that continues to argue that an American and French strike could have catalyzed the regime's defeat, while others noted that a limited air and missile strike was unlikely to have much of an effect on the regime's ability to wage war. This brief saga opened the door for two separate actions that then took place. On the diplomatic side, the United States and Russia sought to address the Syrian chemical weapons issue, reaching agreement on an ambitious and fraught plan to destroy Assad's stockpiles of chemical precursors needed to make weapons. On the military side, the failure to act in response to the Ghouta attack did not end planning, it simply pushed American action into another direction, focused on a training and equipping the Syrian opposition. This effort, at first thought of as a means to pressure Assad in parallel to the CIA effort, eventually morphed into the force that would take the fight to Islamic State.

The American military effort stemmed from a proposal, first articulated publicly by the chairman of the Joint Chiefs of Staff, Martin Dempsey, in July 2013 in a letter to the Senate Armed Services Committee, to consider a program to train, advise, and assist the opposition. The scale of the program, Dempsey wrote, would cost "$500 million per year initially" and "require safe areas outside Syria as well as support from our regional partners" to implement.[59] The issue, as one official described to the author, stemmed from the lack of authorities to take military action against the Syrian regime.

> The issue was, how do we take action against Assad, how do we develop a T&E [Train and Equip] program on a massive scale, with forces that are not vetted, and now how do you do these things outside the security assistance rubric ... we

worked a lot with our lawyers at the time and we knew we couldn't take action without violating the law.[60]

These early efforts never truly advanced beyond planning, but they did frame the follow-on program that began to take shape in early 2015, and which was broadly referred to as the US Train and Equip program in Syria. The program was, at first, a very limited and legally tenuous look at the options to train men to fight Bashar and never really advanced beyond theoretical planning. After taking command of Special Operations Command Central, or SOCCENT, Lt. General Michael Nagata received a request, emanating from the White House to the DoD, asking for options to explore how to put additional military pressure on the Assad regime.

> We wrote a short memo, and the short memo was a Train and Equip program, very similar to the one you are not supposed to talk about, and which would could create a similar structures to identify, train, and recruit Syrians. At the time, I didn't think it had a snowball chance in hell, and then Mosul fell, and then I got a call that said "Nagata turn that into a plan."[61]

In 2014, the planning for the T&E program was in its infancy, and a bit chaotic at its inception. The United States had a basic problem. The authorities given to the DoD to partner with armed actors are premised on counterterrorism goals, and in most cases require working through partner governments. Assad, despite killing thousands of his own people, is not a designated terrorist. "The paper churn, began in early 2014. I want to say March," an official familiar with the program indicated, "but, because of the lack of authorities, these early conversations were never very detailed. There was an understanding that we can't really do this and there was not a lot of detailed operational planning."[62] The first iteration of the T/E effort was guided by lawyers, who were looking at whether Section 1208 or 1206 authorities could be used to justify a T/E program to help topple the regime.[63] Section 1208 authorities stem from lessons learned during the war in Afghanistan and the realization that during the initial invasion, SOF lacked the Unconventional Warfare authority to directly pay foreign individuals to conduct or support US operations.[64]

The National Defense Authorization Act appropriated $25 million for this task and, in later years, the fund was increased to $85 million. These funds come with specific oversight provisions and legally ill-suited for the nascent planning to vet and train elements of the Syrian opposition. The same applies to the 1206 authority, which refers to $350 million in funding to train an ally's maritime and security forces to support and work alongside US forces conducting counterterrorism missions.[65] There were times during this initial process where the DoD also explored whether or not it could use counter-narcotics authorities, but this was found to be legally dubious. At one point, there was also an exploration about whether money was allocated for the Cooperative Threat Reduction (CTR) program could be used after authorities, but the program is intended to provide support to states to secure nuclear facilities, and not train opposition elements to secure clandestine chemical weapons sites in war-torn Syria.[66]

The Catalyst: Islamic State Seizes Power in Iraq

As Washington debated its options, events in Iraq eventually shifted the conversation and hastened planning. "The thing about all these authorities," a current official told the author, "is that without a crisis it is hard to get them. But when there is a crisis, everyone has to move fast and it forces us to speed up."[67] That crisis came in June 2014. The fall of Mosul caught many Americans off-guard and shifted thinking about the nascent planning for a large-scale T&E program. "Here was this ally that we sunk all this money into the Iraqi military and that we thought had problems, but was basically stable, and then it is like, 'oh my god, we have to stop the bleeding,'" a Special Forces officers recounted.[68]

The troubles in Iraq began in Fallujah in 2012, a city of symbolic importance for the Islamic State, and where Iraq's second Sunni insurgency gained steam after it grew from a broader Sunni-led political effort to decentralize the Iraqi state.[69] The catalyst for a broad-based, Sunni-rooted insurgent movement began after the March 2010 election, where former prime minister Nuri al-Maliki's State of Law Coalition (SLC), a grouping of Shia Islamists ran against the Iraqi National Movement, or Iraqiya coalition, a secular and Sunni Muslim bloc, and a third, Iranian-linked Iraqi National Alliance (INA). The Iraqiya coalition won ninety-one seats, compared to eighty-nine for Maliki's SLC, with the INA securing seventy seats. This outcome allowed for Maliki to form a Shia majority of parliamentary seats, which this group was able to increase in 2014 from 159 to 191.[70]

The rejuvenated Sunni insurgency began in December 2012, following the arrest of the Iraqi finance minister Rafia al-Isawi, a native of the former extremist stronghold of Anbar. The arrest prompted a series of protests in the Sunni-majority cities of Ramadi and Fallujah.[71] Maliki handled these protests poorly, alternating between handing out piecemeal concessions and authorizing violence. The protesters were subdivided into two groups, with one linked to Iraq's mainstream Sunni clerical establishment and politicians within the broader Sunni political movement and a second, more sinister, group tied to the Jaysh Rijal al-Taraqa al-Naqshbandia, a neo-Ba'athist insurgent group that would later ally with Islamic State. As the more legitimate subgroup of protesters dwindled, either through apathy or the decisions of its more pragmatic leadership, JRTN eventually remerged as the most numerically representative. Maliki eventually sanctioned more aggressive police action to curtail the unrest, a cycle that ended with the collapse of security in Anbar. From this tenuous position, ISIS, which had retained a presence in this part of Iraq, managed to cultivate ties with JRTN and prepare for its main objective: the seizure of Mosul.

At around the same time that security in Anbar was collapsing, the friction between Jolani and Baghdadi began to manifest in Syria. In late 2012, Baghdadi wrote to Jolani to tell him to publicly announce his affiliation with Islamic State Iraq.

Jolani and the Nusra elites rejected the demand, fearing that any public declaration of fealty to Islamic State Iraq would undermine Nusra's credibility with the broader anti-Assad opposition. Jolani's hesitation eventually prompted Baghdadi to travel to Syria for a meeting, which resulted in ISIS releasing an audiotape that made the announcement on Jolani's behalf. In response, the wary Al-Qaeda leader disavowed Baghdadi's authority; refused to subordinate his group's authority to Baghdadi; and turned to Al-Qaeda leader Ayman al Zawahiri for guidance and financial support. Zawahiri, for his part, ordered Baghdadi to keep the two organizations separate, but Baghdadi refused to abide by his guidance. This intra-Jihadist schism pitted the older Al-Qaeda brand, which had latched on to the broader anti-Assad insurgency (and eventually emerged as the strongest group within the fractured anti-Assad opposition movement), and the more violent Islamic State. In a series of clashes, ISIS defeated its rivals in eastern Syria, consolidating control over the Euphrates River Valley and out to Ninewa province in Iraq, and down through the Anbar desert. From this base, the group executed its most daring act during its rise to power, and seized Mosul; an act that raised alarm bells in neighboring Jordan and prompted Western military action.

The battle for Mosul was brief, but decisive. By May 2014, the Islamic State had released a series of videos online, showing the group conducting raids against security forces and establishing the notion that it was a broad-based social and political movement, committed to achieving its ultimate goal. This set the stage for the group's assault on Mosul. The battle began in early June and ended on June 10. The Iraqi defense of the city collapsed. The rapid collapse of the Iraqi Security Forces surprised many Americans and caught Turkey flat footed. The AKP was wary of the American invasion of Iraq and, in the aftermath of the conflict, tilted toward Sunni-majority political parties. During the campaign for the March 2010 election, Turkey openly backed the Iraqiya coalition, providing political support for two politicians, in particular, Osama and Atheel Nujaifi. Osama previously served as speaker of the parliament, and later emerged as the leader of Mutahidun, the Sunni-majority political bloc that replaced Iraqiya after Maliki secured power after the 2010 election. Nujaifi, in turn, grafted his political ambitions on to the wishes of the nascent protest movement, championing the idea of a Sunni-majority federal zone in Iraq.

The Turkish government supported these efforts, including backing a political arrangement between Osama's brother, Atheel, a former governor of Ninewa, and Mustafa Barzani, the most powerful politician in Iraq's Kurdistan region. As part of this effort to carve out a coherent, and broad-based bloc to oppose Maliki, Ankara concentrated on deepening its presence in Mosul. Ankara's tilt also prompted backlash throughout much of Iraqi politics, given that Nujaifi's proposal was a de facto break up of the state along ethnic and sectarian lines. Ankara's policy choices, ultimately, contributed to the widespread myth that Turkey was an Islamic State supporter. This pervasive myth undermined Ankara's regional standing and, alongside broader tensions over political Islam, hardened anti-Turkish views amongst a faction of Arabs and with the Kurds as Islamic State gained power.

As the security situation throughout Iraq continued to deteriorate, politicians began to preen for the cameras. In one absurd moment, Atheel al-Nujaifi was filmed on a street patrol with a handful of guys, who would later flee the city with Atheel for Erbil. "I remember watching that clip," a journalist based in Erbil explained, "and thinking to myself, what the hell is about to happen here."[72] Ankara refused to evacuate its consulate in Mosul, despite receiving warnings that Islamic State was poised to attack the city's outer neighborhoods. The group, according to Reuters, hoped to take control of a few neighborhoods for a few hours, before they would retreat under fire. They did not expect the city to fall.[73] The security forces in the city, at least on paper, outnumbered Islamic State, with a series of brigades deployed in the city. These units had all been trained by conventional US forces, along with the National Guard and reserve units.[74] "The fall of Mosul was surprising," a current US military official described to the author, "but some of us knew it was possible. We could see the corruption. We knew that there were paychecks going up there, but couldn't figure out who was receiving them."[75]

Perhaps this explains the Turkish response. As early as June 6, Atheel al-Nujaifi had warned counterparts in Iraqi Kurdistan about the ISIS threat. However, as of June 10, then foreign minister Ahmet Davutoglu declared that the consulate was not in any danger and that the diplomatic staff and their dependents would not be evacuated. This decision proved unwise. As ISIS entered the city, and as hundreds of Iraqi security forces fled south toward Baghdad, the consulate was overrun and ISIS took forty-six Turkish citizens hostage, along with three local staff members.[76] Ankara would later trade its own ISIS prisoners to the group in exchange for the release of its citizens, but in the intervening months Ankara's hands were tied as the United States began to assemble the coalition to defeat Islamic State. Turkey was, in effect, cast aside in these early months, as Washington scrambled to ramp up a military campaign to defend Baghdad and Erbil, and then extended the war over the border to Syria.

A Failed Raid: Removing Constraints for Military Action

However, like Turkey, before the war truly ramped up, American hostages held by Islamic State also had to be accounted for. Less than a month after the fall of Mosul, two Black Hawk helicopters carrying Delta operators flew from Jordan into Syria. This small group of elite soldiers was tasked with rescuing several Western hostages, including Americans James Foley and Steven Sotloff.[77] "We did not want to do anything until we could secure those hostages," a member of the military told the author. "This issue tied the hands of the military in those early days."[78] As Sean Naylor describes in *Relentless Strike*, the operation involved flying in the stealth helicopter made famous during the Osama Bin laden raid 200 miles across the Syrian Desert, where they were met by an armed drone circling over an ISIS compound that the United States had been watching for at least a week.[79] The pilot on the mission, who was later awarded a Silver Star, flew for five hours after being shot in the leg by ISIS ground fire, while a member of the Marines Corp. received a

Bronze Star after he came into "close combat" with a member of the Islamic State.[80] The raid proved unsuccessful and the two American hostages had been moved shortly before the arrival of the US operators. Both of the hostages would later be killed and their deaths filmed and posted online by the Islamic State, as airstrikes began in Iraq.

Looking back at this period before the start of major combat operations against the Islamic State, considerable attention is paid to the August 2013 chemical weapons attack, and the Obama administration's decision to include Congress in its deliberations about the use of military force. The American strike would, in all likelihood, have been limited in scope, and limited to the unit that carried out the August chemical attack, and the infrastructure supporting the broader chemical weapons program. The TLAM is a wonderful tool, a weapon designed and perfected since its first iteration was fielded in 1983. The US government, and its closest allies, has come to rely on this weapon to punish adversaries, without having to risk the life of a pilot flying inside the engagement envelope of a surface-to-air missile system, while still being able to accurately destroy almost any target on earth. While the Tomahawk is very accurate, the missile is not magic, and it has not managed to radically alter the behavior of states or terrorist groups.

The role of Congress is often overlooked in the American march to war against Islamic State. However, there was a brief window where, if Congress was so inclined, it could have forced the hand of a wary Obama administration and passed an authorization for military action against the Syrian regime. Instead, the vote was never held because it would have been defeated. As the debate over Libya showed, Congress does not like to be sidestepped, and the effort to unseat Assad has been costly. The Chemical Weapons deal, in this sense, provided a perfect outlet for the critics of the administration, as well as its supporters. It shunted the weight of US effort around a diplomatic mechanism to remove declared Syrian chemical weapons, a worthwhile goal that the administration could support, and gave critics the opportunity to lambast President Obama, without having to actually vote on an alternative course. Islamic State, in contrast, could be defeated with less effort, and without the risk of being drawn into a civil conflict that the United States wanted little part of, and allowed for Washington to curtail its involvement in a way that felt most comfortable: a battle against terrorism.

Chapter 3

THE WILD WEST: THE WAR BEGINS

"Erbil felt hugely insecure, we honestly felt that the city was in real danger," according a journalist based in Iraq during the summer of 2014.[1] After Islamic State bust out of the desert, few places in Iraq felt safe. The United States, hamstrung by its own laws and with little situational awareness, would soon fire the first shot at Islamic State in what would later be dubbed Operation Inherent Resolve (OIR). As would become common, the slow-flying and now-ubiquitous unmanned aerial vehicles (UAVs) struck the first ISIS target, after their manned and distant cousin, the F-15E, "lazed" the target.[2] The bomb hit an American-made armored personnel carrier that the United States had provided to the Iraqis, but which ISIS had stolen and was now using to rampage throughout Syria and Iraq. The war had begun, but it would take months before it was given a name.

After years of instability in the 1990s, the Kurdistan Regional Government (KRG) emerged as a safe haven after the 2003 invasion of Iraq, and the follow-on civil conflict and insurgency against coalition forces. The Kurdish enclave had managed to wall itself off from much of Iraq and through the imposition of check points and rigorous, if illiberal, security measures, ensured that its people and visitors were relatively secure. The divide between the KRG and the rest of Iraq is referred to as the "green line" and snakes around the cities of Mosul and Kirkuk, juts south into Diyala and extends east to the mountainous border with Iran.

Mosul was a violent no-go zone for many non-Iraqis during and after the American occupation of the country. As Islamic State consolidated control and threatened the city, there was still a sense that Iraq would face a violent insurgency; and one that would only gradually and sporadically control places that few would ever visit. This changed in mid-June. The collapse of the city uprooted thousands of local Arabs, pushing them north to perceived safety. The influx of these internally displaced people to Iraqi Kurdistan quickly overwhelmed local capacity, stressing the local government and adding to the panic of the people living in Erbil.

"There was a huge snake of cars at a KRG checkpoint," according to the Erbil-based journalist and "within a very short period, tens of thousands of people were seeking shelter in the carcasses of half-built shopping malls, and in half-constructed buildings." These people, many of whom were Christian, felt abandoned and angry and the mood was turning from concern about a violent insurgency in Arab-majority Iraq to the KDP Peshmerga being overrun and ISIS slaughtering the people it conquered. The Iraqi Kurds, in contrast, felt helpless and struggled absorbing thousands of more people, joining the stream of Kurds from Syria that had also fled the ongoing chaos to the west.[3]

Finding Phone Numbers: Losing Touch and Going Kinetic

The United States struggled to grapple with the fall of Mosul and lacked the situational awareness to truly understand what was going on. In the days that followed the city's collapse, the group pushed east to Tel Afar, through much of eastern Iraq, and down the country's main highway. American forces had left the country in 2011, despite efforts to leave behind some residual forces to advise and assist Iraqis, so at the early stage of the ISIS take over the United States had little situational awareness about the scope of the problem it faced. "Our deployment at the end of 2011 was heavily focused on maintaining pressure on some of the Iranian proxy groups who had bad intentions in mind for the American withdrawal," a US soldier described about the planning to drawdown from Iraq at the time.

> When word came down "to go to zero" we were still white boarding for what it would be like to leave a residual presence of varying levels. We had a heavier end that would have more shooters to continue partnered or unilateral options, while the lower end would be a minimum number of advisors and enablers to allow the Iraqis to execute ops, with U.S. forces remaining in the Joint Operation Center [JOC] to support from there … We would send these things up the chain on residual presence; the same answer kept coming back: "Go down to zero." After three times, it was like, "hey we are actually going to zero".[4]

The "zero" option was driven by domestic American politics and, at that time, intended to repurpose assets in Iraq for the build-up of American forces in Afghanistan. "Overnight the JOC got cleared out, computers and TVs packed up, and palletized. Most of it was shipped over to Afghanistan to support that fight."[5] The United States did have two small twelve-man teams—or Operational Detachment Alphas, or ODAs—that remained in country, but they were funded using Title 22 authorities. These authorities are one of two main funding streams that govern security cooperation. Title 22 funding is appropriated to the State Department, which can then transfer them to the DoD to manage and oversee security assistance programs.

"After the withdrawal in 2011, the only real access and placement was the Title 22 Teams," according to a Special Forces officers involved in OIR. "We had two ODA teams, that fell under the State Department, and basically worked at the school house at the Iraqi Counter Terrorism Service to produce commandos at the onset of initial training. We were not engaged tactically."[6] To engage tactically, of course, would require a different set of authorities and they were lacking in Iraq at this time. These two teams were aware of what was going on and, at different points in 2014, "raised the flag" about the rise of Islamic State and the threat it posed to

Iraq, but the United States lacked the legal authorities to operate in country. Still, as US officials began to meet with their Iraqi counterparts, and efforts were made to try and do something to prepare the Counter Terrorism Service for the rising threat from Islamic State. In 2013

> There was no way CENTCOM was going to get new authority or funding, and so we did what we could, and so we arranged the first set of instruction for Iraqi SOF; so we brought out a bunch out of Iraq because we had no authority to train in country, and we brought them to [Jordan] and we tried to jury rig a new curriculum to deal with a more sophisticated actor.[7]

The legal challenges stemmed from two interlinked decisions, made in two ideologically opposed administrations, and helped along by Iraq's own political schisms. In 2008, President George W. Bush and his counterpart in Iraq, Prime Minister Nuri al Maliki, reached an agreement on a Status of Forces Agreement (SOFA) that pegged passage in the Iraqi parliament to an American withdrawal by December 31, 2011. President Obama, in turn, chose not to push hard to renew the agreement, arguing that the immunity for US forces deployed in the country was not robust enough to pass muster. The road to this impasse began in late December 2007, when Prime Minister Maliki requested that the United Nations Security Council renew the mandate for American and coalition troops to operate in the country.[8] To reach agreement on a bilateral arrangement on the SOFA President Bush compromised on a core demand of any country with which the United States reaches agreement on legal immunity for American forces in country. The Iraqis had sought to subjugate American personnel to Iraqi law, a demand at odds with American practice elsewhere. To overcome this disagreement, the United States proposed compromise language that effectively protected US forces from Iraqi prosecution, albeit in a way that created a mechanism for the Iraqi courts to assert jurisdiction if a number of (near impossible) conditions were met.[9]

This agreement was ratified in the Iraqi parliament, but to win consensus it included a key stipulation: the SOFA would expire on December 31, 2011, and US troops would then be asked to vacate the country. After taking office, the Obama administration had to grapple with its promise to withdraw forces from Iraq during the campaign and how best to navigate the withdrawal deadline. After considerable deliberation and weighing a range of options, the military presented to the National Security Council for consideration, Obama settled on leaving behind a residual force of 5,000 troops, tasked with training Iraqi forces. However, negotiations were slowed by the disagreements following the March 2010 election in Iraq, and the time it took for Maliki to reach consensus with the Shia Islamist bloc to form a government. This political bloc consolidated a broad, anti-American coalition in the Iraqi parliament, which was opposed to renewing the SOFA. The two sides failed to reach agreement in time, particularly over the need to enshrine any executive agreement in each country's legislature. Facing an apathetic White House and an intractable Maliki, the agreement expired per the terms George Bush negotiated and the United States withdrew.

Year 2011 was an odd time to be in Iraq. "We had just conducted a raid and we were bringing back the targeted individual to hand over to the Iraqis. As we banked over BIAP, I remember hearing one of the crusty 160th CW5s up in the cockpit come over the intercom and say, 'look at that fucking waste of money.'" In a sign of what was to come just a few years later, the helicopter this Special Forces officer was flying in was passing over lines and lines of brand new, American-made and US tax payer-purchased Ford trucks.

> There were lines of brand new F-150s, F-250s, and other trucks that had been shipped in and were ready for distribution to the Iraqis. Dozens and dozens of fuel blivets [bladders] and all kinds of other gear. We were just weeks away from leaving for good, and all that stuff was sitting there, not distributed, and ready to be taken by whoever wanted to take it. It was really no big surprise when we saw ISIS running around in stuff we bought for the Iraqis.[10]

As Iraq's security situation deteriorated in 2014, a consensus emerged in Washington that the core problem Iraq faced stemmed from Maliki's authoritarianism and his steady consolidation of executive power in the office of the prime minister. This narrative stemmed from the basic belief in the efficacy of American military action against Islamic State Iraq, Islamic State's predecessor, and the target of significant American and Iraqi pressure beginning in 2006. This pressure, the argument went, forced the Sunni-insurgency out of Iraq's major cities, giving space to the country's leaders to govern more effectively and to address sectarian grievances that drove the insurgency. This narrative failed to capture how Islamic State Iraq had adapted to its precarious circumstances, despite unprecedented American pressure. The group established itself as a hierarchical system, with sub-entities that plugged into the broader organization. These sub-entities, in turn, would assign men control over certain areas, and these people would collect taxes and rent from vulnerable businesses that bought protection from the group. This continued, albeit at a lower level than before, even during the "surge" of American forces and meant that Islamic State was never truly ousted from Iraqi cities. This meant that Islamic State was weakened during the surge, but it still managed to retain a foothold in the core areas that it would later emerge from in and around 2014. To terrorize locals inside these areas, the group resorted to extrajudicial killings, and frequent assassinations of men who collaborated with the Iraqi state. To effectively target the group, the United States, along with the Iraqi government, relied heavily on the Counter Terrorism Services, or CTS. The CTS is a group of elite Iraqi soldiers, built from the ashes of the Iraqi Army the United States disbanded after the 2003 invasion. Without any real guidance about how to rebuild the Iraqi army, US Army Special Forces acted with minimal guidance to build "special" forces, as opposed to conventional infantry.

These forces held the line after Mosul fell, but in the fighting that followed, these elite troops suffered considerable losses. The problems came in 2006, when Prime Minister Maliki began to issue a string of decrees to bring the CTS, the broader Counter Terrorism Command, and three Iraqi Special Operations Forces

(ISOF) Brigades under the prime minister's control. This effectively made the CTS a cabinet-level position in Iraq, with the commander reporting directly to the prime minister. The broader issue, of course, is that the gains made in security required near nightly raids by American and Iraqi Special Forces, working day in and day out to track insurgents in ways that were outside the scope of regular law enforcement. This approach, while needed to quell the insurgency and beat back a group like Islamic State Iraq, is at odds with security in a well-functioning country. The challenge was how to build upon obvious gains in security that were sustainable, without having to rely on a CTS to perform law enforcement functions.

Still, the narrative allowed for upset Americans, caught off guard and surprised by the collapse of the Iraqi military, to assign responsibility for events largely outside of anyone's control to one person: Nuri al Maliki. This blame, then, extended to President Obama for his decision to withdraw in 2011 and for downgrading the threat Islamic State posed. Obama certainly did himself no favors when he described Islamic State as the "jayvee team," compared to the more lethal Al-Qaeda Central, even after it had raised its flag over Fallujah in Iraq.[11] The Islamic State was not the jayvee team, but its resurgence cannot simply be linked to one decision, or Maliki's sectarianism. These two things contributed, but as Carter Malkasian argues, the broader issue with this simplistic explanation is that it overlooks the support within Iraq for the Islamic State, and the uncomfortable reality that the group has latent support in the areas where it managed to retain influence before it surged in 2014.[12]

The suppression of Islamic State Iraq, in retrospect, was dependent on the presence of the US military that beat back the group on behalf of the tribal elements that partnered with the Americans. These conditions weren't sustainable, precisely because they depended on an external power to guarantee their safety from two hostile groups, the Iraqi central government and the Islamic State. Further, after Iraqi politics changed in 2010, the presence of US troops became an issue for Shia political parties to exploit, creating a vicious and no-win situation for the United States, where it found itself acting as a hammer against extremists, but also as an enabler of anti-American actors in the Iraqi political space that had a militant arm that the last vestiges of US troops in Iraq were tasked with pressuring.

The suppression of AQI was a tactical success, but it was a temporary outcome of a change in tactics and how the United States deployed troops. But those tactics were insufficient to change the calculus of the Iraqi leadership. Islamic State took advantage and as the Obama administration prepared for war, it sought to tackle an issue it left on the table: Maliki's tenure as prime minister and the conditions for Americans to return to the country. The collapse of Mosul forced a change in thinking in the Obama administration. The nascent and legalistic planning for a large T/E program morphed into a broader effort to cultivate partners on the ground to fight Islamic State in Syria. The Obama administration, wary of overt military action, had to carve out authorities to fund a conflict against the group, in partnership with the Iraqis and an as-yet-unidentified partner force in Syria. In parallel, the United States had to identify partners willing to fight alongside it, and to host the aircraft and troops that would be needed for the fight.

In June, just days after Mosul fell, Obama reached agreement with Maliki on the terms of immunity for US soldiers. In preparation to send a reported 300 troops to Iraq, Obama settled on Maliki issuing an executive agreement, essentially guaranteeing immunity for the US military. The administration's acceptance of this arrangement came just a few short years after it had rejected a similar compromise when negotiating the extension to the Bush-era SOFA.[13] This effort came as American allies in the Middle East feared the worst and, perhaps for cynical reasons, were concerned that Islamic State was poised to not just take Baghdad, but to expand beyond its strongholds. In Jordan, King Abdullah II's government raised the alarm bell with their American counterparts. As a US official based in Jordan at the time recounts, "There was daily existential dread in Amman that Baghdad would fall and the Toyotas would cross the border and make a run on Amman."[14] Jordan's government, at this time, was "openly fretting about ISIS coming across the eastern border," the US official recounts. "We couldn't tell if it was totally serious, or if it was positioning to get us to pay attention to them," but the sense that Washington and Amman were not in synch on Islamic State was a very real issue that US officials had to grapple with in late 2014.[15]

Whatever Jordan's motives for raising the alarm, the initial planning was, in the words of a former DoD official, a "flail" for those first few months. Up until this point, the United States had presented a myriad of options about what to do in Syria, knowing that the lack of a legal mandate relegated these memos moot before hitting send on the email. "It was then like, holy shit, Mosul. Do something," a former official recalls. "I remember DoD pushing up the chain a simple question to the White House: 'What do you want us to do'? In response, the White House was saying, 'what can you do and we'll tell you what the strategy is'?"[16]

In the skies above Iraq, the US Air Force had begun to shift assets from supporting the war in Afghanistan to monitor the situation in Iraq, albeit without any authorities to act. As the Islamic State expanded its territory, flying high overhead were UAVs, flying in orbits and building a basic ground picture of what was happening. These drones were joined by another aircraft, including what would later become a workhorse in the different assaults on urban towns in Syria and Iraq: the F-15E Strike Eagle. Built around a large radar, the F-15 was initially built as a pure air-to-air fighter, designed with the basic motto of not including a "pound for air-to-ground" missions. The F-15E Strike Eagle, the latest variant, betrayed this lineage, and was designed to haul bombs into a fight and fight its way out with high-end Russian fighters sent to stop it. But in the weeks after Mosul fell, F-15E was doing nontraditional intelligence, surveillance, and reconnaissance (ISR) over Iraq. Lacking the authorities to use force, the pilots on these advanced machines were using their targeting pods to track Islamic State to help build a picture of their "pattern of life," in anticipation that force would soon be used.

These Strike Eagles were flying to Iraq from Al Dhafra Air Base in the United Arab Emirates. "In June 2014, when ISIS was on the rise, and we were watching this … Our squadron was split in half, one day we would be in Afghanistan, then back in Iraq and Syria," a US Air Force Weapons System Officer, or WSO (pronounced WIZO) described. "We had no ground intelligence and we had no authorities or anything for a while. Suffice to say we could not do anything kinetically. We were restricted."[17] The two changes came after the failed hostage rescue of Steven Sotloff and James Foley in Raqqa and, in response to the Islamic State's threat to the Iraqi Kurds. Erbil has long been a way station for elements of the US military. The Kurdish capital city is also home to an American consulate, housed in the Ankawa district just a short drive from the main airport. This Assyrian-Christian district was, at that time, overflowing with displaced persons fleeing Arab Iraq. Erbil is also home to a slew of American oil companies, who have offices in this part of Iraq because of its relative safety.

The concentration of Americans in this part of Iraq created the right conditions to begin the first strikes on Islamic State. President Obama, speaking at the White House, authorized limited strikes against ISIS to protect Americans in Erbil and Baghdad and to break the siege of Mt. Sinjar, where thousands of Iraqi Yezidis had fled near-certain genocide and sexual enslavement.[18] Using the inherent right to self-defense, a standard component of the rules of engagement, which govern the who, what, where of physical actions in combat, the United States determined that if Islamic State breached the bridges to the west of the city, the Air Force would strike in self-defense. On the night of August 8, as the Islamic State reached the Kalak bridge, an American drone watched from far above. As the Islamic State's American-made APC reached the river, the drone released a APX-114 hellfire missile. Due to profile limitations, the missile was guided in by the laser from an F-15E targeting pod. "The very first kinetic event was a [drone] that a Strike Eagle lazed in because it was 'around the corner', which means that the Strike Eagle set up a buddy laze profile. This isn't something we trained to. We just figured it out."[19] The missile slammed into the Islamic State vehicle, holding back the assault on a key bridge leading to Erbil.

Officially, this strike was attributed to the US Navy. This was a ruse. The United Arab Emirates had not yet officially joined the United States in its nascent war against Islamic State and were wary of acknowledging that this opening salvo of air strikes flew from a base inside its territory. "All the early efforts were USAF operations attributed to the Navy. We could not attribute this because of host nation sensitivities, so we said it came from our sovereign territory, the carrier floating offshore."[20] Abu Dhabi, as it would turn out, was eager to get into the fight and used its leverage when the first coalition strikes began later that month.

On the ground, President Obama authorized the limited introduction of SOF in June, some of which were pulled from Joint Special Operations Command (JSOC). It is the command set up in the wake of a failed hostage rescue in Iran to house America's most elite special operations units. Despite having special operations in the title, JSOC does not include Army Special Forces, the forces that specialize in Unconventional Warfare, or the effort to use small teams to cultivate and train indigenous groups to rebel against oppressive governments. As Sean Naylor writes, the "core of [JSOC] was Delta (full name: 1st Special Forces Operational Detachment Alpha)," a highly specialized unit modeled on Great

Britain's Special Air Service (SAS). Delta has a rigorous selection process, and the recruits after undergoing intense and specialized training, along with a litany of psychological tests, go on a six-month operator training course. After completing this course, the soldiers are considered a member of the unit and given the title "operator."[21]

The drawdown from Iraq limited Delta's exposure to the country and, like the pilots flying overhead and almost all of the DoD, there was little situational awareness about Islamic State in Iraq and Syria. "The SOF community was beside themselves at having lost the relationships [with CTS] because there was no SOFA, and no willingness to restart CT enabling or partnering programs. Basically we had been paying these guys, developing these guys, for years, right? And then, sorry, bye." As one Delta Force member recalls:

> [JSOC] was coming in with CONOP after CONOP in the run up to the 2012 election [in Iraq]. They were proposing any number of things to get after these guys. And there was just not a policy appetite to do anything about it ... The unit knew who were looking at, what they were about, and even though we had left, we were still looking. We watched the situation deteriorating and wanted to do something.[22]

The Obama administration simply had no appetite for war in Iraq and planning for operations against Islamic State was stalled at a low level.

The situation had grown more dire by 2013.

> I reconnected with CTS and they started telling me about [Islamic State] ... and these are the best war fighters in the Iraqi military, in large measure because they were U.S. trained, and they have incredible forces, and they were telling me about combat sophistication and weaponry that I did not recognize. I said, you and I fought AQI, and I don't remember AQI being able to do what you are talking about, and they would say that we had never fought anything like this before.

Lt. General (Ret.) Mike Nagata recalled of a meeting in Baghdad with the Iraqi military.

> I went back to CENTCOM, I briefed the CENTCOM and then SOCOM commander and I went to DC to meet the Pentagon, the intelligence community and anyone who would listen, and the contrast in reception between MacDill and Washington was stark. The feedback I got in DC was, "no it can't possibly be that bad" and I even heard, "Nagata, do not you remember we won in Iraq". I felt when I left DC I was being patted on the head and being told to go on my merry way.[23]

Ultimately, it was the Islamic State that forced a change. "Things started to move rapidly," a soldier familiar with JSOC described, after:

We got approvals to go into Iraq. But on my first couple of trips to the region there was a "do not go to Iraq" thing. Once we got those approvals we could send guys in to get boots on the ground. We were able to incrementally increase the presence and then get a better idea of how things were going. But for a while it was to the point of asking for 1-2 people, and that would need the whole USG approval chain.[24]

For the Army, the early days of the Iraq campaign were frustrating. "I had just left, I was one of the last guys out in 2011," a Special Forces officer described. "And here I am going back in June 2014. It was this feeling of disgust, what the hell am I doing here."[25] The Obama administration authorized the sending of one company of US Army Special Forces, which includes six Operational Detachment Alpha teams to Iraq to do an assessment of the Iraqi army, as security was collapsing. The ODA teams are made up of twelve men each and are intended to work autonomously and in cooperation with local forces. This initial wave of Americans also included a company from the Special Force's Crisis Response Element (CRE), along with Navy SEALs to support the possible embassy evacuation, and Marines. "It was pretty tense," a person involved in the initial response described; "there were a lot of people that were pretty apprehensive. State was shitting themselves. There was a sense that the Iraqi army would fold, and that it would get ugly."

The first American boots on the ground weren't sent to fight. "In June, we were directed to do an assessment that involved analyzing the Iraqi positions in Baghdad, and to determine for the President of where we should go with this, and what support they required, and the Iraqi capabilities at the time," a soldier familiar with this effort described. "We went around and met with all the brigades and Iraqi leadership. We determined the Iraqis could hold Baghdad, but not go on offense. That took about 3 weeks. And once that was done we were holding in the Baghdad area until the Mosul Dam fell on August 7."[26] As a second soldier recounts, "There were kinda these ghost structures of units, where, on paper, you had Iraqi brigades, but in reality there was only a couple hundred of guys."

This ad-hoc approach to the opening air campaign mirrored the actions on the ground. From the air, the United States had the very basic problem of marking who was where, and where forces were lined up along the forward line of troops. "We didn't know how to battle track. They are not US forces on the ground and we weren't talking to them, so we had devised a couple of improvised ways to watch the FLOT," a pilot described. "We are just adapting to what we have. The Rivet Joint would mark the communications on certain frequencies, we would put points down like those are the friendly line of troops, they are going west, and then we would see who was moving east. This allowed to know who were the bad guys."[27] As Lt. General (Ret.) Nagata described:

We were doing as much grassroots experimentation about how to advise and assist the Iraqis without getting so close to gunfire that we got our choke chain yanked by leadership. It was happening all over. In the early days, the only forces that were willing to engage in close combat with ISIS were the Kurds in the north or CTS; the conventional force and the police forces were petrified and paralyzed with fear.[28]

The lack of ground awareness remains a significant sore point for the American military. After building the Iraqi military from scratch, and cultivating and training the dependable CTS, the US military had simply lost touch with the Iraqi armed forces. "The thing is that we had lost our network, so we were looking for phone numbers. We spent 8 years in constant contact with these people, every 6 months back with the same partners, and we lost connection to the point where guys were thumbing through their phones looking for someone to call," a US Army Special Forces officer described of the early efforts to reconnect with the Iraqis. "I heard of calls going to anyone, active or retired, who worked with CTS or the Pesh, and asking them if they kept in contact on Facebook, or wherever," a second Special Forces member confirmed.[29]

Despite these challenges, the first wave of Special Forces teams that flew into Baghdad focused their efforts on plugging in to the Iraqi military, and integrating American air power with Iraqi ground units to stop the Islamic State's advance. As one Special Forces soldier recounts, "The first teams to integrate with coalition air power was with the Kurds in Erbil, and then it was Baghdad, and then in Anbar." In Baghdad, the teams "worked with CTS, and we joked that we are the war fighter hotline, if an Iraqi made contact, they'd call us, we'd get real time video over them, confirm it, and then get air power to support their maneuver."[30] From the start of the operation, the United States was working through the Iraqi leadership, rather than accompanying Iraqi units as they marshaled forces for the counter offensive. The partnership was uneasy and the Iraqi military leadership would often hide details about operations from their American counterparts, often because Iranian-linked militias were participating in combat operations. As was common during the war, the fighters on the ground became addicted to US air power, believing it necessary for even basic maneuvers against Islamic State.

First Contact: Defending a Mountain and the First Partnered Operations

At the edges of Kurdish-controlled territory, the Islamic State's expansion led to the KDP Peshmerga collapse in Sinjar. The Kurdish soldiers fled at night, leaving behind an undefended village home to Iraq's Yezidi minority. The Yezidis are sometimes described as ethnically Kurdish, but many disavow this identifier. The group is unique because it practices a pre-Islamic monotheistic religion that worships seven angels, and that Islamic State identified as heretical—and therefore justified killing in large numbers. Outnumbered and weak, the collapse of the KDP forced thousands of Yezidis to flee for the perceived safety of the Sinjar Mountains, a narrow 100-kilometer-long mountain range just inside the Iraqi border from Syria. By August 2, the Yezidi villages just south of the mountain range had come under fire by the Islamic State, as the group pushed west from Mosul and Tel Afar.

The battle was brief, if nonexistent, for control of Sinjar because the residents who could escape chose to flee.

"We were sitting at the Operations Center, back when it was called Team Baghdad, and we were watching Sinjar fall," a Special Forces soldier recalled.

> We had an armed Predator [drone] and we are just watching the Daesh guys lining up Yezidi men in front of a pit they had dug, and we couldn't do anything. They all got shot in the back of the head. One hellfire smoking these guys, maybe the Yezidis would run and maybe some would have lived, or maybe not. At least we would have tried, but we couldn't act.[31]

As the line of cars filled with fleeing families snaked out of Sinjar, and thousands simply walked north to the safety of the mountains, the specter of genocide shifted these planning sessions from debates on paper and in meeting rooms to real life. "By late spring, or early summer 2014, DoD had had several planning meetings about airdropping humanitarian supplies and how best to do it," a former Defense Department official described.[32] The planning for the first airdrop began on August 5, after the Iraqi government requested assistance from United States Central Command. The first step was for the mission planners to receive all the proper clearances and legal authorities, including the vital diplomatic permission to conduct such a mission. One major challenge on this first drop was that the United States typically had troops clear the area before dropping supplies, in order to ensure that the heavy pallets wouldn't land on civilians standing below. The official story, as recounted in *Air Force Magazine*, was that the first night one C-17 and two C-130 Hercules aircraft flew to Sinjar, escorted by two F/A-18s from the carrier George H. W. Bush.[33]

In reality, the escorts were F-15E Strike Eagles. "There was a mountain with a road that zig-zagged up to the top. There were 300 or so vehicles parked on the road. We set up a defensive perimeter to help bring in the first airdrop," an F-15E WSO recounted.[34] The United States had also managed to get some troops on top of the mountain. "We had some special operators that we had inserted up there to help a little." After warning for months about Islamic State, and sending CONOP after CONOP up the chain, only to be met with silence, Delta Force was about ready to find the partner force that it would work through to take down the caliphate. These troops were part of the first JSOC contingent, deployed to augment the defense of the embassy and were on top of the mountain, meeting with the YPG leadership. "We were on Sinjar, doing the recruitment of [YPG commander] Mazlum," a JSOC member recounted.[35]

On that busy first night, the F-15E was called into service to strike an ISIS target near the Mosul Dam. "After the supplies were dropped, we backtracked to Mosul because ISIS was threatening to blow the dam." The German- and Italian-made dam was built during the 1980s on unstable gypsum and sandstone soil that dissolved as water passed over it. The structure needs near-continuous injections of concrete to ensure that it does not leak and, over time, collapse. The foreign engineers knew the structure was unstable, but the equally unstable Iraqi president, Saddam

Hussein, insisted on the location. In 2006, the US Army Corps of Engineers called it "the most dangerous dam in the world," according to *TIME*.[36] In the hours before Obama authorized airstrikes in Iraq, the Islamic State had wrested control over the structure from the Peshmerga. The danger was that Islamic State could blow the dam, or through its negligence it would simply collapse, unleashing a tidal wave of water on villages down river and killing thousands. This strike was the first partnered operation of the war. "We had SOF guys on the ground with the Peshmerga, and this was our first partnered operation, but it was all ad hoc. We could see where ISIS was shooting from and we could just drop near that position."[37]

The actual assault to take the dam was neither straightforward, nor easy to pull off because it required managing intra-Iraqi tensions, even as the Islamic State continued to seize territory from the Iraqi army. "After that first initial strike along that red line we had set near Erbil, a decision was made to assist the Iraqis in taking back the dam," a US Army Special Forces member described. "But at this time, our SOFA, and things like that didn't exist because it was so early." To begin this push on the ground, the United States had to begin the process of moving equipment and supplies north to join the fight. "The Pesh had already been working up there with some American forces with the Task Force. In Baghdad, we were working with the Iraqis. We were taking Iraqis up to Kurdistan to go fight." It would not be easy, largely because Islamic State's control of the highway ruled out the possibility of trucking the armored Humvees needed for the fight.

> We had four C-17 aircraft that were dedicated to moving Iraqi forces to Erbil. The Iraqi CTS have black Humvees that look like vehicles from Mad Max. We had two battalions worth of vehicles that we were able to move up there overnight. So basically those aircraft were doing turn and burns all night, picking up and dropping off. And with no SOFA, we couldn't fly the Iraqis to Erbil, so they flew on their own C-130.[38]

The Iraqi CTS are widely regarded as the country's most elite soldiers. However, in early August, these men were wary of going to fight with the Kurds. "The Iraqis weren't unified. They were not that willing to go and do this mission. They did not see it as saving Iraq, and so we had to explain to them about the Mosul dam and how it could kill thousands." The Kurdish KDP was also wary of working with the CTS. "When the Iraqis landed in Erbil, CTS wasn't welcomed by the Kurds. Having Iraqi forces up there was contentious as hell." These tensions continued throughout the planning of the operation, which began with a meeting with the prime minister, Nechirvan Barzani, and then continued with a series of meetings between the two CTS generals and the Peshmerga leadership. "The Kurds only wanted to meet with the leadership, while the Iraqis wanted to bring a 20 person security detail. That security detail acted like a security detail, and were walking in front of the general. It was like flexing on both sides to show who was boss."[39]

The plan to assault the dam was also contested by both sides. The plan called for the CTS to be the main force and to drive its Humvees down the main road, leading toward the dam, while the Peshmerga would sweep along the flanks to hold territory that had been seized from ISIS. "The CTS did not like this because that main road was where the IEDs were concentrated," a person familiar with the planning recounts. "They interpreted this plan as the Pesh making the CTS eat the IEDs, and then the Pesh would walk on to the battle field and declare victory."

The group of Americans, Kurds, and Iraqis staged for the operation in Duhok, having to take the long way around because the bridges leading from Erbil to Mosul had been destroyed in the airstrikes to blunt the ISIS advance. The group traversed Kurdistan along the mountain road that runs parallel to the border with Turkey, before slicing south to Duhok. From the outset, there was a disparity in equipment. The CTS were dependent on the Kurds for medical evacuation, but only the elite Kurdish units had American-made Humvees. "They were using busses for medevac. It was only the specialized Pesh that had Humvees." Up until the last minute, the CTS resisted executing the plan. "They wanted the Pesh to do it. Basically, the U.S. forces embedded with them had to tell them that they were the premier force in Iraq, so if they didn't lead it and it got out that they didn't want to lead, it would be a shame on them, and a boon for the Kurds when it was all over." This last-minute appeal pushed the CTS into action and, on August 16, the operation kicked off.

The night before, the US Special Forces that had been planning the mission were told that they would not be able to accompany the Iraqi and Kurdish units on the mission. "At the time, we were still waiting on authorities and permissions. We were hopeful that we could go with the Iraqis. But the night before we were told that we couldn't accompany them to the dam. We could only advise and assist too locations behind the forward line of troops," a person familiar with the plan explained.

> We helped them plan, helped them through it, and then we had to tell the Iraqis that we can't go with them. So we then had to deal with that fall out. They kinda got over that, we talked through how they could call us, how they could mark their emissions with the GPS we gave them, how they could call for fire, and then we managed that.[40]

As Lt. General (Ret.) Nagata explained:

> The caution I would give commanders was that I wanted to avoid a rage reaction from policymakers, where we would then end up in more constrained environment than we were in, so it was do what we can to help the Iraqis, but know we are playing the long game, and out of our zeal to help them, do not do something today to make us regret what you did tomorrow.[41]

The assault began with airstrikes, but Islamic States had dug itself in to defensive fighting positions. As would become common for Americans fighting this war, they discovered that the group would conceal heavy weapons in houses, staring down the likely point of advance for the opposing forces. Islamic State forces would open the door to fire down the road and then shut the door to avoid detection from orbiting American aircraft poised to strike at exposed weapons positions. "They had mortars set up in houses in courtyards, they would use the DShK [50 caliber] heavy machine guns inside doorways in houses, look down the main road, and then shoot and close the doors to mask them," a US soldier explained. "A lot of the CTS would take rounds, and we would then task ISR to find where the people were at, and then see where they were taking it from, and then look for them and strike them when we found them to enable them along the route."[42] On that first night of fighting, the CTS fell short of the dam. There was a lot of heavy fighting in the villages and towns to the east of the structure, but by the next night, on August 17, "they started to get in there and to the bridge," a soldier recalls. "The next day they pushed up the western side to secure the perimeter." The battle ended quickly, with hugs between the Pesh and the CTS leadership, a fitting end to the acrimony that dominated the planning phases. The Iraqis suffered 30–40 casualties and returned to Baghdad shortly after the dam was retaken.

As for the effort with Maliki, the Obama administration was close to realizing its goal on the night the strikes against ISIS began. With years of protest, the collapse of the Iraqi security forces, and the loss of Mosul, Maliki's grip on power began to weaken. Both the United States and the Islamic Republic of Iran, the two most influential external actors in Iraq, lobbied for his replacement with a more capable prime minister in the final days of his rule. The United States, seeking to capitalize on Iraq's need for its assistance, signaled that more support would depend on Iraq forming a more inclusive government, and therefore indirectly address the sectarian issue that helped fracture Sunni politics and drove some support for Islamic State. The Iranians, wary of Iraq being overrun by a hostile terrorist group, had grown wary of the mis-management and tactics that allowed a nonstate actor to take over nearly half of the country. In this sense, the United States and Iran, two hostile actors, had a shared interest in defeating Islamic State. This shared interest matched broader trends, led by the concurrent negotiations for a nuclear agreement then Secretary of State Kerry was leading. The synergies, however, were not perfect. In Iraq, Iran's interlocutors to project power were malignant Shia militias; many of which had a history of fighting the Americans. And, in Syria, the Iranian provision of weapons and fighters was at odds with the clandestine, CIA- and regional-ally-led program to force Bashar to make concessions to end his rule. Still, as the battle was ramping up, the United States and Iran found themselves fighting on the same side, a strange outcome for those that had been deployed to Iraq before 2011. The same US soldiers that had been asked to pressure these groups were now looking the other way, as they became a core component of the nascent anti-ISIS effort.

Night One: The War Moves across the Border to Syria

The first coalition mission over Iraq was ad-hoc and thrown together. Four old allies, the United States, the United Kingdom, France, and Australia, participated in the first wave of multinational airdrops of supplies to the Yezidis, still stranded on Sinjar Mountain. "We struck targets in the area, but that night we pivoted to the Haditha Dam," the WSO described of those opening days. "The strikes were defensive to protect the dam," in yet another series of airstrikes designed to ensure that critical infrastructure was protected in those early days. In a signal of Islamic State strength, the two orbiting F-15E were then retasked. "You can't make this up. We had intel that there were 300 suicide bombers crossing the border. Sure enough, we got overhead, we could see them, 300 guys walking into Iraq and we took all of them out."[43]

Without eyes on the ground, the United States was forced to identify targets from the air. This task was made harder because both Islamic State and the Iraqi Army were using the same, American-made equipment. "We would cue up and say, 'I see a tank', but was it good or bad? We couldn't immediately tell. We would be doing road scans to build a data set to know where the Iraqi military is because we weren't talking to them," an F-15E WSO described of those early nights. "ISIS wasn't smart at this time. They were flying the black flag on their vehicles. If they were flying one, and it was a legitimate target, we would hit it. They figured that out pretty soon, so they took the flags off their vehicles."[44]

On the ground, the small number of US ground forces was also handcuffed and had limited authorities to conduct offensive operations. "We just wanted to get out the door and link up with the Iraqi army, and kill these bastards."[45] While the air strikes garnered significant media coverage, the United States also began the process of passing intelligence to the Iraqis for them to strike positions. In one instance, the United States passed targeting pod information to the Iraqis, who then used it to target Islamic State with artillery to slow their advances from east to west toward Baghdad. "Islamic State made it as far as Jurf al Shakar, southwest of Baghdad. And that is where the Iraqi army had started to push back, and it was at the edge of the areas where ISIS had tacit support," a Special Forces officer embedded with the Iraqis described.

> The Iraqi army was starting to wake up, and we got the ability to start bombing. That made all the difference. We were hitting boats as they were trying to push across [the Euphrates River]. It was a pretty good fight. We were doing all this, it was modern. All the people I killed, I did it with my feet on a desk sitting in air conditioning.

As a second soldier bluntly stated about the same time period: "We killed over 600 [ISIS fighters] in that first 3.5-4 months, and that stopped their momentum."[46]

The broader challenge, at this time, was the United States was building a coalition and working to integrate nations offering to help with the fight. These nations were being worked into the emerging plan to formally push into Syria to take the fight to Islamic State. The planning for the first night of airstrikes against Islamic State was spread across America's numerous bases in the Persian Gulf, with air operations controlled in Combined Air Operations Center (CAOC) at Al-Udeid Air Base in Qatar and the F-15E mission planning based at Al Dhafra in the United Arab Emirates. The United States, wary of launching a unilateral, American- and

European-led operation in the Middle East after the disastrous invasion of Iraq, sought to recruit a number of Arab countries to participate in the initial phases of the air war. Planning a multinational air war is not easy. While most countries fly American-origin aircraft, there are various rules governing how the United States can share information with many of its allies. Further, each country can introduce their own caveats, governing how and where they can use force—and under what circumstance they would employ weapons. Further, while each country has—at least on paper—well-equipped Air Forces, the aircraft involved may have differing capabilities to deliver precision-guided weapons, and rely on American-operated aircraft in most multinational operations, and integration is not always seamless.

As the fight continued, well after the first night of strikes, the national caveats remained an issue for planning the air war. Different coalition members had what are known as "red cards," making them a red card holder in the targeting process. This meant that when a target would be nominated for strike, even in a dynamic environment where there is a firefight ongoing, the red card-holding nations would have to have a team review the proposed target at the CAOC in Qatar. In the later battle for Mosul in 2017, this practice got so absurd that the Australian Air Force was carrying inert bombs. As one F-15E pilot recalled:

> We would check in with what we were carrying and, I shit you not, [the Australians] would have to come back with dummy bombs. There was a debate amongst them about limiting collateral damage, so someone came up with the idea of dropping weapons to achieve the same "effect" as a normal bomb, but without any damage. The controller would direct them to the top of the stack after that.[47]

The British Air Force, too, were hamstrung by rules around collateral damage. "It got to the point with them that it felt like they wouldn't bomb anywhere unless SAS [British commandoes] were in a TIC [Troops in Contact] or you were miles away from a mosque."

The United Arab Emirates was an eager ally and keen to join with the United States to strike Islamic State. Over the past few decades, the Emirati government has invested a considerable amount into its air force, with the intent of making it interoperable with the United States. After years of secrecy, in 2017, the United Arab Emirates allowed the United States to reveal that the 380th Air Expeditionary Wing operates an air battle management command, dubbed Kingpin, at the base.[48] From inside Kingpin, American mission planners began to plot out the first wave of strikes against Islamic State in Syria. "The interesting part of it this was that the Emiratis would only let us do the mission if it joined with the United States in the first strike package flown into Syria," one of the strike planners indicated. There was supposed to have been two strike packages, with the United States leading solo, followed by the Arab coalition members assigned lower priority targets, out near the border with Iraq. "But it became a joint U.S.-UAE mission."[49]

The Emirati Air Force had previously flown with the United States in Afghanistan. Between 2012 and 2014, the United Arab Emirates deployed six

F-16s and were cleared to engage in ground-enabled precision strikes in support of American and allied troops.[50] The United Arab Emirates chose Maj. Mariam Al Mansouri, the country's first female fighter pilot, to lead the UAE fighters into battle that night. On the American side, the first fighters to penetrate Syrian airspace were the four F-22 Raptors, tasked with sweeping for any potential Syrian Air Force resistance and striking targets, and the EA-6B Prowler, an electronic warfare platform to jam Syrian air defense. Behind them, four F-15E Strike Eagles, four USAF F-16s, two B-1 Bombers, flying alongside four UAE F-16s, four UAE Mirages, and both American and Emirati tanker aircraft, flying orbits outside the country to refuel the jets.

"This was the F-22s first combat mission. Their targets were in Raqqa and in the further northwest of the country [near the Tishreen dam]. The F-15E and the F-22 struck targets in Raqqa, while the UAE and the B-1 struck near Bukamal, with the F-16s operating in a suppression of enemy air defense (SEAD) role."[51] In a surprising turn of events for the Air Force pilots flying that night, the US Navy also fired Tomahawk land attack cruise missiles from ships in the Persian Gulf and Red Sea at targets in Aleppo.[52] The intent was to strike the Khorrasan group, a reported grouping of high-level Al-Qaeda members then based in Syria.

"We didn't knowing anything about [the Navy strike]," a WSO told the author, even though it coincided with the first wave of airstrikes. Four hours later, the second wave of aircraft began their airstrikes. The participants included aircraft from Jordan, Bahrain, Saudi Arabia, and Qatar. "The second wave was down by the border, and that was all the coalition. These were lower priority targets. Half the coalition does not have guided weapons. Just general dumb bombs dropping all over the place."[53] The air war against Islamic State had officially begun, but it still lacked a name, and the United States was still at a disadvantage. Up until October, the United States was hitting static targets, or bombing specific coordinates passed to the pilots before taking off.

> We were hitting things like vehicle compounds or staging areas; so you are taking out 50 vehicles or so. We also struck some oil refineries so they had less fuel. We actually struck some Syrian airfield. We dropped bombs on Mig-21s that were sitting on airfields. It was a hodge podge of targets, and obviously ISIS wasn't going to fly these aircraft, but we were looking for targets to hit.[54]

The American air war changed in October 2014, or as one person described, "The handcuffs came off" in Kobane. This change also put Washington and Ankara on a collision course. The siege of Sinjar, in combination with the threat ISIS posed to Erbil and Baghdad, pushed the United States to send JSOC to Iraq to begin the process of establishing contact with local partners. In Iraq, this was easier than in Syria. The United States has a long history of working with both the KDP and PUK Peshmerga and, despite losing touch with the Iraqi military, had built the CTS from scratch beginning just after the 2003 invasion. Finding a partner in Syria was not as straightforward. During the battle for Sinjar, a group that few in the United States had ever heard of, the Democratic Union Party's (PYD) militia, the Peoples'

Protection Union, or YPG, had proved to be a bold and aggressive group, unafraid of challenging Islamic State.

The PYD is the Syrian branch of the PKK. Established in 2003, the group's founding stems from changes the PKK made following Abdullah Ocalan's arrest in Kenya in 1999. Imprisoned in Turkey, the leftist militant softened his rhetoric while on trial, abandoning his advocacy for an independent Kurdistan in favor of political autonomy. The ideal political system for these autonomous entities was so-called democratic confederalism, a political idea based on the writings of an odd American intellectual, Murray Bookchin.[55] In his writing, Bookchin argued for an idea he dubbed "social ecology," which was premised on the flattening of social hierarchies and to use classless equality to bring human into harmony with nature.

This philosophy began to gain traction within the PKK movement after Ocalan's imprisonment and his decision to apply them to his own vision of Kurdish-led governance.[56] From prison, Ocalan borrowed Bookchin's concept of "libertarian municipalism," which is a broader treatise on breaking the cycle of parliamentary compromise, and ensuring that power is entrusted to popular committees. This set-up would, according to Bookchin, end top-down governance by bureaucratic elites, in favor of a bottom-up model that empowers people.[57] For Ocalan, this model presented an ideal way to move forward with Kurdish revolutionary politics, and he advocated for the establishment of municipal assemblies that would form a confederation of assemblies in Kurdish-majority areas in Syria, Turkey, Iraq, and Iran.[58] The PYD was part of the broader PKK superstructure, which reported to an overarching committee dubbed Kongra-Gel (KCK), or the Peoples' Congress. This assembly included the major PKK affiliates and is headed by the PKK's leadership and divided equally between male and female representatives.

The PYD had firmly established itself in areas along the Turkish-Syrian border, but was the strongest in Kobane and Afrin, two separate enclaves in northern Syria. The group had less of a presence in Hasakah, the enclave bordering Iraq and Turkey in Syria's northeast, largely because political groupings in this part of Syria had historic links to the Barzanis in northern Iraq. As war came to Syria, the PYD made the strategic choice to remain neutral, turning inward, and choosing not to adopt a platform of regime change. This decision was spurred, in part, by the poor relations the group had with the Free Syrian Army, and the disparate factions that fought under its banner. The Kurds also benefited from the regime's weakness, but were wary of its remaining power and sought to keep all of its political options open. In 2004, just after the PYD was established, there were Kurdish-led riots in Qamishli, following a football match between a Kurdish and Arab-majority team. During the match, some Kurdish fans hoisted the Kurdistan flag and pictures of George W. Bush. The American war in Iraq had paved the way for the recognition of the Kurdistan Regional Government. In contrast, the Arab-majority team countered with banners of Saddam Hussein, the figure associated with oppressing Kurds. These tensions boiled over, leading to a brawl and days of rioting. Order was eventually restored, but the differences over Kurdish political empowerment were never fully rectified.

As violence swept Syria in 2011, the regime faced a significant threat in the northwest. At the outset of the protests, Assad made concessions to the Syrian Kurdish minority, granting them citizenship and promising vague political rights.[59] Ankara was acutely aware of these developments and openly fretted about them. As one senior American official described, "By August 2011, in conversations with Turkish diplomats about Syria, their number one concern, above all else, was: 'do no let this Kurdish thing out of the barn.'"[60] Ankara would adopt a different mechanism to try and manage the PYD throughout the war, but at this stage it was at the mercy of the armed insurgency that it would later move to aggressively support.

In July 2012, the Syrian Army withdrew from points across the border, retaining only a small presence in Qamishli, where it remained in control of the airport and an associated militia patrolled in an area near the border crossing with Turkey. The PYD stepped into this vacuum; at first reached an agreement with Kurdistan National Council (KNC) for some semblance of joint control over Syria's northeast. This agreement, however, came under immediate strain. The KNC lacks a serious militia, while the PYD could rely on the YPG to solidify control over areas the regime vacated by filling basic security structures. The YPG was built by the PKK, which has had a presence in Syria for decades. However, the group began to emerge as a more Syrian-focused entity shortly after the 2004 football riots, and were stood up as part of the movement's focus on providing a local self-defense force. The force grew throughout the decade, albeit clandestinely in small cells inside Syrian regime-controlled cities. As the violence swept through Syria, beginning in 2011, the YPG began to augment its ranks, under the stewardship of PKK commanders.[61]

The YPG played an indirect role in breaking the siege of Sinjar, carving out a corridor to drive men and women from the mount back into Syria. During this operation, the group had support from the Shammar Tribe, a Sunni Arab-majority group present on the Syrian-Iraqi border. The corridor was on the northern side of the mountain and shuttled people to Syria, which by this point was under PYD control.[62] Amidst these chaotic early days, the first contingent of US forces sought to identify a group to work with in Syria. To do so, the United States turned to the PUK and its intelligence apparatus, the Zanyari Agency. "It was Lahur who introduced us to the YPG," according to a current US official.[63] A second official confirmed: "It was Lahur."[64]

Lahur Talabani and the broader PUK intelligence apparatus has a long history of working with the United States. In the months before the invasion of Iraq in 2003, the CIA embedded with the PUK to begin ground planning for the invasion of Iraq and to get a better grip on Ansar al Islam.[65] This cooperation led to the creation of the Counter Terrorism Group (CTG) in 2002. This agency is based in PUK-controlled Sulaymaniyah and is a mechanism for elements of the US government to tap into if needed.[66]

The PUK and the PKK have a complicated relationship. The two groups had an antagonistic relationship up until the KDP–PUK civil conflict, which led to a brief rapprochement between the two groups. The two groups had hostile relations with the KDP. In the years after Ocalan's arrest and the loss of Syria as a safe haven, the KDP has tightened ties with Turkey, based in part on shared antipathy toward the PKK and the KDP's cordial relations with the Turkish government. The PUK, in contrast, does not share a border with Turkey, and its territory can therefore serve as a quasi-safe haven for the PKK. However, clashes between the two groups are not uncommon, particularly during times when the PUK is cultivating Turkish economic support. Still, there is little doubt that the PUK has much better relations with the PKK than does the KDP, even if the groups do have different visions of pan-Kurdish nationalism.[67] For this reason, it is not all the surprising that when the PUK was asked about potential partners for JSOC, it would suggest a "frienemy" that had begun to support Yezidis in Sinjar.

A partnership was born. The Islamic State split its forces after it took control of Mosul and began to push down the main highway toward Baghdad. A contingent of ISIS forces also pushed east, back into Syria with the equipment and material it had looted from the Iraqi Security Forces. The group's goal was to use its newfound equipment to solidify control over the Euphrates River Valley and to push to control more of the Syrian-Turkish border. At this point of the war, Islamic State controlled territory out to Jarablus past the Euphrates River, a key border crossing between Syria and Turkey in the Aleppo province. In Syria's northeast, the PYD controlled three disconnected pieces of territory, dubbed cantons, in Afrin in Syria's northwest, as well as in Kobane, the group's traditional stronghold, and in Hassakah, adjacent to the Iraqi border. At the outset of quasi-Kurdish rule in Syria's northeast, ISIS had besieged two of the cantons. With access to Iraqi Kurdistan, and with Afrin tucked into a relatively peaceful pocket of Syria's northwest, the defense of the cantons was less difficult. Kobane, on the other hand, was isolated, with no access to Turkey, and surrounded by ISIS on all sides. Islamic State took advantage, turning its forces loose on the isolated canton. The battle changed the war and cemented the American partnership with the YPG.

"We finally had some operators inserted at key points. Kobane was a critical point," a pilot described. "In the beginning, Kobane was a defensive operation. But then it became, we cannot let the city fall." By this point, the United States had set up a Temporary Operations Center (TOC) in Baghdad, and JSOC had set up outposts in Erbil and Sulaymaniyah to help with the air war in the north and across the border. Inside Iraq, Army Central Command (ARCENT) was placed in charge, but across the border either JSOC or the Army would play the leading role. "There were times when we had three different 3 star generals in charge, and unity of command became an issue very quickly." The Air Force, in what many would come to regret, ceded command to the army for the overall operation. "The Air Force leadership at that time made the decision that we could not head up a Task Force," a pilot described about the conversations at the time. "This has been a lesson learned for us. This [was] an air war."

From the Ashes, a General Takes Charge: Fighting for Kobane and Tensions with Turkey

As Islamic State besieged Kobane, thousands fled to the porous border with Turkey, enforced at that time with a line of barbed wire strung just inside the railway track built nearly a century before by the Germans. By late September 2014, hundreds of thousands of Kurds from Kobane were allowed to enter Turkey, where they were placed in refugee camps in the area.[68] By November, Kobane and its surrounding villages had been depopulated. What was once home to 400,000 had dwindled to 4,000 total inside the city, along with another 5,000 civilians in Til Seir, just east of the city.[69]

Kobane, like Sinjar before it, mobilized Kurds in Turkey and beyond. In the years before the war, most Kurds in Turkey or Iraq would have struggled to find Kobane on a map. By 2014, this had all changed. The war in Syria, beginning with the siege of Sinjar, had made Kurds in Turkey and Iraq more aware of the plight of their ethnic kin across the border in Syria and raised the fear of genocide.[70] The fight for Kobane took place less than 5 miles from the Turkish border. For Turkey's Kurdish-majority political party, the Peoples' Democratic Party (HDP) advocated for greater equality in Turkey. The HDP was the overarching national structure, under which is a linked political party, the BDP, which ran for election in many of the cities in Turkey's Kurdish-majority southeast. The BDP was the first political group in Turkey to overtly support the YPG's plight in Kobane, sending aid across informal border crossings, initiating programs to vaccinate livestock, and holding rallies from on a hill overlooking the city throughout the siege. These rallies were attended by PKK members, who would provide security for the event and check cars for weapons and bombs.

In certain instances, Kurds would cut holes in the barb wire to cross from the border town of Nusaybin to Kobane. Oftentimes, these Kurds from Turkey would fight for the day against Islamic State, cross back at dusk and sleep at home, and then go back again at sunrise.[71] The rallies, in time, morphed into an informal mechanism to try and lend support to the YPG fighting inside the city. The BDP would sit on a hill, often close to the international media that had gathered to cover the battle, and relay on a simple two-way radio ISIS positions as they moved from the city's suburbs and surrounding villages toward the city center. These rallies soon became a flashpoint in Turkey, igniting intra-ethnic tensions, and helping to end ongoing peace talks between the Justice and Development Party and the PKK. In October, after the Turkish government prevented a few dozen Kurds from crossing the border to fight for the YPG caused civil unrest in southeastern Turkey.

The Kurdish-led riots may have been inevitable, but they unleashed a chasm of growing anger within the broader PKK-sympathetic Kurdish movement in Turkey about the Turkish policy toward Syria. The closure of the border made perfect sense for Ankara. No state can allow citizens to crisscross a border to fight with a militia. However, up until this point of the war, Ankara had not imposed the same restrictions on foreigners transiting the country to join with the Arab-majority opposition in Syria's northwest. The Turkish government did not take effective action to control the entirety of its border until March 2015, a divergence in policy that undermined the government's trust with the Kurdish community. For this reason, many of the PKK-leaning Kurds in Turkey began to accuse Ankara of clandestinely supporting Islamic State, arguing that it was turning a blind eye to the group's presence on the border and not lending support to the United States and the coalition to defeat ISIS.

Inside Turkish cities, this tension was leading to violence. A PKK-affiliated youth group, then dubbed the YDG-H, had begun a quiet campaign to assassinate people it accused of lending support to Islamic State. This effort, often broadcast on social media, often would target elements of Kurdish Hezbollah, which has no relations to the Iranian-linked group in Lebanon, but is instead an Islamist Kurdish militia active in southeastern Turkey. The group's civilian arm, Huda Par, is a small political party that lacks broad-based support. However, its leadership has, at times, sought to cultivate closer ties with the AKP, and the AKP has sometimes reciprocated to try and co-opt its voter base to back its regional candidates. In general, the HDP and the PKK behind it have more broad-based support in Turkey's southeast, but the AKP is the second most popular party in this part of Turkey, and is the only non-Kurdish party that can actively compete for votes in the southeast. The AKP-Huda Par linkages helped fuel the now-pervasive idea that the Turkish government backed Islamic State. The other issue that drove this narrative is that Hezbollah figures would, quite openly, lend support to Islamic State in online sermons and videos, blurring the line between who was and was not an ISIS member in Turkey. And, added to this, the border was left open, a reality that allowed foreigners to join Islamic State almost at will for at least a year. These very real issues got inundated with a bit of conspiracy theory, and then ignited when the Kurdish YPG was besieged by the Islamic State in Kobane and Ankara chose to do nothing about it, beyond accepting displaced people.

The riots in early October pitted the YDG-H against Huda-Par activists, and resulted in dozens of religious Kurds being killed in clashes. The tensions significantly eroded the limited and tenuous trust the AKP leadership had sought to build with Ocalan to reach a peace agreement with the PKK leadership. The result was chaos and a return to violence in Turkey's southeast. For the United States, now turning its targeting pods on Islamic State in Kobane, Ankara's domestic issues were irrelevant. Instead, they were an issue to work around, as efforts began to prevent the city from collapsing. The American effort, in retrospect, saved significant lives. However, in the months that followed the defense of Kobane, the JSOC–YPG partnership that formed would prove to be the key to enabling US partner operations in Syria. It also set in motion a series of Turkish military action in Syria, intended to break this US-Kurdish partnership and to push Kurdish militias off the border.

As Islamic State tightened the noose around the Kobane canton, the US Air Force had to change how it was striking Islamic State. "In the beginning we were striking to try and prevent the city from falling. We could not prevent that," a

WSO recounted. "As it devolved, the elders in Kobane had decided that if they couldn't have Kobane, no one could have it. They basically said level the city, block by block, building by building, and they told us, if we can't have the city, make sure they can't have the city." One such target was a house belonging to Ferhat Abdi Sahin, known previously by his codename Sahin Cilo, a YPG leader from the city. For much of the 1990s, Sahin oversaw the PKK's European operations, crisscrossing the continent's open borders between Belgium, Germany, the Netherlands, and Italy.[72] The Turkish government has accused Sahin of killing 41 Turkish civilians and wounding another 400 in a series of PKK-linked attacks throughout Turkey in the 1990s. Sahin returned to Syria in 2011, where he adopted a new nom de guere, Mazloum Kobani Abdi, and founded the YPG. For most Americans, he is known simply as General Mazlum, the commander of the Syrian Democratic Forces (SDF), and the man the United States relies on to fight Islamic State in Syria.

In October 2014 Mazlum was homeless. As he told the *New Yorker*'s Luke Mogelson, after pitched urban battles with Islamic State, and his house was taken over for a third time, he simply radioed coordinates to the Americans. The house was promptly bombed. This strike, Mazlum mused in 2020, "was when the momentum shifted."[73] Mazlum's house was one of many targets the United States hit. It is doubtful that this strike turned the tables. But his ability to pass coordinates to the TOC in Iraq, who could then relay them to orbiting American pilots, is a procedure that has since been repeated hundreds of thousands of times in this war. "We would do a fidelity check on a water fountain in the middle of the city," a process to set the jet's inertial navigation system (INS) on a fixed point so that the aircraft knows where it is, so that the targeting pod cues to the right location on earth. "We had some special operators in Sulaymaniyah watching the battle from orbiting surveillance platforms, and then they would pass the coordinates to Erbil, who would validate the target before we would strike."[74] The intensity of the campaign grew by the day, as Islamic State kept making itself a target and the city's fate hung in the balance.

According to *Air Force Magazine*, the B-1 bomber dropped the most weapons on Kobane, releasing 1,700 precision-guided weapons. These jets were joined by American F-16s flown from Kuwait, the F-15E, the F-22, and the B-1 based down in the United Arab Emirates.[75] These operations were dependent on constant overwatch from unnamed surveillance assets. In a unique quirk, the Joint Terminal Air Controllers (JTAC) that helped to direct the air campaign were, for the most part, not embedded with the YPG. "Some of our JTACS were in the U.S. We were doing talk ons and target authorities with a JTAC looking at a sensor feed. A lot of these JTACS were at Ft. Bragg in North Carolina," the base home to Delta Force, an F-15E WSO described. "They would get on shift, they would go home, and then another would come on shift." This arrangement was enabled by technology and global satellite communications. "Everything was done remotely, with Kurds in Kobane passing to Kurds in Sulaymaniyah who were embedded with U.S. forces," a US Army Special Forces solider described. "Everything in Kobane was targeted strikes by YPG, who were passing the coordinates to us."[76]

Beyond the mechanisms to use force, the YPG's fight in the city caused political consternation in the White House. On the night of October 20, the United States air dropped 10 tons of medical supplies, along with 24 tons of small arms and ammunition to the YPG in Kobane, according to the PUK's Lahur Talabani.[77] The aid was delivered by three C-130s, flying close to the border with Turkey but without ever crossing into Turkish airspace. Speaking to reporters, then Secretary of State John Kerry expressed sympathy for Ankara's outrage, but said the "crisis moment" dictated action to defeat Islamic State. For his part, President Erdogan condemned the move, saying the action was "wrong" because one pallet of weapons was captured by ISIS and questioned the focus on the city, telling journalists "I have difficulty understanding why Kobane is so strategic for them, because there are no civilians there, just around 2,000 fighters."[78]

"Turkey warned that the airdrop of weapons would be a hostile act," a former senior Obama official described. "There was a debate about the Turkish responses to the drop and what it would mean for the United States. In the end, President Obama made the decision to do it, and then he chose to tell Erdogan why the U.S. did it in a phone call the day after."[79] This call hastened a second effort, designed to augment the YPG with forces that the Syrian Kurds could accept, and which could ameliorate Turkish concerns that the force on the ground was intertwined with the PKK. "It was on the Obama call when we began discussions about bringing Peshmerga from Iraq to Syria through Turkey," a US official described.[80]

As the talks about the Peshmerga continued, air war quickly ran-up against the reality that the United States had not planned for another conflict in the Middle East. "One problem is that by August, we were starting to run out of munitions. We started using small diameter bombs. We were gonna get rid of them anyways, but we just started using them out of necessity and they stuck around because they were a low collateral weapon," a person flying over Syria and Iraq described of these early strikes.

The other issue pilots faced was "reach back," or the ability to distribute real-time ISR around the world, and for commanders sitting in Washington to communicate with a pilot flying over Syria with satellite communications.

> If you were close enough to Erbil, they would capture your feed and retransmit it, and someone back in the Pentagon could watch it. And they would pick out which targets to hit. Sometimes no one would approve, we would ask to release and we'd get no answer. It was like the 3 star went on lunch break. We just didn't have authorities delegated.[81]

The other issue pilots faced throughout the war was the tyranny of technology.

> Technology allowed big brother to be in your cockpit more. It was challenging when a significant leader who has strike authority for whatever you are doing that day would be listening to SATCOM and piggy backing on a [drone feed] and then try to direct you because they think that they have a clear view of the battlefield from their office.[82]

As a third pilot recounts, "It was severe micromanagement. It was a constant, terrible thing, and it was always, 'I know better than you.'"[83]

The talks with Turkey about the Peshmerga proved to be complicated and fraught. About 150 PUK Peshmerga first flew to Urfa, where, after receiving the proper clearances, traveled in a convoy to the border, where the Turks inventoried their weapons and let them cross the border on October 31, 2014, into a narrow pocket, up against the Turkish border. "We were in this position at the time when we did not have access to Incirlik, and we had been trying to gain access, and now we are talking about getting the Pesh through [to Kobane]," a DoD official recounted about talks with Ankara at that time. By early November, the battle appeared to be turning. Islamic State had failed to wrest control of the border crossing, and began to steadily lose ground to the advancing YPG. In retrospect, this was the high water mark for ISIS. They would slowly be ejected, block by block, and building by building in the coming weeks and months. "After we finally got [the Turks] to agree to the Pesh, we all just concluded that this was not worth the effort. And, on top of that, the YPG didn't want [Peshmerga]."[84]

In January 2015, the YPG managed to retake Mistanour Hill, the high ground, and then within a week declared the city liberated of Islamic State. The place was destroyed. But, Islamic State had been defeated, and the once-besieged YPG planned to go on the offensive. For the hundreds of American personnel who watched the fight in near real time from a high-definition drone feed, broadcast around the world, the YPG's tenacity became legendary. "I watched a YPG fighter get shot in the leg, continue to fire his weapon, and hold a position before reinforcements arrived," a US soldier described to the author.[85] As a pilot flying overhead said, "In our community, the [YPG and later, the SDF] were seen as warriors."[86] While the battle with ISIS was won in this part of the world, it was the next phase that proved decisive in shaping how the United States would fight—and how Turkey would seek to frustrate the partnership with the YPG moving forward.

The battle for Kobane was the first decisive victory of OIR. The fighting validated the procedures for the ground war that followed. It also underscored the effectiveness of a small JSOC presence, grafted on to the YPG, using global communications to deliver ordnance on ISIS positions in an urban fight. The airstrikes were overwhelming, but necessary to roll back the group's advance. It also signaled a change in how ISIS would fight later on in the war. Rather than stand and fight for every city, the group would pick and choose where to try and withstand the American and allied forces, paired with the YPG and JSOC, on the ground and aircraft stacked overhead.

These early days of the war also underscored the challenges the airmen and ground troops would face from Washington. The rules of engagement remained strict throughout the conflict and those same capabilities that allowed for JTACS to sit in Iraq or North Carolina to direct an air war also enabled commanders to watch from their office and talk directly to the pilots flying overhead. The political trouble with Turkey, however, would prove to be the main obstacle to the war. The negotiations with Ankara were difficult, owing to Turkish concerns about the YPG and the divergence in goals between the American-led coalition and Ankara's broader efforts to empower an Arab-majority opposition to topple Assad in the country's northwest. The tensions with Ankara would later skyrocket, but not before the joint—and clandestine—effort to topple Bashar finally began to show signs of progress in late 2015.

"2014 was wild, everyday was something wild," a pilot described of these opening months of the campaign.[87] Year 2015 was no different. "Syria was like the wild west. The second you crossed the border. I was in gun slinging mode."[88] The war had just started and things were about to get a lot more complicated.

Chapter 4

COVERT WARS AND OVERT INTERVENTION: THE TWO SIDES OF THE WAR AGAINST ISIS

"I would describe our interaction with Turkey as follows: First, we tried to keep them out of the war, then we ridiculed them for not sending troops, but then got angry when they did send troops, albeit to fight the guys who we had embedded troops with."[1] Washington and Ankara never did resolve their issues over Syria and the tensions that emerged over the battle for Kobane only got worse. For both countries, decisions made in 2015 shaped the future of each country's Syria policy. And, the unexpected Russian intervention upended any nascent planning to work together on counter-ISIS operations and when the first mixed Russian Aerospace Force (VKS) regiment showed up at an air base in Latakia, the war changed again and complicated US combat operations and frustrated American diplomatic efforts.

The Russian presence also complicated American air operations over Azaz and Marea, two opposition-held towns that were to be the jumping off point for the joint effort with Turkey to force Islamic State from its border strongholds in an area dubbed the "Manbij pocket." This offensive failed. ISIS managed to withstand the offensive and eventually prompted a shift in US strategy that deepened the fissure with Turkey. The negotiations with Turkey and the preparations for this battle delayed concurrent planning for the effort to push toward Raqqa, the symbolic capital of Islamic State's caliphate in Syria, and the city where the United States would find itself fighting to control in 2017. To get there, the United States first focused on retaking Manbij. The decision to use the YPG to force Islamic State from this city set in motion ended in an invasion and, ultimately, created the conditions for Ankara to partner with Moscow to pressure its NATO ally.

In September 2014, before the battle for Kobane, the United States and Turkey were embroiled in discussions to gain access to Incirlik Air Force Base, an airbase that the United States has operated from in Turkey since the early days of the Cold War. At the same time, the two countries were negotiating a separate agreement to stand up a T/E program, with a training site in Turkey to support a multination effort to stand up an Arab-majority force to fight Islamic State. These negotiations moved in parallel to the JSOC partnership with the YPG, which had grown close during the battle for Kobane, and which soon was pushing outward to oust Islamic State from the Turkish-Syrian border east of the Euphrates River. The VKS also showed up and began flying strike missions in the same airspace as the Turkish Air Force and American aircraft, which in the summer of 2015 were finally given permission to fly from Turkey.

After the collapse of Mosul and the battle for Kobane, the legal mechanisms that the United States would need to fight a small war against Islamic State were enacted. Before these twin events, and then the replacement of Maliki in Iraq, there were constraints on how the United States could use force in both Syria and Iraq. Throughout the summer of 2014, the DoD and the National Security Council were each working on options for an American intervention in Syria. By August, the Pentagon had settled on a plan to begin a program to vet Arab opposition fighters, train them in regional sites, and then provide them with weapons. This program was to be separate from the CIA effort, which was ongoing in the northwest and which had outfitted thousands of fighters by this point. "We had presented a range of options to [then Secretary of Defense Chuck Hagel], but there were major misgivings and it outlined a ton of potential challenges, and what he had heard was that no decisions had yet been made," a former DoD official recalled.

But then, on September 10, 2014, President Obama announced his administration's plan to defeat Islamic State. The announcement reaffirmed what had already been happening in Iraq and Syria: the war would be fought from the air, with small numbers of American forces deployed to embed with the Iraqi Security Forces and the Peshmerga in Iraq. In Syria, where the United States could not ally with a sovereign government, Obama called on Congress to give the administration the resources to train and equip "the Syrian opposition."[2] Inside the DoD, there was a general assumption that this was the route that the White House would pursue, but the decision came faster than many had anticipated. "[The T/E announcement] was decided way faster than anticipated. and then it was like 'oh, ok, I guess we are doing this absurd program,'"[3] an official involved in the program recalled. The push to do more with Arab-majority groups also stemmed from an initial discomfort about being solely dependent on the Kurds for the US war effort. "My understanding [about that time] was that top level people in the White House and a State were thinking like: 'we need to do something with the [Arab-majority] opposition too, not just these Kurds,'" a State Department official recounted of the early T/E debates in Washington.[4]

The president had first included a funding request for an overt T/E program in a June 2014 funding request for the war in Afghanistan, and the language in that request was focused on the Arab opposition in the northwest. This request included a $500 million allotment for the Syrian opposition for training and the purchase of weapons. By September, the administration had reworked this proposal to include additional authorities to fight Islamic State. This language was eventually included in Section 1209 of the FY2015 National Defense Authorization Act, which provided further guidance about the nascent T/E program. Section 1209 specifically empowered the administration to defend Syrians and allies from the Islamic State, as well as calling for strict vetting of potential trainees for links to terrorist groups. Importantly, the vetting requirement has a presidential waiver to waive elements of the vetting criteria if deemed in the national security interest of the United States.[5]

After the Fall 2014 announcement, and then the subsequent authorities in the 2015 NDAA, the US government went to work standing up the T/E program. As two US DoD officials described, "Once it was announced, we immediately went into T/E planning, ranging from putting together regular reports on the Train and Equip stand up, to provisions on vetting and end-use monitoring of any weapons we would provide." The process also included the prosaic, but vital effort to "select sites for training, which was an exercise in including regional allies in the program, and then figuring out who we would get for the program from Syria."[6] However, as Lt. General (Ret.) Nagata cautioned:

> Authority doesn't mean a lot if you are not given permission to use it. The authorities that were granted were beneficial, but the rate, the speed, and the fullness of policymaker's permission to use those authorities was, at best, slow and inconsistent and, at worst, unserious … We were playing a double jeopardy, wait for the authority, it is here, and now we have to go back to DC to use that authority.[7]

The Turkey Troubles: Finding Ways to Cooperate

The backdrop to T/E was a festering disagreement with Turkey over strategy in Syria. Ankara sought to use American requests to use Turkish territory to strike Islamic State as a leverage to extract concessions from the United States. The tensions crystallized over Kobane and Ankara's tying of greater involvement in the fight against Islamic State to a US-enforced NFZ over much of the Turkish-Syrian border. The initial Turkish denial for US access to Incirlik Air Force base rekindled memories of the 2003 invasion of Iraq. Many of the Special Forces members who were planning to deepen involvement in Syria in 2014 were also involved in 2003, or were serving with men who had been part of Viking Hammer or the follow-on occupation of Iraq, where Ankara's decision to deny the use of airspace complicated and made more risky the US operation in the north of the country.

Shortly after Obama's reelection in 2013, Ankara sought to more closely calibrate its strategy with the Obama administration. It would turn out to be an eventful year. For much of 2011, the United States was mired in its broader effort to drawdown from Iraq, while increasing the number of troops on Afghanistan. As the United States was preparing to leave Iraq, "Turks wanted to have a talk about the Middle East after Iraq, and we confused the hell out of them," a DoD official described. "We really didn't have a strategy. The Turkish establishment was Iraq focused, while we were NATO focused … and this almost religious belief that if we could lock them into NATO air and missile defense, we could push them into a NATO framework."[8] The focus, at this time, was trying to convince Ankara to host an American-operated radar for a Europe-based missile defense system, dubbed the European Phased Adaptive Approach (EPAA). This effort relies on a radar deployed in Malatya, Turkey, which can help provide early warning and cueing information for US-operated missiles in Poland and Romania, designed to intercept Iranian ballistic missiles. Ankara was wary of accepting the radar, owing to its efforts to maintain cordial relations with Iran, and broader suspicions about the intent of the radar.

"The idea was that somehow it would deepen the relationship beyond Incirlik. But then it was just months of negotiations, linked to all kinds of things, from who would feed people at the radar site to who would provide security, to questions about what the radar does, and the operational picture. No one was talking about the relationship."[9] These talks, however, did help with Ankara's request from its allies for missile defense toward the end of 2012, after tensions with the Syrian regime spiked. The relationship had evolved into a series of transactions, unmoored from a shared strategic vision. This reflected the changes that were taking place in Turkish foreign policy. By 2011, the AKP had cemented itself as the most dominant political party in Turkey's history. And, as a reflection of that dominance, its efforts to entrench itself in the bureaucracy were continuing and, on foreign policy issues, Ankara was amidst a concerted effort to establish itself as a regional power. The Arab Spring heightened the contrasts between Ankara's vision for the future of the Middle East and its embrace of a potential regional turn away from an American centric system of alliances and partnerships, anchored around US military guarantees. In this sense, while both Washington and Ankara embraced regime change in Syria in late 2012, both had differing visions for what the overthrow of Assad in Damascus would mean for longer term national interests.

Turkish tensions with the Syrian regime continued throughout 2012. The escalation of violence prompted a wave of people fleeing violence. Ankara made an initial decision to leave its border open, allowing these people to take refuge in Turkey. The Turkish government also made the conscious choice to accept Syrian military defectors, who began to organize the loose, anti-Assad insurgency dubbed the Free Syrian Army.

In June 2012, tensions between the Syrian regime and Ankara sharply increased, after a Turkish RF-4 aircraft was shot down over the Mediterranean Sea. The Turkish government claimed that the RF-4 was on a routine surveillance mission and was flying in international airspace when it was downed with a radar-guided missile. The Syrian regime claimed that the aircraft was flying inside its airspace and that it had downed the aircraft with anti-aircraft artillery (AAA). The event prompted concerns in Washington and Brussels that Ankara would refer the incident to the North Atlantic Council (NAC), NATO's decision-making body under Article 5, the Alliance's collective defense clause. Such action would have split NATO, given that Syria is an out of area contingency, as defined by the territorial delineation contained in Article 6 of the Washington Treaty. In any case, there was little appetite within NATO to become embroiled in the unfolding Syrian conflict, and any Turkish action would risk splitting the alliance.

"We shared the air picture with Ankara; they were a pain to deal with over this," a former US defense official described. "There was this fear that the Turks would escalate with the regime and that we would have a shooting match between the Turks and the Syrians. Maybe, looking back at how many in Syria have been killed, this would not have been such a bad thing." Ankara remained incredulous, at least in discussions with the United States about the shoot down. "The CAOC had to share the air picture. They didn't believe it. It was the same shit over and over again, they wanted more information. It just was the same story, they wouldn't believe what we were showing them that the F-4 shoot down, it appears, was a freak occurrence," an American defense official involved in the joint search for the pilots recounted. "[The jet] was basically shot down by World War II anti-aircraft fire and the Turks just couldn't believe that they could've have lost a pilot, they just refused to believe it was just a freak shoot down."

In the days that followed, the United States sought to assist Ankara with the search for the two dead pilots. By chance, a privately operated exploration vessel, the Nautilus, was docked in Istanbul, in preparation for an exploratory mission in the Black Sea. The ship was rerouted to assist Ankara with the search in the Mediterranean. "The Nautilus just happened to be there, who knows why, but we then arranged to help them look for the wreckage. They did the forensics. [The jet] had bullet holes. And they recovered the bodies. [The jet] definitely violated Syrian airspace. This was Turkish incompetence." Incompetence or not, the tensions continued, albeit through proxies in Syria.

On the international level, Ankara referred the incident to NATO, but did so under Article 4, the mechanism that allows for joint consultation without necessarily triggering a military response. Inside Syria, it sharpened its efforts to topple Assad, while pushing for greater border defense contributions from its Western allies. In November 2012, the Turkish government sent a letter to NATO, formally requesting that the Alliance provide it with Patriot missiles to bolster its defense.[10] In the months after the RF-4 shoot down, the fighting in and around Aleppo and Idlib had led to a series of incidents where projectiles fired at the Syrian opposition overflew their intended aim points, landing inside Turkey. In one specific incident, in October, Ankara retaliated after a Syrian regime mortar killed five Turkish civilians[11] in Akcakale, a border town just opposite Tel Abyad. The Turkish military responded with artillery fire aimed at targets in Syria, a tit-for-tat response that, while grounded in the inherent right to self-defense, raised again the specter of unwanted escalation that could split NATO if Ankara pushed ahead with military action few supported.

The October attack nearly coincided with events in Damascus that foreshadowed the considerable consternation that was to follow between Turkey and Syria. As the war progressed, Turkey gravitated toward extremist groups, overlooking the opposition's ties to the Al-Qaeda affiliate Jabhat al Nusra, while the US military deepened its partnership with the YPG after the battle for Kobane.

In December, just days before Christmas, Ambassador Robert Ford heard the twin explosion in his study.

I was in my study at my house, thinking that "wow this is just like Baghdad" …
the embassy was not open, so we sent over an American team from our security

office to the site of the bombs, and of course the Syrian government had them all blocked off. They got close enough to one of the sites to look at and photograph the bomb crater, and it was sent home, and the assessment came back that it was that a big fucking bomb.[12]

The American embassy in Damascus was in an old apartment building, built decades earlier, and which was placed right on a busy street. The wall dividing the apartment from the road was brick and not rated to stop a bomb blast. The Syrian state, by this point, was unwilling to countenance too much from the United States and refused to completely block the road to traffic. For these reasons, Ford recounts, "We made the decision to close the embassy." The attacks were later linked back to the Nusra Front, Syria's Al-Qaeda affiliate, and which ISIS would later spawn from.

As a senior former official recounts, Ankara's tolerance for Nusra became an issue for the bilateral relationship. "I raised [this issue] with senior Turks," the US official recalls, "their support for Jihadi elements, and in January 2013, at a lunch meeting in Ankara, I [told them] that we are getting reports that you guys are supporting Nusra and Jihadis. And they responded with, 'we are doing it, and the reason is that they are the best fighters and we are trying to bring down the government.'"[13] These ties were, on the Turkish side, clandestine and handled by the country's main intelligence services, Milli Istihbarat Teskilati (MIT). In that same lunchtime conversation, he indicated that the United States delivered a warning: "We basically said, the tool you are using is the wrong tool and that you would have a horrible Al Qaeda entity south of the border, and then asked how that could ever be in their interest. The Turks responded with: 'after they serve their purpose, we will kill them.'"[14]

Ankara had signed itself up for a dangerous game, the official noted, and one in which the CIA eventually turned a blind eye toward with its cooperative arming program based out of Turkey. As it would turn out, this early US warning would prove prophetic because Islamic State and Jabhat al Nusra, two interrelated entities, eventually did consolidate along the Turkish border. These differences were never resolved, but they were raised in a White House meeting that brought together the head of MIT, Hakan Fidan, then Prime Minister Erdogan with Barack Obama and senior American officials in March 2013. It also pointed to a more fundamental issue, linked to later efforts to collaborate more closely on overt military action.

This issue was very much at the forefront of the minds of US policymakers in late 2012 and, after Obama's inauguration, in the first meetings with Turkey in early 2013. In January, inside NATO, Ankara's requests for Patriot air defense were honored. The United States, the Netherlands, and Germany, working under NATO auspices, agreed to deploy Patriot batteries to three different sites in southern Turkey. The German and Dutch units were the first two activated and were deployed at Incirlik Air Force Base and at a site in Kahramanmaras, a small city north of Gaziantep. By January 30, however, the American Patriot unit, deployed near Gaziantep, had not yet been activated due to the ongoing bureaucratic red tape on the Turkish side and ongoing construction at the deployment site. The deployment arrangements were handled bilaterally, with Turkey paying the cost for force protection and supplying the troops, while the deploying nations paid for the costs of their personnel.[15] The units were pulled from Extended Air Defence Task Force (EADTF), which was established in 1999 to improve intra-alliance interoperability and to develop a common set of tactics and procedures, and which has deployed to Turkey twice during the 2003 Iraq invasion and, again, in 2013.[16]

In March 2013, the then chairman of the Senate Foreign Relations Committee, Carl Levin (D-Michigan), endorsed the establishment of a NFZ over northern Syria, using the Patriot batteries to attack Syrian jets, and using manned aircraft to destroy the air defense systems deployed in the north. Ankara pushed for a similar policy and demanded from the United States a similar policy during negotiations over the USAF's use of Incirlik Air Force Base to strike Islamic State. This proposal was at odds with NATO's mandate of self-defense, but it was a salient issue and a point of debate between the United States and Turkey at the outset of the missile deployment.

For Ankara, the one piece of leverage that it had with the United States was the use of its territory, and it sought to use the very real fact that it bordered the civil war to maximum advantage. These issues were all up for discussion in March 2013, when a Turkish delegation visited Washington for meetings with Obama administration. It was during this meeting that President Obama, according to the *Wall Street Journal's* Adam Entous and Joe Parkinson, told Turkish prime minister Erdogan, along with MIT director Hakan Fidan, that the United States remained concerned about the illicit flow of weapons and fighters from Turkey to Syria. This warning was not new, but it was transmitted in a blunt way from the absolute top of the American system. Fidan was used to hearing these warnings. A former American official described a meeting with Fidan in the summer of 2013, where "I raised the Nusra issue again. He responded with: 'give us the names and we'll pick them up before they reach the border.' I replied that this was not about a couple of names, it was about shutting their border."[17]

In the meeting at the White House, the Turkish delegation reportedly responded angrily, but sought to use the meeting to lobby for an aggressive and open-ended arming program, aimed at empowering the opposition to defeat Bashar al Assad.[18] The meeting ended in stalemate, but the talks about joint efforts about ISIS and the tone of the conversation underscored the vast disagreement between the two countries. The main catalyst for increased US-Turkish cooperation against Islamic State was linked to the increased authorities Congress granted the administration in Fall 2014. With the increased authorities, the possibilities for joint action against Islamic State expanded.

By December 2014, the basic plan for the T/E plan had taken shape, but faced a series of potential bottlenecks. The United States and Turkey hammered out a basic proposal, as detailed in the *Washington Post*, to expand cooperation in the Manbij pocket. The basic plan called for American and Turkish airstrikes from bases in Turkey in support of groups on the ground. At one point, the United States and Turkey had extensive conversations about sending in Turkish SOF to relay targets for airstrikes.[19] This proposal, however, quickly ran up against challenges inherent to joint military operations and, more fundamentally, the vast divergences that the two countries were unable to overcome.

For the Turks, the rigidity of the military hindered creative thinking about operations in the Manbij pocket. "On the Turkish side, you had the challenge of their own bureaucratic stove pipes and interests," a senior US official recalls.

> The palace was willing to countenance some activities that Turkish General Staff could not contemplate. So there was this constant theme: We can do this together, we can clear this space, and we would ask for a concept for doing this, and the Turkish General Staff would go to a NATO construct where Turkey would be providing 20 percent of the required personnel, and there would need to be big contributions from the U.S. and other NATO allies. They could not see beyond that.[20]

The Obama administration, of course, was not willing to send ground forces so this back-and-forth was going nowhere. Washington was eager to use the light footprint model and have special forces take on a central role in the plan.

An initial draft of the plan included a role for Turkish SOF. However, "Turkey had a lack of JTAC qualified personnel," a person involved in these discussions with Ankara in 2014 recalled. "They had less than ten [JTACs] from their SOF forces as of 2015, so upon further review Turkish Special Operations Forces didn't look like a great option."[21] The core issue, of course, was that the United States had sought to minimize its own presence in this part of Syria. "The JTAC issue, as I recall, was ancillary to the main problem, which was that the Turks wouldn't go into Syria without us, and they thought the regime would target them if they were alone, and that the regime wouldn't target them if we were with them," a person familiar with the discussions at the time recounts.[22] It would, however, pose a problem once joint US-Turkish operations kicked off in the Manbij pocket a few months later. Yet, for this initial phase of plans, the issue remained that the United States was not yet willing to send Army Special Forces into Syria.

For its part, Ankara was still tying access to Incirlik Air Force base to agreement on the Manbij Pocket and the creation of the safe zone. Ankara did, however, allow for the United States to use drones that it had based at Incirlik Air Force Base after the withdrawal from Iraq to help build a ground picture for future strikes against Islamic State. These drones, flying unarmed, would fly to the Turkish border and then switch on their sensors while overflying Syria. These drones were part of a program dubbed Nomad Shadow, which resulted from an agreement in 2007 to increase US- provided surveillance of the PKK on behalf of Turkey. This agreement culminated in the deployment of drones at Incirlik after the drawdown, and then these drones were pulled into service for the war against Islamic State. The first step toward using them for armed attacks came in February 2016, when the United States and Turkey formalized the agreement to begin training the opposition at a training site in Hirfanli.[23] "It was a great training site and had everything we needed. for bigger live fire training we drove down the road an hour to a main range," a person who visited the site described.[24]

The command structure for OIR was formed around two Combined Joint Special Operations Task Forces, dubbed as CJSOTF-S for Syria and CJSOTF-I for Iraq. The CJSOTF reported to a three-star general, who headed up Combined Joint Task Force—OIR, which was based in Kuwait at Camp Arifjan, where an interagency Task Force had been established. CJSOTF-S was based in Jordan. From the outset of OIR, the "heavy focus was on Iraq. Syria was on the back burner. The predominance of our assets was in Iraq and the focus was on prepping to retake Mosul," a former Marine Forces Special Operations Command officer told the author.[25] CJSOTF-S was responsible for the T/E program. And, separate from both CJSOTF-S and I was JSOC, which many simply refer to as "the Task Force," or TF.

The basic T/E concept was to include the main backers of the anti-Assad opposition and set up training facilities in Jordan, Turkey, Qatar, and Saudi Arabia. The French and the British would send forces to assist with training at these sites. At the outset, the DoD assumed that Jordan would be the first country to acquiesce to the American request, given the monarchy's concerns about Islamic State and willingness to support US foreign policy in the Middle East. In fact, it was Turkey that jumped at the chance to host the training site. "We built the original framework of the T/E program so that each partner could have a veto, and so that all four of the Middle East countries [Jordan, Turkey, Qatar, and Saudi Arabia] would host a training camp. This never happened. But the Turks gave [the military] a training site and access to the border crossing."[26]

The Memorandum of Understanding for the first CJSOTF-S T/E training site in Hirfanli, a lake-side town some 90 miles from the capital Ankara, was signed in January 2015 and the first contingent of US Army Special Forces was soon deployed to begin training men culled from inside Syria to fight Islamic State in the Manbij pocket. "[The Turkey desk at DoD] worked very hard on the MoU and made it a point to constantly remind everyone that Turkey was the first to sign up," a DoD official described. The T/E program was segmented and compartmentalized from the other American efforts in Syria. In the northwest, the CIA was continuing to train and supply weapons to the anti-Assad opposition. In the northeast, JSOC had found a partner, the YPG, and had demonstrated a proof-of-concept for joint operations. The Army's T/E program was to be more circumscribed and narrowly focused on the Manbij pocket and on a separate effort focused on the eastern Syrian desert. These different efforts came with different approval processes. As one of the Special Forces deployed in Turkey described, "T/E was headed up by CJSOTF, or 'white SOF', and with them came 'white SOF' authorities. In other words, we were subjected to a bureaucratic approval process to do anything, while the 'black SOF' were freer to make decisions." White SOF, or Army Special Forces, faced a layer of bureaucracy that sought to micro-manage the early stages of the program, particularly on the vetting of fighters and, critically, on keeping these American troops out of Syria.

The first "white SOF" to go to battle in this area was CJSOTF-S. But rather than deployed in Syria, they first were sent to Jordan to begin to direct an air campaign against the Islamic State between Marea and the Euphrates River. The Americans referred to the staging area as the Marea line and intended to use the forces trained to push Islamic State off the border and out of the Manbij pocket. To satisfy the legal requirements, embedded within the 1209 authorities, the intent of the program had to be Islamic State focused. This required that the Americans receive from any trainee a signed statement, outlining that the intent of the training was to fight Islamic State. The document made no mention of the Assad regime, which for many of the Arab-majority opposition was the actor they cared the most about, but the United States did agree to protect the forces from regime attack if they were engaged in battle against Islamic State.

"The selection process was flawed," a retired Special Forces soldier remembered of these early efforts.

> The program was too long [12 weeks], which meant that any people we would pull out would have to leave the front lines and, potentially, the villages they were defending. Then we said we had to pull individuals, not groups, and by this point, if you are just some random person not affiliated with a group, you have to ask why. And, then, on top of that, we asked them to fight only Islamic State. This ensured we got crap.[27]

The concept of operations (CONOP) for the Marea line push was never truly that ambitious. "Our goal was incredibly limited. We were looking at a tiny map. It was the Marea line, Manbij, and al-Bab, but we would have been popping bottles if they got as far al-Bab. And only then would we start to talk about Manbij," a Special Forces soldier recalls of the program's goals.[28]

The agreement with Ankara for this program came with the stipulation that a Turkish colonel would embed with the targeting cell that vets the targets. This system meant that Ankara was a red card holder, which means that it could veto any proposed strike. The Turkish government also made clear that as part of this arrangement the strikes could only take place within the Manbij pocket so as to ensure that it did not give direct support to the YPG across the river. For the United States, there was a concern that the Air Force would pave the way for a Nusra advance in the area, or the men linked to the group would enmesh themselves within the T/E process.

"We had to recruit people that wanted to fight ISIS and not Assad, and because we were recruiting mostly out of western Syria, which at that time in 2014 was where the fight was still going on with the regime, we didn't want to pull out full groups," a DoD official recounts of the selection process. "We were trying to pull people out of the conflict zone. The vetting standards were high. The reason we pulled individuals, and not groups, was that the groups didn't want to leave. So we tried to pull leaders, send them back, and then stagger the pulling out of the groups out to keep the front line static."[29] Still, the process was not fool proof and many men had familial links to both ISIS and Nusra. "The vetting on the Vetted Syrian Opposition [VSO]; it was basically a joke in my opinion," a person involved in the training recalls. "We had guys that would join the program; they would then admit that their cousins were in ISIS and that they kept in touch, and would make the case for why they weren't so bad. From my foxhole, we were not doing this right, but what was right?"

The men been trained were being formed into a group dubbed Division 30. From the outset, there was a debate about which type of weapons to supply them with, either American or Russian-origin rifles and ammunition. "[The SOF] community did not have a provision to get foreign Soviet Weapons, so we sent them American weapons, which did not go over well," a person familiar with the program recalled. However, the decision to go with US-made weapons was about speed, and trying to put things in motion and figure out the details on the fly. On the weapons procurement issue, the United States ended up using the Special Operations Research, Development Acquisition Center, or SORDAC, to acquire the weapons. "It was a matter of SORDAC being the only acquisition arm that had anything off the shelf and ready to go," a former DoD official recalls. The program's implementers were facing extreme, top-down pressure to move fast. "There was a sense that just getting them weapons, whichever kind, and figuring it all out later was the priority … [The NSC] had zero concept of chain of command. They had this laser focus on minute, tactical details so far outside their jurisdiction in lieu of thinking through a coherent strategy."[30]

The Turkish government was wary of the entire process, but viewed it as a way to try and get more American aircraft into the area to try and wall off a safe zone, and to block concurrent moves the YPG were making with the Task Force. "They never had any objection to Division 30, but they would try to push us towards objectionable partners," a Special Forces soldier recalls.[31] Ankara was not really involved in the vetting process, but did seek to shape which groups could latch on to Division 30 to hasten the operation. "Turkey didn't contribute a significant amount to the vetting but they did bog it down. They wanted us to use groups they 'knew' and most were untouchable," a DoD official remembers. The group that caused the most friction was Ahrar al Sham, a group founded by some individuals once imprisoned in Syria's brutal Sednaya Prison.

Ahrar al-Sham was a nationwide coalition of Islamist armed groups that originally coalesced from a handful of hardline groups in Syria's northwest. In 2011, elements of what would become Ahrar were among the first rebels to take up arms against the Syrian government. Ahrar's original leadership included former inmates of Syria's brutal Sednaya Prison and others who had been involved in various forms of jihadist militancy. Though these leaders emerged originally from a more doctrinaire Salafi-jihadist milieu, they announced at the outset that they were Syria-focused, not transnationally oriented. Over the first years of Syria's uprising they became increasingly critical of more extreme forms of jihadist militancy, including Islamic State. Instead Ahrar adopted what Sam Heller has characterized as "revisionist," Syria-centered version of revolutionary Islamist militancy. Ahrar worked closely with Jabhat al Nusra, but over time the two groups diverged ideologically and became fierce competitors for influence; eventually, Nusra defeated and mostly dismantled Ahrar.

Ahrar was among a number of Islamist factions favored by Turkey, and Turkey attempted to include Ahrar in attempts to take territory from Islamic State along its border. "We would sit with Ahrar and Nusra in Shura meetings in Azaz, and it is [Turkey] that was pushing Nusra to disassociate with Al Qaeda central," a member of MIT told the author at a meeting in Ankara[32] in what was a tacit admission of Ankara's still ongoing efforts to cultivate a broad spectrum of militants to fight against Assad. One splinter faction of Ahrar al Sham, Ahrar al Sharqiyyah, has proved problematic in its own right. It took shape from the remnants of an Ahrar al-Sham unit displaced from its home in Syria's east by ISIS, reforming in Aleppo. It has participated in Turkey's cross-border interventions, in which it has been accused of war crimes. When US troops attempted to enter northern Aleppo alongside Syrian opposition partners, a video emerged of Ahrar al-Sharqiyyah fighters shouting insults and threatening to behead US soldiers.

The final agreement necessary to begin the fight for the Manbij pocket rested with Ankara. Throughout this process, negotiations to open Incirlik to the coalition had continued in parallel to the T/E training program. The United States had managed to keep aircraft over northeastern Syria but the F-15E and the A-10 were flying long-distances from bases in the Gulf. "We had jets down in Kuwait prior to the deployment to Turkey, and then we were told the aircraft were moving. It was a lot simpler logistically to keep over the top of the targeting area when flying from Turkey," an A-10 pilot explained. "The amount of gas to bring a formation up from Kuwait was ridiculous, so it made more sense logistically up to that area to be more flexible."[33] To do so, Ankara had to grant its permission for the US Air Force to operate from Incirlik. Inside Turkey, the country was feeling the effect of the ongoing YPG-Islamic State war that was spilling over the border and its effects were manifesting inside Turkish society.

The Air Tasking Order (ATO) is the mechanism that the United States uses to control coalition air forces in a joint environment. In general, a centralized planning cell, based in this case at Al Udeid in Qatar, would find and vet targets, nominate them for review by Air Force lawyers, before they are then reviewed by the different red card holders, and then passed on to the different squadrons for planning and weapons selection. The Turkish integration into the ATO was a fraught process and beset with mistrust. The problem was twofold: First, the Turks didn't understand the [ATO process] completely and the CAOC was nervous about using their assets without assurances that they'd follow the Rules of Engagement (ROE), according to a DoD official present at Al Udeid.

For the men of CJSOTF-S, the issue was with the priorities of the war at this stage of the campaign. Iraq, as was the case until the final defeat of the Caliphate, was the main military priority, followed by the war in northeastern Syria, and then the emerging T/E CONOP in the Manbij pocket. Before reaching final agreement for the opening of Incirlik Turkey allowed for the US drones to be prepared for armed attack and to fly surveillance missions. These aircraft were being controlled from Jordan from a temporary operation's center in Jordan with a Turkish and American colonel overseeing it. "The operation in Jordan was based out of an ad-hoc hut we had set up with big TV screens," a person involved in this process described of the initial set up.[34]

After close to nine months of negotiations, Turkish president Erdogan and US president Obama reached agreement on the opening of Incirlik Air Force Base in July 2015. On the same day that the news leaked, the Islamic State attacked a Turkish border outpost, killing a Turkish soldier. Ankara responded with airstrikes, both in Syria against ISIS positions and in northern Iraq against the PKK. Thus, from the outset of its involvement in the war, Ankara made clear that it intended to continue strikes against Kurdish targets, even while it dedicated aircraft to the ISIS fight. These twin strikes came after a significant breakdown of internal security inside Turkey, which began to get worse after the October Kobane riots in the southeast. By March 2015, the Turkish government, after years of delay and inaction, began to implement measures to slow down the numbers of foreigners using Turkish territory to cross into Syria.

In the same month, Turkey began to experience a wave of Islamic State-linked attacks, focused on Kurdish-linked targets inside the country that killed more than 275 people in just over a year. The Islamic State cell behind these attacks was based in Turkey's Gaziantep, where they acted as a waypoint for men and women eager to join the caliphate and, it appears, to procure equipment for the group to manufacture explosives inside Syria. As Ankara sought to crack down on these networks, a cell that originated in the Kurdish-majority city of Adiyaman had been operating overtly in southern Turkey since the start of the conflict. The attacks on targets that had tangential links to the PKK appear to have been aimed at inciting intraethnic violence in Turkey. This strategy was effective. In response to this violence, the PKK killed two Turkish police officers in Urfa, abducting them and shooting them in the back of the head the day before Obama and Erdogan were scheduled to speak to finalize the Incirlik agreement. The PKK claimed its actions were to avenge the loss of PKK-sympathetic Kurds, lost to ISIS bomb attacks.[35]

The PKK's rationale of course was a continuation of the tensions that had built up over Kobane, and which led to the October riots that killed dozens. The PKK, by this point in the war, was certain that the AKP was giving direct assistance to Islamic State, as it bombed Kurds inside Turkish territory, and as the battle in Syria was raging for control of the border east of the Euphrates River. In response to the killing of the two police, Ankara launched airstrikes and those airstrikes ended what had been a multiyear ceasefire between the PKK and the AKP.

The opening of Incirlik allowed for Turkish F-16s to bolster the US aerial presence in the region and to jointly target Islamic State in support of the T/E groups. The basic plan was for Turkish and American jets to strike targets, proposed by Vetted Syrian Opposition, which a strike cell, first based at Jordan and then at Incirlik, would vet. The Turkish Air Force sent a colonel, first to Jordan and then back to Incirlik, to work with this strike cell. The Turks retained a red card throughout this process, meaning that they could veto strikes if they saw fit, and to ensure that its aircraft were not used to support the YPG east of the river. Ankara, therefore, had three interlinked reasons for joining the air campaign against Islamic State. First, the United States had been pressuring its NATO ally to take action. Second, Ankara had managed to wrest some limited concession from Washington and, importantly, to use the T/E program has a vehicle to develop an alternative force to the YPG. By this point, the YPG was pushing from Kobane to the Iraqi border, a development that worried Ankara. Finally, the rise of ISIS inside

Turkey created the political space Ankara may have needed to join the coalition. In the end, neither the Turks nor the Americans sent forces across the border. It was up to the T/E guys to do the fighting. It did not go well.

Playing Ping Pong: The Fall of Idlib and Fighting a War through a Soda Straw

After twelve weeks of training, Division 30 appeared ready for battle. "Division 30 went first [into Syria] because of location," a Special Forces soldier recalls. The concurrent US-led effort, based out of Jordan, would soon follow, and like the forthcoming problem with T/E would also fail.[36] Outfitted with American weapons, the group snaked its way down from Hirfanli to Kilis, the Turkish border town just opposite Nusra-held Azaz. The start of the operation coincided with a Muslim holiday, so the group was undermanned. "That first group, when they got reinserted they did not go in as a group because it was a Muslim holiday and some of the folks were still celebrating," according to a US Army Officer involved in the program. "And when they went back in, Nusra came in, and then Nusra took their lunch and their weapons and killed them."[37]

The battle between Nusra and Division 30 wasn't a total loss for the United States. The Division 30 members were able to relay their position to the United States, who then was able to get ISR to verify targets and drop weapons on the Nusra positions. This attack came just shortly after Nusra had also taken prisoner some of the trainees. Ahrar sat the fight out, but a Kurdish-aligned Arab faction, based in neighboring YPG-held Afrin, Jaysh al Thuwar, did respond but it was the American airstrikes that dispersed the Nusra fighters. As one State Department official described, "The Nusra leadership had always expected groups with links to the US would eventually be used against Nusra, so they were paranoid about the T/E groups and were keen to destroy them right away."[38] The group's paranoia stemmed from its own lessons learned from the Awakening movement in Iraq, where many of Nusra's senior leaders were then serving under the banner of Islamic State Iraq. The lesson learned, of course, was to act aggressively and early to prevent any rival from emerging and moving rapidly to neutralize any potential rival.

Some within the American Special Forces community were suspicious of Ankara and believed that the Turkish government had tipped off Nusra about Division 30's crossing. The level of intra-nation distrust was palpable, largely over the still contained—but growing—dissatisfaction in Washington over Turkish acquiesence to jihadist groups, and in Ankara, America's growing support for the YPG. "The Turks believed that we were hiding stuff from them on the YPG, even things like not letting them on SIPR net [the classified Pentagon server shared only with five eye members], was cast in suspicion," a Special Forces soldier recalls. "It was a block to progress ... There were things that we weren't telling them. We knew what was going on at Ft. Bragg with the YPG, but that wasn't our organization."[39]

The United States, in turn, was wary of who Turkey was working with to involve in the T/E program. "We were demanding complete lists of who Ankara had proposed for vetting. We weren't demanding the same types of lists from the YPG," an official recounts. This purported double standard was fed by paranoia about who it was that Turkey was working with in Syria and broader concerns that Ankara's ultimate intent was to create a trip wire for American action against the regime. "Every time we talked to Turkey, the DoD side would be wondering what is the catch? What do they want us to do this with them? Do they want to use jihadis? Will they use this bilateral arrangement to suck us into something more?," an official recounts.[40] These tensions did not, at this time, prevent continued cooperation on the program and the ongoing and iterative planning efforts to try and take the Manbij pocket with non-Kurdish forces. However, the suspicion on both sides was clearly indicative of a fraying alliance, where neither side was particularly keen to work with the other.

On the T/E side, a second wave of Division 30 was found to have turned over the American weapons and vehicles it had received to the Nusra front. The incident was a debacle and led to the program's cancellation, prompting a rethink of the plan to take the Manbij pocket from Islamic State.[41] In early October, after Division 30 had collapsed, representatives from Turkey and the United States met multiple times in Germany and inside Turkey to revamp the plan to push east from the Marea line. The meeting neatly coincided with a significant change in northwest Syria. After years of passively supporting the Assad regime, and providing its Middle Eastern ally with political support at the United Nations, the Russian Federation sent troops and a mixed aviation regiment of aircraft and helicopters to fight on his behalf.[42] The catalyst for Russian intervention stemmed from the military successes of the CIA-led program in Syria's northwest. The CIA had been working with Saudi Arabia, Jordan, and Turkey to train the anti-Assad opposition and, in 2013, the United States began supplying weapons to vetted groups.

By this point in the conflict, the regime had used chemical weapons a dozen or so times, albeit on a scale far smaller than the attack on Ghouta that would come in August 2013. In June 2013, in a carefully worded statement, deputy national security advisor for strategic communications, Ben Rhodes, indicated that the United States had evidence to corroborate reports of WMD use and that in response "the President has augmented the provision of non-lethal assistance to the civilian opposition, and also authorized the expansion of our assistance to the Supreme Military Council."[43] This statement, a former National Security Council staffer recalls, "was coded language to talk publicly about the program we aren't allowed to talk about. This was the most the lawyers would allow us to show about the CIA program."[44] This program was separate from the arming and funding programs that most regional countries were running in parallel to the American effort. By late 2013, the Obama administration debated deepening its support for the anti-Assad opposition through the provision of BGM-71E TOW anti-tank-guided missile. The supply via Saudi Arabia of this weapon was designed to augment the opposition's capacity to destroy regime armor.

The first shipment of these weapons went to Harakat Hazm, a CIA-favored group that the United States had helped to establish, and took place sometime in early 2014. The missiles and other forms of support were designed to empower vetted groups, to the detriment of the extremists, and create an alternative opposition force to fight the regime. At first the standards for which groups received these weapons were strict, but the US government eventually widened the scope of groups eligible to receive payments, weapons, and ammunition. Still, by relatively late in the program, the groups that the CIA was training and equipping remained small, disorganized, and ineffective on their own relative to the more hardline groups like the Nusra Front and Ahrar al-Sham. Moreover, the hardline groups, by virtue of their strength and political acumen, were able to draw most of the US vetted groups into their own political and military orbits. By the time of the 2015 Idlib offensive, in which Nusra and Ahrar led a coalition of groups to capture Idlib City and nearly all regime-held territory in the province, groups wielding American-made TOW missiles had been reduced to anti-armor auxiliary units for the stronger jihadist groups, which remained the most effective forces against the Assad regime.

As one State Department official quipped, "We trained and equipped the anti-armor auxiliary corps for Nusra." For many involved in the CIA-led arming program, this movement was the high point for the effort against Assad. However, for some, the Agency was blinded because of its role in both the arming effort and the analysis of the conflict. "There was an inherent conflict of interest because these guys were in charge of the guns and the analysis, so when asked they would always suggested the program was going well and they had a tendency to draw up these neat maps with shaded areas of color, as if to denote where extremists were and were not."[45] One issue was that the weapons the United States was supplying to the opposition were getting passed around, including to Al-Qaeda-linked groups that operated outside the program, but still benefited from it. "The weapons spread was, at some point, basically formalized," an official indicated. "They would set up these joint operations rooms and the groups would gather and the weapons would proliferate."[46] The arming effort was clearly having an impact on the regime. Assad and his forces were clearly exhausted after years of fighting and, in a tacit admission of weakness, the normally arrogant Syrian dictator proclaimed in a public speech in July 2015 the Syrian Army faced manpower issues and that the regime would focus on holding territory it controlled. For a moment, there was some optimism that the stalemate could prompt introspection, and regime moderation toward elements of reconcilable opposition elements, in return for changes to the country's governance structure.[47]

While the speech may have been the low point for Assad, it did presage agreement with Russia on more direct military assistance. For Russia, the protection of Assad was viewed through the prism of Moscow's own national security interests, rather than a deep-seated affinity for the Syrian dictator. President Putin rose to power in Russia on the back of a hardline, anti-terror campaign following the second Chechen War and a wave of bombings in Moscow. In certain instances, these bombings are blamed on the state and are alleged to have been false flag attacks to build nationalist support for Putin. The concern about Islamist insurgents, active in countries to Russia's south, is considered to be an area of concern for Russian security interests. The spread of Islamic State affiliates, particularly to Afghanistan, was also a concern to Moscow. Beyond this, Russia had made the determination that it would not let Syria go the way of Libya, and had used its diplomatic muscle to prevent the United Nations Security Council from being used as a vehicle to sanction the Syrian regime. Thus, as the CIA program began to show some effects, and the concurrent T/E program began to take shape, Russia viewed the Assad regime's hold on power as being in peril and its interests as being threatened.

At a July meeting in Moscow, the now-deceased Iranian leader of the Islamic Revolutionary Guards Corp, Qasim Soleimani, reportedly discussed with his Russian counterparts the need to bolster support for ailing regime. To date, the Iranians had been supplying the regime with militia fighters culled from its partners in the region, along with advisors and drones to assist with battlefield planning, while Moscow supplied weapons.[48] By late August 2015, Damascus and Moscow had reached agreement for the deployment of a mixed VKS regiment, which prompted the first engineering units to travel to Syria in early September to begin preparations at Khmeimim Air Base in Latakia. The VKS deployment coincided with the early troubles of Division 30 and cast doubt on what was to follow, a CONOP dubbed Agate Noble.

As one former National Security Council official recalls, "We saw the Russian intervention early. We were watching them build out Khmeimim and that led to a lot of discussions about how to respond to it."[49] On September 21, over a week before the Russian Aerospace Forces began to bomb targets in Syria, the Obama administration convened the principals for a meeting. "This meeting charted our response, which included the ramping up of special operations forces deployed in Syria to take it to Islamic State and because it would limit Russian freedom of maneuver in the northeast." The president approved this plan on October 1, 2015, leading to the eventual deployment of US Army special forces in Syria in December and the building up of infrastructure to support them.[50] "The president formally approved the deployment of SOF to Syria's Hassakah on November 15."[51]

The Russian VKS showed up just a few weeks before the United States and Turkey met in Germany to reassess the battle for the Manbij pocket. During that conference, the two sides worked to pair elements of the T/E trainees with established groups, active in the northwest. The distrust was still palpable, with people tasked with managing the relationship with Turkey and eager to build an alternative to the YPG pushing the secretary of defense to make it easier for forces to mass along the Marea line, without having to vet every single individual who could be involved in the effort. "On the one hand, this was because we didn't want to be providing air support to Nusra, but I think there was so much advocacy for knowing for who they were was about interagency rivalries about ownership of proxies," an official recounts. Those rivalries in the United States were, ultimately, about the fight for assets between the Task Force in the northeast and CJSTOF-S in the Manbij pocket. "It was very late in the game that we told them not to send them lists, just to mass and fight."[52]

The integration of the Turkish Air Force into the ATO was welcomed by the members of CJSTOF-S. In a war that was primarily being fought in Iraq, with a secondary effort in Syria's northeast, it was hard to maintain air assets over the Manbij pocket on a consistent basis. For this part of the war, the Rules of Engagement (ROE) for the Air Forces involved were, in general, defensive. This meant that before a bomb was dropped, the force calling for support had to have been shot at, or in some sort of defensive position. Further, in the Manbij pocket, there were no Americans present, nor any trained NATO-level JTAC to do talk-ons to American pilots. This left the pilot to work through a dislocated JTAC talking to them through satellite communications, after having been passed coordinates through a translator, and then sending an ISR platform to go and vet for validity. It was war through a soda straw. It was a slower way of delivering ordnance, but it was the model that had been set up in Iraq at the outset of OIR, and was the model that was used throughout the war. The presence of the Russian VKS made this even more complicated.

As one pilot described, "The Russians showed up around the same time we did, and so that made the experience very interesting and very dynamic. They were the wild card and there was uncertainty over how we would interact with them."[53] The Marea line was the point in Syria where different Air Forces crossed paths. The Russians and the Syrians were focused at this point in the war on the bombing of Aleppo and Idlib, while the Turks and the Americans were focused on patrolling west of Marea. "Part of the struggle up there was that every Air Force merged right there [near the Marea line], you had us there, you had the Syrians there, and you had the Russians there. It wasn't so much that Russia was a threat, it was just the uncertainty that having the Russians in the area brought."[54] That uncertainty impacted the rules of engagement, which dictated how and under what circumstances the US Air Force interacted with the Syrian and Russian Air Forces.

As one pilot described of his experience flying over Syria in 2015, "The ROE were kept deliberately vague, leaving it in the hands of the pilots to interpret ... and there would be multiple instances to shoot down an aircraft, but it didn't happen because of the context and thinking in the cockpit." The vague ROE description of what to do when Russians flew close to coalition aircraft began to manifest itself near the Marea line. As the same pilot recalls, "A Russian Fencer track[ed] towards me to within 20 miles, and the question was what to do. The initial instruction was to get out of Syria. Then they changed that to remaining on mission."[55] Ultimately, what happened was that coalition pilots flying in Syria were often operating within the weapons engagement zone of Russian fighter escorts, the Su-35, that would fly alongside the Su-24 and Su-34 that would conduct the air-to-ground strikes. "We operated well within many Flankers' weapons engagement zone," according to F-15E WSO, and there were many instances where force was nearly used as the two sides came into near-continuous contact along the Euphrates River later. Over the Manbij pocket, the Russians were a constant presence for the coalition to grapple with. "One night north of Aleppo, the Syrian Air Force was active and we were conducting deliberate strike, and we pushed in the high block as what had been declared as U.S. or coalition blocks," a A-10 pilot explained.

To deconflict with the Russian Air Force, the United States adopted a block system of altitude, similar to large training exercises held over the vast ranges in

Nevada, California, and Alaska. The red and blue blocks delineate altitude and are designed to prevent an unintended mid-air collision. As one US official recalls, "We established a hotline of operational air deconfliction." However, it was not perfect and Russia would, at times, test the US Air Force and this mechanism would become more detailed and more robust as the war dragged on. "As soon as we crossed the border we got locked up by Russians, and as we got to the target, the Syrians were below us," meaning that these two A-10s had Syrian aircraft below them, while Russian Flankers circled above them. At this moment, the pilot recalled, "I made the decision to fly down below the Syrians. It was a weird environment. I made the decision to turn all my lights on, let them know I am here—and you do not normally do that—but I wanted them to know that I wasn't a threat."[56] The two-ship of A-10s did conduct this rather unorthodox threat, but it was only after they returned to Incirlik that the flight lead discovered that he had missed his wingman call over the radio informing him that a Russian Flanker had his plane under missile lock for over four minutes.[57]

For the T/E CONOP, the Russian presence threw yet another wrench into the revamped plan. Just after the Turkish government opened Incirlik, the United States rushed to send aircraft to begin strikes. The first strike out of the base was unmanned and was one of the additional drones the United States had sent to Incirlik in May to augment the aircraft deployed in 2011 as part of Nomad Shadow. The first manned aircraft were a small detachment of F-16 fighters sent from Avianno Air Base in Italy. At this time, Secretary John Kerry was interested in pushing for coalition air power to operate west of the Euphrates and north of Aleppo, a US official recalled. Kerry was pushing for something he called a "permissive zone", and he used that term to describe two different kinds of zones: one would be to use the cover of counter ISIS fight to move the envelope west of the river to provide cover for the opposition. And he was linking that to a proposal for deescalation in the southwest.[58]

The Agate Noble CONOP was the plan to create this zone. The United States, in its negotiations with Ankara, had pledged to defend the men it was training if they were engaged in conflict with Islamic State. This protection, according to an official familiar with the planning, would include protection from the regime if they were to interfere in these operations. In Amman, the Russian intervention shifted thinking about the conflict. "Once the Russians intervened, [the Jordanians] put a leash on the southern opposition. They did not want to bring the Russians down south."[59] The Russian-Jordanian entente would later allow for comprehensive, trilateral talks in Vienna. The main thrust of the counter-Islamic State effort was always focused along the Turkish-Syrian border, making Turkish-American interactions more politically complicated.

The first F-16s into Incirlik were deployed on a temporary basis, as preparations were made to move a full squadron to Turkey. "These aircraft were basically a place holder and just something to get into Turkey fast because of the long negotiations with Turkey for the base," a DoD official recalls. "Those guys were there for a short term. The main reason they were pre-positioned was for logistics and once there was approval to drop ordnance from aircraft at the base, it was easier to bring in a full rotation." As a second pilot remembers, "There was an understanding that it would be a short deployment."[60]

The first full squadron was made up of A-10s that had been previously based in Kuwait. This group of twelve jets moved to Incirlik in October and, along with the Turkish Air Force and the unmanned platforms active in the area, were to be the overhead assets for Agate Noble. "We had jets down in Kuwait prior to the deployment to Turkey, and then we were told the aircraft were moving based on it being a lot simpler logistically to keep over the top of the targeting area," an A-10 pilot recalled. By this point, the Strike Cell for the operation had moved to Incirlik. "The JOC [Joint Operations Center] had tons of computers and stadium seating," a person familiar with the operation remembers. In an odd quirk, the Turkish colonel embedded with the Strike Cell, first at Jordan, and then at Incirlik, did not go to the CAOC at Al Udeid. "I was up there in Ankara, and I was trying to find out why this red card holder wouldn't go to the CAOC. An exception was made that because the Turks are in NATO," A Special Forces officer remembers. "We tried to leverage this and work with him to provide additional Turkish aircraft to get us more bombs and more aircraft."[61]

Agate Noble loosened restrictions on groups both Washington and Ankara supported with clandestine assistance in the northwest to move east, to form up on the Marea line to try and push east across the Manbij pocket. "A lot of those other groups showed up and they had shiny new equipment," a person familiar with the operation recalled, in reference to the CIA-armed militias the United States was also supporting. "They were well armed."[62] To satisfy the ROE, the DoD was limited to how it could support these groups. As they massed, a vetted group, dubbed Liwa al-Mu'tasim (LaM), was used to meet the criteria to strike targets. This group had previously clashed with the Islamic State and, by October 2015, was the only vetted Syrian opposition group that the DoD could defend with its airpower. Therefore, to facilitate the push off the Marea Line, the United States would have LaM "drive up and down the line working with other groups," a Special Forces officer recounts. "As long as we could say there was a LaM guy there, we could drop in support. If there wasn't, we could only hold the line," dropping ordnance on Islamic State if under attack. The United States kept tabs on Liwa al-Mu'tasim through the use of a cell phone application, dubbed Android Tactical Assault Kit. This technology allowed for certain individuals within LaM to share geospatial coordinates with the American military. As they massed, to coordinate an airstrike, the group would pass coordinates to the JOC at Incirlik, which would then look again with ISR to clear an airstrike.

The integration with the Turkish Air Force stumbled from the outset, largely because the Turkish pilots being asked to strike targets in support of Agate Noble struggled to strike targets on the ground. The Turkish colonel was eager to show success and was highly regarded by the Americans that worked with him. "The colonel, who was liaising with us was great. He was an F-16 guy, and he was on it. He was one of those guys you come across who is just way above their peers," a person based at Incirlik at the time recalls.[63] To support the push, the Turks were eager to devote aircraft to the fight. "When we would ask for more [Turkish] aircraft, [the Turkish colonel] would take it and add extra." The extra bombs helped, particularly because the CAOC had to prioritize where to send aircraft for the day. "We still had the fight going on in Iraq, all these different places were big at the time, so there were other priorities" that demanded the finite assets deployed to support the fight. The Turkish Air Force sought to fill gaps, but the US side quickly grew frustrated with the Turkish pilots. "We did the first strike using Turkish aircraft, dropping one 500 pounder on a static location. It took 45 minutes for that 9 line. 45 minutes for a successful strike. We were glad it hit, but it took 45 minutes," according to a US Army official.

A nine-line refers to the process to conduct a type of airstrike. It begins with the pilot confirming his or her location, the heading of the aircraft, the distance to the target, the target's elevation, description, and location, followed by how the target has been identified (laser, smoke, coordinates), any friendly positions, and finally where the striking aircraft will egress the target. For this first strike, the JOC at Incirlik had passed grid coordinates from an orbiting drone for the strike. The challenge came in the initial phases of the nine-line and, because of errors in repetition from the pilot, it took many passes to hit the target.

> [The JTAC] just kept repeating the 9 line, and you could hear it on the radio being called back and it was wrong, and it was just over and over. They got a little bit better, and we were down to 20 minutes by the end. Hell, I could use the bombs [in the Manbij pocket]. It was hard to get the bombs up there, but it was so frustrating.[64]

As a second official recalls:

> The JTAC would say something, but at the beginning, the colonel would have to step in and speak in Turkish [to the pilots] and it would go better. I think everybody thought NATO standard, everyone is equal, this should be easy, but it took some time. What I remember is that the pilots weren't doing the read backs the way we do it, so they would read it back, and then there was an error, and so then we had to start over again.[65]

The Turkish red card holder, in contrast, was very familiar with the JTAC process, having worked with them during Ankara's operations against the PKK in northern Iraq. However, it would appear that the finite number of Turkish JTACs, which the United States had flagged as a limitation as far back as December 2014, proved to be prescient and slowed the delivery of ordnance in the area.

> The Turkish colonel was extremely frustrated and upset with the Turkish Air Force. But once we were able to get bombs on targets, and take villages, he was happy that they were finally doing something … he was extremely frustrated with the coalition process, and some of the things we take for granted from the CAOC, like a targeted engagement center annoyed him. He wanted to go weapons loose and get after it.

For the Americans, there was a similar frustration with working with certain coalition partners. "On paper, this coalition sounds good, and then you dig deeper and you have these red card holders, countries debating war crimes and legality, and then we have varying pilot skill within that coalition. We just wanted US aircraft because we knew what we were getting."[66]

For the American pilots supporting the fight for the Manbij pocket, the situation reminded them of the stories they had heard about the First World War. Across the Marea line the forward line of troops had a series of interconnected trenches, just a few hundred yards from the Islamic State's forward line of troops. Behind the trench, each side would set up defensive positions with vehicles behind these trenches and berms, and then behind those to provide protection for the supply lines—and the line rarely moved. To prepare for battle, the United States would dedicate considerable assets to do a "sensor soak" to build a pattern of life inside cities ISIS held. Islamic State adapted to these tactics, hiding in buildings and building a network of tunnels to shield themselves from overhead surveillance.

> ISIS was very good at staying in the buildings and being disciplined. We would have ISR for days, we wouldn't see many ISIS people there, so we would think the villages are abandoned, but on that first operation, and once we had dropped some bombs, and the [Syrian opposition] got in the village, the ISIS fighters pulled out, and they started marching out of the village, and were organized under fire.[67]

As a third soldier described:

> We had constant ISR over the Marea Line that looked for defensive fighting positions, large weapons, and earth movers … Finding ISIS fighters became nearly impossible outside of a firefight. They were making tunnels, staying inside, or moving among civilians. They were also building fake weapons for us to target, just to distract us and waste munitions. It was a frustrating time altogether because we knew we could only be so effective without boots on the ground and doing everything through phones and wifi hotspots.[68]

To fly over the area in manned aircraft, the A-10 pilots assigned to patrol the area had a different set of challenges stemming from the lack of Americans on the ground. Before each flight, the aircrews would get a briefing from the Strike Cell at the JOC to get an update on the position of the Marea line "friendlies" and known Islamic State positions. "When we showed up, we had a team of Special Forces guys on base, and their mission was T/E to go and fight ISIS," according to an A-10 pilot. "We would get fairly regular updates from these guys and every day they would show you the forward line of troops in Iraq. And then in the northeast. And then for the northwest. When the line in the northwest would move, we'd cheer"[69] because progress was often fleeting and the T/E groups, even when augmented with CIA armed entities, struggled to take and hold terrain.

"The Marea Line was a modern day Maginot Line that ultimately remained stagnant," a Special Forces soldier quipped. "Whatever progress we'd make in a day was lost that night when VSO fell back to previously occupied positions, allowing ISIS to roll back in."[70] As a second person recalled, "Our guys wouldn't fire and maneuver. It would be like 50 of our dudes hiding behind a building, with one brave guy firing at an ISIS position. ISIS could hold up the entire plan with one dude firing an AK. Our guys wouldn't maneuver." The lack of willingness to engage with ISIS and then fire and move had consequences for the pilots up above, who would arrive on station from as far away as Iraq, position above a firefight, and then be asked to discern who was who, and where they were located before dropping bombs. The groups that the United States supported remained frightened of Islamic State and would often shrink from a fight, making it harder to support them. "Our guys would turn and run when Islamic State would mass. ISIS would outgun our guys, they would bring up technicals with 40mm anti-aircraft guns, and our guys would take off running. If we got word on it, we could hammer those technicals, but it wasn't guaranteed we'd catch them," a Special Forces officer explained.

In one instance, the United States did get word, but the engagement underscored the challenges of the operation. "We got word that ISIS is attacking, and we slew over the area, and we see two technicals, a Reaper is in the area leaving, and another one is coming on station to replace it. We rifled two Hellfires simultaneously on these two technicals, blew the shit out of them, great, and great our guys held the village." The broader problem, of course, is that the United States had over 100 miles of frontline to patrol, and so air power for these minor engagements wasn't always available. "You are looking through the soda straw at 100 miles of line, and so you don't always know when something bad happens until it happens."[71] The groups along the Marea line needed to be able to act autonomously, and for the Marea line push this never happened, and Islamic State remained motivated to hold on to the terrain it held.

The Marea line groups also proved challenging to support in a firefight. "Supporting [the Marea line groups] was tough because you are talking through SATCOM to someone who is removed from these guys, who is talking with a translator who is talking to the groups, who are trying to do the talk on to the team," a pilot explained.

It was also hard because things were delayed, and then as we are flying, it is complicated to know who was who. Nobody was wearing uniforms. So we would have to look at body language; the things that they are carrying. But ISIS and these forces, from an airmen's perspective, they looked the same. We'd eventually figure it out, but it took time.[72]

As a controller explained:

The A-10 guys did a phenomenal job, they would get approval to do gun runs, and they were willing to get down into it. It was a low threat area, but you always risk a golden bee-bee from ISIS that could get lucky and down a US pilot when they get down that low. You also had to worry about killing the Marea line guys. The last thing you want to do is kill them and ruin the rapport you've built. They were already lookin for any excuse not to go out and fight, so you do not want to give them another reason to stay home and not go out and fight.[73]

In one instance, ISIS discipline got the best of them, when CJSTOF-S had an AC-130 gunship check in on station for a night of orbits in the area. "We had the AC-130 a few times, and when you bring that beast to bear, and you are thinking about ISIS, well 'fuck you', you went to war against a super power." The battle unfolded as it usually did, with coalition bombs hitting targets, followed by Islamic State tactically retreating from the building they were holding. "They road marched to the next village in formation, and the AC-130 had just checked in on station, the crew saw what they needed to see, we had valid targets, and we could keep them all straight."

For all this investment, the Marea line remained relatively static. As an A-10 pilot described, "The Marea line was a tennis match. Every night was back and forth, back and forth." A second pilot used a similar metaphor. "It was disheartening to see the give and take, the ping pong." The challenge, of course, was that ISIS was better motivated to fight than the Marea line groups. They had an esprit de corps that most others lacked and it was this zeal that enabled them to fight to hold territory. They also had geography on their side. "We were never going to break through the Marea Line and clear the Manbij Pocket using [this] strategy," a Special Forces soldier involved in the program lamented. "The ISIS defense in depth was far too developed and their reserves in al Bab and Manbij would always out number our VSO."[74]

Competing Priorities: The YPG Goes on Offense

As Agate Noble stumbled, the debate within the US government sharpened about the plan to take the town of Manbij, which sits just west of the Euphrates River. The city was, before the war, of little strategic value to anyone outside the people who lived in or those that relied upon it for their economic well-being. However, once Islamic State emerged and took control of the city in January 2014 it became an important city that sat at the junction of multiple roads that stretched across Syria. Throughout the battle for the Manbij pocket, the United States was building a pattern of life profile in the city in preparation for the assault of the city. "We were hanging out to the north of the Euphrates, out west from Manbij. If you had nothing to do, we would do non-traditional ISR. We would be sensor soaking ISIS strongholds. To build pattern of life," an F-15E pilot explains.[75] For the A-10 pilots deployed at Incirlik, the planning for Manbij was near constant, but delayed repeatedly because of the T/E groups' struggles. "It was supposed to happen, and then it was delayed and then our squadron rotated out," an A-10 pilot recalled.

The other focus in Syria at this time was Shadadi, the ISIS-held town east of the river that Islamic State had taken control of in 2014. The battle for Shadadi in early 2016 is where the relationship with Turkey began to fray further, presaging the near full break that would come in August 2016 during Operation Euphrates Shield, Ankara's invasion of the Manbij pocket. For the United States, managing Turkey and the war against Islamic State became a dominant issue for policymakers and members of the coalition to grapple with. For the men on the ground in northeastern Syria, the focus was on Islamic State. The Task Force had an inherent advantage over its CJSTOF-S cousins operating from Turkey and Jordan because they were operating in country in partnership with their preferred partner force. "[JSOC] was in country and CJSOTF was not, limiting the responsiveness of the opposition, making difficult to build rapport [with the T/E groups]," a US Army Special Forces member described. These men would not get clearance to enter Syria for close to a year. "Until then we were doing advise, assist, and accompany via Skype."[76]

The Task Force entered Syria sometime after Delta Force linked up with the YPG in Sinjar and before personnel were inserted into Kobane to help defend the city with airstrikes. The battle for Kobane was the turning point, where the defensive mission against Islamic State shifted to offense. "Kobane was Mazlum's top priority," a member of the Task Force recalled. "It wasn't necessarily a bad place to begin. And if it could be a proof of concept for the ISIS fight writ large, well, why not, we were willing to do it."[77] As with the Mosul Dam operation, Kobane proved that a small contingent of specialized US special operations forces that could plug in to coalition air power could take back territory from Islamic State. The YPG, however, demonstrated a different level of tenacity than the groups that fought on the Marea line. As one Special Forces soldier who worked with both the T/E groups and the Syrian Kurds notes, "The [Arab groups] through T&E were not really motivated to do much. Yes, they dislike ISIS, but they preferred to fight Assad... Arabs (T&E) and Kurds (SDF) have a very different culture when it comes to war and motivation to stand up for themselves."[78]

The YPG's rapid shift from offense to defense, however, did catch much of the American policy community off-guard. "There were so many geopolitical factors going on in the region and [JSOC] can move very quickly and move very fast, but for DoD it was like, 'wow, we are too the border, and Turkey is melting apart," a person familiar with the Task Force remembers of the days after Kobane. "It was like, 'we need to find a different partner force' and do Leahy vetting."[79] This process, known officially as the Leahy Law, prevents the provision of funds or aid groups accused of gross human rights violations. The Syria-side of the ISIS war being focused in the northeast came as a surprise to many in the Pentagon. "We were looking at a map of where we [were] dropping, and it was Kobane in late 2014, and then it is its like holy crap, that is where the war is, and, wait, why is the [YPG] moving now."[80] The growing issue was that as the YPG pushed east across the Turkish-Syrian border, it became inevitable that they would connect the two cantons of Kobane and Jazeera, consolidating control over the border and further irritating Turkey.

The symbolic city in the middle of these two cantons was Tel Abyad, a town that the Islamic State had taken control of in January 2014. According to an analysis of over 4,600 unique Islamic State personnel records conducted by Combating Terrorism Center, Tel Abyad was the Islamic State's most important crossing point from Turkey to Syria.[81] As late as May 2015, the Turkish town of Akcakale served as an important waypoint for foreign fighters and the cross-border shipment of fertilizer, which has high levels of ammonium nitrate and is useful for the manufacture of explosives. A study of Islamic State IEDs also revealed that the group was dependent on Turkish-made components and transshipment routes for detonator cord, cables, and allowed for the transshipment of items like mobile phones used to detonate bombs remotely.[82] In a sign of the level of distrust, JSOC believed that Ankara was facilitating the cross-border flow of men and weapons to ISIS-held areas to facilitate attacks on the YPG. "[JSOC] felt that the Turks were allowing and enabling ISIS forces that would attack the Kurds," according to a Special Forces soldier familiar with the Task Force's operations east of the Euphrates. "They would see aVBIED that would originate from inside Turkey to hit the Kurds. And there were so many foreign fighters coming from Turkey."[83] As a Task Force member explained, "The questions we were asking was whether the Turks knew that the people crossing the border were going to ISIS, and whether allowing men and materiel coming across the border was official government policy, or just the action of corrupt border guards and local officials."[84]

For the Task Force, closing down the cross-border flow of foreign fighters and cutting off the Islamic State was an imperative to facilitate the campaign to defeat the group. After Kobane, Tel Abyad emerged as a clear priority and a critical town for the YPG to take control of to sever the Islamic State's link to this one important border crossing. The YPG pushed from Kobane and Hassakah, eventually reaching the Tel Abyad suburbs in late May, before assaulting the city and taking control of it in mid-June. The fall of Tel Abyad severed the Islamic State's links to Turkey in eastern Syria. It also proved that it happened faster than most had expected and further validated the concept rapidly developed to fight Islamic State with a small number of troops deployed in Syria. Further, the YPG was succeeding where the Marea line groups were struggling, making it easy to decide which group should receive priority airpower taskings when competing for finite resources to enable the fight.

The fall of Tel Abyad was not welcomed in Turkey. "Tel Abyad was a game changer because the YPG connected the cantons," a DoD official recalls. "All of a sudden, we started seeing maps and an operational plan that had the YPG going all the way across the border with Turkey, and because they are the TF, that didn't have to go to a policy coordination committee [PCC]."[85] The PCC is one level below the Principals Committee or Deputies Committee, both of which are one level below the president, and allowed for the Task Force's decisions to be immediately considered at a high level within the government. Despite this low-level planning, on the political side, the option to use the Syrian Kurds to push across the entire pocket was never really considered. General Mazlum had wanted this, but the intent was push ISIS out of an important logistics hub—Manbij—to ease the battle for Raqqa for later in the fight. The actual plan was to use the Syrian

Kurds to push down the river toward Raqqa, and still let the T/E program play out so close off the border areas to assuage Turkish concerns.[86]

The strengthening Task Force's relationship with the YPG partnership is what many US officials point to as the ultimate reason Ankara gave in to US requests to open Incirlik Air Force Base. "We had been trying to get them to open Incirlik from the beginning, and they assessed that we wanted it bad, and they wanted us to move against the regime, and held out access to the airbase as leverage," an official recounts. "The YPG was never on the table, and once the U.S. relationship with them deepened, they had to bring us an option on ISIS ... They knew we would be so driven to find a partner and would leave [them] in the dust."[87] Within days of the town falling, Ankara opened the airbase and setting up the CJSOTF-S strike cell in country. "We decided that we would not let Kobane fall, and that we are going to carpet bomb the place. And then all of a sudden the YPG is moving and that is when the Turks start to lose it."[88]

However, the aforementioned "tennis match" in the Manbij pocket was slowing the campaign down against ISIS, at a time when the Task Force had identified a partner force that was willing to aggressively fight Islamic State. The T/E groups, meanwhile, were performing poorly, even when augmented with elements from the CIA program. To try and manage Turkish concerns, the Task Force sought to integrate Arab militias into the YPG, beginning with a smattering of small groups, collectively dubbed the Syrian Arab Coalition, or SAC. "The SAC was a cut out to arm the YPG before we could do it officially," a US Special Forces soldier bluntly stated.[89] In essence, these groups allowed the United States to begin to provide arms to the YPG through Arab groups that worked alongside the YPG so as to meet the letter of the law within the 1209 authorities that funded US lethal support in Syria. "We started discussing this in May, before the opening of Incirlik," a US official recalled. "It was a way to use 1209 and T/E funds for the YPG,"[90] without the president granting a waiver to arm a PKK-linked group. As one soldier described it, "We had to find some groups that gave Ankara enough deniability to politically save face, and so we moved the SAC [east of the Euphrates]."[91]

While Ankara was, in the words of a DoD official, "slightly less furious about the SAC," they still remained committed to building an alternative partner force to try and replace the YPG. However, the YPG was continuing its offensive in Syria's northeast and, by late October, were preparing to take Shadadi. In late October, the Task Force arranged for a drop of weapons to the SAC, as they prepared to take Al Howl, a town that would allow for the push to oust Islamic State from the Hassakah province. In the early morning hours of October 12, a C-17 dropped 50 tons of ammunition in Syria, ostensibly for use by the SAC for the Shadadi battle.[92] However, as was clear from the outset of the drop, the ammunition would be passed on to the YPG. Ankara immediately summoned the American ambassador to Turkey, John Bass, to express displeasure at the act. "The airdrop to the SAC blew it all open," a DoD official remembers. After the airdrop, there was controversy inside the US government after it became clear "supplies went to the PKK. The Under Secretary of Defense for Policy immediately chaired a video teleconference with the Task Force and the guy at the other end was like surprised the Pentagon didn't know this was going to happen. He was like, of course they'll get the supplies, [the YPG] are the only ones with a logistical system."[93] As a second US official recalls, "This is when the Turks start getting super hysterical about the YPG … [the interim Foreign Minister Feridun] Sinirlioglu was telling Kerry that they are super pissed about the SAC resupply. The airdrop thing was controversial, but then pretty quickly we started doing ground resupply on the ground to the SAC" and the operation became less visible.[94]

At the same time, the United States also began construction of what would later be dubbed the Kobane Landing Zone, or KLZ.[95] This airstrip began construction in early 2016. The initial name, however, is another source of internal debate. "It was first being called the Kobane Rojava landing zone," according to a DoD official. Rojava is the Kurdish word that refers to Western Kurdistan, which would imply that the United States was recognizing that there was such a thing as a western Kurdistan. "Luckily we got the paper work changed before the first mission so it never existed beyond a concept, but the only point that swayed DoD leadership was citing that the U.S. Government does not recognize Rojava."[96]

The battle for Shadadi turned out to be less hard fought than initial assumptions. The preparation for this battle began in late October, beginning with the sensor soak of ISR to prepare to retake the town. "There was a lot of prep for what turned out to be a lot of hype, rather than a hard fought battle," an A-10 pilot recalled. "We had so much prep time on that area, we did a lot prior to event forces moving down there; we hadn't taken care of everything, but we had been deploying and watching that city for along time."[97] Still, the battle pushed Islamic State out of Hassakah province, solidifying Kurdish rule east of the river, and validating the Task Force's early work with the partner force it had found and cultivated on that mountain top in Sinjar in August 2014. The final battle in November focused on Sinjar, the place where the Task Force first intervened in Iraq, and where the United States first made contact with the YPG. Like Shadadi, it was a quick operation and Islamic State put up less resistance than assumed. As one Turkey-based pilot noted, "When we first got to [Incirlik], any given night you were probably employing something because the area had been more or less cleared of civilians, and so it was go hunting. Once the Kurds pushed it was a quick operation."[98]

Tidal Wave II: A Desert Oasis and Crippling Islamic State Oil Infrastructure

In parallel to the battle for cities and towns in eastern Syria, the United States also sought to increase pressure on the Islamic State via the targeting of its crude, but lucrative oil infrastructure in an operation dubbed Tidal Wave II. The name was chosen because of its linkage to Operation Tidal Wave, the Second World War era raid on oil refineries in German-occupied Romania in 1943.

The first strikes in Syria in support of Tidal Wave II began on October 21 and involved multiple different aircraft, tasked with destroying oil infrastructure without killing civilians that profited from the illicit oil trade. This strike package began on SIPR, the classified DoD computer server. "[A pilot] had started passing around on SIPR a picture of a truck park. People had been sent to investigate it. It looked like a rail yard, but it was lines and lines of trucks, and they looked like trains, but it was these long lines of trucks in the middle of the desert," an F-15E WSO recalls. For pilots, this target provided an excellent opportunity to hamper Islamic State's oil operation, but there was a deep understanding that the truckers were non-combatants, and most probably innocent Syrians just trying to make a living.

> We thought [the image of the trucks] was too good to be true. Joke was on me, I got called in, and so these guys would come in, drop these trucks off, and ISIS filled them and charged for it to finance the war. The truckers were just dudes, so there was not an appetite to go after these guys, but there was an appetite to go after ISIS.

To try and mitigate the risk to the truckers, the coalition watched the trucks night after night, building the pattern of life that dominated targeting during OIR. Within the coalition, there was a debate about how far the targeting should extend to the middle men who were critical for ferrying Islamic State oil throughout Syria and Iraq. "There were lots of debates about the tribal involvement in the area and how to target upstream," an official involved with the campaign recounted. "It was, how much should we risk upsetting tribes that we were also working with. CENTCOM and Treasury wanted to burn it all down."[99] Ultimately, the Obama administration opted for a policy of restraint, and working to manage from the White House the direction of the war. Later, after President Trump took power, the targeting rules were delegated, allowing for regional commanders to widen the number of targets they could strike.

The oil infrastructure proved to be an easy target for coalition pilots.

> So this truck park was a place where dudes would drop off trucks. They were baby sat by some dudes, and then the guys would come back. It would take days or weeks to fill all of these trucks, so the idea was that we could go after the trucks when the truckers weren't there and only try and target the trucks and the ISIS dudes left behind to guard them.

The remote desert location made the targeting ideal because there were no schools or mosques in the area for the pilots and WSOs to worry about. "It was like Christmas came early, and so word gets out, and then every fighter and strike squadron wants in, and it wound up being two AC-130, four A-10s, and some strike eagles for leaflets and ISR." As it would turn out, the United States had waited a bit too long because the night of mission the number of trucks had decreased from several hundred to just a few hundred, per the estimates of a pilot flying that night.

> The AC-130 was in charge, they had a better communications suite; it was a high profile mission with seniors watching; and it was crowded with aircraft. It looked like some of the trucks had dispersed. They had shut off the pumps, we think. So

there weren't thousands of trucks, there were hundreds. We then had an hour to kill as many as possible. The AC-130 monitored the civilians, and then we had an hour, to just destroy as many as we could.[100]

Operation Tidal Wave II continued throughout late 2015 and until Raqqa was liberated. "We spent a lot of time targeting the oil infrastructure. We would be looking for oil wells, oil sills, and pumps and so we might spend an hour per mission rolling down towards the southeast targeting oil stills, wells, pump jacks, potentially trucks already loaded with oil. We wanted to light money on fire," a second A-10 pilot described. The crude refining mechanism made finding these oil wells relatively easy to spot. A pilot recalled:

ISIS was taking crude oil and crudely refining and they had dozens and dozens of these fields, east of the Euphrates, we would do this mission at night. It was very easy to see. They would light these fires under these oil drums. We would fly over them. If there was fire under them we would get permission to take them out.

Before using lethal force, the pilots would try and scare the people away from the sill or pump jacks. "A non-kinetic marking rocket makes a loud bang. We would put it 100 meter or so from anyone; the people do not want to be around it, and they knew what we were doing, and the people knew to leave. We do not really train for this, but it was just trying to figure out ways to solve a problem." This rocket was a technical innovation, stemming from the addition of a laser guidance kit to make the weapon more accurate and to reduce collateral damage. The A-10 and, later, the F-16 would use a variant of this weapon for strikes inside urban areas.

After taking this action to scare away the people, the A-10 operators would use a low-kinetic weapon like the gun to destroy the oil infrastructure. "We would get intel from the CAOC and assign pump jack and refinery facilities, and it was the same idea. We would apply warning shots, then after people left we would put bombs on them. This lasted until Raqqa finished and once they pushed south, the tidal wave mission kinda finished."[101] By October 2016, just one year after Tidal Wave II began, the air campaign was showing signs of progress. The price of oil inside the caliphate had increased, which suggested to the coalition that the caliphate's supplies had dwindled. After the fall of Raqqa the effort had grown moot, as Islamic State was clearly on the pathway to territorial defeat. But for at least two years, the pilots patrolling eastern Syria were looking for oil-related targets to strike.

The War Turns Hot: Ankara Tangles with Moscow

From the outset of the Russian intervention in Syria, the VKS had sought to challenge the relative safe haven the Turkish- and American-backed opposition had carved out in pockets along the Turkish-Syrian border. Throughout the war,

Turkish air defense units would closely monitor air traffic along the Turkish-Syrian border over the Military Air Distress (MAD) or UHF Guard frequency all air forces are supposed to monitor. "Anybody getting close to the border from the south would be identified," a US pilot flying to and from Incirlik recalled. "It was standard verbiage; [the Turks] would make a call out based on a position from Khmeimim. They would say, you are approaching Turkish airspace, turn south immediately."[102] In at least one instance before November 2015, the USAF had to make emergency diverts to Turkish airfields when the pilots faced an in-flight emergency. During these instances, the pilots would ignore the standardized and enforced flight corridors that Ankara had established to deconflict air traffic flying from inside Turkey over Syria and Iraq. As one F-15E WSO recalled, "I had to divert into Turkey on August 2, [2014] and I ended at Batman. We shut down their commercial airline operations. We had a hydraulic problem and were up there for about a week."[103]

The Russian Aerospace Forces, without question, monitored the guard frequency closely. In July 2017, American pilots and their Russian counterparts, flying in tense mock dog fights would sometimes speak to each other to ease tensions after each side would place the other under missile lock.[104] The Turkish Air Force had aircraft assigned to patrolling the border, as well. The Russian Air Force first violated Turkish airspace on October 3 and October 4 with a Su-24 bomber, which was being escorted by the Su-30 Flanker. As the Su-24 conducted its bombing run on the border, the Su-30 "spiked" (put an opposing aircraft under radar lock) Turkish F-16s that had responded to the intrusion.[105] In response, NATO condemned the action, expressing solidarity with Turkey and warning that they were watching the border closely. The first Turkish shoot down of a Russian-flown aircraft came in mid-October, when the unmanned Orlans-10 crossed into Turkish space and was downed by a Turkish F-16, purportedly as it was monitoring Turkish troop locations just inside the border.[106]

The United States sought to augment Turkish security, sending six F-15Cs and six F-15Es to Incirlik. The C model F-15 is specifically designed for the air-to-air and were quite clearly designed to counter the Russian Flanker patrols going on along the border. The F-15E can also perform this role, but it is ideally suited for the air-to-ground mission. The American jets arrived on November 6, 2015, amidst continuing Turkish-Russian tensions in the air.[107] As one pilot recalls, "They did move some Strike Eagles and C models into Incirlik. Those guys stayed with us for a couple of months. There was a show of solidarity, but immediately the Strike Eagles got pulled to support the fight against ISIS. So we had company on the ramp, it got more crowded. Now you had a couple more squadrons."[108]

These tensions skyrocketed shortly thereafter, when on November 24, a Turkish F-16 downed a Russian Su-24, after it crossed the border on a bombing run for some seventeen seconds. As one A-10 pilot recalls:

> I was flying home when [the shoot down] happened, and it was a long flight. This was before they put tankers in Syria, so we had to push into Iraq, get gas, go back to Syria for mid-vuls, and then back to tank in Iraq, before heading home

[to Incirlik]. As I was heading home, and I didn't know what was happening, but the Turks were screaming on guard, and they screamed a lot, but this time they were warning us about any contacts and to try and get the [hostile contacts] to turn south.[109]

On the ground, the crash site was soon swarmed by elements of the Turkish-backed opposition. The two pilots ejected, but one pilot was killed by ground fire, while the other was captured by a group headed by a Turkish citizen, active in the area. The search and rescue helicopter, then, was destroyed by an American-provided TOW missile. The United States watched the incident from the JOC at Incirlik, feeding information to the CAOC at Al Udeid. "We had situational awareness on the incident. We were providing updates about where the Russians were and what we thought was happening. We knew that one Russian was dead and we knew that the Russian helicopter had been hit by the TOW," a person familiar with the situation recalls. "That was a pretty tense situation for a little while, but in the end, and at the end of the day, cooler heads prevailed."[110]

An American pilot at Incirlik picked up the story. "The [Turks] had been complaining that the Russians had been flying close to their borders, and when we heard about it we had to ask the Turkish colonel embedded with us if the news was true, and he was like 'yes we shot it down. They violated our airspace.'"[111] The worry for the United States stemmed from the unknown: How would Russia respond. "We had to worry about what the Russians would do. After that, we were concerned about the Russian response, they had a lot of surface-to-air missiles and they were co-located with the regime at air defense sites, and so for a time period, we avoided that area of Syria in the northwest." For pilots waiting to get airborne, the base was abuzz following the incident and most assumed that flights over Syria would be suspended. "Here we are, we are sitting on a Turkish air force base, close to where the Russians are operating. It has Turkish fighters on it, there are these concerns about mis-identification, and then I'm thinking 'we are not going to fly for a while,'" an A-10 pilot remembers. "We kept expecting the phone call, do we have to move bases, and that phone call never came, and we went and did our mission in support of the SDF."[112]

In the aftermath of the incident, Prime Minister Erdogan defended Ankara's actions saying that his government would not apologize for the incident and that the military was operating per the ROE it had set after repeated Russian violations of Turkish airspace.[113] Moscow's first response was to deny that it had crossed into Turkish airspace, followed by the rapid deployment of the S-400 (also known as the SA-21 in NATO reporting terms) surface-to-air missile system to Khmeimim Air Base.[114] The incident marked the end of Turkish F-16 overflight of Syria, depriving CJSOTF-S of the extra bombs it had sought to use to support the Marea line push. "The Turks would still drop bombs, but they would do it from inside the Turkish border into Syria, and from the American side, we would drop it from a certain range, and so you'd find time of flight from these bombs were 9 minutes," a special forces soldier told the author. "So we would clear a target, its stationary, and then we had to wait 9 minutes for the bomb to hit. And so we had to be very deliberate about the time and how to strike. And we did have successful hits, and so it would be weapons away, but then we would wait on the screen."[115] After months of negotiations to bring Turkey into the fight, Ankara was subsequently removed from the Air Tasking Order. Moscow had threatened to shoot down Turkish Air Force aircraft that entered Syrian airspace. "The Russians asked us to take the Turks off the ATO after the shoot down," a DoD official recalls. "Our messaging was to de-escalate, but we did send an unintentional signal when we brought the F-15s home, combined with their removal from the ATO" that Turkey was all on its own.[116]

As it would turn out, the twelve F-15s that had deployed in early November were slotted to return to their home base at Lakenheath, England, in mid-December. As the Air Force indicated at the time, the deployment was always intended to be short. As a Turkish official told the author in March 2016, the short deployment was viewed as an indication of American weakness. "Have you guys forgotten how to deter?," a Turkish Ministry of Foreign Affairs official sarcastically asked the author about the incident.[117] Whatever Ankara's interpretation, the reason these jets were pulled is, as one pilot noted, "EUCOM is filled with taskings." The jets were, quite simply, needed elsewhere.

For the Americans, the focus soon shifted more to the east of the river, and in support of the Task Force and the YPG and its smattering of Arab allies. The T/E effort in Turkey and the Agate Noble effort were further de-prioritized. Still, the Russians did take action in response to the shoot down, beyond the threats to down Turkish jets. "The Russians puffed up their chest ... I remember nights where I was flying and there were two Russian fighters flying above me, we knew where they were, but then they would peel off and bomb an ISIS position, and we'd then go and bomb an ISIS position nominated by the Kurds," an A-10 pilot recalls of the post-shoot down atmosphere. "We were also concerned about fratricide coming back to Turkey [from Syria]. We would talk to their forward reporting center so that you didn't get schwacked entering Turkey, but from our perspective, things didn't change all that much."

As a second pilot noted, "The other thing that happened was increased aggression from their air defense and uncertainty that they would identify us. They would do all of the above, intercepts, pinging with Syrian air defense and the S-400."[118] However, for the A-10 community, the shoot down ended up with them flying more hours over Syria because the F-16s that both the United States and Turkey had flown in the area were avoiding the Russian air defenses at that time. As one pilot explained:

Typically the SA-21 uses jet engine modulation, or JEM to identify aircraft. This means you bounce signals off the intake fan of the jets, which allows for the radar to identify the target. Your firing matrix is based on being able to identify what you are shooting at, to avoid fratricide, and when you cant identify an aircraft using the Identify Friend Foe equipment that interrogates encrypted signals from friendly aircraft. A F-16 return looks the same, no matter who is flying it on radar, so [US] F-16 cycled out in favor of the A-10. Why? Russia vowed to shoot down hostile aircraft, and the Turks only fly F-16.[119]

The A-10s use a different engine than the F-16, clearly identifying them as American. Thus, they became the safer option to fly in the area. As one pilot explained, "It ended up with us flying more over Syria because we stopped flying F-16 over northwest Syria."[120]

The war in Syria was now concentrated east of the river, with the Task Force deepening ties with the YPG and its smattering of Arab allies. To move forward with the war plan, the Manbij pocket remained a sore spot, and a strip of territory that the Task Force wanted to take from Islamic State. However, Turkey remained unwilling to tolerate a YPG presence west of the river, pushing instead for a more lenient American approach to some of its favored proxies, dominant in the country's northwest. The battle planning for Manbij reflected the schisms within the US government about the emerging anti-ISIS effort in Syria. The group best suited to take the dam, as a jumping off point to besiege Manbij, was the YPG and SAC. However, at the one-star office level, Manbij was included in the CONOP for the T/E groups.

As the war against Islamic State stalled, following the lightning fast turn of events after Kobane, and the concurrent collapse of Islamic State in Shadadi and Sinjar, the Manbij question loomed large. Ultimately, the battle for this city foretold the next four years of the conflict, with the United States and its Kurdish partners pushing to consolidate territory, Ankara working to undermine that progress, and Russia seeking to exploit fissures between these two allies for its own political gains, even while exploring ways to cooperate with the United States. The war against Islamic State was far from over, but with Manbij, the United States would work out the kinks for the much larger urban battles to come. The minor skirmishes with Moscow, too, would soon grow more tense, as both global powers pushed to control the Euphrates River Valley. And finally, Ankara would renege on its promise to never apologize to Moscow for the downing of the Su-24 in November 2015, and soon each a modus vivendi with its former Cold War rival to try and force the United States to leave Syria for good.

Chapter 5

THE BATTLE FOR MANBIJ AND THE TRAIN AND EQUIP PROGRAM

As 2015 came to a close, Turkey and the United States were at loggerheads over Manbij. Russia, meanwhile, had begun to extend its air campaign to the critical overland supply route linking Gaziantep with Aleppo. The Russian air campaign was, in part, a response to the downing of the Su-24. It also was a military imperative, linked to the joint Russian and Syrian approach to counter-insurgent operations. The Turkish government was also staring down an attempted coup, which few had anticipated before it happened in July. After subduing the insurrection, Ankara still went ahead with a unilateral invasion of the Manbij pocket to block the YPG's westward expansion. The Turkish invasion brought their troops and associated Syrian militias face-to-face with the YPG, which with Task Force guidance had wrested control of Manbij from Islamic State, and subsequently changed its name to the Syrian Democratic Forces, or SDF.

The main thrust of the American effort in Syria in 2015 was the T/E program, which was intended to mollify Turkey and to work jointly on an overt military effort to push the Islamic State from a section along the Turkish-Syrian border. The United States and Jordan also pushed forward with a second T/E program, designed to create a force capable of striking Islamic State positions in the Syrian desert. The fighters were, however, used for an ill-thought-out assault on Bukamal, a town on the Syrian-Iraqi border, and suffered an embarrassing defeat. The Jordanian role in the war would later shift, particularly on the Assad question and the kingdom's efforts to manage the fallout from the ongoing civil war.

As for Turkey, the battle for Manbij was the first contested river crossing that US forces had been involved in since Korea and it was executed by less than 100 men, working to span a strip of river with Soviet-era bridges, and 2,000 Syrian Kurds prepared to fight Islamic State in urban combat. The urban battle plan was the model that the United States would use again in Raqqa. The river crossing, however, upended relations with Turkey, setting in motion an eventual Turkish invasion of the Manbij pocket and a series of failed negotiations to manage US-Turkish tensions.

The Train and Equip Program in Jordan

The T/E program had a second location in Jordan, where US Special Forces, working alongside British conventional forces and Jordanian Special Forces, put a series of Syrian recruits through a three-month-long training program. For Jordan, the training site was of secondary importance to the broader effort to win security guarantees from the United States for the Islamic State. The centerpiece of that concession was the basing of American and coalition jets at Muwaffaq Salti Air Base, known to most of the Americans as Azraq. The small F-16 base was expanded throughout the war to accommodate the growing number of aircraft deployed there, ranging from large cargo planes, aerial refueling jets, to the heavier (as compared to the F-16) F-15E Strike Eagle. "As we got past the 2014 and 2015 ISIS crisis," a State Department official recounts, "the Jordanians were relieved. They also got a significant and carefully modulated presence there that between the build out at Azraq, which was the much bigger component to the counter-ISIS efforts, and Tanf," a small Special Forces manned outpost first built inside Jordan to control the flow of people at the tri-border area where Iraq, Syria, and Jordan meet.[1]

The training site for the Jordanian component of T/E was near Aqaba, the seaside resort town popular with tourists. The actual training site was tucked into the desert, placed deliberately out of sight from any potential onlooker. "We had a nice training camp in the desert, 5km x 20km was the space to train in," a trainer based at the site recalled. "We shared the space with Bedouins. We would go out and deconflict with them and then do the training the next day. We often used the bedouins as force protection, we hired young men from their tribes to do our laundry and our dining facility and to watch for tourists."[2]

For the first T/E class, men were pulled from Turkey and brought to Jordan for training. As was the case in the north, the group of men was poorly motivated and had a tense relationship with the American and British trainers at the base. The second wave was culled from a single eastern Syrian tribe and these men were more properly motivated. "We had a good relationship with the Syrians and told the command that we would be comfortable crossing with them, and this was different from the guys in Turkey, where there was significant distrust." The training was intended to be three months, but as the program began, the CONOP for these trainees had not yet been drafted. "We spent 6 months with these guys. It was supposed to be 3 months, but there was a delay on the CONOP that was going up through different levels of Operation Inherent Resolve, and when we get to the three month mark, we still didn't have a plan to get them across the border."[3] The overarching issue, by this point, is that the CONOP being envisioned was asynchronous with what the T/E group was actually capable of achieving. "A lot of the Syrians wanted to quit. We finally got the CONOP, we took them to Tower 22" to raid a small, ISIS-held border crossing.

At the political level, the importance of this small garrison grew in magnitude because of how Jordan's view of the conflict was changing. Beginning in mid-2013, the Jordanian government began to close the border to Syrian refugees and limiting the number of border crossings by which people were allowed to cross from Syria to Jordan. By 2015, this had resulted in a build up of people at the remote, desert area of Rukban, which is close to Tanf and that the military referred to as the berm. "If you looked at what they did in 2015, which was when [Jordanian government] stopped letting in more Syrians. Folks were getting in to the country near Tanf, and they were able to communicate to people in Syria, who then speak it back through their networks that this was the place to cross."[4] As a result, people began to move to this area, just opposite the berm and a make-shift refugee camp popped up and become home to thousands of people.

At this point of the war, the Obama administration imposed restrictions on the Special Forces groups deployed near the berm, and tasked them managing a potential southern front in the ISIS war. For missions longer than a few hours inside Syria, the Special Forces needed approval from the national security advisor. To manage this issue, the United States sought to work through allies that had different rules for how it operated in country. "The Norwegians had been in Iraq, and their tier one special operations forces operate like our tier one guys," a Special Forces member recalled. "The Iraqis made them identify their guys. That pissed them off. They still wanted to do something, so they ended up leaving the country and coming to Jordan and worked through Tower 22."[5]

Tower 22 was the infiltration and exfiltration point along the Jordanian-Syrian border. By 2016, the T/E groups inside Jordan were ready to seize the border garrison from Islamic State. In January 2016, the group moved to the border, in preparation for the seizure of the ISIS-held border crossing. The battle for the garrison was short and straightforward. "They shot some mortars and integrated with coalition air power, which they used to target the border guards," a person familiar with the operation recounted. Islamic State lost control of the border in March 2016, but beyond this operation, the forces that were being trained had little capacity to do much else. As one person familiar with the Jordan-based T/E program explained:

> These guys were for small missions to hit ISIS and move. They didn't have the assets to set up a permanent base. They could just hit a base, perhaps with indirect fire, and maybe follow up with airpower. If there was an ISIS checkpoint, they could hit that. They were trained to be an antagonizing force to hit ISIS; a longer term-specialized force for desert raids, and not an infantry force to maneuver and seize terrain.[6]

However, after the seizing of the border post, the T/E groups were used to try and establish a second front in the war against Islamic State. As one State Department official quipped, "Tanf is amazing. It's an amazing example of mission creep."[7] That mission creep began after the basic CONOP was altered. "A concept was sold that Tanf could be as a base of operations for a desert movement to one day overthrow Bukamal," a Special Forces officer remembers. Bukamal is a town on the Euphrates River in the Deir ez-Zor Governorate, 145 miles north of Tanf and on the border with Iraq. "We were going to try and paint a big blue arrow north, and one day have our allied force assault the city, and through some psychological operation with social media, the people of Bukamal would be primed and ready to rise up and support us. It was a horrible plan from the beginning," a person familiar with the operation remembers. As a second person involved explained, "They were not ready and they did not have the air power to support them … They were an expeditionary force to exploit ISIS weaknesses in the desert. They can't seize a town. They weren't trained for that."[8] The operation turned out to be an embarrassment. As the group moved north, they seized an abandoned airfield and began the psychological component of the operation, broadcasting messages to the local population on a local radio station. Islamic State soon counterattacked, killing men from the T/E group, seizing US-provided equipment, and then killing more in an ambush as they retreated to Tower 22.[9]

As had become common up north on the Marea line, the T/E group was joined by men the CIA had trained and equipped in the separate, clandestine arming program. Still, the combined force allowed for the United States to provide air strikes if a vetted group was present in the combined group of forces. During the battle, air assets were tasked to target an Islamic State convoy that had left Fallujah after the coalition had taken control of the city in neighboring Iraq. The retasking of air power was a common occurrence in OIR. The main issue with the T/E push to Bukamal was with the plan itself. "This was rolling the dice and using hope as a method," a Special Forces officer explained. The plan was flawed from the outset and incongruous with the capabilities of the T/E groups deployed into the desert. As one State Department official recalls, "[Tanf] was never intended to be anything other than the 'ragged edge of the D-ISIS fight.'" However, as the war continued, the base became a flashpoint for American interactions with the Russian, Syrian, and Iranian air forces. It also would become a sticking point for officials from the Trump administration that sought to use the base in its broader effort to pressure Iran, and as a mechanism to sell President Trump on the necessity of retaining a presence in Syria, despite the American president's desires to withdraw all combat troops.

From Tishreen to Manbij: The Move West of the River

For the Task Force, the entirety of 2015 effort against Islamic State was a high-wire act. JSOC was hunting for Islamic State leadership targets in both Iraq and Syria, but had to balance broader efforts to simply watch and map the organization, or to take action and kill those that needed to be removed from the battle field. The group also had to manage the broader, geopolitical tension that the fight was causing with Turkey. The weapons drop to the SAC and YPG in late October 2015 caused significant friction with Turkey. However, by November, global events superseded Turkish concerns and increased the urgency to push Islamic State off the border and to hasten the war effort.

In late October, President Obama authorized the first acknowledged US Special Forces presence in Syria. The first overt US "boots on the ground in Syria was in December 2015," a person familiar explained.[10] This deployment came as the urgency to hasten the war against Islamic State grew in Europe, but there were differences between the Army Special Forces and the Task Force. As one Task Force member observed, "The [U.S. Special Forces] were driving vehicles we had purchased for the partner force, and had to use Delta stuff for beyond line of sight communications. They had to use local houses, and the various commanders were very cautious and careful, and if they go to Syria, they wanted to ensure that it looked like we weren't going to stay, and to ensure that once they were in they wouldn't get yanked for political reasons. I could feel the restrictions with them."[11]

On Friday, November 13, a group of Islamic State gunmen and suicide bombers roamed the streets of Paris, killing people at a concert hall, the national stadium of France, and at various restaurants and bars. The terrorists killed 130 people.[12] The mastermind behind the attack, Abdelhamid Abaaoud, was a Belgian national that had traveled to Syria to fight with the Islamic State. The other members of the cell were all ISIS sympathizers and linked to the same network that would conduct a series of attacks in Brussels in March 2016 that killed thirty-two.[13]

For the United States and France, two close allies, the attacks served as a catalyst to hasten the campaign against Islamic State. For the French, the first move came in the form of airstrikes on targets in Raqqa. After this mostly symbolic response, the French deepened their support for the coalition, eventually deploying forces alongside the United States in northeast Syria, and introducing the Javelin anti-tank missile with its special forces deployed in country. The Paris attacks forced an introspective conversation with President Obama about the pace of the campaign. At this point, the T/E campaign had mostly stalled, hobbled by the poorly performing groups that were charged with defeating Islamic State. To the east of the river, the YPG was moving much more quickly, and with the Task Force's assistance had taken control of the border from the Euphrates River out to Iraq. It would later emerge that the Paris attackers used Manbij as a way station on their journey to and from Syria.[14]

After these first waves of meetings, the Task Force began to plan the operation to move west of the river and force Islamic State from the city. To do so, the Task Force would first have to cross the river and in so doing would violate a clear Turkish red-line. As one pilot recalls:

> Manbij had been heavily bermed, and heavily prepared in a defensive manner, and there was uncertainty on the avenue of approach and how to get into the area. The other challenges were about the supply lines and that the bridge was down and bombed out. So we had to look south, and the only place to cross was the Tishreen dam.[15]

Before the Paris attacks, Tishreen was included in US-Turkish discussions about Agate Noble and the T/E CONOP. As one DoD official recalls, "We were doing planning with the Turks in Germany when the Russians showed up in Syria. And the output of that planning session was a plan that included what we were going to do with Tishreen with the Turks."[16]

The operation for Tishreen with the Syrian Kurds in the lead kicked off in late December 2015. The battle was brief, with US airstrikes assisting the YPG and SAC as they pushed across the river and consolidated control over various small villages lining the banks of the river. The issue, by this point, was that "[the US had] agreed at the 1 star level, that it was something that Tishreen was going to handle at the T/E," a DoD official recounts. "The path of half truths runs right through Tishreen."[17] For Ankara, the river had long been a red-line and a barrier to further Kurdish territorial expansion. In October 2015, Turkish prime minister Ahmet Davutoglu warned that Ankara would not tolerate the YPG crossing west of the Euphrates River, or from pushing east from the then YPG-held canton of Afrin. That same month, Ankara shelled YPG positions near Kobane and Tel Abyad after it attempted to cross the river before the December 2015 Tishreen offensive.[18]

The T/E guys just weren't up to it and the urgency had grown following the attacks in France and the feeling that ISIS had a large number of sleeper cells it was soon going to activate. After Tishreen fell, the SDF had entrenched itself along the eastern portion of the Turkish-Syrian border. "At night, you could see SDF outposts out in the open, every 10 miles or so, and in contested areas it was every kilometer or so, and so you could see the forward line of troops from the Tishreen area to Iraq," an A-10 pilot recalled.[19] However, the offensive then stalled for months, as the United States and Ankara continued to negotiate about the partner force to use in the Manbij pocket. By May 2015, the Task Force had made preparations to launch a second effort to cross the Euphrates River to prepare for the fight for Manbij. The SDF favored a pincer movement in all of its offensives, approaching targets from two sides, taking bits of territory and then clearing the areas it had taken of Islamic State loyalists left behind. The United States and the SDF had secured Tishreen, but General Mazlum had pushed for a second crossing point. Tishreen was to the south of Manbij, while the Qara Quzak bridge was to the city's north. The bridge had been destroyed and so was not in service. The Islamic State believed that the bridge was impassible and had not built rings of defenses around the crossing point. Tishreen, in contrast, was well defended and with belts of IEDs lining the expected route the SDF would use to push further west.

The SDF had initially proposed crossing even further north, but the route wasn't deemed feasible by the Task Force because of its proximity to the Turkish border. To set up the offensive, the United States needed access to a highway to move the heavy equipment that the SDF would use to assault the city. On the hills opposite the Qara Quzak, Islamic State had built up a defensive perimeter to cover the bridge crossing. "This was the first opposed river crossing since the American-led war in Korea," a person involved in the operation recalled. The airstrikes on the ISIS positions opposite the dam lasted for three days, while US Special Forces supported the SDF and Task Force with mortars fired on ISIS positions at night. The goal was to establish a position on the western side of the bridge to prepare to bring heavy vehicles across. "After footholds were secured, the Task Force fashioned a makeshift ferry using old pontoon bridge sections to shuttle SDF militia members and heavy equipment, such as Russian T55 tanks, armored personnel carriers, construction equipment for defenses, and trucks, across the river. The construction process was about 72 hours of balls out work, absolutely mission critical to the success of Manbij."[20]

The entire operation was carried out by seventy-six men and a handful of excavators and managed to help place 500 SDF members on the western bank of the Euphrates in just under five hours, and then built that number up to around 2,000 SDF members by the day's end. On the western bank, the United States had an AC-130 gunship flying and providing air cover. The area was sparsely defended. Islamic State had not sent men to guard a bridge that had been destroyed, but providing cover was necessary because the SDF were being ferried across in inflatable zodiacs and were susceptible to attack from the western bank.[21] While the United States and its local partners had crossed at a second point along the river by May 2015, the challenge remained in managing Turkey and trying to graft the T/E mission on to the Task Force push with the Syrian Kurds. By this point, it was clear that the goal of using the T/E groups to close the Manbij pocket was going to fail. "The [Vetted Syrian Opposition] wouldn't fight for whatever reason, and all of a sudden the YPG had taken tens of more kilometers," the DoD official recounted. "And you can't argue against what they are doing, what are you going to say, 'stop, do not kill ISIS'. The more trouble there was with T/E, the more it just became a fait accompli that the YPG would be asked to do it."[22]

Ankara's Growing Concerns: The Potential "Terror Corridor"

Ankara was not just grappling with the United States. In the northwest, the Russian air campaign was enabling a YPG offensive from positions in Afrin into Aleppo. This bombing allowed for the Kurds to push east and take control of the formerly Arab-held territory of Tel Rifaat and Menagh Airbase. In response to these moves, Turkey began to more aggressively shell YPG positions near Tel Rifaat and Menagh, as well as on YPG forces threatening Azaz, the border town that Ankara had used to supply its allied proxies in Aleppo.[23] For a few months in late 2015 and early 2016, Ankara had to grapple with the potential that two larger powers, the United States and Russia, would each independently facilitate the connection of the Kurdish cantons, creating what Turkish officials had begun referring to as a terror corridor running from Sinjar in Iraq to the Mediterranean Sea in Syria's northwest.

The final issue was that security in Turkey was deteriorating. During the summer of 2015, PKK-affiliated groups in Turkey were digging trenches in different urban centers, proclaiming that these places were autonomous and governed per Ocalan's democratic confederal principles. In Silopi, a destitute town on the Iraqi border, the PKK's youth group, the YDG-H, took similar action. By August 2015, the group had dug trenches and filled them with improvised explosive devices to hinder the Turkish military in any future cooperation to retake areas the YDG-H declared as sovereign. According to Ayla Albayrak, a journalist for the *Wall Street Journal*, "Each day, Turkish special forces play a deadly game of cat-and-mouse with armed Kurdish youths, firing tear gas and live rounds in a bid to reassert control of several neighborhoods."[24]

In Diyarbakir's Sur district, the same phenomena took place. By August, the YDG-H had dug tunnels in the city's ancient quarter and erected barricades. The youth had dug up the city streets and stacked the cobblestones up to create cave-like structures and hung sheets and blankets across the narrow streets to protect them from snipers and aerial surveillance. The YDG-H did the same in Cizre and Silopi. The YDG-H coordinated operations with WhatsApp to shuttle fighters between different cities in the southeast and coordinate fighting inside cities.[25]

Between August and December, the political dynamics in Turkey limited the AKP's response to the uprising. During that summer, former prime minister Ahmet Davutoglu pursued coalition talks with Turkey's opposition, after his party failed to win enough seats for an outright majority in the June 2015 election. Davutoglu's efforts to govern in coalition ran afoul of Erdogan's overarching effort to further centralize power and the powerful Turkish president sought to subvert any coalition and aimed to hold new elections in the fall. Davutoglu was also a proponent of the peace process with the PKK, which had allowed for the government to diffuse similarly tense situations in years past. In March 2015, Davutoglu spearheaded the so-called Dolmabahce meeting, where representatives from Turkey's pro-PKK Kurdish movement and the government met and agreed to a ten-point document outlining the broad contours of any resolution to the decades-old insurgency.[26]

The pre-November 2015 clashes followed a familiar pattern in all three cities: the bulk of the fighting took place between the YDG-H/PKK units and police special forces and the gendarmerie units tasked with security in the southeast rural districts. The pending November 2015 parliamentary election appeared to have acted as a restraint on more aggressive Turkish military action. Things changed in December, just as Tishreen was about to kick off, and in near-lock step with the increased Russian airstrikes along the Marea line. The Turkish military placed Sur and Cizre under twenty-four-hour curfew in December 2015; one month after the AKP reclaimed its parliamentary majority. Silopi was placed under twenty-four-hour curfew in January 2016. To support the YDG-H's urban insurgency, the PKK embedded more experienced fighters with the youth fighting in the towns. As one journalist who spent time in Silopi recounted:

> The YDG-H were "kids" in ragged clothes with old weapons. One night, we were taken outside the city, close to the Iraq border, where the YDG-H met PKK fighters sent from Iraq. The PKK fighters drove Toyota Hilux pick-up trucks across the border and were led by Faruk Aydin. Aydin, known locally as Heval Kemal, was native to Silopi before he went to Qandil for training with the PKK.[27]

As one State Department official quipped, "Whatever we thought was acceptable [to Turkey in Syria] before the end of the ceasefire, things had changed."[28] To prepare for the Manbij offensive, there was an effort to make the YPG more palatable to Turkey. Within the US government, the Task Force sought to ensure that the group assumed a new name, the Syrian Democratic Forces (SDF). As one member of the Task Force told the author, "For internal USG parlance, we made the decision to call them the SDF … we gave them a new patch and we would use the new name, but even if Mazlum was officially leaving his PKK card at home, its not like he is not a card carrying PKK member."[29]

Over a series of National Security Council meetings, Obama was briefed on the plan for Manbij, and efforts to mitigate the likely political fall out with Turkey. As part of this effort, the United States identified militia members that had worked with Turkey in the past on an operation to move the tomb of Suleyman Shah, the grandfather of the founder of the Ottoman Empire, Osman, and whose mausoleum was adjacent to the Qura Qawzak bridge in Syria. The area had been overrun by Islamic State and the small Turkish garrison was besieged. "We got wind of the Turkish operation to move the tomb," a US DoD official described. "A person at the embassy instantly recognized that this was going to be a problem because any foreign military equipment that we saw rolling into Kobane we were going to strike." In response, the United States began talks with their Turkish counterparts before the Suleyman Shah operation began and the two sides jointly planned it. "We ended up providing them ISR for the mission," the official recounted, "but they did surprise us. After they retrieved the tomb, they didn't bring it back to Turkey." The Turkish military left the tomb in a small make-shift mausoleum just inside the border with Syria and in territory that the YPG controlled.[30] "The lesson here," a second official explained, "was that the Turks and the YPG could work together on small tactical things."[31] To facilitate the crossing, Ankara coordinated with Mazlum, ensuring that the YPG would not fire on the convoy as it drove across the border, which would risk Turkish retaliation. The United States never publicized its role in the operation and, to this day, Ankara maintains that the mission to move the tomb was done entirely on its own, with its own reconnaissance assets.[32]

As part of the ongoing effort to assuage the Turks, the Task force used many of the YPG elements involved in Suleyman Shah operation as the nucleus to stand up the Manbij Military Council (MMC). These non-YPG Arabs were allied with the Kurds, but were not "card carrying PKK members" and mostly culled from the Manbij area.[33] The MMC was officially formed in April 2016. "The SOF guys were trying to get the Turks to meet the SAC," a US official recalled. This eventually happened at Incirlik Air Force base, when the MMC leadership met with Turkish officials in early April. This effort was almost certainly destined for failure, but it was an important exercise to try and ease tensions and, if possible, recreate some of the synergies that had existed during the Suleyman Shah operation. "The Arab parts of the SDF didn't matter to Turkey. If you wanted to make a distinction, you could have used the SAC as a fig leaf. The Turks saw no real difference." The urgency, however, was still driving US decision making and the T/E effort had stalled, leaving the Kurds as the only real viable option for a local partner force to assault an urban target.[34]

As one official recounts of the discussions during Agate Noble, "We would push and say to the Turks that ISIS is at its weakest when it has to fight on multiple fronts, so we could push from both sides, with the SDF from east and the opposition groups from the Marea line. It was a non-starter."[35] Still, with the renewed urgency from the Paris attacks, the hastening of the war against ISIS in Syria had gained new urgency, and with the river crossings, the YPG and its Arab allies were the partner force closest to the city.

After countless meetings in the White House, "President Obama told Erdogan on May 18 that we are going to go forward with the Manbij operation," according to a US official.[36] The battle for Manbij began in June, after months of planning and preparation. The basic battle plan, as one US Special Forces soldier described, was to use a "double envelopment, with one large envelopment surrounding Manbij from both the north and south axes, and then a smaller scale double envelope on each axis. Typically, the SDF would surround summary enclaves via this double envelopment, besiege the area, and then systematically clear the area. Once finished, we'd move to the next village."[37] During the run-up to the battle plan, the United States sought to assure Turkey that the YPG would not remain in the city after its was liberated, and would turn over basic governance to the MMC. "All of the military planners believed that Manbij would make Raqqa easier, because it cut them off from the logistics hub," an official recounted, "but the initial plan was to just go to Raqqa. The Paris attacks changed that."[38] The YPG fighters involved in the operation would withdraw east of the river, observing Turkey's red-line, while simultaneously clearing the city of Islamic State fighters. The definition of YPG fighter remained a significant point of contention between the United States and Turkey long after the city fell and precipitated a series of bilateral mechanisms to try and resolve beginning in 2017, ultimately dubbed the Manbij Roadmap.

The battle for the city served as a template for the Task Force and informed its later planning for Raqqa. "The SDF would establish new lines and they would plow the forward line of troops to create berms and trenches, and they would have several check points and a defensive fighting position they would be fighting from." As a second person recalled, "Manbij was the model we used later for Raqqa, right down to allowing a corridor for the last remnants of Islamic State to leave the city. This allowed us to follow them out and strike them where they regrouped."[39] In quirk of the air war, the targeting authority for operations in support of the SDF were different from those for the Marea line. A Turkey-based pilot could support the SDF, but to do so the pilot would speak to the targeting cell in northern Iraq, whereas the targeting cell for the Marea line was still at Incirlik. "It took a lot more coordination and awareness working with our dislocated forces who are coordinating directly with the SDF to figure out where people are at," a weapons systems officer recalled.[40] This quirk stemmed from the fact that Manbij was a Task Force-led operation, while CJSTOF-S remained confined to operations within the Manbij pocket, outside of the unfolding battle for the city.

The American presence on the ground for this operation also sped up the targeting process. As one person with the process explains:

> We would send up a drone, get a grid, and hammer a guy. Because they were
> on the ground, they would just pull up a grid and that method of engagement

worked really really well. What we were doing prior, and on the Marea Line, was that we were having the Syrians give us grid coordinates, we would verify them with ISR, and then we do a direct engagement with the Predator or Reaper, or call in the fast movers.

The process of working with men on the ground with the SDF shortened the process between identifying targets and launching weapons, cutting out an element of the process that was common throughout the war on both sides of the river.[41]

The SDF besieged the city by mid-June, but per the battle plan began to slowly clear the urban areas block by block, using the double envelopment method; biting of chunks of territory and then clearing it behind rapidly built berms and trenches. By August, the city had fallen, and the SDF had entrenched itself west of the river in defiance of Ankara. Ostensibly, the end of combat operations prompted the YPG to withdraw, leaving behind the MMC, which was part of the broader SDF grouping of militias. However, the fighters within the MMC were still subordinate to General Mazlum, and therefore still unacceptable to Turkey. As one senior official remembers, "This is where JSOC got into fine grain lawyering, renaming militias, and again the Turks had enough intel to know that these things were going on in the city."[42] Still, after the city fell, the United States extended an invitation to Turkey to visit the city to try and further assuage Ankara's concerns. The invitation was similar to the engagement between the Turkish government and the MMC in Incirlik before the start of the operation. "We would say, 'come to Manbij, check things out for yourselves any time,'" a State Department official remembers. "They came once and never came again. It didn't help."[43]

The United States also had to work through its own legal processes to determine if it was possible to provide reconstruction assistance to a local council linked, even if indirectly, to a US-designed terrorist group, the PKK. "State's lawyers made a determination that we basically could not work directly with certain SDF-run councils because of the PKK influence. It was illegal," a US official recalls. "And State also determined we could not tell DoD that, nor release the legal reasoning laying it out. So what ensued was this constant barrage of accusations from DoD that State just loved Turkey and didn't get it. And State was like, uh, well, let's talk about something else."[44] For the Special Forces that provided fire support for Tishreen, assisted with the crossing at Qura Qawzak, and helped plan the assault on Manbij, this news was not welcome. "Everyone knew the game and that there was PKK influence. General Mazlum was PKK for fuck's sake. We would talk with YPG who were wearing PKK patches," a soldier recounted. "To hide behind some bullshit legal opinion is bush league and weak. So, per our own government, it was okay to train, equip, and advise them militarily to kill ISIS, but not ok to give them money to rebuild what we destroyed?"[45] Eventually, the issue was resolved, per an official from the United States Agency for International Development, or USAID. "There was legal guidance on the [SDF council issue] but we found ways to circumvent it. We would try and make sure funding didn't go the PKK specifically."[46] This process, however, took time and sped up after the United States moved development people in country later on in the war. "We worked through various outside entities and then eventually through parts of the Kurdish administration's apparatuses that were deemed acceptable enough."⁴⁷

As the MMC consolidated control over Manbij, General Mazlum was eager to continue to push west to al Bab, the ISIS stronghold in central Syria and a key jumping off point for further offensive operations along the Turkish-Syrian border. As the battle wound down, and per the plan the Task Force had established, the last vestiges of Islamic State fighters holed up in central Manbij were allowed to leave through a dedicated corridor. The fighters drove to al Bab, where some stayed and others moved further south down the Euphrates River. Almost immediately after the end of major combat operations in Manbij, the SDF established the al Bab Military Council, modeled on the MMC for Manbij, and announced the intention to liberate the city. For the United States, al Bab was not a priority, largely because the focus remained on Raqqa and the town was still ostensibly part of Agate Noble CONOP and slotted for CJSOTF-S. "The SDF created both the Jarablus and al Bab councils to try and entice us to keep moving west," a Special Forces soldier recalled.⁴⁸

While there may have been some low-level planning for such an assault, at the political level, the idea was to still work through Turkey in the Manbij pocket, while the SDF consolidated its positions from Manbij out to the Iraq border and down to Raqqa. Despite the lack of political support, the Task Force was also looking to put pressure on Turkey to do more to stem the flow of fighters across its border en route to join within the Islamic State. A senior TF official visited Ankara in 2016 and, according to an official familiar with the Task Force leadership, "would say 'Dabiq in a week.'"⁴⁹ Dabiq is the city that Islamic State suggested in propaganda as the site for an apocalyptical prophecy where the armies of Islam and Rome clashed, and where the new armies of Rome would once again fight against a holy army.⁵⁰ It is located north of Aleppo and inside the Agate Noble area of responsibility and was a clear suggestion that the United States could keep pushing west, if the Manbij pocket was not closed.

For Ankara, the Manbij operation was the deal breaker, and prompted more serious planning for a unilateral cross-border operation to ensure that the Syrian Kurds did not take advantage of an Islamic State collapse and overrun the brittle coalition of Arab groups along the Marea line. Ankara's concerns were magnified by Russian actions, which had enabled the YPG to push east to Menagh and Tel Rifaat, and were simultaneously focused on severing the Turkish overland link to Aleppo. The signs were ominous for Ankara, as it risked being cut off from northern Syria, and shunted into Idlib, where its allied forces had lost momentum and appeared unable to topple Assad. This chain of events forced a change in Turkish planning and to reassess its security interests. This process eventually settled on three interlinked approaches, designed to give Turkey leverage with Moscow and Washington. The first required military action to prevent any further YPG movement along the border. Second, Ankara would have to engage with Russia to ensure that its forces were not targeted and the situation devolved into conflict. Third, Turkey would have to cultivate its own Arab forces, independent of the SDF, to give Ankara a set of more capable proxies to throw at the Kurds and to retain pressure on Assad.

As this planning began, a faction within the Turkish military was plotting against state in an act of treason that nearly resulted in the killing of President Erdogan by rogue officers. However, by August, Ankara was ready for war, and was intent on unilaterally pushing to create the safe zone it had long advocated for in negotiations with Washington. The plan was a near-carbon copy of the T/E CONOP, including the liberation of Manbij from the forces Washington had just supported to take it from Islamic State. Washington and Ankara were now on a direct collision course in eastern Syria, and Moscow was poised to try and exploit fissures to capture Turkey and enmesh it in a diplomatic process that Russia needs to end the war on terms it deems favorable. As the war progressed in the summer of 2016, the stage was set for Ankara to partner more closely with Moscow, on the ground in Syria, but also in the diplomatic arena after Ankara's prize passion in the war, Aleppo, fell to regime-allied forces.

More Trouble in Turkey: From a Coup to an Invasion

By January 2016, the Turkish conflict with the PKK in the southeast of the country had mired Kurdish-majority cities in chaos. The conflict in Turkey's southeast had resulted in multi-week sieges, where the armed forces would declare a twenty-hour curfew, confining residents to their houses. The battles were decidedly in the Turkish armed force's favor, but the challenge of operating in an urban environment was apparent from the start. As one Turkish intelligence official explained to the author, "We will destroy the PKK in the southeast. The world will condemn us, human rights organizations will call us out, and, you know what, we will not care. Our army may not be the best in the world, but it is an army, and the PKK is a militia."[51] These words were prophetic. The urban fights left an entire generation of Kurdish-youth dead or wounded, and sparked an exodus of others to join the PKK in Iraqi Kurdistan. Some probably crossed to Syria to fight Islamic State.

The urban insurgency in Turkey further radicalized the Turkish national security state, leading to the eventual appointment of more hardline figures to the interior ministry. However, for the United States in Syria, yet another issue to grapple with was the unexpected—and unforeseen—coup attempt that nearly thrust Turkey into extended factional fighting that would have destabilized the country. Instead, the coup attempt failed, leading to an authoritarian turn that made the Kurdish issue Ankara has faced for decades even more difficult to solve and opened the door for a series of cross-border interventions that upended the American war against Islamic State.

Just nineteen days before the coup attempt, Ankara began to implement its changed policy in Syria. After pledging to never apologize for downing a Russian Su-24, the Turkish government did just that, with President Erdogan writing a formal letter that "expressed regret" about the shoot down the previous November.[52] The letter was necessary to ensure that Turkish military forces could cross the border, in what was ongoing planning for an offensive into the Manbij pocket to ensure that the SDF could not push further west to connect the cantons. To ensure that its vehicles weren't targeted by orbiting Russian jets, which remained active near this area during the summer, Turkey needed Russian acquiescence for its offensive.

The planning for Operation Euphrates Shield was ongoing when elements of the armed forces revolted. The actual coup attempt in Turkey kicked off earlier than the plotters had planned. The putsch coincided with Erdogan's family holiday, which he often took just after Ramadan. On the afternoon of the coup attempt, the Turkish national security bureaucracy met to discuss intelligence that suggested a coup plot was being hatched. The events of that night remain murky, even though hundreds have been prosecuted and a detailed timeline of certain actions has been produced. The then Chief of the General staff, Hulusi Akar, and the head of MiT, Hakan Fidan, were present. After this meeting, the plot was put into motion, apparently after Akar returned to his office. His aide, Levant Turkkan, eventually took Akar hostage and under armed guard escorted him through the building and on to a waiting helicopter to take him to Akinci airbase, just north of Ankara, and where the coup was allegedly being overseen.

The Turkish president was staying at a hotel in Marmaris, a Turkish sea-side town popular with local and international tourists. As the coup unfolded, there are differing accounts of when Erdogan was informed. Whatever the case, at 9:15 p.m. a WhatsApp group was created for the putschists to communicate, and shortly thereafter Turkish military trucks parked at 90 degree angle on the bridges connecting Istanbul's European and Asian sides. Nearly simultaneously, Turkish F-16s accompanied by tankers were flown from Incirlik Air Force base to keep the aircraft airborne for hours. For Erdogan, the news of the coup forced him to address the nation via FaceTime, as he debated whether to board his private jet to leave Marmaris for the capital Ankara or Istanbul. Ultimately, Erdogan chose to get airborne, a decision that ensured that he evaded a military team sent to kill or capture him at his hotel. After taking off, the presidential plane circled over the Black Sea until such a time as Umit Dundar, the head of the first army headquartered in Istanbul, guaranteed the president's safety, allowing him to land at Ataturk airport in Istanbul. The coup plot began to fall apart, shortly after Erdogan left Marmaris.

In a last gasp, the rogue F-16s began to bomb targets in Ankara, including the national police and the parliament building. In tandem, attack helicopters opened fire on the intelligence building. "Bombs started dropping and then tanks are in the streets," a US official present in Ankara that night remembers.[53] In Istanbul, the F-16s made a series of high-speed passes, breaking the sound barrier to initiate a series of sonic booms. For many in the city, it felt like bombs were being dropped every time the jets would break the speed of sound.

As the putschists were rounded up, and order restored, the atmosphere in Turkey changed again. For the United States, elements within the Turkish government that the United States had come to work closely with were upended, as the AKP began a massive purge of men and women suspected of having links to Fethullah Gulen, a Pennsylvania-based cleric. The AKP and the Gulenists had entered into a political alliance in 2002, designed to replace what many in both camps viewed as hostile bureaucratic entities in Turkey's historically Kemalist-oriented judiciary and armed forces. Within the armed forces, the Gulenists managed to claw their way to the top of the promotion board, beginning a process of ensuring that their loyalists were promoted to positions of power. In tandem, the trials of officers in both the Ergenekon and Balyoz cases, two cases that revolved around allegations of coup plotting, allowed for the rapid purge of senior officers loyal to the movement between 2008 and 2011. These purges were based on forged evidence, but nevertheless allowed for both the AKP and the Gulenists to protect themselves against a coup by hardline, Kemalist-leaning officers.

However, it was after the AKP and the Gulenists fell out, beginning in 2011 and accelerating in 2013, that the coup-proofing efforts that both had overseen began to backfire for President Erdogan. The fall-out between the AKP and the Gulenists began in 2011, as both men began to vie for more power. This touched off a series of political power struggles that culminated in the December 2013 release of a series of recordings of Erdogan, his family, and members of his cabinet engaged in serious graft totaling well into the tens of millions of dollars. In response, the AKP moved against the Gulenist media empire, shutting newspapers and television channels the movement controlled, and forcing into exile or arresting scores of members. This chaotic time was slowed by the then still-viable Turkish justice system, which hindered some efforts to revamp the judiciary. This changed after the coup attempt.

In the months leading up to the coup attempt, Turkish media began to report of a looming purge of the Gulenist officers that had rose to power during the AKP-Gulenist entente. Thus, as the annual August meeting of Turkey's senior staff loomed, it was rumored that many officers would not be promoted, or outright purged from the senior ranks of the armed forces. Faced with being purged, it is likely that a core cadre of Gulenist officers, perhaps joined by elements of vehemently anti-AKP secularist officers, conspired together to topple and kill Erdogan. They nearly succeeded, except for the actions of Hulusi Akar, who despite being held hostage refused to issue an order for the armed forces to assist with the putschists.

Whatever the case, the outcome of the coup attempt was terrible for US-Turkish relations. As one senior US official remembers, "You can't overstate the corrosive impact of the coup attempt on bilateral ties, and everything after the coup attempt we were trying to do was made exponentially more difficult." For many in Ankara, the links back to the United States were undeniable, giving rise to a conspiracy theory that Washington must have been involved in trying to topple the Turkish government. The aerial tankers that supported the rogue F-16s flew from an airbase that hosts American forces and many in Turkey believe is American run. Gulen is also present in the United States, living comfortably in a palatial estate in rural Pennsylvania. "We had a huge reservoir of distrust, and lots of senior influential Turks in the palace and in society believing that we had allowed Gulen to plan it, and that we had conspired. And I believe Tayyip believes it."[54]

The purge of the Turkish judiciary and the police force began almost immediately, along with the arrest of scores of members of the military. It also impacted internal Turkish bureaucratic squabbles over which entity controlled the Syria file. Up until then, and continuing to this day, MiT was the dominant actor in Syria. As one senior US official notes, "MiT was more nimble on Syria and [MiT Director Hakan] Fidan had Erdogan's confidence, whereas where the [Turkish General Staff] did not." Following the coup attempt, this official recalled, "Akar's stock went up, and it gave it more space to argue its case" because of the loyalty elements of the officer corps showed to Erdogan.[55]

Ankara also began the process of filing for Gulen's extradition from the United States, sending boxes of evidence to the United States. Washington sought to help Ankara with this process, recognizing that the coup attempt was traumatizing experience for the Turkish leadership and that the extradition of Gulen was an issue that had the potential to upset relations. As one US official explained, "The Department of Justice worked very hard to meet America's substantially more rigorous evidentiary status." However, it was becoming evident that the post-coup purges had elevated inexperienced officials, eager to report up the chain within their own bureaucracy positive efforts to realize a goal Erdogan had pushed for. "We had to assume that the significant diminution of the legal ranks impacted the quality of who they were sending to Washington and who the Department of Justice was meeting with," a US official recalled.

> As purges went on, we were dealing with less skilled counterparts, and anxious counterparts—I mean who wants to sign the paper that said this was the final submission to the Department of Justice, knowing that DoJ may so no to the extradition request. So they just kept throwing boxes at us. I didn't envy those Turkish officials. It was a lose-lose for them, and a lot like the lottery. If you keep buying tickets you may win.

The coup attempt had a negative effect on flight operations from Incirlik in support of the ongoing war against ISIS. During the coup, the power was cut to the base, forcing the American and coalition members on the base to rely on generator power. "The place was very paranoid after the coup," a person on-base remembers. "The government would come into the base and remove people." For the Task Force inside Syria, the coup attempt was not something anyone was thinking about before it happened. "The coup in Turkey was unexpected, it was like 'what the fuck is going up there.'" The immediate, negative operational impact was apparent to the United States and other NATO countries used to working closely with Ankara. Inside NATO, the Turkish military began to recall officers for ostensible links to Gulen. "[After the coup attempt] Turkish manning was at about 70 percent of their allocated NATO Command Structure (NCS) posts. This was amongst the lowest for Allies, and it was uncharacteristic for Turkey," a NATO official remarked at the time.[56] The negative impact was most felt in the Air Force, where the purges were the most widely sweeping. More than 300 F-16 pilots were purged, resulting in a cockpit to pilot ratio of 1.25 pilots per one aircraft to 0.8.[57] A 1.25:1 ratio is the accepted norm for sustainment in numerous air forces, leaving Ankara scrambling to make up the gap.

The Russian Federation recognized the value of expressing solidarity with Turkey, and doing it quickly following the coup attempt. Just hours before the coup attempt was thwarted, Russian president Vladimir Putin was the first to call President Erdogan to express his condolences for his plight the night before. Turkish officials seethed at the American response, which many viewed as overly focused on the purges, and not empathetic enough to tragedy that had just unfolded. Further, the United States and Turkey squabbled over the official to send to Turkey to express solidarity, with Ankara wanting a high-ranking, cabinet-level official and Washington being slow to react to carve out time in these peoples' busy schedule. The first person to visit Turkey from the United States was the chairman of the Joint Chiefs of Staff, General Joseph Dunford, who met with his Turkish counterpart, Hulusi Akar, and also toured the bombed out Parliament building. During this meeting, the two sides did discuss Syria and the Marea line efforts, but the mood in Washington was that Ankara would probably regroup after the events of July 15. This proved not to be the case.

As the SDF consolidated control over Manbij, and continued to agitate for operations further west in al Bab and Jarablus, Ankara began to reach out to the Assad regime's allies to clear its looming offensive. On August 9, 2016, Presidents Erdogan and Putin met in St. Petersburg in what was dubbed a "clear the air summit." The meeting was Erdogan's first trip abroad after the coup attempt.[58] The two men expressed their desire to improve relations and, behind closed doors, likely discussed the operation that Ankara would dub Euphrates Shield. Ten days later, on 19, Foreign Minister Mevlut Cavusoglu visited Tehran, where he too was likely to have discussed Operation Euphrates Shield with the Islamic Republic of Iran. Washington was the last to be told, but within the US government, intelligence had revealed the Turkish operational planning a bit before Ankara officially chose to inform the United States. Thus, even though Ankara had sought to keep this secret, Washington was aware that Ankara was planning something.

Amidst this build-up, the Obama administration had tapped then Vice President Biden to visit Ankara, where he was to meet with Turkish officials, express solidarity after the coup attempt, and reassure Ankara about the tactical nature of the American relationship with the YPG. The date for the Turkish invasion coincided with his visit: August 24, 2016. The choice of date was not an accident. As the vice president traveled to Ankara, Turkish tanks began to cross the border, where they faced little resistance from Islamic State. After landing, Vice President Biden sought to convince Ankara that the United States was empathetic about the failed coup attempt and, in a public speech, warned there will be "no [Kurdish] corridor and that We have made it absolutely clear to... the YPG that they must move back across the river [from Manbij ... and under no circumstances will get American support if they do not keep that commitment. Period."[59]

The vice president's words were meant to reset the relationship, but they instead underscored the intense legalese ongoing as to who and what really was the YPG, and what was a separate entity working with the SDF. Whatever the case, the issue soon became moot as Ankara pressed on with its offensive, circling al Bab as the goal of its operation. In this sense, Operation Euphrates Shield was the CONOP that both Washington and Ankara envisioned when planning in Turkey and Germany for the Marea line. However, as Ankara undertook this operation alone, it risked undermining the recently finished operation for Manbij, and eventually brought Ankara and Moscow into closer alignment.

For the United States, the invasion prompted a debate about what to do as it was happening. As one senior State Department official recalled, there was an initial concern that US personnel could be accidentally killed. "As [the Turks] pushed south, and they started to get to the Manbij forward line, we had some pretty challenging days of respective proxies starting to shoot at each other, and some folks being concerned about American casualties, in part because they had been quite aggressive in pushing to U.S. forces as far forward to dissuade movement south." These clashes between the SDF and the Turkish military were concentrated along the northernmost portions of SDF territory between the narrow Sajur River and the much larger Euphrates inside the Manbij pocket. "We were able to manage those [clashes] and prevent the worst possible outcomes, and then we settled into a new delineation of who would control what," the senior State Department official recalls.[60] As a member of the Task Force described, "There were constant conversations with Mazlum at this time and tremendous diplomatic work by [the special envoy to the counter-ISIS coalition] Brett McGurk to try and keep the Turks back and limit the scope and scale of their advance." By the end of August, the two sides reached a ceasefire agreement that divided Turkish from Kurdish territory along the Sajur River, a natural barrier between the two sides. However, "the strain on the partner force cannot be overstated," a Task Force member recalled of that time.[61]

The tensions between the Turks and the SDF and Task Force ran hot in August to September 2016. "The Task Force was spoiling for a fight," an official recalls. "It was a mess. It is only because there were smart people on the ground at the time that things didn't get really out of hand."[62] As a Special Forces officer explained, "We had significant risk placed on tactical operations. [Later], there were regular U.S. forces in Manbij doing the patrols ... but in those early days, having SOF there was critical to manage risk. It was on a razor's edge most days."[63] As the Turkish offensive to the north of Manbij stopped, it continued along the border, clearing the small villages that the Agate Noble operation had struggled to hold for the previous few months. However, the post-invasion status quo remained tense and unstable.

Washington was also playing catch-up, after having been essentially caught off guard by the Turkish invasion. "After Euphrates Shield happened, essentially without our knowledge, and the Turks proved they could move the Arabs with some embeds, we agreed to put some people in."[64] Those people were Army Special Forces members, first deployed inside Turkey to observe the start of the operation, who had a link to Liwa al-Mu'tasim, the vetted group that CJSTOF-S had supported during the Marea line operation with airstrikes. "The overall idea was to get more involved for insights and influence," a DoD official recalls. "We were playing catch up."[65] However, as the first men entered Al Rai, a militia involved in Euphrates Shield, Ahrar al Sharqiyyah, the Ahrar Al Sham splinter faction, was captured on camera threatening to behead the US soldiers sent in to Syria from Turkey. "The optics of that video were bad," a US official remarked. The US Army Special Forces did, however, eventually link up with elements of the Vetted Syrian Opposition. "The groups were fluid, you could double count them, some guys were fighters in one group and commanders in another," a person familiar with the US presence in Euphrates Shield said. "We sent some guys across and they did link up with guys and started to help them clear territory, particularly around Dabiq, but the Turks started to get paranoid and did not want us in there anymore. They wanted control of everybody and they wanted control of everyone and who went where and when and they are dealing with everyone."[66]

Beyond the video, the trust deficit between the two allies hindered cooperation and prevented the open sharing of plans between the two sides, particularly as Russia began to bomb to the south of al Bab, in support of a regime offensive launched to solidify a forward line of control just south of the city. As one official recalls:

> The communication was not great and the details still so uncertain that we only agreed [to send U.S. forces] to a 20 kilometer depth. All the same problems with the Marea line operations persisted in Euphrates shield, and so we weren't going to press on to al Bab with so little planning and so little certainty about regime and Russian intentions and the viability of the Arabs to provide the bulk of the ground forces and bear the brunt of the fighting.[67]

This line of thinking proved prescient, particularly as the Turkish forces push past 20 kilometers and prepared to assault al Bab, and the operation bogged down and the Turks faced a significant challenge in assaulting the city.

The Turkish Russian Entente: The Fall of Aleppo and the Battle for al Bab

By November 2016, the Turkish military had carved out a buffer zone along the border, stretching between Azaz to the Euphrates. The zone extended south, through Dabiq. The city fell to Turkish forces in mid-October 2016, but the battle was about to get messier. A senior US official recalled about Operation Euphrates Shield:

> Euphrates Shield kicked off, then it goes poorly because it is not in [the Turkish military's] skill set, and because everything that preceded the operation militarilly, there are not a lot of people in the U.S. military lining up to give advice to the Turkish about how to do better, and added to that, the Turks are not interested to ask for help because it undercuts their own image of the lethality of their own military, and so it was a nasty dynamic.[68]

To the west of Manbij, the relatively porous forward line of troops provided the SDF with room to push west, beginning with an operation to take the small town of Arima. Ankara reacted to the Kurdish move with airstrikes and shelling, while to the west of al Bab, the YPG and the Syrian regime were pushing toward the city. Thus, what started out as a Turkish move to take the city to sever the Kurdish overland route between the two cantons was now at risk from Kurdish moves on the ground. In late November, Presidents Putin and Erdogan spoke over the telephone, which led to the freezing of tensions to the west of al Bab and what appears to have been an agreement for Turkey to take the city and stop, while the Syrian regime consolidated its position to the south of the city to block any further advance. The telephone call was the latest example of warming Turkish-Russian ties, despite concurrent losses in opposition-held Aleppo.

In Geneva, where American diplomats were meeting with representatives from Moscow to discuss the situation in the northwest, one US official recalls how Ankara's diplomatic approach to Russia had changed, even as Aleppo was being besieged. "The Turks stopped putting up a fight with the Russians. They were silent, we even went a few times to small group meetings, which was the important players, and the Turks were silent."[69] This change stemmed from the agreement reached over the summer to enable Euphrates Shield, and presaged the diplomatic entente that Moscow and Ankara would enter into to pressure the United States, and to try and create a bilateral mechanism to end the war in Syria.

As Euphrates Shield entered its 100th day in early December, the Turkish military and its Arab allies were prepared to assault al Bab. To the West, the Turkish-backed opposition in Aleppo was also facing defeat in Syria's second largest city. The Russian air campaign, backed by an infusion of Iranian-allied militiamen, enabled the regime to besiege the city, and then storm individual neighborhoods. At this time, a US State Department official recalls, "The Russians were negotiating with [Washington], the armed opposition groups in Ankara, and with groups in Aleppo through Khmeimim [airbase]. At the same time the Iranians were negotiating with armed groups inside Aleppo. There were all these channels and it was sort of chaotic."[70] Ankara was also involved, with Foreign Minister Cavusoglu visiting Tehran in late November, along with frequent calls between Presidents Putin and Erdogan.

On December 13, 2016, a Turkish-Russian agreement to evacuate the city took hold, with Moscow declaring an end to the four-year battle for control over the city.[71] The agreement, a US official recalls, "wasn't much different from the evacuation deal we wanted … The Russians saw at some point that they could get their evacuation without us and then blame us for being useless. They were also getting mixed signals from us and probably thought the Americans were confused and it is not useful to talk to them."[72] Ankara, in contrast, was in a position to implement an agreement with the groups besieged in Aleppo and arrange for them to be transported to Idlib, where Ankara was also a dominant external player, and the primary sponsor of the opposition in the area. The agreement suffered a setback when the buses being used to transport the fighters from Aleppo to Idlib were set on fire as they traveled to the city from Idlib, and two besieged Allawite towns, Fuaa and Kafraya, were shelled, leading to another round of negotiations with Iran to ensure that these two areas were also freed from siege and residents allowed to leave.[73] With these details sorted, the evacuation of Aleppo finished on December 22, 2016. Just one week later, Turkey, Russia, and Iran announced that they had reached agreement on a general ceasefire in Syria and would hold talks in Astana, Kazakhstan, to formalize the process. The Astana process, as it would become known, stemmed from failed negotiations with the United States on a similar arrangement for Aleppo and, importantly, on a mechanism to coordinate airstrikes on United Nations-designated terrorist groups.

During this same time period, Turkish armor suffered a serious setback on the western outskirts of al Bab, signaling the start of a longer-than-expected effort to retake the city. The Turkish-backed opposition, too, was split across two different frontlines, which allowed for the SDF to expand further west from its positions in Manbij. On the al Bab front, Turkish mechanized forces pushed from west to east to take up a position on Sheikh Akil hill, which overlooked the city from the west. Throughout Euphrates Shield, videos suggest that Turkish armored units supporting SOF and a smattering of FSA groups demonstrated poor combined arms tactics and would attempt to push into towns with armored elements with little to no support from infantry units. The lack of infantry proved deadly. Just days before Christmas, Turkey lost at least eight Leopard 2A4 tanks, one Sabra M60T tank, two Otokar Kobra vehicles, and two armed personnel carriers in an Islamic State counterattack with anti-tank-guided missiles and vehicle-borne improvised explosive devices.[74] The attack killed over a dozen Turkish commandos from the 1st Commando Brigade,[75] and prompted the government to pause the offensive and appeal for outside assistance. In a press conference less than a week after the loss at Sheikh Akil hill, Ibrahim Kalin, the Turkish Presidential spokesperson, appealed for support, saying, "The international coalition must carry out its duties regarding aerial support to the battle we are fighting in al Bab. Not giving the necessary support is unacceptable."[76]

In response, Ankara first reached agreement with Moscow on a deconfliction mechanism and to share targeting information for airstrikes in the city. However, the agreement appeared to be predicated on Ankara's acceptance of an agreed forward line of troops, which the Turkish military would share with the Syrian regime. In early January, the VKS began to bomb targets in support of Turkish forces. To do so, Russia informed the United States of the strikes because they were in close proximity to US air operations near Manbij.[77] For the United States, the issue was more fraught because any US air operation in the area would be intermingled with the VKS and Ankara had sought to keep a tight lid on the targets they were proposing to be struck. The forward line around Manbij would, with Moscow, emerge as a flashpoint in ongoing negotiations in Jordan about how to delineate a line of deconfliction for aerial operations. At this point in the war, the deconfliction line was still being formalized, with protocols and air blocks for flights outside of just basic altitude and communications mechanisms. "We helped on the ground and the air … The Turks always wanted our help to do things their way. That was part of the problem. Their way never worked"[78] or comported with the constraints on US operations in Syria, or the legal restraints on combat operations.

The Turkish struggle in al Bab also freed the Syrian Kurds to take control of Arima, the small town it had pushed to control in late November. This outpost would, after the battle for al Bab, give Moscow a foothold in SDF-held territory that it would later exploit in 2019. The Turkish forces eventually pushed to surround the city, repeating the classic pincer movement that the SDF had used in Manbij. There were signs of friction between the Turks and the Russians during this phase of the campaign, giving rise to a disputed airstrike that killed three Turkish soldiers. The Kremlin blamed the strike on poor coordination and improper grid coordinates provided by the Turkish military. Ankara denied the incident. A US official blamed the event on poor organization, saying, "the Russians also bombed and killed two Turkish soldiers because the Turks went past al Bab. It was emblematic of the shoddy organization and why our guys couldn't go as far forward as they wanted."[79]

Al Bab fell to the Turkish military in late February. Ankara then turned its attention to the frontlines with Manbij. As pressure increased on the SDF, the group's leadership allowed both the regime and the Russians to move in to Arima from their strongholds, just opposite Manbij. The tensions over Manbij were the backdrop for a trilateral meeting, held in Antalya, Turkey, that the Turkish military organized with the United States and the Russian Federation. It was at this summit, a US official recalls, that Moscow "embarrassed" the Turks and "essentially ended Euphrates Shield." As one US official recalls of the meeting, "The Turks made these powerpoint decks and Russia would simply say, 'no, that is not going to happen'. It was uncomfortable to watch."[80] One day after the summit, the Russians and the regime moved into Arima formally, creating what the United States eventually dubbed the Arima extension. As one US official recalls, "They had been on the perimeter [of the small town]. They moved into a place we called the Arima extension, which was a name to have physically on a map, and their presence there grew around 2018 following tweets from President Trump."[81]

The end of Operation Euphrates Shield coincided with significant changes in the war east of the river. The SDF had not been sitting idle as Ankara struggled around al Bab. Further, inside the United States, the November 2016 election resulted in a surprise victor: Donald J. Trump. The ground war was poised to expand to Raqqa, but before then, the recently elected president would have to make a decision about the American relationship with the Syrian Kurds. For Turkey, Operation Euphrates Shield prompted changes in how future military operations would be conducted, but it did give Ankara the foothold it needed to put pressure on the SDF and to begin to expand its control of the border through follow on invasions, dubbed Operation Olive Branch and then Operation Peace Spring. The Russian-Turkish entente, beginning with the negotiations over the Aleppo surrender and evacuation and then the formalized mechanism, later dubbed the Astana process, also created a backlash with Arab elements of the coalition, prompting counter moves that the United States would engage in with Moscow and Jordan. Finally, the Turkish struggles around al Bab allowed for the SDF, angered at the incursion but nevertheless willing to continue working with the Task Force, to begin the shaping operations for the battle for Raqqa.

2016 was a decisive year in the war. Manbij had fallen, but Agate Noble and the T/E program had proved incapable of fulfilling the mission it had been assigned. Ankara had also simply lifted the plans for its own incursion, a fact that would repeat later in Operation Peace Spring. Year 2017 would prove to be a much more intense period for US-Russian interactions in the air and on the ground, leading to a series of near shoot downs in Der Ezzour. The US presence at Tanf, built around "the berm" and near Rukban, would also take on a greater role in the campaign, not because it had anything to do with the war against Islamic State, but because it was a useful tool to keep a disinterested president engaged in a war many thought was necessary to pressure the Islamic Republic of Iran. Finally, Islamic State was losing. The war had shifted and the caliphate's day as a physical entity was numbered, but the penultimate battle, beginning in Raqqa and then pushing down the river, was only just starting.

Chapter 6

THE DIPLOMATIC PROCESS: TALKING WITH RUSSIA AND TURKEY

Just days after intervening in the Syrian civil war, the Russian government made overtures to the United States to begin a series of meetings in the once-divided city of Vienna. The talks served as a mechanism for the two sides to discuss the troubled political process in Syria, as well as to hammer out agreements to deconflict combat operations. The second venue for talks with Moscow was in Geneva, the lakeside city in Switzerland. The disagreements in either European city would often reverberate in the skies over Syria, where the battles for Tabqa and Palmayra brought the American and Russian air forces into near daily contact. As tensions increased over deconfliction arrangements, there were multiple incidents where American jets nearly downed jets from the VKS, and vice versa.

The change in US leadership also impacted the war. President Obama, who was deliberative and thoughtful and whose National Security Council was seen as overbearing and prone to micromanagement, gave way to Donald Trump, an erratic president committed to withdrawing American forces from Syria, but overseeing a bureaucratic process so shoddy that his own appointees would ignore the wishes of the world's most powerful man. The war plan did not change, despite these differences, but President Trump's insistence—against the advice and actions of his own appointees—created an incoherence in US policy that was not present during the Obama years. The Turkish-Russian entente also deepened, building off of the talks around the evacuation of Aleppo, and building into a formalized diplomatic process. These talks, however, prompted an Arab counter reaction, given the general disdain throughout much of the Arab world for Turkish president Erdogan and his affinity for the Muslim Brotherhood and political Islamist movements, and eventually leading to the conclusion of a ceasefire in the south of Syria. Finally, American and Iranian forces also came into contact, south of the river, around the small garrison of Tanf and a second, unacknowledged Special Forces base north of the "berm." These tensions escalated to include a failed Iranian missile strike on a US Special Forces garrison, dubbed Bowling Green, and a F-15E shooting down the attacking drone, along with a Navy F-18 downing a Syrian-flown Su-22, albeit after the Syrian Air Force bombed an American position.

From Vienna to Geneva: Negotiating with Moscow

Just days before a Turkish F-16 shot down a Russian Su-24, representatives from Moscow and the United States began to meet in Vienna in a quiet back channel to try and feel one another out over the direction and scope of each side's Syria policy. As one US official explained, "The meetings with the Russians began in Vienna in late October 2015, basically right after their intervention and it seemed to us that the initial goal was to stabilize the front lines and prepare to fight only on one front."[1] For the United States, the Russian intervention prompted caution for the pilots flying overhead, but also a bit of hubris about Moscow's ability to shape the outcome of the conflict. Quite quickly, the debate in Washington shifted to whether or not the Russian armed forces had signed itself up for a military quagmire that it would not win. President Obama, for example, warned in early October 2015 that "Russia and Iran [are] just going to get them stuck in a quagmire ... and they will be there for a while if they don't take a different course."[2] However, efforts were underway to try and reign in the Russian aerial attacks and to ease civilian suffering. "There were two meetings in Vienna with the Russians. The first was on October 30 and the second November 14. The third one was in December in New York just prior to the ratification of United Nations Security Council Resolution 2254 in December 2015," according to a US official involved in the talks. The focus was on getting to a Cessation of Hostilities to freeze the fighting, but even that effort was marred by a divergence of American and Russian goals.

The American debate about Moscow's intervention initially overlooked Russia's immediate military goals, which were focused around a narrow, tactical objective, which was nested within a broader worldview inside the Kremlin. The narrow tactical objective was to defend the Assad regime from collapse, following the success of the CIA's program in Idlib, and in near-lock step with the American-Turkish agreement on the T/E program. For Moscow, the combination of its own growing military capabilities, combined with its commitment to prevent the fall of an ally, even a difficult one, to a Western-backed force drove its decision-making. And yet, for close to three years, Russia was cautious, choosing to limit its involvement to the provision of equipment and advisors, in lieu of a direct, more forceful intervention on behalf of the Assad regime. This changed during June 2015, when an exhausted Syrian state was signaling it could hold the line in places where it was on defense, but would be unable to launch offensive operations to take back territory lost. The other actor that deepened its support with Russia was Iran, which had sent men and materials to aid in previous battles, but decided to increase its commitment through the provision of more militia members to aid in Assad's defense.

To this point, the United States and Russia had been involved in negotiations dating back to 2011, ostensibly aimed at suspending violence in Syria and working toward some modicum of political accommodation between the state and the insurgency. The first such effort began in Geneva, under the direction of Kofi Annan, and was focused on securing agreement on negotiations to each agreement on a transitional governing body to exercise full executive power over the country. As one of the American negotiators, Fred Hof, wrote the document that the two sides agreed to, the Geneva communiqué, was a consensus document that required Russian approval. Therefore, the document did not make any mention about Assad, nor was the transitional governing body contingent on his removal or overthrow. Moscow, to the surprise of none of the negotiators, has sought to exploit the vaguely worded document to its benefit and ensure that Assad's rule was never threatened.[3]

There were others in the US government that thought that Geneva Communique was, in essence, a regime change document, even if the language was not directly spelled out. "The early stuff, and the Geneva communique especially, was basically predicated on the idea that Assad was going down," a State Department official suggested, underscoring how the document could have different interpretations of the same text.[4] This diplomatic process underpinned the internal deliberations within the Obama administration about how to gain leverage over Assad, to force him to make concessions, and to push Moscow into a corner to accept the Western interpretation of the Geneva communique.

The intent of the CIA program, as Ambassador Robert Ford recalled, was to use the provision of arms to try and empower the moderates within the broader anti-Assad insurgency toward this end. However, this effort quickly became subsumed by the concurrent effort to empower the moderates versus the blossoming number of radical groups that had enmeshed itself with the Syrian opposition. As Ford recounts of his talks with the opposition at this time, "[I told the leadership] you have to distance as far as possible from the Nusra front, and if you work with them, we can not work with you. And you need to condemn them. [The leadership] yelled at me saying that the U.S. was more worried about Sunnis killing each other, but not getting killed."[5] The issue turned more sectarian, particularly after the Iranians began to insert themselves into the conflict, and jihadist groups leaned on anti-Shia tropes to justify the use of violence.

In Washington, the arming debate morphed into two prongs, with the first being focused on using the weapons as a means to unify the opposition, and the second to empower groups against the radical elements that were taking over the movement. The opposition, however, proved to be riven by division and unable to unite politically, or on the battle field. By 2013, the purported leaders of the Syrian opposition were at a disadvantage because they had no influence over events inside Syria, were weaker than Nusra, and the war had taken a turn. The Syrian regime, backed by Hezbollah, the Iranian-linked party based in Lebanon, helped the regime take control of Qusayir. The United States was also in negotiations with Russia over the destruction of Syrian chemical weapons, following the regime's August 2013 attack in the Damascus suburbs that killed 1,400.

The Obama administration had its own division over the efficacy of arming the opposition, but both Hillary Clinton and John Kerry, both of whom served as secretary of state, pushed to arm the Syrian opposition. As Ford recalls of Kerry, "[He] was extremely supportive [of arming the opposition], and so he raised it with the president. And he finally got permission, in February 2013, to begin material assistance, but non-lethal, delivered through the state department."[6] The lethal aid was supplied through a different channel. In any case, the aid steadily ramped up, leading to the fall of Idlib in 2015 that had the unintended effect of drawing Moscow directly into the conflict.

With the Russian intervention, things changed. As was the case throughout much of the administration, Obama tapped Secretary Kerry, who sought to negotiate with Moscow on a ceasefire and, later, on a mechanism to embed Russians and Americans in Geneva to share targeting data for air strikes against certain groups in Syria. It was these three efforts, the push toward a Cessation of Hostilities, the inconclusive talks over the Aleppo surrender, and the talks on the sharing of targeting data, that dominated 2016. It also created the momentum to begin to have direct, bilateral talks with the Kremlin about the Syrian war.

The city Geneva sits in a depression, surrounded by mountains, and at its lowest point empties in Lake Leman, which straddles the Swiss-French border. The United Nations, or Palais, is just off the Avenue de France, wedged between the international airport and the lake. Opposite the entrance to the Palais is the Intercontinental Hotel, where the American delegation would often stay during talks with Russia and other parties involved in Syria. The hotel also played host to the various delegations for the Iran nuclear talks, both of which competed for Secretary Kerry's time and focus. Between 2012 and 2015, the bulk of the focus of the American outreach to Russia came in reference to the Geneva communique, and trying to wrangle Moscow to use its influence with the regime to ease violence and to cajole the regime to attend the talks with the opposition representatives at the UN in Geneva. After the Russian intervention, the scope of the talks expanded, pivoting away from narrow efforts to implement the Geneva communique and toward a more sustained effort to try and create a mechanism to end the conflict. This effort moved, first, with the establishment of the International Syria Support Group (ISSG), which was stood up in Vienna after rounds of negotiations in Germany.

"The ISSG was born of the realization that Iran and Russia were going to have a say and that there needed to be a new process to both accommodate their views and interests, and also to convince them of the need for a transition," a State Department official recalls. The interaction between the Iranians and the Americans was, in part, eased by breaking of the taboo on direct meetings between government officials during the Iran nuclear talks: Secretary Kerry and the Iranian minister of Foreign Affairs, Javad Zarif. The US discussions with the Russians in Vienna resulted in the drafting of a declaration of intent to push the various parties to the civil war to adhere to a ceasefire and begin preparations "for a Syrian-led process that will, within a target of six months, establish credible, inclusive and non-sectarian governance, and set a schedule and process for drafting a new constitution."[7] The document, while making reference to the Geneva communique, did seek to water down the language. It notably left out the reference to the transitional governing body and replaced the word with the word "governance."

"Russia liked the references to elections," a State Department official recalled of the talks. "They also liked the idea of constitutional reform."[8] Within the US government, there was a debate about whether or not the word "secular" should have been included in the ISSG Statement. However, the use of such word risked losing support from elements of the Syrian opposition, many of which were Islamist leaning and were wary of secular governance. The ISSG language created the pathway for Moscow to focus more intently on a process it could control, the reformation of the constitution, without having to grapple seriously with the focus on the transitioning governing body, which Russian elites viewed as tantamount to regime change. The various ISSG members also diverged on the definition of terrorist groups in Syria. "There was this whole Russian backed effort to get ISSG consensus on which opposition group were terrorists and which were not. The Jordanians worked with [Russia] on this, and so the Jordanians were floating around different lists of who was and was not a terrorist," according to a US official familiar with the talks. "They made a matrix and they put a red dot next to a country and cross referenced to a terrorist groups, and so the Russians had a lot of red dots, but the UAE had a lot more red dots than the Russians."[9] The language ultimately reflected the United Nations Security Council (UNSC) definition of terrorists because the language is vague and not very specific.

These talks led to the issuing of a statement in November 2015, which was later incorporated into UNSC Resolution 2254. The meetings empowered Saudi Arabia to host a conference for the opposition to try and unify the differing factions the official negotiators sought to represent. This led to the creation of the High Negotiating Committee, or HNC, which was to represent the opposition at later peace talks on December 10. "By December 15, Kerry went to Moscow, where he was mainly focused on airspace deconfliction and smoothing that out and also the political track ... Kerry and Lavrov were talking multiple times a week by this point," a US official recalled.

In mid-December, the ISSG statement was codified in UNSC Resolution 2254, which made reference again to the transitioning governance body, but which also included a clause at the end underscoring the intense legalese about what it is that the council would be and how it would take shape. In UNSC 2254, the language reaffirmed the need for a transitioning governing body, but one "which shall be formed on the basis of mutual consent while ensuring continuity of governmental institutions". This reference, it appears, was a Russian addition to rearguard protection against using this language as a mechanism to pressure to the regime.

The Russian plan was similar to a proposal put forward by Iranian foreign minister Javad Zarif, and was quickly dubbed the Zarif plan by US diplomats. "You basically had the opposition and its backers plan for a transition based on the Geneva 1 communique; and then you had for years what was known as the Zarif plan, which was nationwide ceasefire, constitutional reform, and then elections."[10] These divergences would plague the two sides during forthcoming negotiations, but was the fulcrum around which US and Russian negotiations would pivot for much of 2016 and early 2017. The efforts on the ISSG and 2254 framed meetings in Munich, where meetings were being held to reach agreement on a broad ceasefire to try and freeze the violence. By early February, the ISSG reached agreement on a broad-based Cessation of Hostilities (CoH), which included language to ensure the provision of humanitarian assistance and the urgent implementation of a nationwide ceasefire, with exceptions made for military action against Jabhat al Nusra, Islamic State, and UNSC-designated terrorist groups.[11] The entire process, beginning with the standing up of the ISSG, the decision to include Iran, and then passing of 2254, capped off by CoH took considerable effort and diplomatic acumen. "The ISSG and UNSCR 2254 was a very involved and skillfully done diplomatic exercise that involved lots of personal involvement from Kerry," according to a US official.

The process was aided by frequent meetings between the United States and Russia, first held in Switzerland and then moved to Austria. On the Russian side, President Putin appointed a special envoy for Syria, Alexander Lavrentiev. This appointment created a parallel position to Brett McGurk, the special envoy for the counter ISIS coalition. These two men spearheaded direct, face-to-face talks, first in Zurich, and then moved to Vienna. The "Vienna Channel," as it would be dubbed, morphed into a venue to have back channel discussions about the conflict. The channel sometimes included representatives from the Russian Ministry of Defense, who would meet with their counterparts from the DoD. The American team usually included Brett McGurk and his Russian counterpart, Lavrentiev, who would also be joined by Sergei Vershinen, the then head of the Ministry of Foreign Affairs' Middle East and North Africa Department. "We met in Zurich for the first time on Feb 4, 2016, and we called it the Zurich channel for a while, before it shifted to Vienna. The view was for de-escalation," a US official involved with the talks recalls.

"The talks with Russia were sensitive at the time. It was bilateral and we thought we could get something done. That was the thinking behind it. We were working with the Swiss because it is easier to do things secretly with them," a US official recalled. This first meeting, according to the official, was focused on reaching agreement on humanitarian access for aid, in preparation for the larger talks to be held in Munich. "At this first meeting," the official recalls, "the Russians brought a written Cessation of Hostilities text." With the draft in hand, the US team took the document back to Washington, where it was heavily edited and presented again to Moscow. "This back and forth initiated a process for what would become the Cessation of Hostilities that was rolled out in February 2016."[12] The text was finalized on February 19 and was codified in a telephone call between Presidents Obama and Putin on February 22. The CoH statement was later included in UNSC Resolution 2268, which called on the external parties to the civil conflict "to use their influence with the parties to the Cessation of Hostilities to ensure fulfillment of those commitments and to support efforts to create conditions for a durable and lasting ceasefire" that began at midnight on February 26.[13] One provision within the CoH called for the establishment of a Task Force with over a dozen countries to delineate the territory that terrorist groups control in Syria and to create a communication mechanism to share and report ceasefire violations.

The Task Force still meets, even though the CoH has long since broken down and violence has ravaged the country. It was only after the Covid-19 global pandemic halted global travel that the Task Force stopped meeting in person.

"These task forces have proved to be a real lesson in institutional momentum," a State Department official quipped, even though they had long outlived their original purpose, or even reached basic agreement on the maps delineating which groups controlled what territory.[14] The Cessation of Hostilities took effect and remained shaky and unevenly enforced and, by May, fighting around Aleppo had escalated, despite efforts to manage the growing crisis in the Vienna Channel.

During the decrease in fighting, there were a series of meetings that Staffan De Mistura convened in Geneva, the first of which was held in late January. There were three rounds of this in 2016 run by the United Nations Envoy, Staffan de Mistura, a US official recalls. "The first round was right when Azaz was being cut off, so it was not a conducive environment for talks." The second round, the official recounted, took place after the CoH had reduced violence. "They convened the second round from March 14-24 ... It was more successful than the previous rounds. De Mistura issued points of commonality between the two sides, and it was like a lot of mom and apple pie stuff, but it was an effort to establish some common ground."

However, as a second US official suggested, the progress was minimal and remained beset with considerable tensions. "In 2016, there was these Geneva rounds that went nowhere, and we were just there all the time." Beyond the violence taking place inside Syria, the main problem for the Staffan de Mistura was that the opposition and the regime remained fundamentally at odds and unwilling to sit in the same room with one another. "De Mistura was always trying to reorient the talks to create a mechanism to get the regime and the opposition to talk to each other. They never agreed on any foundational process and it was basically the opposition saying that the Assad has to cede power, and Assad saying they need to accept him first before talks."[15]

Secretary Kerry worked closely with his counterpart in Russia, Sergey Lavrov, to overcome American and Russian differences and reach agreement on a ceasefire to freeze the violence. His intent was to create space for peace talks and the remaking of the Syrian constitution. "Kerry was always talking to Lavrov and there were these periodic envoy and ISSG meetings and it eventually led to Kerry conceding that Assad could stay in a transitional period, and that was a minor concession," according to a US State Department official.[16]

It was during this lull in violence that Russia sought to shape talks about the future of Syrian politics. "We met in Bern in mid-March," a US official recalls, "and at this meeting we were pushing them hard on transition, and they hated that term. It was the 'T' word." The United States, at this time, was floating a number of options to try and win support from Moscow. The first was that Assad would simply not run in the election mandated in UNSCR 2254, a choice that would necessarily lead to a transition away from his rule. The United States also suggested having Assad delegate power to vice presidents. Moscow, in contrast, had drafted a Syrian constitution just days before the meeting in Bern and maintained that the choice both countries faces was Assad or chaos.

"We eventually decided to pursue both tracks, a new constitution and a transition. Kerry went back to Moscow on March 25, where this was discussed," according to a US official. The United States took the Russian draft home and edited the document and brought it back to Zurich for a meeting with the Russians on April 7. "This meeting did not go well because there was no progress on these two parallel tracks." On April 10, the regime announced its intention to retake Aleppo, a statement that the Russians had to walk back. The announcement coincided with the third, and final, De Mistura held meeting between the opposition and the regime in Geneva in 2016. "It is about now that the CoH starts to go off the rails," a US official explained. "The CoH is basically being openly undermined, but we did try and reboot it in the Amman Channel."

This avenue for discussion began in February 2016, when a trilateral meeting was held in Jordan to "lay out all the maps and got down to brass tacks." This channel would serve as another vehicle for US-Russian dialogue, and foreshadowed a trilateral initiative to reach a ceasefire in the southwest in 2017. "We held a few different meetings the Amman channel where we did try and reboot the CoH, and we got some traction in areas, but it was clearly falling apart. It was like pushing on string."[17] The American concession did not completely end the violence in Syria, but it did create more space to deepen negotiations with Moscow over the future of Syria. One outgrowth of this engagement was sustained talks in Geneva about a joint military agreement to share information about locations of Islamic State and Al-Qaeda-linked elements in Syria, with the intent of creating a mechanism to coordinate airstrikes.

By May, the fighting in Aleppo had increased and the ceasefire agreed to in February had frayed. The United States and Russia met again in Bern, where the two sides engaged in negotiations on a step-by-step process to revive the CoH. The Bern negotiation ended up in the drafting of a joint statement that recommitted each side to the CoH and agreed to jointly monitor the implementation, rather than do it remotely from Khmeimim Air Base and Amman. "We started a Cessation of Hostilities cell in Geneva to share information about what was going on the ground. There was no support from DoD or CIA to do anything with this," a US official recalls. "There was nothing classified, nothing operational, and it was basically just designed to have a conversation. The Russians were hoping for mil-to-mil cooperation. This was their whole dream. Kerry was willing to do it if we could get rid of Assad and get on the political track."[18] During the same meeting in Bern, Russia also proposed a mechanism to deepen the deconfliction line that had been in place from when the VKS began air operations in the country.

> The Russian military reps proposed something: They said you are in the northeast, why don't you coordinate with us on Raqqa. You push on the city, and we push on Der Ezour to the west of the river. They never wanted to draw lines on a map, but this was the first conversation about this and using the Euphrates as a deconfliction line.

This proposal was the first of many discussions over deconflicting air operations, and a series of tense interactions around Der Ezour that nearly resulted in numerous shoot downs of each side's aircraft.

The monitoring cell in Geneva for the CoH also became a template for an even bolder proposal, following the May 9 declaration. The United States began to consider creating a mechanism to try and ground the Syrian Air Force, leaving the bombing of Nusra and Islamic State to the VKS and the Coalition. This process, known as the Joint Implementation Group (JIG), was an outgrowth of the Kerry–Lavrov talks and designed to try and limit the scope of the Russian air campaign. The basic idea began to take shape in late Spring 2016 and shared the same basic premise that the only groups that should be targeted were Islamic State, Jabhat al Nusra, or any United Nations-designated terrorist organization. "On May 20," a US official indicated, "we made public a proposal that Lavrov had briefed to [Secretary Kerry] on the phone a few days prior."[19]

"The basic concept was we could share intel and do battle damage assessment and that certain areas would be no-bomb zones. The JIG was to eliminate Nusra and ISIS from the battlefield. And at some future date, we would figure out how to reconcile the western backed groups and the Assad regime," a US official involved in the talks explained.[20] From the outset of these talks, the DoD participated against its will and sought to limit its involvement. The other issue was that the United States was being asked to "demarble" the opposition, the term adopted to describe efforts to separate Jabhat al Nusra and its successor groups from the opposition. This task, a US official recalls, turned out to be impossible. "You can't do it. The opposition didn't make the distinctions themselves. We would say there is no Nusra in an area, and then two days later a Nusra guy would show up on Twitter in the same area, and so we just couldn't get around this."[21]

The legal issue was also a major sticking point. There is a federal statute that prevents bilateral military cooperation with Russia. The Russian VKS was also bombing hospitals, raising the moral cost of working alongside them to jointly destroy targets. Despite DoD's hesitance, the JIG nearly succeeded in getting off the ground because it had the strong support of Secretary Kerry, who was effectively overseeing US diplomacy to help end the conflict. "Obama farmed Syria out to John Kerry and Kerry felt he had the writ pursue it as he wanted," a US official recalled. "At the Pentagon, we were against the whole deal, and we thought going in with Russia was us folding our hand."[22] As another US official succinctly put it, "[Secretary of Defense Ash] Carter and DoD didn't want to work with Russia."[23]

By the summer of 2016, the talks had accelerated in Geneva at the United Nations. While DoD was hesitant, a US official recalls that there was consensus on the need to try and establish a mechanism to limit the Russian air force and slow the bombing campaign. "On the Russian military side, they had an advantage over our side," an American involved in the negotiations recalled. "Alexander Zorin, [the Russian defense ministry's envoy to Geneva] was the lead guy for two or three years, they had institutional memory, while our team rotated every 30 days or so."

During the talks with the Americans for the JIG, Zorin, the Ministry of Foreign Affairs was placed in a subordinate role, with that task going to Maria Khodynskaya-Golenishcheva, the Russia representative to the ISSG. Zorin was involved in most, if not all, of Russia's work with the ISSG and outreach and relations with the armed opposition. He has a military background and some US officials suspected that he was a GRU officer. As one US official who interacted with him recalls, "Zorin was very involved in all aspects of Russian diplomacy and military activity during this whole period ... He's professional. Does his job and toes the line well, but it is possible to work with him on the technical details when things get serious." As for Maria, she was less focused on technical details, but would often be called in to deliver talking points in the afternoon sessions of the JIG meetings.[24]

During the summer of 2016, the two sides began to hold meetings on a regular basis to reach agreement on a shared map, delineating Al-Qaeda and Islamic State presence and reaching agreement on the Terms of Reference, the document that would define how the JIG would operate. The map negotiations advanced further than the Terms of Reference, but were plagued by differing interpretations of where Jabhat al Nusra was located, and the conditions where the group could be targeted. "The map meetings went fairly well and there was a lot of progress on that line of effort," a US official involved in the process recalls. However, reaching agreement on a precise definition of terrorist proved difficult. "Russia would claim everyone is Jabhat al Nusra. For the Russians, it didn't matter, any Sunni group was eligible for strikes. That was the sticking point."[25]

The fundamental challenge for the United States was that Nusra was so deeply enmeshed with the opposition at this point in the war that it was hard to point to areas where they did not have at least a small, token presence. This ceded leverage to Moscow because they could point to intelligence that showed some presence, even if it was minimal and relatively inconsequential compared to the totals of fighters affiliated with non-UN designated terror groups also active in the area. According to a US official:

> We were trying to demarble [the opposition]. And then the Russians would bomb in an area where there were 2-3 groups located, including Nusra, which was the biggest and strongest. Then they would target the U.S. backed group, and the U.S. backed group would seek protection from Russia from Nusra, and then Russia would say the groups are clumped together, and bomb again.

As another official remarked, "Every time the Russians would talk about making efforts to separate the moderate opposition from the extremists, that was a reference to conversations Lavrov would have with Kerry, and accompanied with a tongue in cheek, deadpan Russian-style satire: 'there are no moderates, get it.'"[26]

In one incident in Geneva, Zorin dropped his guard with his American counterparts, darkly referring to Moscow's targeting of hospitals in its air campaign. During negotiations over the map, and talks about delineating where Nusra was present, the American delegation reiterated that hospitals were off-limits and not to be targeted. In response, Zorin quipped:

> Every time we role up on a hospital, there is some Dutch guy with glasses, and he says this is a protected facility and standing behind him is a bunch of guys with beards. So we know what is up ... The implication was that the NGOs are harboring fighters. They had cynical attitude towards these places .... and while

they never admitted to bombing them on purpose, they made clear that they thought they were harboring terrorists.[27]

Zorin was also adept at pushing back against American criticism, citing the bombing of Dresden in the Second World War, the accidental bombing of the Chinese embassy in Belgrade in 1999, and the firebombing of Tokyo to deflect criticism of Russian actions in Syria, a US official recalled of these exchanges.[28]

Zorin would also blame the United States for issues the Russian military faced during its campaign in the northwest, blaming American weapons for an accident with a Syrian helicopter that two Russian test pilots were flying. "They accused a U.S. backed group of shooting down their helicopter, with either a TOW or Stinger. During the test they are firing rockets off the fin, you could clearly see from videos online that one of the rockets malfunctions, and as the pilot tries to shoot it off the winglet, something hits the tail rotor," according to a US official.

> They claimed that we had done it, put it out to the press. We put together a series of rebuttals, including with the ground footage, and we presented the information to Zorin, and he goes, "yeah that is probably right, maybe his wing man shot him down," and just moved on. They knew it was a lie, and maybe thought it would get us to chase our tails for a few days.[29]

The incident underscored how Russia was willing to use subterfuge to keep American negotiators off balance, but also how they would capitulate on these non-vital issues when presented with incontrovertible proof. Despite the disagreement about the Terms of Reference and the mutual distrust permeating throughout the discussions, by the summer the two parties had pushed forward with the selection of a site to host American and Russian personnel to operationalize the effort to strike designated terrorist groups. "We had picked out a dacha outside of Geneva," an official recalls. Yet, beyond the site, there were still numerous issues to work through. "It got close in that the JIG would have been stood up, but what did not get close was that the U.S. would not have been able to share any useful information with the Russians," a DoD official recalled. As a second official remembers, "We couldn't do secure communications in the proposed building, so we would have had to go to another facility for that type of work, but there was a fair amount of technical work that was done."

The DoD, wary of the talks from the start, tried to hide behind legalese to ensure that the JIG would not succeed. The threshold for targeting, an official recalls, was written in such a way that it would have been near impossible for Russia to meet them. The DoD, this official recounted, was also frustrated at the lack of broad-based familiarity with the targeting process and how sharing intelligence with Moscow was both unlawful and unethical. Despite this, by August 2016, the two sides were exchanging papers about the precise wording for the JIG, and by September the negotiations continued and centered on how long a ceasefire was needed to be observed before the process could be implemented. The challenge was that violence around Aleppo was increasing, precisely at the time when

Secretary Kerry was pushing hardest to try and reign in Russian air strikes using this process.

"On our end, we decided that we needed a week-long ceasefire," an official recalls. "This was part of DoD's pressure." As a second official recalls, "We decided we needed a week-long real ceasefire to know if the other side was serious. That ceasefire began on September 13, 2016 to try and stop the regime from bombing the opposition, allow unfettered access of aid, and freeze the conflict. The hope was that after a week, the JIG could begin to operate and the US and Russia would each bomb only Islamic State or Al Qaeda-linked elements."[30] The ceasefire came under strain almost immediately. As one US official quipped, "The regime couldn't be restrained for more than six days." However, the real nail in the coffin came a few days later, when American aircraft accidentally bombed regime vehicles in Der Ezour that the Coalition had misidentified as belonging to the Islamic State. During a series of strafing and bombing runs on the vehicles, the Russian side alerted the United States through the deconfliction channel and the strike was called off, but not before sixty-two Syrian regime soldiers were killed.[31]

In response to the strike, Russia convened a meeting of the UNSC, which resulted in the Russian representative walking out. The US ambassador, Samantha Power, described the act as a "stunt."[32] In a nod to the JIG, Sergei Rudskoy, the head of the operations directorate of the Russian Armed Forces' General Staff, suggested that the incident stemmed from poor coordination with the Russian armed forces.[33] The final nail in the coffin came just a few days later, when two Russian Su-24 bombers destroyed a UN aid convoy in the opposition-held territory.[34] The airstrike coincided with the Assad regime declaring an end to the ceasefire. As one US official bluntly stated, "We accidentally bombed the regime guys, and then the Russians bombed the UN convoy and the regime declared the ceasefire over. That ended the JIG."[35] In his farewell address to the United Nations General Assembly, the former director general, Ban Ki-Moon, described the attack as a "sickening, savage and apparently deliberate attack" carried out by "cowards."[36]

Kerry and Lavrov met after the UN strike, but the momentum for the joint Russian and regime offensive for Aleppo was building. During the summer negotiations for the JIG, the United States had sought guarantees from the Russians on the provision of aid to the city. The main conduit for such aid was Castello Road, which the regime had cut when it besieged Aleppo in July 2016, and connected the city to the Turkish border. The regime and Russia began to bombard Aleppo in late September and kept at it until declaring a pause in the campaign to try and force a surrender. Despite the JIG's collapse, the United States still sought to limit the Russian advance and reimpose a ceasefire. In Geneva, the United States gathered a small group of the most important external countries involved in Syria to try and increase the pressure on Moscow to halt its bombing campaign. However, by this point, Turkey had "gone silent and abandoned East Aleppo," a US official recalls, as it became clear that Ankara and Moscow were negotiating concurrently about Operation Euphrates Shield.[37] From this process, Ankara and Moscow deepened their negotiations, which created conditions Washington would seek to exploit to freeze the conflict in Syria's southwest.

However, that process began after a radical change in American electoral politics: The election of Donald J. Trump as president of the United States in November 2016. The election ushered in a new era of American diplomacy, deepened the relationship with the Syrian Kurds, albeit only to try and assuage a war-skeptical president, and touched off a huge intra-American schism about the relationship with Russia.

The March Down the River: The Battle for Tabqa and Donald Trump's First Decision

Operation Euphrates Shield created a series of problems that the Task Force had to manage with the SDF. With the installation of a ceasefire in the early days of the conflict, the tensions became more manageable. The Turkish operation was, at its core, the realization of the Agate Noble CONOP, albeit with one major exception: Manbij. The territory the United States held west of the Euphrates River would remain a diplomatic challenge, both with Ankara and with the Russian Federation, and at different points in the war, both countries would threaten to attack US-backed forces. The third sliver of territory, built around "the berm" and the Rukban refugee camp, dubbed Tanf, was also a sore spot for Moscow and Iran. This odd dynamic created overlapping interests between two American foes, Russia and Iran, and a US ally, Turkey, about the need to force the United States to lessen its involvement in the Syrian conflict and to ensure that the SDF did not carve out a truly coherent autonomous entity in Syria's northeast.

The American campaign against Islamic State moved in fits and starts, largely because of external concerns about mollifying Turkey. The initial thought was the United States and the SDF should focus on taking Raqqa and Mosul simultaneously, while leaving Manbij to be mopped up by the T/E elements. The Paris attacks shifted the momentum and prompted the decision to use the SDF to cross the river, a planning deviation that hindered relations with Ankara. In any case, Operation Euphrates Shield effectively cleared the Manbij Pocket of Islamic State, and through Russian interference, Ankara and the regime shared a large stable forward line of troops that extended from Aleppo to the Euphrates River. During Euphrates Shield, the SDF began its push down the Euphrates, beginning the preparation for the siege of Raqqa. The Obama administration had pushed to accelerate the war in Syria, but fell short of the goal of liberating Raqqa before leaving office.

Donald J. Trump came into office with firm and well-developed views about US foreign policy and the American presence in the Middle East. During the campaign, then candidate Trump reiterated his commitment to ending the American-led wars in the Middle East. In a revealing interview with the *New York Times*, Trump suggested that American interventions in the Middle East had left the region and the United States worse off and that the countries that benefit from American security guarantees should reimburse the United States for the protection they receive.[38] Trump was also fond of suggesting that American foes, like Russia and Iran, benefited from the war against Islamic State because they free ride on the back of American power without contributing to the war effort. In this sense, Trump draws little distinction between American ally and foe, suggesting both are equally involved in taking advantage of US military power. This transactional approach is fed by extreme ignorance, which makes Trump susceptible to overtures of leaders keen to take advantage of him. From the outset of his candidacy, the AKP in Turkey and Putin in Russia quite clearly understood that the American president was easily corruptible and someone they could manipulate and both leaders pushed for his election.

On the campaign trail, Trump did speak about the need to finish the war against Islamic State, promising to "bomb the shit out of them,"[39] seize Syrian oil, and mused openly about setting aside the effort to topple Assad because both countries had a shared interest in defeating ISIS.[40] The American president sought to follow through on each of these campaign promises. To do so, he had to first grapple with the war plan that was left behind to seize Islamic State's hub in Syria, Raqqa, a feat that entailed making a decision to arm the YPG directly. In the waning days of the Obama administration, United States Central Command began to prepare for a change in government. For the civil servants that would transition from one president to the other at the National Security Council, the focus between November and January was preparing for a transition.

As one National Security Council official recalls, "The prep on the Turkey/Syria was extensive. Once we knew the new administration would make the decision on arming the YPG, our goal was to lay out the issue and the pros and cons of the policy choices."[41] On January 17, 2016, President Obama authorized his national security team to turn over to the incoming Trump national security team a plan to issue the appropriate waiver to meet the regulations in the 1209 authorities to begin to arm the YPG directly. The Obama administration had suggested the incoming administration could rapidly approve the arming plan and, within six months, have taken control of Raqqa and then begin to rein in the SDF. The intent, the administration argued, was to let the Trump administration blame the outgoing Obama administration for arming the Kurds in talks with Ankara, and then use the withdrawal of support as a way for Trump to reset relations with Ankara. "We envisioned the war ending after the lines of contact froze," a former senior Obama NSC official remembers. "We saw it, at the end, as negotiating with Russia and Iran over freezing the conflict and then continuing negotiations."[42]

The decision to arm the Kurds directly was fraught, but relatively straightforward in purpose. To assault Raqqa, the SDF would need heavy equipment to move forces into a large urban area, but any such action would further enrage Turkey. Rather than pick up the Obama plan immediately, the Trump administration held off and initiated its own review. As one person who worked for both administrations remembers, "Transitions are always messy, no matter who is overseeing it. The Trump team was particularly messy because there were just so few people that had been appointed to step in and take over."[43] A Trump official told *The Washington Post* anonymously that the plan the Obama team presented was too risk-averse and bound to fail and blamed this on "poor staff work."[44] As one official responded to the author, "We could have gotten some things wrong, but that process was meticulous staff work."

Upon taking up the position of secretary of defense, James Mattis issued a review of the counter-ISIS effort to date, and was tasked with presenting options to the president for his review. For much of 2016, the United States and Turkey had remained in contact over the looming battle for Raqqa. The tension and distrust between the two countries had deepened since Operation Euphrates Shield. Along the forward line that separated the de facto US-controlled zone in Manbij and the Turkish-controlled zone in Euphrates Shield territory, skirmishes were common. "We would often get shot at while on patrol," a US special forces soldier recalled of the patrols along the Manbij forward line. "It was very tense and we had to try and ensure that the SDF didn't shoot back because we didn't want to give the Turks any pretense to invade. It was a tinderbox and something we had to manage every day."[45]

In those early days, Secretary Mattis was looking again at whether a viable, alternative partner force existed to assault Raqqa. The Turkish plan for the assault revolved around using Arab groups it had paid and trained, rather than the SDF. Ankara proposed two plans to Washington: The first, and more practical of the two, envisaged Turkish-backed Syrian forces entering Tel Abyad and moving to Raqqa's outskirts, where they would then plug into the Task Force effort to liberate the city. The second, and more questionable proposal because of the presence of regime forces in the area, would use Turkish-controlled al Bab as the launching point. The Turkish plan, according to a person familiar with them, also included "clearing Manbij, which was an indication that the plan proposed was not really about the defeat ISIS mission, but was also aimed at clearing SDF elements from the border."[46]

In one visit, the chairman of the Joint Chiefs of Staff, General Joseph Dunford, visited Ankara to meet with the then chief of the Turkish General Staff, Hulusi Akar. The meeting was part of the iterative discussions held between US and Turkish officials over the Raqqa plan. On this visit, according to a US official, Akar took Dunford to visit a training site, where the Turkish-supported opposition received training.[47] Beginning with Agate Noble, American officials had grown disillusioned with Turkish claims about forces it could muster to seize and hold territory. One key issue was that Ankara was supporting groups that were enmeshed with radical elements, who would pose force protection and vetting concerns for the US forces that would be asked to accompany them. The other was that the forces Ankara promised were just never large in number.

"We would meet with the Turks," a US official recounted, "and we would go through a slide deck of the force requirements for Raqqa. We would hear in the meeting that they could not brief this up because the numbers of fighters required was too large. We would convene again and see that the slides had changed. We were never sure Erdogan was fully briefed on what was required for Raqqa."[48]

The frustration with Turkish promises eventually led many within the US government to refer to the proposed alternative force for Raqqa as "Erdogan's ghosts" or the "unicorn" army and eventually included some to have coffee cups and shirts printed with a unicorn on it. "It was the ghost brigade," one official bluntly stated.

The Trump administration's review of the proposed plan for Raqqa was completed in early May, before Secretary Mattis traveled to Copenhagen for a meeting with the members of the coalition to defeat Islamic State. About ten days later, on May 19, Mattis outlined the new approach. In essence, the battle plan was unchanged from the one the Obama administration left behind. The SDF would be used to assault Raqqa. However, in his remarks, Mattis mentioned that authorities would be delegated and that Islamic State would be besieged in urban areas and "annihilated."[49] As one US official recalled, "It took three months just to stamp the plan they already had in hand from the previous administration. The only real change was to delegate authority down to battalion commander and to loosen strike restrictions on civilian casualties."[50]

During this timeframe, the recommendation was made to arm the YPG directly, knowing that such action would result in Turkish condemnation. To do so, President Trump would have to issue a national security waiver because of the YPG's links to the US-terrorist-designated PKK. As one official familiar with the president's thinking at the time recalls, "Trump was sold on the idea of arming the Kurds because it would end the war faster. He was willing to take the hit on Turkey, but was confident he could manage the relationship on a personal relationship, and focus on bilateral trade."[51] As for Mattis, one official remembers that "he seemed genuinely disappointed that the YPG was our only choice and looked to offset that with concerted support to Turkey on PKK."[52]

In early May, just two days before the coalition met in Copenhagen, a Turkish delegation visited Washington. The delegation included Hulusi Akar, Hakan Fidan, Ibrahim Kalin, Erdogan's chief spokesperson and foreign policy advisor, and Justice Minister Bekir Bozdag. The delegation was in Washington to prepare for Erdogan's visit, which was scheduled for mid-May to Trump. During this trip, the White House informed the Turkish delegation that the United States would be arming the YPG directly. Erdogan visited Washington for two days on May 16 and 17. The trip ended up being a disaster for Turkey because on the second day, just before leaving the United States, Erdogan's bodyguards assaulted protesters outside the Turkish ambassador's residence. The incident soured public opinion of Turkey inside the United States and in Congress and has hardened anti-Erdogan views amongst American lawmakers.[53]

For the Trump administration, the choreography for the event was sketched out during the Obama administration and designed to try and send a strong political signal that Turkey remained a steadfast American ally, despite the frictions over Syria. Erdogan was invited to stay in the Blair House, the president's official guest house, and a place reserved for official head of states to stay when visiting Washington. Erdogan and his entourage typically stay at the St. Regis, an upmarket hotel just up the road from the White House, so the change of venue was intended to be symbolic and indicative of the strong bilateral relationship that would endure far beyond American support for the YPG.

On the military side, the United States also came prepared to increase its support for Turkish efforts to target the PKK's leadership and training sites. The venue for such cooperation was Operation Nomad Shadow, the program set up in

2007 amidst disagreement about the PKK during the American occupation of Iraq. "[The Secretary of Defense] swapped the 1 line of MQ-1 for two lines of MQ-9," a person familiar with the decision recalled.[54] This swap increased the number of aircraft involved in doing combat air patrols over Iraqi Kurdistan from two to four, and the MQ-9 is larger than the MQ-1 and can stay on station longer than the first-generation MQ-1 and has better sensors. "We let the [intelligence, surveillance and reconnaissance] platforms facilitate kinetic strikes," a second person recounted.[55] The increase in ISR coverage for Turkish strikes against the PKK, however, still faced considerable limitations. "They gave us very little in terms of starting points, ... so we bore holes in the sky with these premium assets doing little to nothing," according to a US government official. As a second official recounted, "Yes, they gave little and because [the Turks] weren't the best at utilizing our ISR it wasn't used to the fullest capacity, but when it did lead to a strike, it mattered [politically] ... at the tactical level, they were appreciated and thought it valuable."[56] As a third official suggested, "You can imagine why they didn't want to give us any of their good stuff on PKK, either they thought we could tip them off, or we would get too much insight into their sources and methods. They also could have just not known that much about the PKK."[57]

The United States agreed to provide Turkey with an eight-number grid reference, which would allow for Turkish assets to know about targets somewhere within 10 nautical miles. This arrangement meant that the US assets were not actually targeting the PKK, but "would help them target things they define as national interests," according to a person familiar with the process. "We help get them closer and trust that they will have procedures to mitigate civilian casualties and only strike when there is near certainty, which they have committed to doing in a way consistent with [US] standards, like zero CIVCAS and near certain positive identification on PKK."[58] Without precise starting points and a clear priority of targets to hunt for, Nomad Shadow, as one official described it, "like flying around looking at a myriad of haystacks guessing where some needles may be buried. At best, we got lucky when we found stuff."[59] The intelligence would lead to around one or two strikes per month and usually involved a Turkish asset replacing the American drone to finish the strike.

This arrangement was also marred by mistrust. "They always assumed we knew everything about the PKK and just weren't sharing," a US official recalled.

> But we cared about Al Qaeda and Islamic State. The United States government is not focused on the PKK. This would annoy senior [U.S.] leaders because they felt the Turks weren't appreciative for the support. It was common for us to remind Turks who wrote the talking points for key leader engagement to say thank you and not complain about this ... The MQ-9 does not grow on trees.[60]

The other two promises to Turkey were that the United States would keep Ankara informed of the weapons transferred to the YPG and, where feasible, collect them once the conflict ended. The weapons collection plan, however, quickly fell by the wayside. "The Task Force just put all the weapons collection in the non-feasible category and moved on. Neither the Special Operations Joint Task Force, nor the Combined Joint Task Force were in a position to provide oversight on the weapons," a person recalled.[61] This action rankled people inside the US government, some of whom felt that the Task Force in Syria was ignoring an order from the secretary of defense. "In short, the Secretary of Defense gave very specific guidance and attached conditions to the arming and was then just ignored."[62] Still, every month the Task Force would send up an updated monthly list of the weapons sent to the YPG. "The Task Force reported to SOJTF, who then reported to the Combined Joint Task Force, and then up to CENTCOM. It was one big distribution list with the breakdown of what was 'divested,'" according to a member of the Task Force. The weapons provided were also calibrated to try and minimize the risk to Turkish armor. "We didn't provide heavy weapons, which we define as nothing for the anti-tank role and nothing larger than 14.7 millimeters. We did give rocket propelled grenades," according to a US official, but "no artillery larger than mortars. We gave [the SDF] infantry stuff." Arguably, the most valuable equipment the Americans provided were heavy earth-moving equipment and medical supplies. As one person recalled, "The funny thing was that the special forces guys were so under resourced that they often kept some of the 1209 equipment for themselves, like trucks."[63]

With the issuance of the waiver, the United States had cleared the final hurdle, and was prepared to begin the operation to liberate Raqqa from the Islamic State. However, the problems with Turkey were continuing to fester, and would soon come to a head over Manbij, Ankara's threats to invade the city, and President Trump's ultimate decision to abandon US positions along the border in December 2018 and, again, in October 2019. Trump's decision-making reflected schisms within his own administration largely between the impulsive president's penchant for issuing orders, only to have his staff try and walk it back when presenting him with options to carry out his wishes after the fact. For the US military, the battle for Raqqa presaged near conflict with Russia, largely over the deconfliction mechanism for ground and air operations. These tensions also played out in back channel meets in Vienna, where a channel to discuss a ceasefire in the southwest was the closest the United States ever came to abandoning its de facto goal of regime change, in favor of a more managed policy of trying to mitigate violence. This process came about after Russia and Turkey, working with Iran, sought to build their own diplomatic mechanism to manage the conflict after the fall of Aleppo.

From Astana to Amman: Competing Zones and Imperfect Ceasefires

The fall of Aleppo forced a change in American and Turkish policies toward Syria. For Turkey, the collapse of the imperfect ceasefires in the spring and summer 2016 and the near certainty that Aleppo would fall forced Erdogan to alter his top-line priorities in the conflict. The Russian-Turkish entente ultimately led to the standing up of a rival political process to the one taking place in Geneva. In December 2016, Russian foreign minister Sergei Lavrov hosted talks with his Turkish and Iranian counterparts, which resulted in the drafting of the "Moscow

Declaration" to establish Turkey and Russia as the guarantors of the opposition (in the case of Ankara) and the regime (in the case of Moscow). The process, Russia announced in December, would be held in Astana, Kazakhstan.[64]

For the United States, the election of Donald Trump prompted staffers to try and wrap American strategic aims in Syria around the goals the president expressed during the campaign. It was, quite literally, an effort to operationalize the "make American great again" approach to foreign affairs. The fall of Aleppo also marked a turning point in how the United States viewed the conflict in Syria. Before this event, American diplomacy was centered on two interrelated efforts. The first, centered in Geneva, was designed to bring the opposition and the regime together, under UN auspices, to work to enforce the Geneva communique. The stumbling block with Moscow was over the authorities of the transitional governing body, the role of Assad within that body, and the inability of the opposition to fully back the western effort, and to account for the actions of groups like Jabhat al Nusra and its later iterations.

Geneva II was formally held in Montreux, the idyllic Swiss town on the eastern edge of Lake Leman in January 2014. During the run-up to the meeting, the United States was constantly engaged with the Syrian opposition to try and convince them to attend. Washington and Moscow had also reached agreement on the disposal of chemical weapons, following the August 2013 attack in Ghoutta. As one US official indicated, "The chemical weapons agreement [with Russia] created a technical process to work through. It was a success, in that we removed most of the weapons. It also led us to United Nations Security Council Resolution 2118."[65] The four months between the August 2013 chemical weapons attack and the holding of Geneva II underscored within the US government that diplomacy would be the main line of effort with Moscow. This approach stemmed, as one person involved with Geneva II recalls, Secretary Kerry's deep-seated belief in the necessity of engaging Moscow on issues that both countries had an interest in. "Kerry came in with a committed idea that we could engage with Russia as a partner. He carried the flame that by engagement you bring these countries into the international order, you make them stakeholders and shape them. And he really believed this with regards to Russia, and definitely with Iran."[66]

From that point on, a US official recalls, the second prong of Syria policy was to increase American leverage through the provisions of arms to the opposition. This approach gained more traction after Geneva II failed and the opposition and the regime still retained maximalist positions. "After Geneva II, everybody decided that the Russians and the regime were not serious, so we have to change their calculus," a US official recalls of the internal debate in Washington about Syria policy.

We have to put more pressure on them, so that marked a massive uptick in the provisions of arms through the program that shall not be talked about, and we also got the neighbors on board and started coordinating better. This was the starting point when Jaysh al Fateh in March began to take Idlib and obviously what we are building to is the Russian intervention.[67]

The Russian and regime victory in Aleppo was another critical moment for the Obama administration. It reframed the debate again, pivoting away from the focus on pressure to get movement on a transitional governing body, in favor of mitigating the violence inside the country and focusing on reaching local ceasefires. "We had gotten into this thing in Syria, and the Russians had re-raised, and we weren't gonna call them. We were not gonna intervene, and so we got pantsed. What options did we have," an official remembers. "It finally altered the bureaucratic trajectory ... What we said was we can not argue for a negative. It will not fly in blob politics, but what you can argue for is to engage with Russia, especially with Kerry. You can proactively make the argument for engagement with Russia as a means of addressing the conflict and implementing 2254."[68]

As a second official recalled:

> After Aleppo went down, some of us got together and started talking about how this construct is doomed to failure, so maybe a local ceasefire could be pursued ... so we talked to the embassy in Jordan and those that were interested in the Syria file, and so we suggested that if we are going to start on a ceasefire, maybe we should look at the south.[69]

President Trump also inadvertently gave ammunition to the Russians in January 2017, when in response to a question posed by ABC News, he suggested that he would support de-escalation zones in Syria for internally displaced people.[70] Trump's remark was actually tied to his forthcoming Executive Order to bar all admissions of refugees from Syria, along with caps and restrictions on people migrating from a handful of other, mostly Muslim-majority countries. But the off-handed statement impacted Syria policy.

"Trump used the term de-escalation zones and the Russians ripped it and took the phrase before the first Astana meeting," a US official recalled.[71] The first tripartite meeting between the Turks, Russians, and Iranians was held in late January, just a few weeks after the inauguration. The Astana trio invited the United States as an observer and the State Department did have a team ready to send, but ultimately the Trump administration chose not to send anyone to Astana. "All of the [other] Special Envoys went, and we didn't send anyone because it was so close to when Trump took power," a State Department official recalled. The United States chose to send one person to the second Astana meeting as an observer in February 2017. With little else to do, the United States chose to float the idea of a separate track of negotiations between the United States, Russia, and Jordan. "The Jordanians sent Nawaf Tell, the current ambassador to the Hague, and some guys from the [General Intelligence Directorate] to keep an eye on any talks on the south," a US official familiar with the Astana talks recalls. "We proposed our own ceasefire, and the response was: 'absolutely, there is no reason the Turks or the Iranians should have any say over the south.'"[72]

This proposal moved forward despite a flare-up in tensions between the United States and Damascus after the regime's use of chemical weapons in Khan Shaykun on April 4, 2017. As part of the regime's efforts to clear the city of opposition militias, the Organization for the Prohibition of Chemical Weapons determined that Sarin nerve agent was used. The regime attack killed at least ninety people, one third of which were children, according to Human Rights Watch. In response to the attack, President Trump told reporters gathered in the Rose Garden "crossed a lot of lines for me. When you kill innocent children, innocent babies, little babies, with a chemical gas that was so lethal," then that "crosses many lines, beyond a red line, many many lines." Secretary Tillerson also shifted his tone, suggesting that "there would be no role for [Assad] to govern the Syrian people."[73] As a State Department official remembers of Tillerson's thinking at the time: "[Tillerson's] own personal sentiments on Syria just changed after the Khan Shaykun attack."[74]

The Trump administration fired fifty-nine Tomahawk land attack cruise missiles at targets in Syria, including Shayrat air base in Syria, the location where the Khan Shaykun strike originated from. The missile strike was intended to be calibrated and to signal that the United States would not attack the regime, but would respond to the regime's use of chemical weapons when used. The cruise missile strike did not change the trajectory of the war, nor prevent the future use of chemical weapons. However, the event created a fissure within the US government, allowing for elements of Trump's national security team to dissent from the disengagement option Trump supported on the campaign trail. Despite the flare-up with the regime, the efforts to reach agreement on the south continued on.

In April 2017, a month or so after the meeting with Jordanian officials in Astana, the United States proposed the ceasefire to Russia at a meeting in Vienna. "We brought the ceasefire up with the Russians in April," an official recalled. "We made clear that we wanted to work on the southern ceasefire and that it be separate from Astana. The Russians were amenable and we told them to expect something soon."[75] The soft agreement from both Jordan and Russia prompted another round of staff work in Washington. That same month, Secretary Tillerson signed off on an action memo, which is a type of document prepared for when the Secretary is needed to make a decision. The memo asked for permission to hold a meeting on April 29 about the proposed ceasefire zone, inform Israel of the proposed ceasefire to ensure that the arrangement meets their security requirements, approve a meeting in May to get interagency approval on the proposed ceasefire, and approve a subsequent meeting in the Vienna channel for a trilateral with Russia and Jordan to begin negotiations. The action memo also included an accompanying paper, which spelled out what it would likely to take to win approval for the ceasefire. In that paper, the Trump administration concluded that the final arrangement would likely require the opposition recognizing the sovereignty of the Syrian Arab Republic, allow the regime to raise the flag in the area, regain control over the border crossing, and to resume control over Deraa city.

"The Jordanians were in lock step with this process, 100 percent. They loved it and very relieved to wash their hands with the south, and to eventually open the border with Syria," an official recalls. The document was noteworthy because it was, for the first time, an acknowledgment from the United States that the Syrian regime would have to be tolerated in any ceasefire. The Israelis were also briefed on the proposal and, per the design of the talks, Jerusalem was a de facto member of the trilateral, despite not being involved in the negotiations. The Americans would brief the Israelis before and after every meeting.

"We met with the Russians on May 7 in Vienna," a US official recalled. "We told the Russians that Israel and Jordan are on board with [the ceasefire], and we asked what they thought—and this was before we had the [policy coordination committee]—and we gave them a version of the concept. They said ok to starting the trilateral process." After this meeting, back in Washington, the PCC was held, and the implementation plan was agreed to across the US government. The timing of this agreement came as the recently appointed Secretary Rex Tillerson began his tenure and his efforts to change how the State Department does business. As part of his effort to streamline the way Department does business, "Tillerson decided to use policy planning [S/P] as the policy issuing arm of the State Department, which meant that they would issue directives for the bureaus to implement."[76] This arrangement allowed for opponents of the southwestern ceasefire to more easily influence the process and to use the Khan Shaykun response as a mechanism to force a hardline shift in American policy. This process resulted in a strange outcome, wherein President Trump was eager to end the war quickly and remove US troops and turn the conflict over to the countries in the region to manage, while his advisors sought to use the American presence in Syria to pressure the Islamic Republic of Iran, pursuant to the administrant's focus on what it dubbed as "Maximum Pressure." This policy used economic sanctions to try and force the collapse of the Iranian regime and argued that denying Tehran a victory in Syria could enable this outcome.

This schism led to a series of internal Trump administration disagreements that eventually culminated in a hasty withdrawal of most of the American forces in Syria 2018 and then again in late 2019. This withdrawal, however, would only come after the war against Islamic State in Raqqa and the Euphrates River Valley was mostly finished. "The initial direction was more or less to disengage from Syria, per the President's general instructions and campaign rhetoric ... but you had [NSC officials] fabricating 'statements of conclusions' for PCCs to reshape policy to become what it is today. And Tillerson, for some inexplicable reason, decided to use S/P as the policy directive issuing arm of the state department," an official recalled of the schizophrenic process. This weird set of factors ultimately distorted American policy in Syria, away from the early emphasis on disengagement and toward one of hardline retrenchment.

"There were big fights in State over where things were going, but most of that whole year we had the most productive discussions with the Russians in the Vienna channel that were ever had," an official recalls. Those discussions on the southwest ceasefire officially began in late May in Vienna, where the United States, Jordan, and Russia met to discuss the American-drafted ceasefire concept. Before the meeting, the United States met with both the Israelis and the Jordanians, marking the first time all three convened to discuss the southwest ceasefire concept. Before this meeting, the United States had written an implementation plan, which they shared with the parties. "This was our bottom line position. There were no tricks ... It was a serious proposal that could not be negotiated in one sitting, so the process was split into a series of technical working groups."

In the interim, the three sides agreed on the need for a ceasefire, which was agreed to on July 7. "After this, there was a series of trilaterals at the technical level, and then the higher levels, where the mapping and the monitoring center were worked on," an official familiar with the talks recalled. "These talks led to a memo of principles, which spelled out a no foreign force buffer zone, with detailed maps, and a Russian pledge to remove the Iranians, and humanitarian access and how we would jointly fight terrorists."[77] To implement the agreement, the CIA needed firm instructions to the station in Amman to halt the arming program that had continued unabated since it was stood up in 2013. The negotiations continued until October, when the three sides reached agreement on the Amman Monitoring Center (AMC), per the terms July Memorandum of Principles reached. The AMC was "based on a common battlefield picture, the collection of potential violations in a fully staffed location, manned at all times by all three nations, and which could be augmented with a variety of technical means by the participants, possibly including U.S., Jordanian, Russian, or other countries' ISR recourses."[78]

At a meeting in Vietnam, Presidents Putin and Trump officially endorsed the ceasefire and the Amman Monitoring Center in a statement that the US envoy in charge of the Vienna trilateral had drafted. The statement turned out to be the high watermark for the southwest ceasefire. As implementation slowed, inside the US government, the mood had shifted from one of managed de-escalation to a more hardline approach, premised on the notion that Washington could deny the regime total victory. This denial, the argument went, could be paired with sanctions to exacerbate economic uncertainty in regime-held areas to force capitulation. This change was crystallized in a speech Secretary Tillerson gave at Stanford University in January 2018. The speech, as it would turn out, was one of the last Secretary Tillerson would give before he was fired and replaced with his more hardline successor, Mike Pompeo, and the effort to turn Syria from a theater in the fight against Islamic State into a node in the broader effort to collapse the Iranian regime.

Chapter 7

THE BATTLE FOR RAQQA: URBAN COMBAT AND RACING RUSSIANS

President Trump campaigned on ending America's wars in the Middle East and curtailing financial commitments around the world. However, the bombastic American president did promise the American voters that he would "knock the hell out of ISIS." Upon taking office, the president sought to do both things. On the war effort, the Trump administration adopted the Obama era war plan, albeit with one noteworthy change: certain authorities were delegated to the battalion commander to speed the ground effort and to loosen the restrictions on airstrikes. The second was Trump's cancellation of the covert arming effort the CIA had led since 2013 and the ending of funding for USAID programs in Syria's northwest. These three interrelated decisions focused the American effort on the war against Islamic State and, at least in theory, freed the president and his team to explore a modus vivendi with Russia, purportedly in pursuit of a broader effort to remove Iranian forces from Syria. In actuality, the Trump administration's Syria policy was marred by chaos and dysfunction, a by-product of the mismatched intentions of the president and the men he appointed to run point on Syria policy.

The battle for Raqqa, in contrast, was a straightforward affair. It was the culmination of lessons learned from the war to date and the partnership between the SDF and the Task Force. The battle for Raqqa coincided with a Russian countermove, launched from Palmayra, a historic city that the regime had retaken from Islamic State in March 2016 during a lull in fighting with the opposition in Idlib. The United States ended up having to grapple with the Russian decision to try and match the American push down of the Euphrates River to deny Washington a deeper foothold in eastern Syria. This decision severely taxed the deconfliction mechanism built for earlier flight operations and required negotiations for a similar arrangement for ground forces. Russia was also eager to try and set the terms of the negotiations during this period and sought to cross the Euphrates River on multiple occasions, an action that the United States resisted. Finally, Turkey also complicated things with a decision to invade Afrin, a Kurdish-held enclave in northwest Syria in January 2018, just a few months after the battle for Raqqa ended.

Urban Combat: The Syrian Democratic Forces Fight Block-by-Block

The preparation for Raqqa involved action to isolate the city from Islamic State reinforcements from territory the group still controlled to the south of the Euphrates River. During Operation Euphrates Shield, the United States and the SDF had pushed south to the outskirts of Tabqa, a town on the southern side of the Euphrates River, where a large dam had finished being built in 1973. The Tabqa Dam was off-limits to airstrikes, given the danger of collapse. However, it also allowed for Islamic State to crisscross the river to reinforce its positions. The dam was also a strategic location that the SDF had an interest in taking control of because control of major infrastructure could be used as leverage, both for the internal Kurdish effort to establish governing structures to cement its autonomy.

Initially, the Task Force and the SDF explored replicating the river crossing at Qura Qawzak and using boats and barges to cross Lake Assad to the north of the dam built across the Euphrates. However, the lake was 11 kilometers wide and the boats that could be used had a top speed of 4 nautical miles per hour, so the crossing would have taken more than an hour.[1]

The operation settled on airlifting the SDF to the southern side of the river. The operation included elements from the Yekineyen Anti Terror, or YAT, a JSOC-trained, counterterrorism force within the YPG. These fighters had received training from the beginning of US operations inside Syria, relying on Title 50 authority to circumvent the 1209 restrictions. "[YAT] is the group that knows the terrain, the language, and the people. So they do a lot of the intel work, too," according to a US official familiar with the YAT program. As of May 2017, YAT was equipped much like other US Special Forces-trained anti-terror units, including advanced combat helmets, digital camouflage uniforms, Patagonia cold-weather attire, chest rigs that hold ammunition, body armor and first-aid kits, plus M4 rifles with various modifications, including infrared lasers used for targeting during nighttime raids, according to Shawn Snow of the Military Times. The photos of these fighters emerged during the fight for Tabqa, underscoring how they were part of the first wave of local forces to assault both the dam and then the neighboring airbase.[2]

The assault allowed for the United States to gain a foothold on the western bank of the river and to deny Islamic State access to Raqqa from the bridge. The coalition had targeted the bridges that had crossed the river, leaving the city isolated and besieged. With Trump's order to directly arm the YPG in May, the stage was set for the battle to begin. "The plan called for thirty thousand militia men," an official recalled. "We would go to Ankara with that number and it is it the number that we had to build up to by the end of the Obama administration."[3] The bulk of the force would be used to besiege the city, while a smaller force would be used to spearhead the urban assault. "We planned Raqqa for a year," a US official familiar with the planning explained.

Basic Army doctrine for an offensive rests on surprise, concentration of forces, audacity, tempo, and speed. In the case of Raqqa, there was no surprise, but it was important to be able to mass fires without large groupings of troops, which the

United States and the coalition did with the provision of artillery and air support to the SDF. The tempo is the speed at which the offensive proceeds, while the SDF would have to prepare and plan for where to take risks to be audacious in intent and scope. The final component, speed, was dictated by the SDF losses during the assault and Islamic State counterattacks, which were frequent and enabled by the urban terrain. "Mazlum understood all this," a Task Force member recalls. "He controlled [concentration] and [audacity] through his command and his ability to control forces loyal to him. The pace and speed were relatable to U.S. support, with the artillery and airpower."[4]

The pacing of the mission was dependent on the United States and coalition assets, but the ground operations were completely reliant on the SDF. This symbiotic partnership was the culmination of the US partnership with the SDF and underscored how both Washington and the SDF were co-dependent by this point of the war. The Islamic State had had months to prepare for the assault and set about making life as difficult as possible for the coalition to assault the city. "The main avenues of approach were rigged with tremendous numbers of improvised explosive devices and vehicle borne improvised explosive devices, as well as numerous concentrated fire points," a F-15E WSO involved in Raqqa operation recalled. As was the case years prior in Mosul, ISIS would use the urban terrain to its advantage, concealing VBIEDs and anti-aircraft artillery and shoulder-fired missiles in garages. The Islamic State would open the garage door, shoot at orbiting aircraft, and then close the door to shield them from orbiting aircraft. "Islamic State had also built a series of tunnels," a person involved in the operation recalls. "The front line would end up being porous and Islamic State would be able to get behind SDF. They would also let the SDF, in certain instances, assault a building. They would then use the tunnels to get underneath it and set it on fire, forcing the SDF to egress into sniper fire."[5]

To overcome the challenge of IEDs, the coalition and the SDF agreed to strike two points along the city's ancient walls. This would allow the SDF to push into the city, without having to drive down the main roads, where they were acutely vulnerable. The two strikes took place in the early morning hours of July 4, enabling the forward movement of the SDF. "Just after the ancient wall fell," an A-10 pilot recalled, "Raqqa went full speed."[6] As the SDF pushed into the city, an odd dynamic evolved. The city had been completely cut off, so Islamic State sought to evacuate some of its equipment across the river on boats, or send reinforcements up the river. "We would hit boats," a coalition pilot recalled. "The robots [drones] have really good optics, so we could identify weapons, even under their clothes, or they were squirters from a different airstrike trying to flee." In one surreal scene, coalition pilots described half the city as being under Islamic State control, while SDF-liberated areas were full of people swimming in the river during the day, or trying to arrange to move their vehicles across the river in makeshift barges.[7]

The battle space posed numerous challenges for coalition air forces. Islamic State had covered the streets with sheets, a cheap and effective way to prevent US drones and surveillance aircraft from seeing movement on the streets below. The group had also brought anti-aircraft artillery (AAA) into the city, placed them underneath the sheets, and further concealed them inside buildings. "ISIS did have the ability to contest our maneuver and airspace with AAA," according to a coalition pilot, "They would put a canopy over the streets, they would pull out the AAA to fire, and then cover it. It made it hard to target them." The threat was, according to the same pilot, at medium altitude and was something that the pilots had to respect, even though it was often more of a nuisance than a real threat. "The CAOC, I would say, was incredibly risk averse in terms of descending [into range of AAA]. They were not going to allow any fighter pilot to be shot down for a non-American partner. From a tactical perspective, you honored the AAA, but I was never worried it would hit me."[8] As a second pilot recalled, "We would take quite a bit of AAA, but ISIS was not a great shot, but they would still shoot. They would open a garage, role the AAA piece out, shoot at us, and then pull back in. If we could find and fix them we would take out the garage."[9]

The other challenge was the city itself and pilots adapting American tactics to the urban environment. "It is hard to maintain custody of a target in an urban canyon, to maintain a target in and amongst the buildings," an A-10 pilot recalled. "The weaponeering to destroy buildings was not in our back pocket when we deployed. [Most of us] grew up in Afghanistan and we were not allowed to touch a building. And then here I am, where if nominated, we were expected to level a building."[10] The F-15E community, however, had trained to level buildings and during this conflict had devised a way of bombing that the pilots referred to as "knee capping." This process, according to an F-15E pilot, would be to use a "2,000 lbs GBU-31 to hit the base of a building at a 30-45 degree impact angle, which would topple the building's top stories." This tactic, the F-15 E community dubbed, "was like kicking someone behind the kneecap." The name stuck.

As a second pilot explained:

> The urban fight is a huge challenge because you can't identify much. If you are working in open areas, you can see things from fifteen to twenty thousand feet, whereas in the urban area, you are relying on the guys on the ground to guide you on to bad guys. We worked with the SDF and our folks on the ground.[11]

In a typical bomb run, a coalition pilot would typically get clearance for an airstrike from 8 miles away from the target and release the weapons from between 3 and 5 miles from the target. To do this, the pilots would work with the Task Force on the ground and rely on imagery from the numerous ISR assets orbiting overhead. "We would set up in a wheel, stacked at different altitudes," a pilot recalls. A close air support, or CAS wheel, in Raqqa would typically be a constant 30–40 degree bank that would subject the pilot and his WSO to 1.5G. These wheels would be somewhere between 5 and 10 nautical miles in length. The pilots would then wait to be directed to an airstrike, or would be looking for muzzle flashes or a positive identification to roll in and strike targets. "The battle damage assessment is hard to ascertain from the air," a pilot explained. "We had to rely on the guys on the ground because of the buildings." As a WSO explained, "The bomb would drop and the JTAC would say 'good hits, stand by BDA'" and if there were fighters that were not killed in the strike, "we would be cleared for immediate re-attack on southern squirters."

In a city like Raqqa, the advantageous high ground for Islamic State was the top levels of buildings, where snipers could be deployed and significantly slow the SDF and their Task Force enablers. "This is why they were leaning towards destroying buildings and not the people near buildings," the pilot recalled. In certain instances, however, more finesse with the weapon was needed to ensure that building would not collapse, or that the fragmentation from the bomb would not injure coalition troops or SDF militia members fighting in close proximity. As one F-15E pilot recalled, "We were dropping danger close all the time." The term danger close refers to dropping weapons close to friendly troops, sometimes within 50 meters of their positions. In one such instance, just inside the ancient wall, an American JTAC on the ground with a Task Force team was pinned inside a house, 50 meters or so away from a building, where Islamic State was holed up on the second floor shooting down at the advancing troops. "We decided to drop a GBU-31(V)3," which is a bomb designed to penetrate hardened structures, "at an 85 degree angle with 35 second fusing delay. The bomb took the second and some of the first story completely out, but the blast was mitigated perfectly, frag went everywhere but the friendly house."[12]

The 85 degree impact angle, a pilot described, "creates plus shapes of frag. So you would see plus signs all over during the day. At night they would show up in the infrared spectrum There was a lot of bombs being dropped." A secondary challenge stemmed from the different coalition partners that were active over the city and planning for how each nation could use air power. "Each nation from within the coalition had their own objectives and their own requirements and their own procedures, and so resolving those amongst them appeared to be a challenge," a pilot recalled. The Task Force on the ground was extremely professional according to two pilots who worked with them to deliver bombs. "Their engagement authorities were usually better. And there was less coalition nonsense," a US F-15E pilot recalled.[13] "The JTACs were extremely professional and that was one of the more rewarding aspects of the Raqqa campaign," according to a different F-22 pilot.[14]

During air operations, the Russian VKS would also fly in close proximity to the city, usually in support of the Syrian Arab regime forces operating on the southern side of the river. The other potential flashpoint was the US garrison at Tanf, just inside the Jordanian border in southern Syria. The US presence at Tanf expanded under Donald Trump, largely because of the decision to delegate decision-making down to the battalion commander. This removed the restrictions on US troop presence in Syria that were present during the Obama administration. The garrison became a flashpoint of tensions between the United States, on one side, and Iran and Russia, on the other.

In May 2017, the United States conducted the first of what would become sporadic attacks against regime and Iranian allied forces near Tanf, purportedly in response to their probing around the base's perimeter. The first strike raised awareness within the US military about the need to create a better mechanism to deconflict with Russia in Syria. However, by this point of the war, Russian forces were far removed from Der Ezour city and were only making sporadic contact with US forces near Raqqa. Iran retained a presence in the desert near the garrison and would use proxies to challenge the United States. To manage these actors, Washington relied on Russia, who could pass words to its two main allies in the conflict. On May 9, according to *Foreign Policy*, Russian aerospace forces bombed within 14 nautical miles of the garrison, which led to negotiations with the Russians to provide advanced warning if they were going to bomb inside a 55 kilometer bubble that enveloped the outpost.[15]

The strike on regime and Iranian technicals on May 18 signaled that the United States intended to use the right of self-defense to strike targets that moved inside a 55 kilometer deconfliction zone that ringed the garrison. "This all got complicated," a Department of Defense official noted, because "there is just all sorts of 'red' actors and also a host of different 'blue' actors all in the same area, albeit with different priorities and interests."[16] The declaration of this zone created a safe haven, from which elements of the anti-Assad opposition were protected from external attack. These militias, while small in number and linked to both the CIA program and the US T/E effort, had competing agendas and different priorities.

"The Army guys all hate the [Jaysh Maghawir al-Thawra, or MaT]. They steal goats from locals and then charge the Special Forces guys for the goats they steal," according to a US military official familiar with the station at the Tanf garrison. A State Department official was more blunt in his assessment: "The MaT is made up of gangsters and smugglers, who extort locals, and is comprised of a lot of Rukban males."[17] The camp, therefore, became synonymous with the US garrison and, also, fell under its de facto protection, even though Jordan was eager to ensure that these people did not cross the border.

In June, the tensions continued to escalate around the garrison, beginning with a misunderstanding that escalated to another round of airstrikes and an Iranian counterstrike that nearly killed US Special Forces in a small outpost dubbed Bowling Green. On June 6, the United States again destroyed regime and Iranian-aligned militia-operated technicals once they entered the 55-kilometer zone. The strike, however, purportedly stemmed from an attack on a different US-supported group, the Lions of the East, carried out against a regime checkpoint that had been allowed inside the 55-kilometer zone in what was a series of tit-for-tat moves the United States and Russia were overseeing. "After we established the 55km circle, there were still regime inside it that we said could stay but shouldn't move toward Tanf, and they would have to leave eventually," according to a US official familiar with the chain of events. "After the Russian strike, the regime sent in more technicals to reinforce its position inside the 55 kilometer zone. Then DoD struck the site, against instructions, and which then sent the whole U.S. government system through the roof with anger."[18] The US-backed groups were testing the limits of the VKS, using the bubble as a launch point for attacks on regime targets in the area. "The MaT kidnapped an Iranian and then they were trying to interrogate him and killed him, and they tried to make it look like he wasn't actually dead," according to a US military official. "We called it the 'Weekend at Bernies' incident because it was like the movie."[19]

In response to this strike, the Iranians vectored a Shahed-129 drone toward a US position that had been established outside the 55-kilometer zone. The Bowling Green outpost was isolated and not well defended. "The Weekend at Bernies' incident is what pissed a lot of the dudes off. The MaT drew first blood and the Iranians and the Syrians had the place surrounded."[20] The Shahed-129 is an Iranian-made UAV comparable in size to the American predator and capable of carrying air-to-ground missiles. On this flight, the Shahed-129 fired a missile at Bowling Green, but the weapon failed to detonate on impact. "We were just lucky the air-to-ground missile didn't fuze," a US pilot recounted. After the missile was fired, a two-ship of F-15E tracked the Shahed using nontraditional techniques because of the way in which radar works and how the Shahed flies. The F-15E downed the Shahed, but during this process, two Russian Su-35 jets had settled in above the American pilots. "The Russians had hard spiked the F-15E two-ship taking out the Shahed," a US pilot familiar with the incident recalls, using the radio term for when a hostile aircraft has placed a friendly aircraft under missile lock to prepare to fire.[21]

As a pilot recalled of the incident, "We had two Su-35 spiking into us at six thousand feet in trail, and we had picked up a Su-22 at 300 feet and visual flight rules direct to Bowling Green." Running low on fuel, the American F-15E two-ship passed off responsibility for Tanf to two NAVY F/A-18 that were beginning their regular patrol, but had arrived on station late. "The NAVY rolled in on the Fitter and locked him up," according to a person familiar with the incident, "but they then watched him do a pop up attack and he dropped his bombs on the ODA guys," according to an official familiar with the incident. "The F-18 didn't shoot down the Syrian because the Russians had locked up the F-18, as well and were prepared to fire."

The incident was never reported, most likely because both the Shahed-129 and the Syrian Su-22 failed to kill any Americans. The incident, however, underscored the vulnerability of US outposts to aerial attack under the tight rules of engagement that governed US flight operations.

It also set up the downing of a Su-22 later on in the war in yet another incident involving Tanf. "After this incident, the commander on the ground was pissed. Every fighter squadron in the area of responsibility got a visit after this and he told us: 'if you think that an American is gonna die, you shoot down who you need to shoot down. Kill whoever needs to be killed.'" The change was, in the words of someone briefed:

Amazing, because up until that point it was micromanagement like you've never seen. To shoot down a Syrian aircraft, they would have to have to first dropped on a US position within 600 meters, and while he was circling back, we would have to visually identify that that he was still carrying bombs before taking action. We did the math on this and it is just impossible.

This talk, the person familiar recounted, "was senior leadership affirming that they had our back."[22]

After the bombing of Bowling Green, the United States had to devote more air assets to protect Tanf. "After the shoot down, we were flying defensive counter air patrols over Tanf all the time," according to a mission planner involved in protecting the base.

> And because it was a defensive counter air mission, we had to get the F-22 involved. So think about all the resources this was taking to stand-up a 24/7 DCA cap with the tanker tracks and everything that goes along with that. The F-22s were stationed down at Dafra in the UAE, so they had this incredibly long journey and they had to get gas along the way, so were talking about a nine hour Sortie just for a four hour DCA.[23]

As one F-22 pilot described, "The Su-35 is a tremendous airplane, and one would not be incorrect to say, that if a Su-35 is in the air, and a Raptor isn't, the Russians could have the advantage." However, the strange way in which the air war was being fought limited how US pilots could take action. "It was a tough balance … We weren't truly protecting people in the classic definition of a DCA because people were in a weapons employment zone … But we are not at war … so it was up to the pilot to make a judgement call."[24]

For close to ten days, a US pilot recounted, the situation in the air near Tanf was "like a Mexican stand-off. We were all hard spiking into each other." The Russians, however, soon made a move to de-escalate the tense situation.

> The Russians pilots made an interesting move. They started flying close to us and rocking their wings, which is a signal to show that they wanted to join up in close formation. The U.S. pilots responded by rocking ours back, telling them that it was ok to rejoin. They rejoined and spoke on [the emergency frequency], telling us that they "weren't dangerous". They told us we had a 'beautiful' jet, asked where we were from, and chit-chatted as if we were simply having a couple beers at the bar.

The Russian move momentarily calmed what had been a very tense situation, but the United States was signaling that it would no longer tolerate hostile action inside the 55-kilometer zone, or over any US position near the river. However, a pattern had emerged that the Russians would challenge American-controlled territories south of the Euphrates River, largely in pursuit of a broader political effort to limit the territory that the SDF controlled inside of Syria.

The Tabqa operation was important to block Islamic State from crossing the river, but it also led to a US and SDF presence south of the Euphrates River. As with Tanf, this American presence irritated the Russians and the regime, both of which thought that the expanding American position in Syria's northeast was untenable and antithetical to their own interests. The Syrian Armed Forces, along with the Russian air and ground forces, conducted operations in the area against Islamic

State. The Russian activities grew in frequency, following the American assault of Raqqa and decision to peel off some forces from the fight to push toward Der Ezour in September. "We had offered Tanf to the Russians during this period," a US official quipped. "We proposed this in the Vienna channel as a bargaining chip to settle on the river as the dividing line. The Russians weren't prepared to discuss this, so they let an opportunity get away."[25]

In mid-June, a Syrian Su-22, the same type of aircraft that had recently bombed Bowling Green, was flying within 11 nautical miles of a coalition and SDF position near Tabqa. As the pilots described, the American aircraft settled in to an orbit near Tabqa and checked in with the TAC to let him know that they were "on-call" to provide close air support for friendly forces on the ground. As had become common in this part of Syria, a Russian flanker had settled in above the stack of US aircraft and a Syrian Su-22 was operating in the area.[26] As one Air Force pilot described, "We had been watching the Su-22 day in and day out," suggesting that the flight of the SyAAF aircraft in that area was common. The Syrian jet was pointed at a friendly position on the ground, so the pilot decided to take action. The first missile missed the Su-22, most likely because the weapon was old and coming to the end of its service life. The second missile impacted the Su-22, leading to the pilot ejecting. "U.S., French, British special forces were 10-15 km away from where the fitter was downed," a coalition pilot familiar with the shoot down recalled, but the use of force remains controversial with the fighter community.

American interactions with both Russia and Syrian pilots were common and the line between taking action and holding fire was not clear-cut, requiring that the pilots evaluate the threat in each interaction and use force accordingly. The shoot-down was the first for the Navy since the first Gulf War, but for some in the Air Force it was an overreaction to the Bowling Green incident. "The fitter was hitting an ISIS target so it was not justified at all for the dude to shoot it down." After taking action, the US Navy jets jettisoned their ordnance and external fuel tanks and flew into Turkey to meet up with a US tanker, albeit without flying through the corridor established to avoid friendly fire accidents. The shoot-down was an example of the fog and friction of war inside Syria, but also underscored the need for the United States and Russia to fully flesh out the deconfliction arrangement for operations along the Euphrates River in eastern Syria.

The Battle for Der Ezour: Clashes with Moscow Intensify

The battle for Raqqa was an urban grind and dependent on overwhelming US firepower and a committed subset of the SDF fighting block to block to wrest control of territory from the Islamic State. During the summer, the United States was focused on the urban fight. By September, "we were close enough to the liberation of Raqqa to peel off forces to clear the east bank of the Euphrates River," according to a source familiar with the battle. During the battle inside the city, the United States widened the scope of targets the air force could hit. "One thing that we did," a pilot described, "was to begin to target Mosques." This was a controversial tactic, but the United States believed that the Islamic State had relied upon these sites to shield itself from airstrikes. "They thought we wouldn't strike them, so they were using them as a safe haven and using them to hide weapons."[27] By the end of the campaign, only hospitals were off-limits, as the urban fight dragged on.

As ISIS defenses collapsed, the group turned Raqqa hospital into a final refuge, where they were protected from coalition bombing. "They all holed up in the hospital," a pilot described of the situation in September. In one of the final fights of the ground war inside the city, "A British SAS guy got into a super dynamic situation," a person familiar with the ground battle described.

> There were muzzle flashes everywhere, people running everywhere; the SDF was only 30-40 meters away, and ISIS was trying to fight as close as possible with some pretty serious firepower ... Our British buddy was trying to manage it and have us strike, but the situation was too dynamic for the process in place, we ended up dropping within 40 meters of the SDF. It looked like they were getting overrun and the buildings we hit seemed to contain a few suicide bombers because there lots of big secondary explosions.[28]

The disagreements over US positions south of the river and the events around Tanf and Tabqa underscored the need for a more comprehensive deconfliction mechanism to govern US and Russian air and ground operations along the river. However, the DoD was reluctant to proactively engage with Russia until they approached the river and came close to US operations in Der Ezour. "The situation got very tense in August," according to a US official. The Russians and the regime had planned to break the Islamic State siege of the regime's Der Ezour military base, which remained under tenuous regime control after the city fell to Islamic State control in 2014. "The Russians came to us in August and said, 'We have this operation that is getting ready to start to relieve the siege of the city and so we need to operate on both sides of the river.'" The issue, of course, was that the United States had already begun to deploy forces eastern bank of the river, in preparation for the push to the Iraqi border with SDF. "Our response was 'no' and to reiterate that the line was the river and signal that once they got within 60 kilometers of DeZ we could talk again." In response, the Russians appear to have decided to raise the stakes for coalition air operations in the area and ensure that talks about deconfliction would continue. The regime also sought to rapidly take back territory, pushing rapidly to expand lines of control to the western edge of the Euphrates River and, eventually, to cross it to block the SDF from any further expansion.

"The Russians would fly combat air patrols on the Syria-Iraq border by the Euphrates," a coalition pilot described. "This one time, two vehicles blew a check point near Bowling Green, so we rolled in, but on the way in, a Russian Su-30 spiked us again and it was clear he was trying to escalate things." The two American jets were not pointed at the Russian Flanker, a signal that they were not hostile. On this occasion, the Su-30 angled toward the US jets, flying on a collision course toward the Americans. "We didn't have the gas to mess with him," a US pilot quipped.

But, by this point in the conflict, the F-22 had set up in a near permanent position near Tanf, so they were asked to roll in, and they came "booming in at their ridiculous speed from the west and they spiked into the Su-30. The Russians broke off, but the Raptor couldn't do much with the vehicles on the ground" because of limits to the aircraft's air-to-ground capabilities. These tense moments would become commonplace in September 2017 as the two sides negotiated a more comprehensive deconfliction mechanism to more tightly control air operations in such close confines along the eastern and western banks of the Euphrates River.

"It ended up being a bit of a race [with the Russians]," a person familiar with the operations in Der Ezour recalled. "The deal that General Mazlum made with the Arabs," the same official recalled, "was that in exchange for Arab fighters sent to Raqqa, Kurdish fighters would go down the river." The Russians, however, were wary of an expansive American-controlled zone and sought to block the SDF from any advance outside of Raqqa and its suburbs. "During the operation down the east bank of the river, the Russians started bombing the SDF. They wanted to deter their movement, so they would fire artillery and bomb positions. This was the status quo until September 17."[29]

In mid-September, just one month before Islamic State negotiated a surrender in Raqqa, the Syrian regime had tried to cross the Euphrates River east of Der Ezour to establish a foothold, in anticipation of a bilateral meeting between the United States and Russia in Amman. "The night before we were slated to meet with the Russians, the Syrians tried to cross the river, but they sucked at it. A bunch of bulldozers fell in the water and their bridges were swept away. The Russians then just went ahead and did it for them."[30] The Amman meeting was, in general, meant to carve out a more robust de-escalation arrangement, but the two sides remained at odds over the territory the SDF would hold east of the Euphrates and the regime presence in that part of Syria.

"The mid-September [2017] meeting was about de-escalation," a source familiar with the negotiations recalls.

> They came with a map and a proposal about SDF withdrawal from the river, to which we replied that we wouldn't withdraw in the face of the enemy. We suggested that we were both fighting ISIS on either side of the river, and we agreed to allow the regime to have a 1 by 4 kilometer box, where they had just crossed the river because we were south the river at Tabqa and Tanf. The Russians sorta agreed, but the proposals was not finalized until October.

During these negotiations, the tensions in the skies over Syria noticeably increased and there were numerous close calls between Russian and American pilots.

In early September, a pair of F-15E were responding to a troop in contact, or TIC, where a small group of US soldiers were receiving fire from an Islamic State position south of the river, when the Russians decided to mix it up with the USAF. As the F-15Es were responding to the coordinates to strike the Islamic State position, a Russian strike package made up of the the Su-34 bomber and a mixture of Su-35 and Su-30 escorts had taken off and were approaching the river to support

Syrian regime forces also present in the area. "We figured we were deconflicted," a US pilot recalled, in a nod to the frequency with which the two countries' air forces would come into contact. The weather that night had a broken cloud layer and Islamic State was firing 57-millimeter anti-aircraft at the Russian's aircraft. "The Russians would do this one attack run in max afterburner. You could see their afterburner and ISIS would shoot at it. It was amusing to watch," a pilot recalled of that night. However, during this bombing run, the Su-34 pointed the nose of his aircraft at the US pilots and dropped his ordnance within 1000 feet of Task Force members operating on the ground, who were working with a U-28 surveillance aircraft and the AC-130 gunship, flying beneath the fracas above. "The Russians are in the pattern and another Su-34 comes in and it looks like he is going to drop again in the same spot," a person familiar with the incident recalls.

"The pilots told the AWACS that they would head butt the Russians because they were hitting a U.S. position." A head butt refers to flying in front of a jet to destabilize it with the violent wake to deter the pilot from flying along the same route. "We were convinced that the Russians were making a mistake, but the U.S. jets were being jammed, had an older mechanical radar, and were having trouble talking with the Russian jets because of the electronic attack." As the United States flew into position, Islamic State began to fire the 57-millimeter anti-aircraft guns at the jets as they got closer to the Russian Su-34. The head butt maneuver worked and the Su-34 broke off his attack, but the fighter escort "spiked a F-15E and used his target illumination radar," which is an indication that he was preparing to fire. In return, the US F-15E locked up the Russian Su-30 and the two aircraft merged, meaning that they passed each other nose on nose at high speed. "We were holding each other's lock and we end up merging into head aspect merge, beak to beak at night, and he passed within 200 feet. I felt his afterburner rattle the canopy," the pilot involved in the incident explained. "The Su-30 is super maneuverable," the pilot continued, "but it looked like the Flanker lost sight of us because he gimbaled his radar, and our wingman happened to lock him at the same time." A second Su-30, during this exchange, crossed the Euphrates River and, in response, "AWACS told us that we were cleared to engage the Russians." A third Su-35 had placed the AC-130 gunship under missile lock, leaving two F-15Es with one Su-30 under missile lock, a second Su-30 flying over the river, and the Su-35 holding the AC-130 under missile lock, as each side determined whether force was required. During this entire interaction, two F-22s were flying over Tanf, protecting the base after the incidents in May and June. "The F-22 was doing bullshit defensive counter air patrol over Tanf and they heard this going on on the radio, and they were requesting to role to our area," a pilot described. "They could have been there in 5 minutes, but they were told no and to stay put." A second two-ship of F-15Es ended up being pulled from Raqqa, and each side decided to stand down, with each aircraft breaking off.

The incident prompted a series of calls between the United States and Russia and heightened the need to reach conclusion on a more robust deconfliction mechanism. "The initial Russian proposal on deconfliction was 15 km circle around Der Ezour city," a State Department official recalls. "We were prepared to accept this," the same official continued, "as part of a deconfliction plus arrangement with the Russians." The pace of the SDF's advance, however, moved faster than the US–Russian negotiations. "The SDF had cut these deals with Arabs on future governance," the official explained, "so they could not easily give back territory to the regime, and they were telling the U.S. that they would keep pushing down the river." The Russians, working through various channels in Amman and Vienna, came back to the Americans with a proposal that had a series of interlinked, 30-kilometer spheres that ring fenced the river, and required the SDF to withdraw.[31]

"The whole situation is dicey," a pilot described of the situation at the time.

I watch the regime shoot at the eastern bank [of the river] at ISIS targets, and then I watch SDF shoot into the western bank of the river at ISIS targets. The regime thinks that they're taking fire from the SDF, but it's actually Islamic State's hit and run mortar teams that shoot out of buildings with holes in the roof. So the regime then shoots at the SDF. The Russian's are just 5 miles away from all this. It's all messed up.[32]

The inconclusive talks about the deconfliction plus arrangement continued into October, where tensions continued near the Der Ezour city.

"We had to head butt Russians again," a pilot quipped about air operations on October 1, 2017. "A Russian Su-34 was flying at the aircraft's normal weapon delivery altitude," the pilot explained, "and then he released his weapons a few miles before his launch acceptability region, which meant that the bomb impacts were just a few miles from a Task Force position." On this flight, the Su-34 ended up crossing the river and over flying the America position, leaving the pilots on patrol that night to respond. "We ended up locking up the Su-34, as our wingman did a full afterburner pass in front of the Russian. The move didn't even phase the guy," the US pilot recalled. The situation eased, as the Su-34 continued moving north, away from the US ground positions, and continued to release ordnance on Islamic State positions in support of the Syrian regime's forces. "The Russians were losing ground around this time," a US official recalled. "They were bombing all the way up to Mayadeen, which was strange for them. They nearly had a mid-air collision with the 'mayan droids,'" a US pilot indicated, referring to the US Predator drones doing a sensor soak on the city in preparation for the looming battle for the city.

In mid-October, representatives from Russia and the United States met again in Amman to finalize negotiations about deconfliction that began in mid-September. "In mid-October we met again and the goal was to get a more comprehensive agreement that codified the river as the deconfliction line, with the Russian cut out for the small box they controlled south of Der Ezour city," according to a US government official. The US and Russians sent representatives from the Combined Air Operations Center in Qatar and from Khmeimim Air Base. These two sides reached an agreement that would allow for strikes on either side of the river with notification, which helped to facilitate an agreement and allowed for the US side to begin drafting a document to share with the Russians. "We did their staff work for them," a US official quipped.

> We had an English and Russian language version that we prepared for the meeting the next day. And when we came back, it was clear that the Russian side had been drinking all night. So they took the Russian version, barely glanced at it, said it was fine and said they needed to send it back to Moscow for approval. We sent our draft back to DC, and then we all so said 'ok, good, we are done'.[33]

In Washington, the State Department and the Office of the Secretary of Defense objected to some of the language, suggesting that the original draft could go against the law against cooperation with the Russians, instead of being narrowly defined and built around deconfliction. "The changes," a US official indicated, "did not change the Russian translation, but during the six weeks of back and forth, it held and allowed for us to get closer to the border [with Iraq]."[34]

The Russian and American aerial interactions did not stop with the demarcation of the river as the deconfliction line. "The reality is that the river is, what, a thousand feet wide, give or take, and then you have to understand that we are moving around 500 miles per hour or so," a US pilot described of flying near the Euphrates River.

> So, at basic cruise you are going nine miles a minute, and so every six to eight seconds you have travelled a mile, and then you got to think, the weapons we carry go three times faster than that, so every time you step into that jet you do your best to interpret guidance, especially when you get a Syrian or Russian that points at a friendly force on our side of the river.[35]

As a second pilot described, "The Russians would fly a single ship, usually a Su-35 near the river. And, look, the Su-35 would mop the floor with a Strike Eagle in terms of maneuverability, but we would usually have two jets, compared to their one Flanker," according to a F-15E pilot. "But most of the time, [the Russians] would just fly around inside their orbit, and it mostly felt like they were doing the same shit as us. Flying orbits over their dudes and probably looking at us saying the same."[36]

This one night in October, a third pilot described, "I was flying on my side of the river, when I see a Su-24 heading for a U.S. position on the ground. I do not even think he knew I was there, maybe they were told to go and scare the Americans on the ground, I do not know, but the first guy he ran into was me." In this interaction:

> I turned into him, and it scared the shit out of me because I am in an A-10, but I am sure it scared the shit out of him because he didn't see me; and I ended up in the more advantageous position, but I was not going to fire. He ended up breaking off and crossing back over the river.

The incident, while relatively common, underscored how agreements on paper couldn't realistically account for the types of interactions the United States and the Russian Federation would come into contact in such a congested environment.

We weren't treating Operation Inherent Resolve like a contested environment. We train to penetrate complicated integrated air defense systems and to use all our assets to do this task. That is not how we treated air operations in Syria. But then we learned quickly that it kinda is contested, and I do not want to say it caught people off guard, but it did require us to adapt tactics to meet that challenge.[37]

Negotiating a Surrender: Islamic State Leaves Raqqa

The war inside Raqqa officially ended in mid-October, after the group and the SDF reached an agreement to leave the city in a slew of chartered buses, beginning on October 12. The agreement was revealed publicly shortly after it was concluded, leading to public consternation, but the convoy that departed the city remained under close American surveillance after it left. "What happened with the busses," an official recalls, "is that the Der Ezour tribes took ownership of these people and they weren't sent to Islamic State territory." Still, over the top of the convoy, US jets would keep an eye on the buses. "I remember flying the last few days of the Raqqa campaign, when the locals evacuated by bus, and we stopped employing munitions," a pilot recalled. The convoy eventually snaked its way down the river and stopped in the desert, seemingly with nowhere to go. "The busses look like junk," a pilot indicated at the time they were idle towards the end of the Raqqa campaign. "There is a bunch of personal shit all around. We watch some guys come out, smoke cigarettes, take a pee, but they are just sitting there." The convoy eventually moved on, but the fighters that they were carrying did little to stem the momentum the SDF had at this point of the war.

Still, as the first civilians began to enter Raqqa, the scope of the damage from the air war was overwhelming, signaling the challenge the SDF would face when rebuilding the city.

"[Raqqa] was completely ruined," according to US State Department following his first visit to the city in 2017. "The SDF didn't have a lot of heavy weapons or armor, so anywhere and anything that an ISIS fighter could shoot from was hit. And that was basically the entire city." The heavy airstrikes, a necessity to enable close urban combat, were "shocking" for those that did not know what to expect before entering the city.

I would think how utterly clueless the diplomats and officials in New York and Washington were on their high horses, weeping for Aleppo and gnashing their teeth over the Russians … while I knew no one would be lifting a finger to provide a dime to rebuild Raqqa. Our crazy demand for, essentially, regime change as a prerequisite for reconstruction started to look like the worst and most cowardly kind of cop out.

The development of the knee-capping tactic, which pilots had perfected to hit the base of a building to topple the top stories without collapsing the structure, changed the urban landscape. As one official described, the ruined structures had a "sort of like a heroine lean," in reference to the addicts hunched over from an opium hit. The city, the same official believed, may have been forever altered.

> What we heard from a handful of people was that the prominent and richer families who lived in Raqqa all left for regime held cities before rebels took the city, before ISIS too over. Then more people fled after ISIS took over. So by the time we came and destroyed the place, a couple waves of militia control had already depopulated the place.[38]

As a second senior official describes, "We had defeated ISIS in Raqqa, but the city was in complete shambles. Miles of destruction." However, as the area was cleared of explosives, both officials remember people returning to try and carve out a life amongst the destruction. "The population had started to come back and, by mid-2018, we estimated that number of people topped one hundred thousand, but for that first year it was a struggle to restore essential services, clean water, and electricity. People, to this day, are still purchasing generator power, but basic services did come back."[39] As a second official recalls, "every time I went back, there were more people. They would set up shops in the bottom floor of ruined buildings, so life was returning."[40]

However, the difficult challenge of post-conflict governance was also taking hold, particularly within the SDF and the power structures between Arab and Kurds. The SDF had come to rely heavily on Omar Alloush, a Syrian Kurd that was the key interlocutor between the YPG's core leadership cadre and the Arabs it was training to fight alongside them in the battle against Islamic State. As one official described Alloush, "he had links to the PKK going back to when [PKK leader Abdullah] Ocalan was based in Syria. He is Kurdish, but he knew the tribal and familial structures of the Arabs in the northeast. He did the outreach to local tribes and families that fled ISIS and, or Nusra and regular Syrian opposition in areas after Assad lost control."[41]

During the buildup to Raqqa, Alloush was a critical part of the broader effort to expand the number of the SDF's Arab fighters. "It was three-step process, beginning with CJSTOF-S, followed by Alloush reviewing the names, and then a final review by a YPG council," according to a US official. "The idea was to incorporate groups that weren't wedded to regime change into the SDF structure."[42] The United States did not train every Arab in the SDF, only those that the SDF nominated for the program. The group that was not nominated would be sent to a separate, YPG-led training track. The YPG would also pay the salaries of the fighters, a process probably designed to keep a tighter control over the groups that fought under the SDF banner.

After the fall of Raqqa, "there was this SDF retinue, some of whom were running check points and commanding these little bands of Arabs," an official described.

> When we would visit the city, we would have these SDF minders. They were mostly Kurds, with some not even from Syria. When the locals realized that some of us spoke Arabic, they would find moments where the minders were out of ear shot and complain about the Turkish Kurds running check points, tell us how we were making a mistake, and then make some vague ask for direct support to Arabs.[43]

Despite these challenges, the prominent families that did stay in the city during the war chose to cooperate with the SDF-appointed Raqqa council. The two sides did have some tensions, but prominent families that stayed inside the city during the war did seek to work with the SDF, viewing the group as the better alternative to regime or Islamic State rule.

The battle for the city magnified challenges that the United States still had to work through. The SDF had forced Islamic State from its most important urban holding in Syria, but the war would still have to push down the river to the Iraqi border. The Islamic State's defeat in Raqqa also freed Ankara to begin its own operations to challenge the YPG in Syria, beginning with the invasion of Afrin in January 2018. The Trump administration was also divided internally over the wishes of the president and the policy that the United States should pursue once the caliphate was defeated on the battlefield.

Chapter 8

THE TIN CUP CAMPAIGN: AMERICAN DYSFUNCTION AND A TURKISH INVASION

President Donald Trump did not oversee a functional White House, or preside over a coherent policy process. Trump's aversion to organization undermined his efforts to shape US policy in Syria and to oversee a withdrawal of American forces from a region that the American president once described as "sand and death." The internal American dysfunction allowed for foreign actors to manipulate the American president and to use the United States' presence in Syria's northeast to their own advantage, or to try and stoke divisions within the American bureaucracy to force a total withdrawal of American forces.

The liberation of Raqqa was a seminal moment in Operation Inherent Resolve. The Syrian Democratic Forces would, without any doubt, continue their march to the border with Iraq, and Islamic State fighters would be dispersed into the Syrian desert and its leadership hunted by the Task Force. The pending Islamic State defeat also created the political space for Turkey to invade Syria because its actions would not detract from major combat operations. The Turkish-American spat over Manbij remained a flash point, and the two sides would enter into sustained negotiations to try and manage tensions and forestall a Turkish invasion of the city. These interlinked issues, eventually, culminated in President Trump ordering a withdrawal from Syria, but then agreeing to delay the removal of US forces after Prime Minister Benjamin Netanyahu personally lobbied the president, most probably in coordination with National Security Advisor John Bolton to retain a US presence at Tanf.

The race to secure foreign funding for American actions also included what some officials dubbed "the tin cup campaign" to try and secure Arab backing to underwrite the American presence in the country. President Trump's Syria policy was abstract and hard to define, a reality that allowed for his appointed staff to insert their own policy preferences into the process to try and mold the president's thinking about Syria and limit his options. Trump, while never fully enmeshed in the details of the conflict, was eager to end the American war against Islamic State and to withhold funding for reconstruction.

Cutting Spending: Ending Covert and Overt Assistance

From the outset of the civil war, the United States' aid apparatus was based in Turkey. This setup reflected the initial American focus on the northern part of the country, where much of the anti-Assad rebellion was located. The American aid program was divorced from the military effort, largely because the US war against Islamic State did not begin until late 2014 and did not expand until early 2015. The clandestine CIA program was active in Turkey, but that effort was kept separate from the provision of aid to internally displaced people and governing and media assistance doled out to the opposition groups that had residence along the border.

President Trump was skeptical of the American aid effort, arguing that it would benefit the Assad regime and making clear that others should pay the United States for its war effort. After taking office, the Trump administration cancelled the Timber Sycamore program in July 2017.[1] "CIA director Pompeo came to the view that we didn't want to give money to Al Qaeda. And Trump bought that," according to a senior US official. Trump's National Security Council, however, was completely nonplussed by the decision, believing that the program was a fundamental pillar of the American war effort to topple Assad. "The NSC was upset and distraught," an official recalls of the decision.[2] The schism, of course, was that elements of the NSC were pushing to undo the president's order [to cancel the CIA program], while the United States and Russia were just beginning negotiations on a southwest ceasefire. "It actually would have been nice to keep lethal support as a bargaining chip, but we didn't have it."[3]

The other pillar of American policy in the northwest was the provision of governing assistance to groups in the northwest. In February 2018, former Secretary of State Rex Tillerson traveled to Kuwait, where he announced $200 million in stabilization funding for Syria.[4] President Trump was opposed to giving reconstruction assistance, a US official recalled of his deliberations at the time. In a call with a foreign leader, this official recalls, "he called Rex a 'dummy' for proposing $200 million in U.S. assistance to Syria" and suggested that any money to "help Assad rebuild was a gift."[5] Secretary Tillerson and Donald Trump were an odd political pairing, given their distinct ideological differences. Tillerson and Mattis formed a close partnership, perhaps as part of a concerted effort to impose some modicum of order to the chaotic White House process.

Despite Tillerson's antipathy toward Trump, his tenure at State Department created the bureaucratic mechanisms to work at cross purposes with Trump's campaign promises to wind down the American presence in Syria. "The NSC would piece together a mosaic of Trump statements to suggest a policy that was quite similar to the Obama-esque status quo, which were then presented to Tillerson by policy planning for review," a US official recalled. This process became the nucleus for a speech Secretary Tillerson gave at Stanford University, designed to explain the Trump administration's Syria policy. The speech was a hardline recitation of maximalist outcomes, framed by UNSC 2254, but which also reaffirmed the commitment to Assad's removal from power and expanding the American priorities in Syria to include the removal of Iranian-backed forces.

"Tillerson was back on to hardline regime change," according to a US official. "The Secretary had flipped and, after that speech, everything stalls with the southwest ceasefire and the trilaterals with Russia and Jordan ended."[6]

The speech also underscored the necessity of providing "stabilization assistance," a reference to the necessity of providing support to different areas throughout Syria to ease suffering and try and counter violent extremism. "In the summer of 2017," a US official recounts, "we established START Forward, which came from people who had worked in Iraq and Afghanistan, arguing that up to this point we had been doing remote programing, outside of a few examples earlier in the conflict." With the war against Islamic State progressing, this official continued, "we had troops on the ground. There was a need for stabilization assistance in liberated areas, and we wanted civilian agency to take the lead." However, any such effort to bolster territory the SDF controlled ran afoul of Turkish interests and subverted Ankara's indirect control over the streams of aid being trucked across the border. As part of this effort, the United States began to explore alternative areas to work from, outside of the small 8-person START Forward team that was based in northeast Syria.

> We did a reassessment and Lebanon and Jordan were immediately off the table. Amman said 'absolutely not', and the experience we had was that the government, and the intel services, really micro-managed assistance. And Lebanon didn't allow cross border assistance. Then the next logical place was Iraqi Kurdistan, but intra-Kurdish tensions made this difficult, so we ended up setting up in Berlin.[7]

As the United States evaluated its aid program, President Trump remained fixated on the rich, Gulf Arab states paying for the US presence. As far back as December 2017, President Trump reportedly asked Saudi Arabia's King Salman bin Abdulaziz Al Saud for $4 billion to stabilize Syria.[8] "The initial plans was to ask for $2 billion," a US official recalls, "but at the last minute Trump said 'double it', so we went to $4 billion."[9] The two sides did not reach agreement during this call, but it foreshadowed a later effort to get Saudi financial support for US operations. In March 2018, the internal tensions between elements of the US government had expired, and President Trump was dissatisfied with the lack of progress on winding down the US mission in Syria. The American outreach to the Saudis, between 2017 and 2018, was reflective of the challenges bureaucrats faced in trying to operationalize the "America first" foreign policy Trump had sought to pursue. The Trump administration was riven by division and, absent a coherent policy process, various factions could interpret presidential statements as they saw fit.

In general, it was clear that Trump wanted Arabs to pay for the war effort. "There was an effort to bring the SDF into the orbit of the 'orb Sunnis," a US official quipped, in reference to Trump's first visit to Saudi Arabia and his photograph with King Salman and Egyptian President Sisi touching a glowing blue ball. "Our pitch was that these people [the SDF] are not under Iranian control, so it is a way to have influence."[10] The Saudis, this official described, would always politely demure, but never outright tell the American president no. "It felt like we were going door-to-door in the GCC. We asked Qatar for the same."[11]

On March 13, 2018, Trump fired Rex Tillerson, ending what had been a drawn-out drama between the two men over divergent policy interests and, critically, the report that Tillerson had privately called Trump a "moron".[12] That same month, President Trump spoke at a rally in Ohio, where he caught his staff off guard and announced that the United States "will be coming out of Syria like very soon. Let the other people take care of it now."[13] Just hours after the Ohio rally, the Trump administration froze the $200 million slotted for stabilization assistance, again taking his staff by surprise and forcing retroactive bureaucratic moves to catch up with the president. In the aftermath of these twin decisions, John Bolton, the former National Security Advisor, sought to shape how the United States would implement Trump's withdrawal guidance. The cancellation of the aid, too, forced the State Department to consider its options in Syria moving forward.

"The decision to suspend aid was not necessarily wrong, it was just the way it went. It was pure Trump," a US official familiar with the assistance program recalled.

> By this point, the northwest had been run over by extremists and there was so little room to operate. We had been working with local councils and providing them with heavy equipment. Over time, the number of local councils had dwindled because the council had become so weak that they cooperated with Hayat Tahrir al Sham [HTS], or they were HTS directly.[14]

The National Security Council tried a different approach after the Ohio Speech. "The NSC produced this memo that included two options for the president," an official recounted. The options were written in such a way to try and stall the withdrawal. "It was basically, you can withdraw and it all collapses, or you can keep forces in Syria and you can achieve all of these objectives, like countering Iran, defeating Islamic State, and on and on. Well, he chose option 1, which was leave right away." The meeting was contentious, according to a second US official. "No one was giving Trump what he wanted, so he just asked how long the military needed, and when he didn't get an answer, he just said, 'can you finish in 6 months' and people responded in the affirmative."[15] During this same meeting, Trump excused himself to call Israeli Prime Minister Benjamin Netanyahu, where the two men discussed the withdrawal. "The call was about the intelligence Israel had seized from Iran," which would turn out to be files documenting Iran's nuclear weapons program. "He asked how much time he needed to release that information, Bibi said he can probably have it ready in 4 months, and Trump ends the call and comes back to the meeting and says Bibi needs 4-months. This is how we ended up with a 4-6 month timeline to leave Syria."[16]

The arbitrary decision-making process was not tethered to any measurable outcome, but was instead reflective of a frustrated president committed to withdrawing US forces. However, after issuing this order, the implementation was again marred by Trump appointees trying to use the policy process to walk back the president's decision. In the State Department, the focus turned to two interrelated issues. The first, stemming from a directive from the National Security Advisor, was to secure financial support from the Saudis and the Emiratis to share the burden of the American presence in Syria. The second effort was to narrow the effort in Syria to focus only on the northeast, where US forces were active in the battle against Islamic State. "We were like 90 percent of the way done with the ground war," an official recalls, "so the backdrop to all of these crazy decisions was the near end of the campaign."[17]

By the end of April, a US official recalled, "There was a general agreement that there was no defeat-ISIS relationship to assistance programs in the northwest." The State Department was amidst its own leadership change, with Pompeo coming on board to replace the recently departed Tillerson. "[Secretary Pompeo] agreed that State should try and argue for D-ISIS efforts in the northeast or other key programs, like the White Helmets, but we could neither tie Northwest programs to D-ISIS nor have any confidence in our ability to effect outcomes given the situation on the ground … [the Secretary] agreed and the termination memo was approved."[18] The cancellation of this assistance and the specter of the withdrawal prompted a series of half-baked initiatives to protect US interests in the northeast, ranging from finding an Arab coalition to take over for American troops, to demarching European governments for more troops and funding for the operation.

"The Trump decision started the tin cup campaign where we would go begging to different countries about contributing to the ISIS fight. It got pretty pathetic," according to a US official. "At one point, the Swedes mentioned something about Syria, and then someone jumps on a plane to try and get funding. Did this result in funding? Absolutely not. This led to futile engagement with the Europeans."[19] This whole period, according to a second official, "was both funny and pathetic. There was this tracker—an excel spreadsheet—that was color coded with red, white, and green, with green being countries likely to contribute, yellow was maybe, and red was a no." However, "if you really looked hard the countries coded in green, you quickly realized that what they were really saying no in polite 'diplospeak'."[20]

Almost immediately after the cancellation of the funding, Special Envoy McGurk visited Riyadh and Abu Dhabi to ask for funding to sustain START Forward in the northeast and to keep some US aid presence on the ground. "Brett immediately went to Saudi and the Emirates," a US official recalled, and "that is how we ended up with $100 million [from Saudi Arabia] and $50 million [from the UAE]." The Gulf Arab pledges totaling $150 million were not universally welcomed. "This $150 million just appeared one day and we were all skeptical," a former US official remembers. "The Saudis, we knew, never paid their pledges. The whole operation was running on fumes; we were hoping that Trump can unlock this foreign pledge, but then Khashoggi happens, and the cash shows up the next day." Jamal Ahmad Khashoggi was a Saudi journalist, living in exile in the United States and Turkey, and after years of loyalty to the Kingdom had turned on its new de facto ruler, Crown Prince Mohamed Bin Salman. At the Saudi consulate in Istanbul, Khashoggi was applying for paperwork to marry a Turkish woman, but upon a follow-up visit he was murdered and dismembered. To this day, Turkish authorities have not found his body, but the national intelligence service had the building wired for sound, recording the murder and capturing the movements of the assassination squad during a brief stay in Istanbul using closed-circuit cameras.

"We call the $100 million our blood money," according to the same US official. As a second official described, the foreign funding created a very transactional foreign policy and left unanswered questions about who was actually in charge. "We were living off other people's money, so people would always ask: 'what if Riyadh says we'll fund these education programs, but you are going to need to buy the books we tell you', or the UAE says we can't work with a tribal group because their leadership is in Qatar."[21] The United States had, essentially, signed up to a mechanism for a third country to pay its government employees. For many, it was a low moment.

There was also an effort, primarily by people at the National Security Council, to replace US forces with Arab troops. "There was this Bolton thing," an official remarked, "to build the 'great Sunni army in the northeast' to replace U.S. forces." The proposal, according to the *Wall Street Journal*, sought to incorporate an Arab-led force, made up primarily of Egyptian troops, with special forces sent from Saudi Arabia, Jordan, and the United Arab Emirates to work with the Syrian Democratic Forces.[22] "This was all the NSC," an official recalls. "We would get calls from the Egypt desk at State asking, 'like what is going on'. It was all a neo-conservative wet dream." As another official quipped of the proposal, "I was like: dudes, if its Egyptian troops they are going to Damascus."[23]

A Turkish Invasion: The Battle for Afrin

The acrimony about the American presence in Syria coincided with Ankara's decision to invade YPG-held Afrin, a disconnected Kurdish stronghold that had been relatively violence-free for much of the Syrian civil war. The Turkish build-up of forces was slow and deliberate and, as was the case with Operation Euphrates Shield, Ankara reached out to Moscow to deconflict its operation with the Russian Federation. The venue for these discussions began in Astana, where the two countries, along with Iran, agreed to establish a series of observation posts to monitor the Idlib de-escalation zone. The agreement created a mechanism for Ankara to begin to insert troops along the Afrin-Idlib divide to ring-fence Idlib turn over to Turkey the task of "de-marbling" the oppositon". The meetings in Astana did not grapple with the terms in the Geneva Communique, argue over the terms of a Transitional Governing Body, or directly address the status of future Assad governance. Instead, the process focused on two Russian-favored vehicles, the reformation of the constitution and elections, and has stumbled over Turkey's inability to corral the opposition and strip it of extremists. This process is fraught and probably impossible, perhaps ensuring its ultimate failure. However, in the short term, Ankara's deeper ties to Russia created a mechanism for the two countries to reach agreement on the Turkish invasion of Afrin.

The American relationship with the Syrian Democratic Forces was always a high-wire act of legalese to avoid recognizing that Washington was working closely with the Syrian representative of the Kurdistan Workers' Party, a US-designated terrorist organization. The United States framed its cooperation with the SDF as necessary for war against Islamic State, but sought to distance itself from Afrin, which was under YPG control. The Turkish military's poor performance during Operation Euphrates Shield impacted how Ankara planned for Operation Olive Branch, the name given to the January 2018 invasion of Afrin. In mid-October, the Turkish government sent troops across the border, after reaching an agreement with Hayat Tahrir al Sham to ensure safe passage. The optics for Ankara were not great, given that the small Turkish military convoy was being escorted by a militia with links to Al-Qaeda. Still, the first four military outposts Ankara established in late 2017 allowed the Turkish military to effectively blockade Afrin, in preparation for the planned invasion.

Just days before Ankara was planning to invade, the coalition announced that it intended to train a 30,000 strong "border force," deployed along the Turkish and Iraqi borders, as well as deployed along the Euphrates River along the line of contact with the regime.[24] The announcement prompted a harsh Turkish reaction, with Erdogan accusing the United States of forming a "terror army" and saying that "our mission is to strangle it before it's even born."[25] The announcement was premature. As one US official described, "the Combined Joint Task Force was still figuring out the plan for the SDF's force structure and they just said too much." The gaffe enraged Turkey, but it also created a mechanism for State Department's European Affairs Desk (EUR) to wrest more oversight over US policy in Syria. "After the Border Force, there was a freak out, and more things had to be run by EUR because it fit this narrative that the Joint Task Force was trying to pull a fast one."[26] The American announcement about the SDF border force was framed as the catalyst for the Turkish intervention, but the reality is that the Turkish military had been planning for such an operation and negotiating with Moscow to open the air space to allow for armed overflight. However, the announcement could have moved up the planning because of growing Turkish concerns that the American partnership with the SDF would endure after the territorial defeat of Islamic State.

The basic tenets of the Turkish-Russian entente in June 2016 were premised on the understanding that the Russian VKS controlled the skies over northwest Syria, extending out to Manbij. The Turkish Air Force would fly along the border, but its overflight was dependent on Russian permission, commiserate to the understanding reached before the Astana process began to meet regularly. The YPG believed that both the United States and the Russian Federation would deny Turkey armed overflight, leveling the playing field and raising the potential cost of any Turkish invasion. The YPG leadership was, undoubtedly, judging the poor Turkish performance during the battle for Al Bab as illustrative of the military's capabilities, and had convinced itself that it could withstand the Turkish armed forces. As it would turn out, the YPG misjudged Russian intentions vis-a-vis

Turkey and was overconfident about its own capabilities to withstand a Turkish invasion.

On the opening day of Operation Olive Branch, the Turkish Air Force reportedly dispatched seventy-two fighter jets to strike targets in Afrin, a figure that represented 25 percent of Turkey's total fighter inventory.[27] The claim was meant to dispel the notion that the Turkish Air Force had been significantly weakened after the failed coup attempt and the purge of hundreds of fighter pilots after it was put down, resulting in a calamitous ratio of fighter pilot to aircraft ratio. The initial Turkish claim, however, was met with skepticism. "Per our estimates," a European official noted, "the maximum capacity of Turkish Air Force is 20 sorties a day, so the opening day sortie rate was a one-off."[28] The Turkish national security elite was, in private, signaling that they would continue the operation until the YPG was defeated, but were less jubilant about a quick victory than the public rhetoric would have suggested. "At this closed door meeting for European diplomats," an official with knowledge of the private lunch recounted, "the former Justice Minister had a slip of the tongue and told the audience that he expected the Afrin operation to last as long as Euphrates Shield, so about 8 months, and the Ministry of Defense told everyone that there would be no negotiations with terrorists and that they would 'cleanse the border.'"[29]

The YPG, meanwhile, was caught between the Russian Federation, the regime and the Iranians, and the advancing Turkish military. "Olive Branch put Mazlum in a tough position," according to a senior US official. "The Syrian Democratic Forces wanted to deploy [to Afrin], but it was the YPG based in Afrin, and so Mazlum had to take off his SDF hat and put on his YPG hat. He told us he had to stop what he was doing in Raqqa."[30] As such, the invasion halted combat operations in the Euphrates River Valley, frustrating the Americans tasked with finishing the ground war as quickly as possible, given Donald Trump's desire to end the war.

The Turkish armed forces had learned some of the lessons from the struggles at al Bab. For Olive Branch, the overall command was given to Erdogan and based out of his palace in Ankara, while the tactical command was given to the second army based for the operation in Hatay, near the border. The Turkish intelligence service, MiT, once again oversaw the operations of the Turkish Supported Opposition, which Ankara deployed with its armed forces. This arrangement gave less weight to the Special Forces command, which had been in charge of Euphrates Shield. "The biggest thing was the Turkish air. It just wrecked [the YPG]." Despite this disadvantage, "Mazlum was under pressure, he was saying, 'I have to support Afrin. I need to something. It doesn't matter if every force gets ground up, I have to do this'. We did manage to talk him off of the ledge, but it was tense."[31]

Moscow sought to use Operation Olive Branch to its diplomatic and military advantage in the country. At the outset of the conflict, Russia opened its airspace to Turkey, most certainly agreeing to not target Turkish jets that fly inside an agreed to area of territory to support combat operations. The YPG, caught off guard by the Russian decision to allow Turkish overflight, almost immediately began to appeal to Moscow to close the airspace. "The Russian position on Afrin, per their talks with the U.S. on this topic, was that they were clear with both the

YPG and the Turks: The key to closing the airspace is the return of the regime to government buildings and subsuming of the YPG under Assad control." This position, however, was untenable for the YPG, which retained a relatively strong hand in areas where the United States was present east of the Euphrates River. "The YPG wanted regime forces to move to the border, but not into the city areas, thereby leaving urban areas under de-facto Kurdish control."[32]

Moscow did, ultimately, force Ankara to pause its combat operations in Afrin, albeit for reasons unrelated to a broader agreement with the Syrian Kurds. In early February, a Russian Su-25 ground attack jet was downed by a shoulder-fired missile. "We assumed it was an FN-6 because a Russian Su-25 would have had the flare cocktails for Russian shoulder fired missiles, but not necessarily for a Chinese missile," according to an Air Force officer familiar with the incident.[33] The cocktail refers to the types of flares an aircraft carries to confuse certain types of shoulder-fired missiles and they are generally configured to confuse the systems that country produces. The Russian pilot did eject from the Su-25, but was killed on the ground by the militias. In response, Moscow closed the airspace of northwest Syria for close to a week, freezing Operation Olive Branch and demonstrating that it could severely curtail Turkish overflight if it chose to. Eventually, Russia reopened the airspace, allowing for the operation to resume.

The Turkish invasion also suggested that there were differences between the Russian and Iranian positions on the offensive. "[Turkish Foreign Minister Mevlut] Cavusoglu was telling embassies in Ankara that it was the Iranians that objected to Turkey's presence in Syria, not the Russians," according to a European official.[34] In mid-February, for example, Syrian regime-affiliated militias began to enter Afrin from regime-held areas. The movement of forces flying the regime flag raised the question about whether the movement of Syrian forces was sanctioned by the Russians and whether it would, again, freeze the offensive. "There was a side agreement with groups in the regime-held Zahra and Nubul, but the agreement went ahead without direct Russian control and it wasn't in large enough numbers to stop the Turks."[35] The Turkish military ended up targeting the convoys, stopping them from entering Afrin and signaling that without Russian protection Ankara would continue to push ahead with its offensive.

The United States also faced its own bureaucratic challenges after the Turkish operation. The invasion suspended operations in Der Ezour, slowing the final phases of the ground war against Islamic State. The SDF was peeling off units to travel to Afrin to reinforce its position. "There was a moment when the YPG broke away from the SDF to reinforce the YPG," a senior official explained, "and we had to flag that if they were carrying body armor, bleeder kits, radios, bulldozers, or other equipment we provided them for the ISIS fight, we would be legally obligated by the terms of the waiver to cease our partnership with the SDF."[36] The Task Force was also faced with having to manage its partner force, which was putting pressure on the military to try and slow the Turkish operation. However, the basic guidance issued was that the United States could not seek to use Russia to undercut the interests of a NATO ally, even though Turkey's actions were hindering the final phases of the ground war against ISIS.

For the YPG, the experiences of the PKK inside Turkey informed their decision-making, after it became clear that Afrin would fall to Turkish forces. "The YPG were stunned about the Russians," an informed source explains, "and they have not trusted them since." As the Turkish military besieged Afrin City, the YPG leadership remained wary of engaging in urban battles. "They were aware of what happened in Cizre," where the Turkish military besieged and destroyed much of the urban center, and killed almost all of the PKK youth involved in the fighting. Rather than stand and fight, the YPG chose to withdraw to regime-held Tel Rifaat and has since been waging a low-level insurgency to destabilize Turkish rule ever since. The fall of Afrin hardened the YPG's anti-Turkey bona fides and further complicated the American relationship with the SDF. For Ankara, the offensive emboldened its policymakers to push for resolution on Manbij, the city that Ankara remained intent on controlling, despite it having fallen to the SDF. With the battle in Raqqa finished, the United States would once again find itself embroiled in negotiations with Ankara and having to balance its relations with a treaty ally against the needs of the last phases of the ground war against Islamic State.

Talks with Turkey: The Manbij Roadmap

At the start of Operation Olive Brach, President Erdogan indicated that Ankara would eventually expand its military operations to include Manbij. In March, as Turkish forces were entering Afrin City, Erdogan suggested that "we will continue now to Manbij, Ayn al-Arab, Tel Abyad, Ras al-Ain and Qamishli until this corridor is fully removed."[37] In a follow-on speech, Erdogan directly threatened American troops, using coded language to suggest that US troops wearing YPG patches would be buried in the trenches the group had inherited from Islamic State and dug along the forward line of troops with Turkey after Operation Euphrates Shield.[38] In response to the Turkish threats, two senior US military officers, Maj. Gen. Jamie Jarrard, the Special Operations commander for the American-led coalition in Iraq and Syria, and Lt. Gen. Paul Funk, the Commanding General of Operation Inherent Resolve, visited Manbij with a reporter from the *New York Times*. During the much publicized visit, General Funk issued a veiled threat to Turkey, expanding on Jarrard's comments indicating that he was "proud" of the American presence in Manbij and "[wanted] to make sure everybody knows it." Funk expanded on this comment, saying if "You hit us, we will respond aggressively. We will defend ourselves."[39]

The rhetoric belied the vulnerable position the United States was in, should Ankara choose to ignore the American warnings and use force to oust US forces from the city. "We simply were trying to hold them back," a Task Force member described. "We would have guys drive Strykers, flying huge American flags, turning their flank towards Turkish forces as they drove. They would then turn hard south, go over the horizon line, get out and re-arrange the gear being carried, move the flag, and then do it again to give the appearance of more forces than we actually had."[40] The Turkish threats risked upending the American war in Syria, not just because the Kurds would freeze the fight against Islamic State, but also because a full-scale Turkish-Kurdish conflict would challenge the status quo that allowed for US operations with the SDF. "Working with the YPG was predicated on them not aggressing Turkey," but any such attack would entail clashes and call into question the American position in the country.[41]

The tensions over Manbij prompted bureaucratic tensions inside the US government. Inside State Department, the Tillerson-era empowerment of policy planning created a mechanism to sideline the Special Envoy to the Counter ISIS Coalition, Brett McGurk, and his dominant role in shaping policy in Syria and to push policies that were more accepting of compromise with Turkey. In early February, "Policy planning and EUR wanted to send a Manbij hand over plan to the Secretary." The proposal was "shot down hard, but S/P was pushing to totally align with Turkey, redraw areas of SDF control, create institutions with the Arab members of the SDF and the Turkish backed opposition, and cease talks with the Russians."[42] In response, a separate draft was circulated that more tightly held to the promise former Vice President Joe Biden made during his August 2016 trip to Ankara, which was a commitment to be "very specific about who is going across the river and who is staying in Manbij, per the promise to ensure YPG doesn't remain in the city." The idea, as an official described at the time, "is to craft something that appears reasonable internally, but will be hard for the Turks to accept, which will then help smother the transition ideas."[43]

The American vision for Syria was shifting away from the prioritization of reaching local accommodation with Russia, such as the southwest ceasefire, and in favor of a harder line policy to deny the regime victory. "There were elements on the NSC that were in favor of ratcheting up demands on the regime," an official recalls:

And there was this thinking that the Arab anti-Assad opposition was effective and the key to his removal. These hawks at the NSC were not happy that Trump cancelled the program we cannot mention, but settled on a "get tougher" approach of escalation. But because military options weren't on the table, their policy amounted to bellicose rhetoric on the regime, sanctions pressure, and doing anything they could to prevent the President from withdrawing U.S. forces from Syria.

This policy was broadly in line with thinking inside S/P, where "one idea that had been percolating for a while was to basically transform eastern Syria into an opposition-aligned area," an official explained. "For Turko-philes in S/P who had the Secretary of State's ear, that meant handing the area to Turkey and its proxy militias." The thinking underpinning this proposed policy shift is heavily rooted in the American experience in Iraq, where many of the Trump administration's senior National Security Council officials served as military officers. This generation of officer remains enamored with the "surge" and the problematic notion that regional problems and counterterrorism can be boiled down to empowering Sunni Muslims, so as to ensure that they are not disenfranchised and can be coaxed with political and economic incentives to refrain from supporting a group like Islamic State. "There was an affinity between the NSC hawks with a Sunni fetish and the Turkophiles in S/P," the official explained, "which continued to drive U.S. Syria policy" during the Trump administration.[44]

The Syria portfolio was also in the midst of staffing changes that presaged the harder line turn that the United States was set to adopt. Joel Rayburn, a former army colonel and an appointee to the National Security Council, had been tapped to move to the State Department to take over as the Deputy Assistant Secretary for the Levant, a role that allowed him to push for his preferred policies in Syria. Richard Outzen, a member of policy planning, was also slated for a role in the Special Representative for Syria office. These two men shared an interest in engaging with the Syrian opposition and finding a modus vivendi with Turkey to support the policy of increasing demands on Assad and trying to diversify the opposition forces the United States was supporting. "These were signals," an official indicated:

> That Brett McGurk's position and views on Syria were less influential. The military, at this point, was starting to prepare for the final battle in Baghouz and the tensions with Turkey were leading the SDF to frequently pause the campaign. These pauses would then give ammunition to those pushing the narrative that they were a bad partner and that it was time to divest a bit from them.[45]

Within this cadre, a document emerged, later dubbed the Manbij Roadmap, which sought to create a mechanism to forestall a Turkish invasion of the city, but also begin a dialogue process to replace the major SDF-backed governing structure inside the city with a council more palatable to Turkey. "The roadmap was yet another effort to square the circle on the inherent tension between our long-standing and deep partnership with the Turks and their passionately held view about the nature of our relationship with the SDF/YPG," according to a State Department official familiar with the negotiations with the Turks.[46] The February talks included an agreement to set up two technical working groups, the first of which was focused on the Manbij issue, while the second discussed other areas of tension between the two countries. This included Turkey's failed efforts to extradite Fethullah Gulen, the exiled Imam Ankara accused of masterminding the July 2016 failed coup attempt, the Turkish imprisonment of an American pastor Andrew Brunson, and Ankara's purchase of a Russian-made air and missile defense system. The problem, according to a second official, was that "Outzen drafted [the Manbij roadmap] and presented it to the Turks in a bilateral setting before it was properly internally vetted."[47] This whole effort, a third person described, "started out as a sideshow and was pursued in such a way to deliberately keep Brett [McGurk] and the Special Envoy's office out of the process" and pursued within the Manbij-focused working group.[48] After months of negotiations, the two sides endorsed the deal in early June. However, it was clear from the start that the two sides remained at odds over the intent of the document.

The Manbij Roadmap was simple in concept, but the terms being discussed were certain to be difficult to implement. The discussions swirled around two disparate issues, both linked to addressing Turkish national security concerns about the Manbij Military Council inside the city and its links to the YPG. The roadmap proposed joint Turkish-American military patrols and a process to vet the members of the MMC and to graft Turkish-backed elements on to the governing structures inside the city. As one official described, "Turkey's problem wasn't just that there were card carrying PKK members on the MMC—and there were—it was that even if we forced those members to leave, what would be left behind is a PKK aligned political entity." The Task Force, in contrast, sought to again use legalese to circumvent Turkish complaints, repeatedly arguing that the MMC was made up of Arabs, so there were no PKK members on the MMC. "The Task Force was credulous and clueless. There were people there that could barely string an Arabic sentence together." The problem, however, was that any effort to integrate Turkish-backed militias and political figures into the city risked moving the fragile frontlines established after Operation Euphrates Shield into the city. "It was oil and water. Can't mix them. It was a formula for violence, fighting, rivalry, and ultimately weak governance and instability."[49]

The text, however, was vague and each side had differing interpretations about the scope of the agreement and the pace of implementation. The US bureaucracy also had two different visions for the document, with S/P, European Affairs, and the Special Representative for Syria's office all viewed the document as a mechanism to cultivate closer relations with Turkey and to begin to replace the YPG as the main American partner. As one official privately noted about the YPG, "if we could just get rid of those rat fuckers, we could work more closely with Turkey."[50] This is why, a second official noted, "the Manbij roadmap was disingenuous because it wasn't really only about Manbij, it was about getting rid of the 'rat fuckers' completely and doing more stuff with Turkey east of the river."[51]

After announcing the agreement, it became immediately clear that the United States and Turkey had vastly differing expectations about the agreement. The United States made clear that there would be benchmarks to implementation and that Turkish military presence would not enter the city, but instead be confined to rural roads dividing the Turkish and American-controlled zones near Manbij. The text was so ill-defined that much of the implementation was left to the military because they were in charge of organizing the joint patrols and had a role in vetting members of the MMC. The military almost immediately sought to manage expectations, with the former Secretary of Defense Jim Mattis indicating that much still had to be discussed between the two militaries about how to conduct joint patrols. The first step, Mattis indicated, would be to conduct independent patrols along the forward line of troops. "Those first meetings," a US military official noted, "were designed to get on the same page about joint training for the patrols and to settle on things like which military would be in charge and the rules of engagement." The Turkish side, in contrast, framed the agreement as having a set time frame for each phase of the agreement's implementation. Turkey's former

Deputy Prime Minister, Bekir Bozdag, suggested that the agreement would need six months to be implemented and that it would result in the elimination of YPG-linked individuals in the MMC. Turkish foreign minister, Mevlut Cavusoglu, went further, suggesting that the agreement would be "replicated in other areas."

"We took out the mention of other areas [in the agreement text]," an official recalled, "but even though we did sand down some language, we did release publicly that we would continue to work on joint planning with regard to other areas as mentioned in the Manbij Roadmap."[52] The United States, in a press call, was more vague about any hard timelines, telling reporters that the agreement would be implemented as quickly as possible, but the Turkish timelines were not concrete and progress would be conditions-based.[53] For the military, the immediate challenge was ensuring that the document did not hinder operations with the SDF, which remained ongoing against Islamic State in the Euphrates River Valley. "The actual operational details have not even been discussed let alone agreed to," an official noted at the time of the agreement's announcement. "During the negotiations, the timelines the Turks wanted were watered down: things were made conditions based; we lowered expectations of replicating Manbij model elsewhere; and took out stuff implying completely new Manbij government structures."[54]

The two sides began implementation talks in Germany, eventually agreeing to host training for the joint patrols at "Site G," a Turkish military facility that the United States sent forces to begin training for joint patrols. "Site G," according to a US Special Forces soldier, "was an absolute must have before starting joint patrols. Without the joint training, there was just too much risk to let yourself die on these patrols."[55] From the outset of the military-to-military talks, Ankara sought to rotate the leadership of each joint patrol. "We just could not support that," a US military official recalled. "Our overarching concern was how a patrol would respond to a potential SDF action. We did not want to have a scenario where a Turkish patrol leader would exercise Turkish rules of engagement in reaction to Kurdish action and then shoot someone. That would have put the U.S. in an impossible predicament." For this reason, the United States demanded that it be in charge of every patrol and at all times to manage any potential situation and ensure that any potential escalation could be managed.

The Turkish military had also not been involved in joint patrols with the United States, despite both militaries being NATO members. "We were being asked to put two foreign infantry platoons together, so everyone needed to be on the same page," an official described. "It was a no brainer at the tactical level because if bullets started flying, we needed to be able to rely on everyone being on the same page. This meant that we needed to ensure that we could react to contact and communicate through military radios," an official explained. The United States and Turkey trained to these scenarios at Site G, using basic US doctrine and training concepts during the preparation. "Washington just couldn't grasp all this," a US special forces soldier explained. "They just wanted to jump into the patrols and so CENTCOM did a good job of explaining this up the chain. On the ground, the Turkish military enjoyed the training, said it was some of the best they received, and we did build camaraderie."[56]

The Turkish military had its own set of demands during these talks, including the potential use of national air assets to respond to incidents if they were to arise. "They wanted to use their own air force if they had a troops in contact, or if they felt that the coalition's response was too slow," an official involved in the talks recalls. "We couldn't have Turks flying around, but we didn't object to Turkish air support so long as they were flying on the Air Tasking Order and the Combined Air Operations Center could control the airspace." The Turks also reserved the right to detain people, per the national authorities they used for the patrols, an official described. "We couldn't really argue against this, but this was one of the reasons why the break contact under contact training was a big deal." The patrols, as it would turn out, were instructed to "break contact if there was any contact," meaning that if they were shot at, the standing instructions were to drive out of harm's way. "There was no way we wanted to be engaged with anyone, whether it be the Turkish backed opposition, the YPG, or the Russians, because it would have put the young leadership in charge of these patrols in an impossible position."

"That first patrol," an official recalled, "was in no man's land, near Sajur, between the Turkish supported opposition and the MMC controlled territories."[57] These patrols, a second official recounted, were built around "a line in the sand that the U.S. drew northwest of Manbij. All of the patrols covered the same swathe of land, so they were more symbolic than anything." The two militaries would meet at a predesignated time and spot and then go up and down the same roads, hitting checkpoint after checkpoint." Throughout this process, the United States repeated its long-standing offer to accompany a dismounted Turkish patrol inside the city. "We wanted to show them how secure it was because their intel reports would say there was terrorists and chaos everywhere."

The Turkish-backed groups, a person familiar with the patrols, would still fire at the American patrols.

> Those shots were done purposefully. Everyone knew where the FLOT was. The MMC didn't fire back or initiate fire because the U.S. told them not to and the SDF commander knew that this wasn't in their interest. It was those pot shots that contributed to the instability Turkey claims is in and around Manbij, not the current security and governance organizations.[58]

The second component of the Manbij roadmap was focused on vetting members of the MMC. In December 2018, six months after the roadmap was signed, the first list of some 170 members of the MMC was sent to Turkey for Ankara's review and to begin the vetting process. "A 250 or so person list was sent to Turkey," an official said at the time, "Turkey will now review the list and make determinations about who is PKK." The United States would then investigate Turkey's objections to make a determination about whether they would be removed from the city. During these early days, "the goal was to establish a basic criteria that both sides could agree on, and then throw the names at that criteria."[59] The Turkish position remained that these people would then need to be replaced, or as the United States argued, "just leave the city. We knew that there were considerable negotiations still to take place," a US Special Forces officer indicated at the time.[60] As it would turn out, the Turkish-American talks would deviate wildly, following a telephone call between Presidents Trump and Erdogan in December 2018.

The American Withdrawal: Trump's Deadline Expires

In April 2018, President Donald Trump told his staff that they had four to six months to withdraw from Syria. His staff ignored him. As it would turn out, Donald Trump was more flexible. He ordered a withdrawal some nine months after his speech in Ohio, which should have given the bureaucracy an extra three months to implement his policy directive. This never happened. The Manbij Roadmap was, at its core, a mechanism to delay Turkish military action, in order to allow the SDF to continue its fight against the Islamic State. For S/P and EUR, along with the recently appointed Special Representative for Syrian Engagement, Ambassador James "Jim" Jeffrey, the roadmap was a mechanism to resolve US–Turkish tensions, rebuild trust, and begin the process of incorporating Ankara into the American-occupied zone in northeastern Syria. The Turkish government had other plans. Ankara was not entirely opposed to cooperation with Washington, it just was committed to ensuring that the terms of any agreement were implemented per its interpretation of any written agreement.

The United States was methodically implementing the Manbij Roadmap, but the execution of the agreement was far less than Ankara had demanded before the conclusion of the text, and not in line with public statements about how the deal would be implemented. By December 2018, Ankara was again threatening to invade Syria, citing the lack of progress with the United States on the Manbij Roadmap. The Turkish government was also pushing forward with the threat to invade because of its long-standing discontent about the so-called "terror corridor" of SDF outposts along the Turkish-Syrian border east of the Euphrates River. In response, US forces in Syria built a series of small military bases along the Turkish-Syrian border in November, just as the first patrols with Turkey near Manbij began.

The establishment of these small outposts was designed to reassure the SDF that the United States would deter a Turkish invasion east of the river, so that the fight against Islamic State would continue. In public, Secretary of Defense Jim Mattis suggested that the observation posts were intended to monitor the border to reassure Ankara that the United States would prevent cross-border attacks and also reassure the SDF that the United States stood in between it and the Turkish armed forces. As one senior official recalled, "We had these observation posts that we put out there on the border within half a mile of Turkey. You could see the border and they had these scopes and sensors to look into Turkey, so you could see what was coming." During this time period, the official recalled, "The Turks, slowly and very visibly built up their military forces and it was obvious that this wasn't for show."[61] As this was happening, Ankara's rhetoric sharpened, signaling an invasion was imminent. In a speech on December 12, 2018, President Erdogan explicitly said, "We will launch an operation east of the Euphrates within a matter of days to save it from a separatist terrorist organization" and that "the purpose of these U.S. observation posts is not to protect our country from terrorists but to protect terrorists from Turkey."[62]

As had become custom, as Erdogan ramped up his rhetoric, his office quietly requested a phone call with President Trump. It had become a pattern that US officials had grown accustomed to. The Turkish president would increase his rhetoric, threaten military action, and then seek concessions in private from the American leader to tamp down the tension. As one State Department official recalled, "We had reached agreement on the roadmap and it was moving along, if slowly. The briefing notes for the president's call with Erdogan were, essentially, 'to remind Turkey which country was the super power and to stay out of Syria.'"[63] The call did not go as planned.

As the two men began their call, Erdogan continued to hammer the United States for the support it was giving to the SDF. During this call, the *Washington Post* reported, Trump finally relented, telling Erdogan that "You know what? It's yours … I am leaving."[64] The abrupt announcement appeared to have caught Erdogan off guard, whose aims before the call were most probably to get some movement on further talks on replicating the Manbij Roadmap in cities along the Turkish-Syrian border east of the river. Ankara intended to carve out a 30-kilometer buffer zone. Ankara had little interest in taking over the mission against Islamic State, even if Erdogan used that talking point to try and convince Trump.

"Shortly after that call," an official recalled, "there was 'new' guidance from POTUS on Syria policy, and by that, it was the same god damn guidance he has always had, which was to wind this thing down." The debate that ensued thereafter pivoted around the maximalists that still sought to retain a US presence in Syria and to slow walk following Trump's guidance, as they sought to convince him to change his mind. The other camp was more realistic, arguing that the US position was tenuous in Syria, and without American protection the Turks would invade and destroy the SDF. "This incident underscored how full of shit people were who kept claiming that Trump had given them a mandate to get tough in Syria and to use American forces as leverage." Ambassador Jeffrey and his team's position at the Special Representative for Syria office was to "meld the Turkish backed opposition with the opposition elements in Syria and turn it over to Ankara, but it was chaotic, and the principles in charge of U.S. foreign policy were still debating what to do days after the phone call."[65] Ambassador Jeffrey, an official suggested, was adamantly opposed to the option of encouraging the Syrian Kurds to reach an agreement with Assad to allow for the regime to return and to deter Turkish action.

The abrupt withdrawal order prompted Secretary of Defense Jim Mattis and the Special Envoy to the Counter ISIS coalition to resign from the administration. "When Mattis and Brett resigned," an official explained, "we had people on the inside going around and telling people that they thought things would get easier because the withdrawal would be slowed down. Joel Rayburn was going around saying that 'all we ever needed to do was replicate the Manbij roadmap east of the river'. It was like living in la-la land." Still, a plan was coalescing to try and slow the withdrawal and essentially walk back the president's guidance and seek to implement elements of the transition plan that was initially proposed to manage the tension in Manbij before the negotiations over the roadmap began. This position was in line with thinking about turning over swathes of the northeast to Turkey and its Arab proxies to bolster the American position against Assad throughout the country. "Rayburn would claim that DoD was going rogue if they moved to implement the withdrawal order," according to a US official.[66]

"Jeffrey," an official recalled, "had visited Ankara in early December, before the phone call. During this meeting, he tried to convince the Turks that the American presence was in their interests and that if they actually did invade, we wouldn't stand in the way and that Trump would probably just order a withdrawal." The SRS team had drafted paper before the phone call, describing their view on options for the northeast. The draft plan, an official described, was "essentially premised on 'ensuring stability in northeast Syria' and called for gradually minimizing YPG influence, having local elections to increase the Turkish and Turkish backed opposition role in the northeast, as well as push for intra-Kurdish reconciliation between the Barzanis and the PKK." "It was after this visit", the official continued, that Turkey really upped their rhetoric and it was this rhetoric that forced the phone call, suggesting that the meeting may have catalyzed plans to coerce the United States into more concessions. "Before the call, everyone was very nervous because they realized if Trump got the whole story about Syria and the plans to stay, he would just pull the plug on the whole thing. And that is what happened."[67]

> It got really chaotic, at one point there was this Sykes Picot map that was floated. It had these random blobs of color with these vague descriptions, like the 'Arabs' would run Raqqa, and Kurds would get Kobane and Hassakah, and parts of Qamishli. And by these Kurds, the map makers meant some blended Kurdish entity that includes Barzani linked Kurds from northern Iraq.

Amidst this chaos, Ambassador Jeffrey and National Security Advisor John Bolton sought to "break Tanf off" from the ordered withdrawal; a position that Ambassador Jeffrey also supported, and which was framed as part of a broader American effort to block an Iranian "land bridge" connecting Iran with Lebanon via Iraq and Syria.[68]

In early January, Bolton traveled to the Middle East and to Turkey to slow down the withdrawal. Speaking from Israel, Bolton suggested that the United States had attached a series of "conditions" on withdrawal, a turn of phrase that suggested the withdrawal would be slow and deliberate. "They were principles, not conditions," according to an official, "but at that time, no one was allowed to even repeat the things he was saying because we had no idea where they were coming from." This period also ushered in some internal government censorship, particularly from officials who expressed skepticism that Turkey could finish the job against Islamic State by deploying troops hundreds of miles from its border near the Iraqi-Syrian border just north of the Euphrates. "There were efforts to suppress cables that called into question whether Turkey was able or even really willing to do what Trump thought they had signed up to do vis-a-vis fighting ISIS."[69]

Ambassador Bolton's use of "condition" to describe the withdrawal was intentional, designed to shape the US bureaucratic process to slow roll the President's decision. "There was a Bolton memo outlining the expectations of Turkey," a person familiar with the haphazard process recalled. "But DoD and the intel community both said it was unworkable." Still, what emerged from this process was a set of five interlinked principles. These principles reiterated that the United States was leaving, but that force protection was a priority during the withdrawal; As the United States withdrew, it would finish the fight against Islamic State and would coordinate with Turkey on this effort; Washington would strive for a negotiated settlement to the Turkish-SDF issue, and opposed mistreatment of 'opposition forces that fought Islamic State, as well as to protect civilians living in these areas; the United States reaffirmed the desire to see Iran withdraw from Syria, and to remain at Tanf; and, finally, foreign Terrorists Fighters that the SDF had detained would not be released (although there was no concrete plan on what to do with them).

The five conditions were in tension with one another. A Turkish role in the northeast would undermine security, ensuring that the risk to US forces would grow, and thereby detract from the focus on force protection. Ankara viewed the SDF as a terrorist group and would use force to dislodge the group from the border, a reality that ensured that the principle on protecting militias that fought the Islamic State would not be carried out. Finally, the United States did not have the means to oust Iran from Syria, but sought to use the Iranian issue as a mechanism to retain troops at Tanf, reappropriating the desert garrison from a small appendage to the counter-ISIS campaign to a central node in the Trump administration's broader effort to isolate the Islamic Republic. These decisions did, ultimately, slow the withdrawal. It also signaled a new phase in American diplomacy. In the coming months, the United States and Turkey would once again enter into negotiations about border security and discuss options to create a mutually agreeable border force inside a small strip of territory east of the Euphrates River. The United States would, again, send a slew of demarches to European governments to try and bolster their presence in the northeast to take the place of US forces that slowly left the country. These efforts were never successful. Finally, Russia managed to take advantage of the chaotic American policy process, expanding its presence near Arima—the area that Moscow had occupied during Operation Euphrates Shield—and beginning a process of sustained outreach to General Mazlum to increase pressure on the SDF to reach agreement with the regime to facilitate its return to Kurdish-controlled areas.

The Russian Role: Testing the Limits and a Flare-Up with Mercenaries

The American-Russian relationship in Syria was complicated and could vacillate from intense dialogue to military-to-military confrontation. "They are much more willing to take and accept risk," a US military officer explained, "and their application of force has grown more sophisticated since when they first rolled it out during the invasion of Crimea and then applied lessons-learned to Syria."[70] As part of Russia's agreement with Turkey at Astana, the two powers sought to deny the United States overflight of Idlib, and to hand the task of managing the insurgency to Ankara in 2017. The United States chose not to test this de-escalation zone directly, but never did stop striking targets in Idlib. "We use all sorts of intelligence to find high value targets and then we would use stand-off munitions, like the JASSM, to strike them." The Joint Air-to-Surface Standoff Missile is a long-range cruise missile that can fly semi-autonomously along pre-programed waypoints. "The missile would fly along these waypoints, making turns along the way so that when it entered Idlib it was flying in a way to mask its radar signature," a person familiar with the strikes explained. "We would take the shot from east of Hassakah or from inside Iraq. The Russians would complain that we were breaking the agreement, but we would counter that we didn't overfly Idlib."

"The JASSM strikes," a USAF officer recounted, "were to just to tell them that we could still do this and there was nothing they could do to stop us."[71] But, as a person familiar with the targeting process explained, one major limiting factor was high-level bureaucratic concerns that if the strikes were too frequent and Russia complained too loudly, it would run afoul of President Trump's personal affinity for Vladimir Putin. "We conducted these strikes in a way that would not rub the Russian's noses in it," an official recalled, "and our targets were bad dudes; that we both agreed were bad dudes. We didn't take credit for them. But we did want to make them feel as small as possible."[72]

The Russians were also eager to test the United States in Der Ezour along the Euphrates River. In the skies over Der Ezour city, the USAF and the VKS engaged in some of the most aggressive confrontations of the war. In February 2018, the Russian private military contractor, the Wagner Group, tested the ground deconfliction agreement by looking to expand the Russian presence east of the river. The United States retained a small garrison near the Conoco Oil plant. As the Russian build-up began, the United States dispatched Delta Force to the area to augment the Special Forces and Army Rangers already in place, and to bolster any potential defense of the US position. "The Delta guys were sent there," a person familiar with the incident explained, "and they were looking at river crossings." As it would turn out, the Russian force crossed at the crossing point that the US had agreed to in the talks over deconfliction. "They launched this operation from that same 1km by 4km river crossing that they had carved out in 2017."[73] The Russians got pretty close and we were talking to them on the deconfliction line. "The first call," the official continued,

> was just explaining to them what we were seeing. We were seeing artillery and a Multiple Launch Rocket System throwing rockets around, and so on the second call we asked again: Is that you? The Russians said it wasn't us. We reiterated that the next call would be to tell them that we are taking action. The Russians again responded it was not them.

The trigger, as it would turn out, was that the Wagner Group began to bracket fire the American outpost with artillery, which refers to using spotting rounds to calibrate the aim to then walk the shell on to the target. "Once the rounds fell in front and back of the guys, we knew we were being bracketed and it was clear that this was self defense. At that point, a radio call went out: 'cleared hot' and everything just started to evaporate."[74]

The American response included F-15E Strike Eagles, AC-130 Gunships, attack helicopters, and armed drones. "The robots were winchestered," an Air Force officer quipped, using slang to describe how the armed drones flying overhead ran out of missiles. "The controlling JTAC was out of breath from doing so many 9 lines." During the fracas, "Russian Su-30s launched but were held far away by U.S. pilots who had targeted them, but had held fire as the other assets were striking targets on the ground." The Su-30s were pinned down, an official explained, "because they were spread on azimuth," meaning that each aircraft was flying directly off the wing of the other at a range of between 500 and 3,000 feet, which, because of "bleed over" from the radar, makes it easier to place under missile lock.

"The Russians didn't have any surface to air fires," the official continued, so with the Su-30s pinned down there was little to stop the American onslaught.[75] The engagement, an official explained, "was not quick, but it was decisive and once it was green lit there was little left on their side." The fight ended when the Russians called the United States on the deconfliction line, asking for a ceasefire for humanitarian reasons. "They called back and asked to collect the bodies on humanitarian grounds across the river. We stopped, but told them that if there were any further moves towards U.S. troops it would start again."[76]

The Wagner Group reportedly lost over 200 men in the fight.[77] "As this was going down, we got a Russian speaking individual crying and the quote was the Americans are beating us like children. That quote become pretty legendary." To this day, it remains unclear why these forces were sent across the river. The explanations range from a private act to try and wrest control over Syrian oil fields to an official decision to try and use nonaffiliated forces to try and force the Americans to abandon a facility Moscow coveted. Whatever the case, the assault failed, and the tenuous order that prevailed in eastern Syria continued.

This order, however, would soon come to an end. After months of slow rolling the ordered withdrawal, President Trump would again push for the rapid implementation of his guidance. Although, in the next instance, the catalyst was a looming Turkish invasion that Ankara intended to carry out to finally carve out a contiguous Turkish control zone along the border with Syria. The Turkish invasion changed the American mission in Syria, pushing the United States to withdraw under fire, and leaving behind a smaller number of troops focused on retaining an American foothold in the eastern part of the country, and working through both the CIA and the Task Force to hunt for dispersed Islamic State targets.

Chapter 9

FINISHING THE FIGHT AND MANAGING WITHDRAWAL: THE AMERICAN WAR ENDS IN SYRIA

President Trump's December 2018 telephone call with President Erdogan upended American policy in Syria and forced the United States to grapple with the need to withdraw, while also still trying to ensure that the battle against Islamic State was completed. The final battle was in Baghouz, a small village on the northern side of the Euphrates on the Iraqi-Syrian border. As the US military prepared for this final battle, American diplomats continued to debate how best to secure American interests in Syria's northeast. The resignations of Secretary of Defense Mattis and the Special Envoy McGurk entrenched within the State Department a cadre of bureaucrats, committed to retaining a US presence in the northeast of Syria and working more closely with Turkey to ensure that Bashar al Assad did not retake areas the SDF had cleared of Islamic State. This effort fell flat, but dominated the American diplomatic effort throughout much of the Trump administration's last two years in power.

The United States and Turkey never did overcome their disagreements in Syria, despite serious efforts to replicate elements of the Manbij Roadmap east of the river. Trump never did oversee a complete withdrawal. The general incoherence of effort, however, did make life more difficult for US forces, as their mission was reappropriated from fighting Islamic State alongside the SDF to retaining an American foothold to safeguard Syrian oil facilities, a legally tenuous mission, and one that appears built around a separate Trump campaign pledge to "take the oil" from countries the United States occupies, and dressed up to ensure that not all troops were withdrawn. This mission, however, failed to deter Turkish action and Ankara's invasion of the northeast upended the hard-fought deconfliction mechanism reached with Moscow, and allowed Russian and Syrian troops to cross east of the river and to occupy Manbij. The result has been tense US-Russian interactions on the ground, while Turkish troops occupy a codified box of territory seized during Operation Peace Spring. For the Task Force, the mission has also shifted, and its operators, working with the CIA, hunted Islamic State leadership. This effort did, eventually, lead to the killing of Islamic State leader, Abu Bakr al Baghdadi, in a raid near the Turkish border in Idlib, and again unlocked American overflight of Idlib for armed drones.

The Battle for Baghouz: Sensor Soaks and Missing People

The final battle against Islamic State centered on Baghouz, a town that group used as a way station as it traversed between Iraq and Syria. The Islamic State, by this point in the war, had been badly beaten and its leadership was in disarray. Nevertheless, the last six months of the ground campaign went far slower than the United States had assumed. The war's final battle was indicative of the broader challenges the United States faced throughout the conflict. Islamic State proved adept at avoiding American sensors, using the surrounding terrain to its advantage and remaining indoors with women and children to deter air strikes. The SDF was also exhausted from its years of fighting, and was eager for offensive operations to wrap up, so that it could transition to basic governance and give its fighters a rest. Finally, the SDF's Kurdish core, the YPG, remained politically problematic and the United States remained wary of any banner being used that didn't feature the SDF logo, lest they invite further Turkish condemnation and risk more pronounced US-Turkish diplomatic efforts that could complicate the ground war.

"During the lead up to the final battle in Baghouz, there were like six small towns in the surrounding area that were going super slowly and the government was getting frustrated," an official explained. "Eventually, Mazlum had to send in more YPG members to finish the fight because the Arab SDF members just were not going fast enough."[1] The basic battle plan had different areas assigned to different Arab-majority militias within the SDF, an official recalled, and each of these militias would interface with an American advisor that worked with a small, US and SDF staffed Joint Operations Center, or JOC, at the Omar Oil field. The JOC had a small dynamic targeting cell, much like the operation based at Inclirk for the Marea line push, where US and SDF personnel would interface with the orbiting assets to help direct the air campaign. "The U.S. was always pushing to use local guys to spearhead the fight," an official recounted, "but if it got gnarly, you would surge YPG."[2]

Despite being pushed from all its strongholds, the Islamic State remained a potent adversary, using explosive-laden vehicles to destroy the SDF's heavy equipment and earth-moving equipment. "The SDF's bulldozers were getting chewed up by these 'Mad Max' type vehicles blowing everything up. At one point, the Iraqi Counter Terrorism Service nearly jumped into the fray, but the U.S. quickly stepped in and asked them no to get involved because there was a concern that Iranian linked Shia militias would also get involved." The final variable was that throughout this campaign the Turkish government continued to threaten to invade Syria, splitting the SDF into factions to defend the border and to continue the fight down near the Iraqi border.

Despite these challenges, the battle was poised to begin in February and the remaining Islamic State fighters were destined to die in battle, or be captured and held in SDF-run prisons. The city was surrounded in February 2019 and the battle was expected to go quickly. However, as it would turn out, the battle turned into "a very slow strangle because Islamic State was packed into a small area," an official recalled. "The SDF didn't want to kill everyone in the city and undermine its credibility with the local population."

As had become routine, the city had been "soaked" with sensors before the battle began, but even with all of the assets thrown at the fight, the estimates about the numbers of people inside the small city turned out to be off by a large margin and the battle moved more slowly than expected. "Baghouz had unfavorable geography," a person familiar with the ground campaign explained. "The river and the surrounding cliffs and caves gave the fighters respite" and allowed for them to hide from orbiting sensors trying to get a grasp of just how many people were left in the city.[3] The other challenge was that the estimates of fighters and civilians were off by a magnitude of thirty. "We thought there were 2,000 people in the city, but it turned out there was 60,000 plus."[4] Islamic State, an official explained, had learned to surround itself with civilians. "We would see them move between caves," an official explained, "but quite often they would go out with women and children in tow, so we would not strike."[5]

Despite all the technology that was brought to the fight, the United States never did truly have a grasp of how many fighters were on the battlefield. Each agency, an official explained, had different methodologies for counting, so the estimates would vary widely. "Baghouz was a slog," a Task Force member described. "The population appeared to be mostly civilians enmeshed with Islamic State fighters, and the SDF believed that the women filtering out of the city were just as committed to the caliphate as the men that stayed behind." The United States was faced with waves of people leaving the city, where they would surrender to SDF forces. "We didn't have enough prisons for these people, precisely because we didn't know that there were this many still inside." The Marines were in charge of security and, as a person involved in operation described, "The Marines had no idea what they were witnessing. The people coming out of that city were teenagers and kids. Some of the women were wearing suicide vests. There were a lot of Uyghurs. Some Kazakhs and some Uzbek too, but the largest foreign populations were Russian and Turkish."[6]

The process entailed that these people would move through a series of checkpoints, beginning with a basic search, and then to a place where their basic information was recorded. After this, they were shepherded to a third location for biometric screening. They were then segregated by gender, with children remaining with women, and each being sent to different detention facilities. "It was extremely impressive in terms how to manage sixty-to-seventy thousand people and not losing track of them completely on the fly. But the people that were coming out were extremely destitute and it was hard not to feel some sympathy for them." US personnel would, at points along the way, talk to these people. The women, in particular, suggested that they had been brought to Syria against their will, traveling to Turkey for a family vacation, only for them to then end up in Gaziantep or Hatay, where they would cross to join Islamic State. "A lot would say that they did not necessarily want to leave their home countries, but that their husbands had made the decision and they had to follow. In some cases, they were tricked and told that they were going on vacation."

> We initially thought this was going to be a few thousand hard core guys and all of a sudden we have 100,000 men, women, and children to deal with, and the prison capacity at that time was already maxed out. It was so unexpected that we had to figure out what to do. There was no plan. How could there be. We had no idea.

The women and children, it was decided, would be sent to the Al-Hol refugee camp. "These people," a senior official described, "were put in vans the Self Administration had contracted, and the vans transported some seventy-thousand civilians up to the Al Hol camp."

The military aged males were sent to a slew of recently upgraded buildings to detain them. "We were close to max, but then all of a sudden we had to figure out what to with all of these other people, many of them were foreign." The existing SDF prisons were operated with assistance from the Task Force, which assisted with prisoner intake in ensuring that they were taken care of. "We did the biometric enrollment, and assisted with the provision of medication for guards and prisoners, jumpsuits and clothing, as well provided the money to modify buildings, cameras, bars, locks and riot gear, including the helmets, shields, and shot guns." The Task Force also provided water trucks and air conditioners, guard towers, and oversaw the training.[7]

The United States could not, by law, use the funds Congress appropriated for the Train and Equip effort for the construction of new buildings. The funding could be used to improve existing structures, or repair or rebuild damaged buildings. "The make shift prisons that house ISIS detainees," a person familiar with detainee operations recounted, "were identified by the SDF and built up with American funding." The British, an official explained, had a different set of restrictions and could not use funding in ways similar to the United States. They could, however, "build new structures, but were leery of building a prison in Syria that could one day turn into Assad's next torture chamber, so they repeatedly proposed to the SDF to build temporary structures."[8]

The Task Force was pleading for help from the State Department; specifically the Bureau of International Narcotics and Law Enforcement Affairs, or INL. This bureau within the State Department's core competency is to assist with the management of competent and legitimate criminal justice systems, including detention and imprisonment issues. "INL just wanted to stay out of Syria. There were people trying to get them involved for years, but they had no authorities to work with sub-state groups like the SDF. The Trump administration wanted them working in Latin America, and they had had a terrible time in Iraq training the national police between 2003-2011."[9] As a result, the United States never did arrange for a civilian entity to assist with prison management. The Task Force eventually turned over its oversight of the prisons to the Special Operations Joint Task Force, its Special Forces cousins, at the end of November 2019.[10]

Baghouz fell to the SDF in late March, ending what the Department of Defense dubbed the ground war against Islamic State. This verbiage, while not official, was intended to signal that the group's ground soldiers had been rendered militarily ineffective, but that the allure of the now defeated caliphate would likely endure and an insurgency could form to challenge the SDF. The final ceremony to mark the fall of the caliphate, however, exposed the continued tensions inherent to the American partnership with the SDF and its core leadership cadre, the YPG. In the ceremony to mark the fall of Raqqa, the SDF had unfurled a large picture of Abdullah Ocalan, inviting criticism from Turkey and making American officials uncomfortable with the group's iconography.

The day of the ceremony the stage that had been set up was flanked by two large YPG and YPJ flags, forcing the Americans to warn the group that if they didn't take them down, the senior US officials slated to attend would not show up. "The YPG were very upset," an official explained. "It was like, after all this, we still could not recognize them." The US officials eventually threatened to cancel American military and diplomatic participation at the ceremony, prompting the SDF to cover the YPG and YPJ flags with the SDF flag, but because of the difference in colors, the two militia flags continued to show through the SDF flag draped over them. This led to another stand-off and, eventually, to the complete removal of the two flags and the replacement of the entire backdrop.

Coordinating with Turkey: From the CJOC to Peace Spring

As the final battles against Islamic State were taking place, the US diplomats in charge of Syria remained fixated on trying to manage the ordered withdrawal of American troops from Syria. In early 2019, as Ankara ramped up its hostile rhetoric, the United States sought to manage the threat of a Turkish invasion, while creating conditions to allow for troops to remain in Syria for the foreseeable future. These plans were, in some respects, an effort to align the divergent views about the American role in the civil war. President Trump had, since the Ohio speech in March 2018, directed his staff to withdraw from Syria. This staff, however, would take advantage of the lack of bureaucratic follow through and seek to mold these words into an outcome that fit with their preferred outcomes for the Syria conflict.

"There were actors," an official explained, "that claimed that the Department of Defense was completely rogue whenever they moved to implement the withdrawal orders." In place of the withdrawal, the Special Representative for Syria office began to entertain plans to replace US forces along the border, and to do so with militia elements that could be acceptable to both the SDF and the Turkish government. The idea was to create a de facto buffer zone along the border, designed to push the SDF off the Turkish-Syrian border and to replace them with fighters that Ankara would feel more comfortable with. The United States, in turn, could, then vacate the area, but still remain in the country with smaller numbers of troops and provide air protection for the northeast, extending a no-fly-zone over the US- and Turkish-controlled areas in Syria.

In mid-January, following yet another phone call with President Erdogan, Trump tweeted that he would devastate Turkey if it attacked the SDF, but also indicated that the two countries would work together on the creation of a "20 mile safe zone" along the border. The Turks had, hitherto, pushed for a 30-kilometer safe zone along the border, modeled on the basic outline of the Manbij Roadmap. In response to the president's tweet, the Turks then increased their ask to 32 kilometers, or 20 miles, of territory. The terms of the debate, therefore, had shifted. Washington was no longer in the position of trying to deter a Turkish operation, as had been the case with the establishment of the Observation Posts in November 2018 and with the Stryker patrols along the border. Instead, Washington and Ankara were now negotiating how to allow Turkish or Turkish allied forces into an area the SDF controlled.

In January 2019, Ahmed Jarba, the leader of militia-for-hire, proposed such a plan to US officials at a series of meetings in Istanbul. Jarba had sought to profit off the war by allying his small cadre of fighters with the winning side, deploying forces with the SDF during the battle for Raqqa, only for them having to be removed for incompetence as the fight was ongoing. "He's an influence pyramid schemer. He tries to secure some bit of interest in some initiative of his, then goes to someone else to use that to generate more interest in it and so on and so forth," according to an official who interacted with him.[11] During this meeting, Jarba proposed that his forces monitor the border from a series of garrisons. In a paper drafted for US officials, the Jarba plan called for fifty-seven observation posts placed along the border between the towns of Ras al Ayn and Tel Abyad. To staff these posts, he argued, there would need to be twenty individuals per shift and three shifts per 24 hours, totaling 3420 militia men. An additional 180 men would be needed for logistical support, for a total of 3600 men that the United States would then have to train and equip and pay their salaries. Jarba, an official explained, "was asking for training on mobile and fixed patrols, investigations and studies, surveillance, information evaluation, source recruitment, and border crossing security in Tel Abyad, among others. None of this was feasible, but there was this thinking inside the U.S. government that these types of counter-ISIS alternatives were never seriously pursued, so the exercise had some value." General Mazlum did give indications that he would be amenable to some sort of compromise, so long as Turkish troops were kept out of the buffer zone. "He would tell us he was open to some small stuff," an official explained, "so long as the U.S. stayed."[12]

During these early talks, the United States and Turkey still remained involved in implementing the Manbij Roadmap. The vetting process had continued. Of the 170 or so names Turkey had been sent, Ankara had reviewed sixty-seven by mid-January 2019, and had deemed all sixty-seven to be a threat and demanded that they leave Manbij. The United States, in turn, reviewed the Turkish dossiers on the sixty-seven names and concluded that twelve were too closely linked to the YPG. That list, then, was shared with Mazlum, who objected to two of the twelve names, leading to the removal of 10 people from Manbij.[13] "We presented the list to Mazlum and he was not happy with it. Mazlum talked to his advisors and they were less happy, but then he made the decision to remove them ... these people were based mostly in Ain Issa, and they were not happy that they had been forced out of Manbij."[14] The tensions around Manbij did not subside, but were engulfed in the broader Turkish effort to carve out its own zone east of the Euphrates River. As part of this effort, Ankara would routinely cite the pace of implementation as a problem, and as a promise that the United States had broken and needed to fulfill to ensure harmonies relations.

Between February and August, the United states and Turkey stood up what was dubbed the safe zone task force, a bilateral mechanism to discuss sharing security responsibilities in territory east of the river. As one official described it, "there was this period of high level meetings to address key issues, and it was these meetings that laid the foundation for the 'Security Mechanism' agreement in August 2019."[15] From the outset of negotiations, the two sides differed on the depth of the proposed zone along the border. The Turks were pushing for 32 kilometers deep that the Turkish armed forces would control in partnership with the United States, while the United States had settled on a 15-kilometer deep zone under control of a third party, perhaps with small Turkish observation posts nestled inside this area. "During these meetings," an official explained, "we would table non-papers to try and reach a common understanding on the proposed zone, but the Turks wouldn't ever table a non-paper and they wouldn't budge from their maximum positions."[16] The Turkish position, in contrast, was to bring in large numbers of its own forces to control the entirety of the zone. As a US official explained, "They didn't present the zone as being under their control. They said they wanted to go in with us. But the forces that they were considering bringing in only meant one thing: Turkish control."

To try and manage this issue, the United States continued to try and find a third-party alternative to deploy along the border, allowing for Washington to withdraw some troops and to signal to the Turks that the Kurds would be pushed back from the border. This effort was intended to forestall a Turkish invasion without actually having any permanent Turkish military presence in the proposed buffer zone. In mid-February, the United States demarched its European allies, asking for troop contributions. As one European official explained to the author, "you guys demarched us yesterday [April 2, 2019] and during this demarche, the U.S. diplomats apologized because we were in the second group, and not the first group of countries you all asked for to send troops to Syria." The first US request was sent on February 24 to France and the United Kingdom, which had troops deployed in Syria already, and to other members of the broader counter-ISIS coalition. "The French agreed to stay," an official explained at the time, "but all the others demurred or asked for more information" to delay actually telling the Americans no. The European countries Washington was demarching required American logistics and command and control to sustain their presence, so any non-US force inside the buffer zone would require some American component to assist with targeting and logistics. The Europeans had been left in the dark and not consulted before Trump announced the withdrawal of US forces in December 2018, so there was considerable irritation at not being consulted about an issue that was of profound importance to their national security.

The high numbers of European citizens that traveled to Syria made the risk of returning fighters more acute. For France, in particular, the attacks in Paris underscored the potentialities of returning foreign fighters and the ability to wage attacks in their country of origin and within the European Union. The chaotic American decision-making process raised the risk for much of Europe and undermined trust in Trump's commitment to sharing the burden on managing the threat from Islamic State after the collapse of the caliphate. Tensions with Turkey were also rising and Ankara's intransigence, first on border security, and then on acquiescing to the SDF presence in the northeast because the group is critical to suppressing the ISIS threat. For these reasons, there was deep skepticism about a large Turkish role in the northeast, but also profound disappointment about the haphazard decision-making process that led to the disorganized way the American withdrawal was handled.

During the negotiations for the safe zone, Ankara again began to build up forces along the border to signal that they were prepared to invade if the talks broke down. The tensions increased during the summer, culminating in Erdogan threatening to invade, indicating in a speech, "We entered Afrin, Jarablus, al-Bab. Now we will enter the (area) east of the Euphrates."[17] The threats were intended to hasten American acquiescence to the Turkish demands. As one US official described, "The Turks, throughout this process, they never budged, so by definition what was happening is that our position was getting closer to their position."[18]

For many in the US government, the concern was that Ankara was going to invade, regardless of the effort to stop it. Therefore, it was in Washington's interest to try and shape the Turkish role in the northeast. This effort was, then, split between bureaucratic factions. There was a faction that saw Ankara's role as a net positive for the United States and a benefit to the broader effort to challenge Assad, push back against the Russian role in the country, and pressure Iran. For the second faction, the intent was to manage risk for US forces on the ground and to try and reset bilateral relations, which would have post geopolitical benefits for NATO. A third faction argued that Ankara needed to be actively deterred and that Ankara should be warned of significant costs should it risk the lives of US forces.

The risk grew so acute that, just days after Erdogan warned of invasion, the two sides reached a basic agreement to conduct joint patrols east of the river and to stand up a combined joint operations center, or CJOC, in the Turkish city of Sanliurfa. These patrols would take place between Ras al Ayn and Tel Abyad and extend from 5–14 kilometers deep into Syria territory. The depth was determined by the road the two sides would patrol and was relatively arbitrary, but nevertheless symbolically important because the agreement enabled a Turkish presence east of the river. "The agreement in August was never actually finalized," an official explained. "There was still bracketed text, but then it was dumped on DoD to implement quickly."[19] The agreement also entailed concessions from the SDF. The group was required to remove fortifications from the Turkish-Syrian border and withdraw forces from the zone, ceding de facto control to the United States and Turkey.

The rapid implementation stemmed from ongoing disagreement about the Manbij Roadmap and the inability of the two sides to ever settle on a common understanding of the agreement's text. "In an ideal world," an official indicated, "we would have had a buttoned down and rigid implementation agreement, but the Turkish threats prevented this. The goal was just to stop an invasion."[20] The urgency led to an agreement to quickly implement the unfinished agreement. "Implementation was put on turbo charge," an official quipped. Ankara kept up the pressure during this time period, with President Erdogan announcing over and over again that he had imposed an end of September deadline to implement the agreement and absent full compliance on Turkey's terms, the Turkish military would invade. The deadline coincided with the United Nations General Assembly meeting, where Erdogan would speak and try and meet President Trump to reach agreement. "Our goal was to tie them up in process," a senior official explained, "because every day that we were talking was another day that they stayed out of Syria."[21]

The first such effort to implement the agreement was to stand up the CJOC, but even that facility was marred by mismatched expectations. Ankara viewed the agreement as a stepping stone toward instituting its vision for the northeast.

> There were two issues, right from the get go that we had to grapple with: The first was the lack of U.S. forces in the country. The whole agreement happened at a time when forces were leaving the country, or tied up in the counter ISIS fight elsewhere, so we didn't have many to spare. The other was that the Turkish government did not allow the U.S. to stage forces on Turkish territory. We rehearsed in Turkey, but that meant we had to go back and forth every day.[22]

The agreement was dubbed the "Security Mechanism," but Ankara's willingness to countenance a US presence on its territory had waned since the Manbij Roadmap. "We requested that they consider expanding existing training sites and they did offer something in Urfa, but it couldn't support what we needed and they showed no willingness to expand it." The American and Turkish militaries, then, would meet a preplanned point along the border. The Turkish military would remove a section of border wall and drive across and meet up with their American counterparts. For the joint helicopter patrols, the two sides would meet in the air and patrol together along the preplanned road. The exception, an official explained, was with the first patrol. This joint helicopter flight was heavily photographed and had senior leadership involved. "We met in Turkey for that first patrol, but the subsequent ones met in Syria."[23]

The Security Mechanism also included a provision for Turkish overflight of the northeast, so long as they were part of the Air Tasking Order. The Turkish Air Force had not been part of the coalition's ATO since November 2015, when they were removed after shooting down the Russian Su-24. "It was a big step to bring them back in," an official explained.

> The unilateral Turkish Air Force flights were pissing everyone off, so the CJOC worked hard to coach them back on to it ... they could specify the type of assets and the types of missions they would like to support, just as long as they

supported the rules of engagement. The first on the ATO was their surveillance flights, followed by their F-16s.[24]

This arrangement formalized Turkey's overflight of the area with surveillance drones, a practice that Ankara had used to map out the SDF fortifications in preparation for offensive operations. "The Turks had great maps," an official explained, "they knew exactly what was going on and people who were suggesting otherwise were kidding themselves."[25]

From the outset, there was disagreement about whether the SDF was adhering to the letter of the agreement about the removal of fortifications. The Task Force moved quickly to remove fortifications and berms, broadcasting much of the work on social media to underscore that the two sides were working in good faith. However, outside of the photos for social media, there was debate about the removal of fortifications. "In meetings, there were divisions over the construction of defenses and whether the SDF was publicly removing berms, only to be quietly building more defenses. Some of these positions were being built by civilians, but defining who was who along the border remained a challenge."

The more divisive issue was over Ankara's demands to build a series of bases inside the security zone, a demand that the Turkish government had pushed for during the entire time it was in talks with the United States. "The way this would all work," a person involved in the talks explained,

> was that we would propose something. Ankara would accuse us of stalling. We would try and explain why the proposal was in their interest. They would dismiss it and threaten to invade. We would push back. And then mix in more threats and some foot dragging on our side and then we would end up compromising. None of it was sustainable, but the idea was to just string this out as long as possible and it got the point where some of us just wanted them to finally rip the band aid off and get it over with.[26]

During the United Nations General Assembly, Erdogan proposed an internationally funded safe zone project in the northeast, complete with Turkish-built apartment blocks and soccer pitches, and a policy of resettling Arab refugees from Syria's northwest in the northeast. "The proposal was absurd. There is no local economy, 70 percent of the refugees were from the northwest, and anyone settled there will be forced to return to Turkey," an official lamented at the time.

> It showed their true intentions and it would make its way down to the tactical level. The Turkish proposals for permanent bases overlapped with the planned settlement blocks. It would get down to the CJOC and the Turkish military would end up repeating the party line, and we would propose a counter and it was rejected because it was out of synch with the pro-government press.[27]

As the two sides reached an impasse, it became clear to many US officials that the agreement was destined to break down and Ankara would invade. "The CJOC

would transition to coordinating only for the purpose of protecting U.S. forces …
and we made clear we wouldn't move aircraft, especially if we were retrograding
because it risked letting the Russians come in to the airspace."[28] By October 6, it
was clear that Ankara had given up on the Security Mechanism and would invade
Tel Abyad, the town that the YPG had liberated from Islamic State years earlier.
The war had, in essence, come full circle: the Kurdish takeover of the city prompted
Ankara to reevaluate its own policy and to acquiesce to airstrikes from Incirlik Air
Force base, but now Ankara was poised to invade and occupy it to push out the
forces that it deemed unacceptable.

Before launching what would later be dubbed Operation Peace Spring,
Erdogan, once again, requested a call with Trump. The conversation was intended
to hasten the implementation of the security mechanism, but instead devolved
into yet another venue for the Turkish president to push for an advantage he knew
he already had. In previous phone calls, Trump made clear his desire to leave
Syria and his willingness to hand over responsibilities for Syria to neighboring
countries. "In one of his calls," an official explained, "Trump told Erdogan that 'we
are almost done with ISIS, then seriously we will be gone, and you won't have a
problem … don't fuck up [the counter-ISIS campaign] and then we'll be gone."[29]
Thus, as Erdogan pressed his advantage, it took no great feat of diplomatic acumen
to understand that the American president was frustrated by the slow pace of
withdrawal and was intent on leaving Syria and that Ankara had an opportunity to
manipulate the American president.

The phone call took place on Sunday, October 6, 2019, and, just like in
December 2018, took the American national security establishment by surprise.
During the phone call, Trump ordered the United States to withdraw from the
border with Syria, removing troops from the likely Turkish invasion routes, and
pushing to remove all troops from Syria. Chaos ensued. Just hours after the call
ended, military commanders contacted the SDF's General Mazlum at 3:00 a.m. to
inform him of the president's decision and to warn him about the pending Turkish
invasion. The United States, per multiple officials, never intended to stand and
fight the Turkish military. However, there was a sense that the American presence
would deter Turkish action because of the possibility that military action could
accidentally kill a US soldier. As it would turn out, Ankara was less concerned
about the presence of US troops than many policymakers had assumed.

The Turkish invasion began on October 9. "They called the Combined Joint
Task Force Operation Inherent Resolve representative in Ankara to inform him
about the operation, but then the person didn't actually tell anyone," an official
explained. "As this was building up," a US pilot recalled, "we would ask what to
do if Americans get caught in the cross fire. We were told to not worry about it.
And then as this thing kicked off, we were doing 100 foot passes over the Turks
and their proxies." The invasion route was, as an Army officer quipped, "perfect for
tanks" and few doubted that the Turkish military would rapidly advance to the M4
highway that parallels the Turkish-Syrian border. "We had Turkish F-16s flying
south, Russians flying north of the river, you had Turkish armed UAVs; we tracked
them because they had strayed out of the box we had agreed to during the security

mechanism, and meanwhile you have pockets of Americans that you are trying to protect. It got crazy with Turkey pushing south."[30]

The Turkish military fought with a menagerie of militias. As the fight dragged on, these militias would set up checkpoints on the M4 highway, raising force protection issues for US soldiers that were exiting Syria. As one soldier indicated:

> The YPG didn't need sophisticated equipment to defeat Turkish armor, they had set up tank ditches and other turning obstacles. These are classic infantry tactics. The basic rule is that you place a tactical obstacle and you cover it with fire. The turning obstacle forces the tank to turn, canalizing the attacker and allow for max effect of your weapons. The Turkish main battle tank, the M60, doesn't stand a chance once its weaker armor is exposed. This is why Jim Jeffrey's negotiations, which included the dismantling of obstacles along the border was such a 'win' for the Turks. It lowered the risks for invasion.[31]

Ankara, as it would turn out, had used the CJOC negotiations to its advantage. It had reached an agreement that removed the main obstacles for its main battle tanks and deprived the YPG of any tactical advantage without having to fire a shot. The Turkish tactic during Peace Spring was to put their proxies in front of their armor, but "these guys don't know much about combined arms maneuver and the Turks quickly found out these guys weren't some professional force and they would lose tanks. This is why they pushed so hard to remove the YPG's tactical advantages in talks with us."[32]

The Turkish invasion also severely tested relations with the US military inside Syria and, at points in the brief conflict, American forces nearly used force to protect themselves. In one exchange near the Turkish-Syrian border, Turkish artillery bracketed a small US outpost, raising the ire in Washington and prompting a series of calls to stop the artillery barrage. "There was a small outpost that took fire that night," a military official explained. "It was close enough to get a response from our side, but the rules of engagement were very sketchy. There was also YPG in the area." As a second official explained, "[The Turks] intentionally bracketed our observation post. They knew it was there. The barrage lasted for a long time and we nearly shot back." The other flash point happened near the Lafarge Cement Plant, or LCF. This coalition base was stood up in 2015 for British, French, and American special operations forces, working alongside the SDF.[33]

The base had separate areas for each military. The French, an official who spent time at the base said, "had a French chef and they had locally sourced food," while the British had a bar.[34] The Americans, a second official explained, were not allowed to drink at the British bar because of the rules governing the drinking of alcohol during combat.[35] The base also had a separate training site for the SDF, where the group flew the YPG flag. "There was a YPG section with personnel and flags that were essentially co-located with SOF," an official explained. For the Task Force elements at the base, the overarching concern was that they could come under attack, or the Turkish-backed opposition elements could pose a threat to the base's security. "We had operators with Javelin [anti-tank guided missiles] locked on Turkish armor," a person familiar with the Task Force explained. "We could have wiped out a battalion of tanks and that was without air power we could have called, and the rules of engagement for such a call is delegated pretty far down."[36] As a second person remarked, "We also had orbiting Predators locked on to their armor. It go really, really close. But they just stopped."[37]

The Turkish advance stopped short of the base, but during the operation the YPG withdrew from the base, leaving on the foreign operators. Eventually, they too would withdraw and coalition struck a few sites. "We blew up $50 million worth of munitions," an official explained. The YPG blew up one of its buildings without telling the US officials, causing soldiers on the base to duck and cover, thinking that they were being targeted by artillery and prompting concerns that things with Turkey "were about to kick off."[38]

The other flash point was on the M4, where the Turkish-backed opposition had taken control of segments of the highways. In one such instance, "there were guys egressing on the ground," a pilot recalled, "and they called up because there was a check point that had been set up and the Turkish opposition was dragging people out of cars and executing them. They asked for type 3 control because the groups were killing people and were coming close to U.S. forces." Type 3 control is an engagement where the risk of fratricide is low and ground forces are allowed to authorize the use of as many weapons as necessary. Again, the United States held fire, but did witness numerous atrocities. In one instance, a Kurdish politician, Hevrin Khalaf, was executed after her car was stopped at one of these makeshift checkpoints and she was hauled from the car and shot, alongside her driver and bodyguards. The attackers filmed the events and the footage was published online, leading to accusations that Turkey was responsible for war crimes due to the actions of its proxies.[39] "We did keep a dossier of these reported war crimes," an official explained, "but it was probably in vain and nothing ever will be done."[40] The United States closed the CJOC in mid-October, less than a week after the start of Peace Spring. The invasion also ended the Manbij Roadmap patrols, which had remained in place right up until the Turkish operation.

Amidst the chaos of the Turkish invasion, the Russians and the Syrian regime reached a separate agreement with Mazlum, allowing for the deployment of Russian and Syrian regime units along the border, and in areas where Ankara had planned to invade. In Manbij, the Russians moved quickly to take the place of the departing Americans, moving from the Arima extension that they had occupied at the end of Operation Euphrates Shield to quickly take over facilities the United States had left. By October 15, Russian patrols had replaced the US military around Manbij, patrolling along the forward line of troops, dividing the Turkish forces from the Manbij Military Council. The envelopment of Turkish forces by Russians did freeze the Turkish offensive, creating conditions for the United States to push for a ceasefire with Ankara.

On October 17, 2019, the United States and Turkey reached agreement on a ceasefire that formalized Ankara's gains, including formalizing Ankara's military control over the zone it controlled and calling on the YPG to withdraw from the Turkish-controlled zone.[41] Five days later, Turkey and Russia finalized their own agreement, calling for the YPG to withdraw from a 30-kilometer buffer zone from the entirety of the border and instituted joint patrols, similar to the US–Turkish agreement for Manbij and with the Security Mechanism. At the end of the month, the "Turks demarched us," according to a US official. "They asked for Mazlum's arrest and his extradition."[42] The joint patrols with Russia began on November 1, 2019, and have continued ever since. The patrols prompted locals to throw rocks at passing vehicles, leading the Russians to augment them with helicopters to ensure force protection.[43]

In early November, Ambassador Jeffrey led a delegation to Ankara for a face-to-face meeting to reiterate the commitment to the ceasefire and to try and overcome the differences between the two countries. The United States had not yet settled on a cohesive policy. The Task Force in Syria and Central Command remained at odds with Turkey over the invasion and the risks to US forces. Ambassador Jeffrey, in contrast, led a group within the Special Representative Syria that viewed the invasion and the ceasefire as an opportunity to reset US–Turkish relations and to pursue a policy collaboration on pressuring Assad. "SRS was giddy and the thinking was that now that Turkey had beaten the YPG and the U.S. and Turkey were on the same page we could fight the regime together."[44]

For others, the Turkish invasion was both an obvious outcome and also a serious detriment to continued US operations in the country.

> The sense was that the president talked with Erdogan and did not show enough push back, and Erdogan took it as a permission slip … It was pretty awful that first week. I do not think the Turks had good control over [their proxies] guys because some atrocities were committed. It was a very ugly, sort of military campaign that first week, and then it settled in to more of a drawn out process … and then following Peace Spring the Russians got bolder with their patrols and they started to bump up against our guys.[45]

After the Turkish invasion, the United States withdrew 60 percent of the forces it had deployed to support the war effort. The withdrawal left behind a skeleton force, unable to properly conduct the types of advice and assist missions that the United States had been conducting. The deconfliction mechanism with the Russian Federation was upended because Russian forces were able to break out of the deconfliction box and push north to the Syrian-Turkish border with air and land forces. For the SDF, the erratic US decision-making process undermined trust, but the group had few good options other than to try and balance its relations with Washington and Moscow. "The Turkey operation, and how we handled it, almost destroyed the relationship with Mazlum and the SDF," a senior official recounted. "All the SDF senior leadership felt that we abandoned and betrayed them, and in the wake of that, we eventually salvaged a policy that we would stay. Mazlum is a pragmatic guy and he swallowed it because he was desperate for a U.S. presence, but ever since there has been a sneer and broad resentment for what happened."[46]

The failures that contributed to the October invasion largely stem from Trump's own political appointees, who sought to circumvent presidential guidance for well over a year. Donald Trump was let down by his own chaotic governance and his abject failure to stand up a coherent policy process that worked in harmony to implement his directives. Instead, in the absence of any clear process, people he empowered interpreted his guidance as they saw fit and twisted the president's words to support a hard-line, anti-Assad position that the commander in chief was disinterested in pursuing. Trump was, ultimately, the final cog in the system, and it was his two discussions with Erdogan—in December 2018 and October 2019—that marked the end of the US presence along the Turkish-Syrian border.

The aftermath of the invasion, again, exposed the radical divergences in thinking about the US role in Syria. The Special Representative for Syria office saw the post-invasion landscape as potentially beneficial to US interests because Ankara's elimination of the immediate YPG threat could allow for the two countries to cooperate more closely on Assad. For the men and women more involved in the fight against Islamic State, the invasion was quite rightly viewed as disaster for relations with the SDF. It also ushered in a new reality, wherein the Russian presence east of the river was more pronounced, and Moscow was able to put more diplomatic pressure on Mazlum to acquiesce to regime rule and to force the Americans out of the country. The US-led war against Islamic State was, again, headed for another turn and for the basic mission to change from a methodical, surrogate-led ground war to one of simply showing the flag in the northeast, why the Task Force narrowed its mission to hunt for Islamic State leaders that had fled their former caliphate and had ensconced themselves in areas where Ankara was in de facto control in the country's northwest.

Taking the Oil: A Token Force and Targeting Islamic State Leaders

President Donald Trump has never shied away from expressing a core belief that the United States should "take the oil" to pay for the wars it fights in the Middle East. In a 2016 interview with the *New York Times,* then candidate Trump was explicit, arguing, "I've been saying, take the oil. I've been saying it for years. Take the oil. They still haven't taken [Syrian] oil. They still haven't taken it."[47] Faced with a haphazard withdrawal and a collapsing US position in northeastern Syria, following the Turkish invasion, the American president settled on a policy of "guarding Syrian oil fields." This policy was shaped by a daring raid, conducted deep in Idlib that killed Abu Bakr al Baghdadi, the Islamic State leader.

The Baghdadi raid was, in the words of a US official, part of a number of targeted operations that the Task Force conducted amidst the chaos and uncertainty about the future American presence in Syria. The raid that ultimately killed the ISIS caliph began in Iraq, where Delta Force and other US SOF elements are based, and often fly helicopters to and from Syria. On this raid, the United States brought in specialized helicopters, similar to the ones used during the raid that killed Osama

Bin Laden in Pakistan. As the raid was taking place, the United States informed both Turkey and the Russian Federation so as to deconflict air operations. "The Russians non-concurred with the operation," an official explained, "but we went ahead anyway."[48]

"For a raid that close to the border," a special forces soldier explained, "we had to notify the Turks so that they don't shoot at us. The same with the Russians."[49] As it would turn out Baghdadi had taken refuge in a compound 13 kilometers near the town of Barisha, near the city of Idlib, and far from the group's former strongholds in eastern Syria.[50] "The operation was dubbed Operation Desert Fire," a person familiar with the raid told the author. "It was only fitting that the compound was left as a burning hole in the ground."[51] The raid was later described in detail by President Trump, who indicated that the ISIS leader had run from the compound into a cave and detonated a suicide vest as trained dogs approached him. However, the authorities to conduct the raid that had been delegated to a colonel, an official explained, and the team that conducted the raid rehearsed in theater, rather than in the United States. "The operation didn't require presidential approval."[52] The information that led to Baghdadi's capture, Trump indicated, was aided by sources the SDF had cultivated, but that the monitoring of the compound was mostly done with electronic intelligence.[53]

"The raid allowed us to unlock Idlib because it showed Moscow how bad guys had moved into the area," a person familiar with the US-Russian discussions said. "We didn't make a big deal of it, but we reached a basic agreement on some aspects of flying in the area, such as no overflying Russian bases, and we basically agreed to begin targeting high value targets." The other area that the United States unlocked was deeper cooperation with Turkey. The CIA, which has people inside Turkey, moved back into the country to assist with the gathering of intelligence to target ISIS leaders. The Task Force and the CIA, in turn, began to work in parallel with one another, with each side operating armed MQ-9 drones for the hunter-killer mission. The return of US assets increased the frequency with which senior ISIS and Al-Qaeda-linked individuals were targeted in drone strikes.

The context of the war had also shifted to Moscow. The Russian Federation was no longer staring down sustained urban combat in Aleppo, but instead has perfected its strategy of forcing the opposition to submit, or face starvation or certain death in a series of sieges and bombing efforts in towns and cities outside of its control. The Turkish government, too, has achieved its narrow objectives and its issues in Syria are now centered in Idlib, where a mass exodus of people could overwhelm and aid officials along the border. Ankara closed its border with Syria in 2015 in a move that Turkish officials once said was impossible during the contentious discussions with Washington over basing access. The Turkish-Russian dynamic had also shifted from one of close partnership to symbiotic entanglement. The Astana process had locked the two countries into a partnership, wherein Moscow had thrust the responsibility for representing the opposition to Turkey, while Ankara had come to rely on Russia to moderate the regime's behavior. The two sides had built their relationship around shared antipathy toward the United States' policy in Syria and a recognition that each side needed the other to achieve their interests in Syria. The relationship, however, was premised on a Russian demand that Ankara represent the fractious opposition and eventually negotiate its surrender.

As part of the Sochi Memorandum signed in September 2018, the Turkish military established a series of observation posts ring fencing Idlib. In early 2020, the Assad regime besieged a series of these observation posts, cutting off Turkish troops from resupply from the border. The regime, too, was amid an offensive that the Turkish-backed opposition was unable to stop. In February, President Erdogan issued an ultimatum to the regime's forces, warning that they needed to retreat to the original lines agreed to in the Sochi Memorandum and withdraw from the areas around Turkish bases that they occupied. On February 29, 2020, the deadline Erdogan gave to the regime to withdraw expired, signaling that Turkey was prepared to take more aggressive military action.

"In meeting with the Turks during this time," an official explained, "the Special Representative's office was telling Ankara to 'put more steel into the defense of Idlib', implying that the U.S. was prepared to back them." By this point of the war, it is almost certain that Ankara had little trust in the United States, but "SRS thought that this could stop the Assad offensive and there was a hope that a Turkish-regime clash could force a crisis and force Trump to contemplate some form of intervention on the Turkish side."[54] A Russian-backed offensive in Idlib, the thinking went, would drive a wedge between Moscow and Ankara, giving Washington an avenue to win back Turkish support and to cooperate more closely on the purported shared goal of pressuring Assad. "These guys were fantasists, but there was this deep seated belief that Assad was fragile, and each thing fed on the other and became self-reinforcing."[55]

The Turkish military began to target regime armor in late February with armed drones, flying orbits over the frontlines. The Turkish government would quickly publish successful drone strikes on social media, showing repeated strikes on Syrian air defense systems and clumped together armor and artillery pieces. For SRS, the Turkish air campaign was seen as another indicator of regime weakness. "The mantra was 'every day Assad is more fragile than ever, he could be gone at any moment' and that this offensive, along with is economic woes could be the 'straw that crumbles the regime."[56] The Turkish air campaign did destroy a large number of regime assets and had some success against the short-range, Russian-made air defense system, the Pantsir S-1. The videos of these missile strikes were quickly uploaded online, creating yet another feedback loop to reinforce the Turkish narrative of military prowess and capabilities in rolling back the regime. To this end, Ankara did prove capable of using unmanned systems to target the Syrian regime, but the Russians responded with airstrikes to prevent any territorial losses.

In one instance, a Russian bomber struck a Turkish military base, killing dozens of Turkish soldiers deployed near the frontlines. The airstrike did prompt Turkish appeals to the United States for the forward deployment of a Patriot air and missile defense system in southern Turkey to deter Russian overflight along the border. The intent was for Turkish forces to build three tiers of air defense, beginning with the shoulder-fired missiles it had deployed inside Idlib with its forces, a second tier of air defense, the HAWK, deployed inside Idlib, and a third, US-operated long-range air defense operating just inside the Turkish border with the radar pointed at Syria.[57] "The Patriot request was a non-starter," an official explained at the time. "It would have had to have been U.S. crews operating those missiles and we weren't going to shoot down a Russian jet. Period."[58]

The Turkish Air Force, throughout this brief conflict, did not fly any manned jets over Idlib, owing to concerns about escalation with Moscow. However, the Turkish Air Force did manage to shoot down three Syrian regime jets, denying Assad overflight over Idlib. Ankara, however, was unwilling to shoot down Russian jets, allowing for Moscow to fly with impunity over the forward lines of contact. This continuous Russian presence ultimately allowed for the regime to settle this flare up on its terms, leading to a return of loyalist forces to the M5 highway and a mechanism for the Russian and Turkish militaries to jointly patrol the M4. This ceasefire further enmeshed the Turkish and Russian militaries in Syria, despite the tensions that had led to clashes in late February and early March. After dozens of Turks were killed, the outcome that Ankara accepted was to accept continued besiegement of its Observation Posts and to hold to a schedule of joint patrols with Russian forces, while Moscow continued to call for the removal of radical elements from Idlib. This outcome has still placed the diplomatic onus on Turkey to deliver the opposition to Russia, a task Ankara has proved incapable of carrying out.

The ceasefire remains tenuous and, as the Turkish-Russian patrols have become routine, radical elements within Idlib began to target them with roadside bombs. Eventually, Ankara evacuated its observation posts and reinforced positions inside the two main highways. The force protection issues both militaries face underscore how violent Syria still is, outside of areas the United States controls, and far from the frontlines in the war against the remnants of Islamic State.

Taking the Oil: America's Nebulous Syria Policy

For the United States, Idlib is a diplomatic side show and a means to try and graft broader policy desires onto an incoherent US strategy. In the wake of the Turkish invasion, a senior official explained, "We have about 40 percent of the number of forces that were present in Syria before the Turks came across." However, one idea that the Trump administration gravitated toward was to deny the Assad regime access to the oil field that the United States and the SDF controlled. Syrian oil, the argument went, would be necessary to reconstruct the country and, without it, Assad would be unable to ever completely win. Thus, the United States could use its presence to simply deny Assad victory, increasing the cost for his continued rule and for that of his two sponsors, Russia and Iran. "After the Turks invaded the northeast, there was this idea that YPG could sell Turkey the oil from Der Ezour and that this would add to the overall 'Maximum Pressure' campaign that the administration was pursuing against Iran and its regional allies. It was crazy."[59] Crazy or not, the oil issue created a pretext to sell Trump on maintaining a skeleton force inside Syria to patrol near Syrian oil fields and to extend those patrols to areas south of the M4 highway.

***

The Turkish invasion of northeastern Syria forced the United States to grapple with its broken policy process. President Trump had, since his speech in Ohio in March 2018, made clear that he was keen to see a rapid drawdown of US forces from the country. His political appointees resisted, trying to steer the policy process toward an outcome that gradually withdrew troops and retained US forces inside the country indefinitely. This dichotomy eventually ended in Trump acquiescing to the Erdogan demand for a buffer zone. This decision threatened the lives of American troops, who were caught between an advancing Turkish army and increased Russian and regime elements coming across the river to the up position along the border.

The outcome has been to further muddle the post-combat phase of the war against Islamic State. With the ground war over, the Task Force used bold action to force Russia and Turkey to reckon with the reality that Islamic State leaders had sought safe haven in areas Ankara controlled. The Baghdadi raid unlocked American overflight and created a narrow mechanism for the United States to target ISIS and Al-Qaeda leaders without Russian interference. Moscow also ended 2020 having increased pressure on Turkey to grapple with the extremist issue inside Idlib and ensconced the regime along the two main highways. The United States, in turn, has maintained its small presence south of the M4 and at the Tanf Garrison. The mission remains countering Islamic State, but the war has slowed down for the forces deployed. The men and women deployed to support Operation Inherent Resolve in Syria have far less to do these days than at the height of the conflict, but the diplomatic activity that defined 2017 has stalled and it appears inevitable that Russia will again renew its offensive on Idlib to further pressure Syria.

CONCLUSION: A LIMITED WAR AND A DIPLOMATIC CUL-DE-SAC: THE WAR IN RETROSPECT

The war in Syria is truly revolutionary in tactics and strategy. The basic premise was plugging in American enablers to assist the Iraqi senior leadership to better target Islamic State fighters. In Syria, the war was different, and hinged on a smaller subset of the American military, led primarily by specialized US SOF operating under the Task Force, to cultivate a ground force willing and capable of fighting an entrenched insurgent group. In Iraq, the war was fought with the support of the Iraqi leadership and with the backing of the Iraqi military, which, while weak, still formed the main core through which the United States could enable offensive operations. Within that military, the United States had built a truly capable partner force, the Counter Terrorism Service, that was able to step into the void and launch an early operation around the Mosul dam to begin the long fight to retake the country. In Syria, the United States had no government support and fought the war in parallel to a large, semi-clandestine effort to overthrow the Assad regime.

The war in Syria was a series of push-and-pull effects that, together, led to a series of diplomatic and military outcomes that the United States never truly accounted for as it rushed to war in 2014. The start of overt, American combat operations was dictated by the authorities the president had available to him to conduct combat operations without an authorization from Congress. The basic blueprint for the war in Syria was to keep the total number of troops to a minimum, embed them with a local force, and then use air power to enable offensive ground operations. The United States did not plan to go to war with the YPG, a PKK offshoot, and the source of tension with Turkey that few in Washington foresaw as being the main source of diplomatic hand holding has the war pushed ahead.

Instead, in the battle for Sinjar, which helped to trigger the start of the American campaign in Iraq, a small Delta Force and Special Forces attachment met with the Syrian YPG leader, following an introduction from a second, long-standing American ally, the PUK, brokered an introduction. This introduction fostered the partnership that would eventually lead to the toppling of the Islamic State's caliphate in Syria. However, the decision to partner with the Syrian Kurds prompted backlash from Turkey, and Ankara's insecurity ultimately led it to invade Syria three times. The combination of American support for the SDF and Ankara's effort to upend that partnership severely strained bilateral ties and led to close Turkish-Russian cooperation.

The American military relationship with the Iraqi Kurds dates back to the first Gulf War and was entrenched during Operation Viking Hammer, the pre-invasion combat operation against an Al-Qaeda sympathetic terrorist group that once gave safe haven to Zarqawi, as he was on his own personal journey to inspire the group that eventually morphed into the Islamic State. The partnership with the Iraqi Kurds was critical to finding General Mazlum. It was then that the Islamic State's efforts to capture Kobane provided the United States with the main opportunity to begin to strike targets inside Syria with more frequency and to insert Task Force members to help coordinate the air campaign. Mazlum was eager to push the Islamic State back, so American aircraft were given more leeway to strike targets. The civilian population had mostly fled, lowering the risk of unintended deaths. This three-part, interrelated set of circumstances ensured that coalition air power could push back the advancing group.

The battle for Kobane was also a watershed moment in the allocation of resources to the fight. The American war against Islamic State was, in essence, three different sub-conflicts against the group. The main focus was in Iraq, with northeast Syria emerging as a second-tier priority, followed by the smaller Train and Equip effort that began later on in the campaign in the Manbij pocket. These three sub-conflicts were each dependent on the same set of finite air assets, tasked to enable targets of convenience or to strike pre-planned targets. It was during Kobane that the American respect for the YPG deepened, as dislocated JTACs and targeting officers would watch the battle unfold in real time from orbiting ISR assets, and see up close the tenacity of the ground fight. For the pilots, the YPG— and later the SDF—were the warriors on the ground, who they never spoke with, but for whom they would drop bombs or conduct strafing runs. This partnership began with Kobane and it never ended. The YPG and YPJ tenacity also earned the group respect from Americans deployed inside the city to assist with airstrikes, as well as the armada of enablers connected digitally to the battlefield.

At this stage of the war, few in Washington knew much about the Kurdistan Workers' Party—and knew even less about the group's branch in Syria, the Democratic Union Party. It was an accident of history that the United States came to depend on them to fight the war against Islamic State. However, as the war progressed, they were the only serious candidate to wage such a fight. The group ticked every box: The Syrian Kurds were, in general, favorable to fighting with the United States, guaranteed the safety of US forces deployed alongside them, shared an interest in fighting Islamic State well beyond its traditional strongholds inside Syria, and the group had a strong, top-down hierarchy that enabled them to deploy fighters and manage logistics. The YPG's motivations were, of course, driven by the group's ingrained support for Kurdish nationalism and the achievement of a quasi-independent state, ruled with little interference from the governing authority in Damascus. The broader anti-Assad Arab-opposition, in turn, had groups hostile to the United States, was riven by division and factionalism, and had little interest in dedicating the bulk of its forces to fighting Islamic State. This asymmetry of interests ensured that the United States and the Arab-opposition groups would not fight well together against Islamic

State. It also drove tensions with Turkey, who maintained that Washington was backing the wrong group in Syria.

The SDF's linkages to the PKK, as well as its overarching political ambitions, ensured that America's NATO ally, Turkey, would resist the US strategy to defeat Islamic State. The United States sought to manage these differences, reassuring Turkey that its partnership with the Syrian Kurds was temporary and tactical, albeit while giving the YPG open-ended support and training that Ankara feared would later be used to make the group more lethal inside Turkey. The broader and more pressing concern for the Turks was how the YPG had moved from semi-pariah to accepted international actor, an outcome that upended the decades-long Turkish effort to win support for its effort to list the PKK as a terrorist group. These tensions could never be overcome and, as Ankara's own position vis-a-vis Assad crumbled after the Russian intervention, the Turkish government sought to manage a quasi-regime victory in the northwest, while working with Russia to complicate the US relationship with the SDF.

In retrospect, the major American oversight in the conflict was overlooking the Russian willingness to use force in support of the Assad regime. The main US effort to topple Bashar was handled by the CIA, in partnership with allies and partners in the Middle East. The conventional wisdom holds that the United States acted in a relatively restrained way and sought to provide only enough support to the anti-Assad opposition to put pressure on the government to capitulate and agree to the terms of the Geneva Communique. In reality, the program was far larger than is widely understood and, by 2015, was showing signs of success. This success, however, was predicated on a faustian bargain, wherein the United States acquiesced to extremists spearheading operations and the groups that it supported having a presence in the areas these groups helped to clear. The extremists were not interested in sharing power, but instead imposed their own version of governance that created safe haven for offshoots of the same groups that the United States had pledged to fight. The weapons the United States was providing to the opposition were also proliferating widely and, in some cases, the spread of these small arms was accepted as necessity because it enabled closer coordination between the divided factions Washington had sought to unite. The United States accepted this, arguing that these outcomes were necessary to support a negotiated settlement that, if implemented, would require the Assad regime to give up power and turn governance over to the very same men that had pledged to topple the leadership. This bargain was untenable and was anathema to Russian national security interests.

The collapse of the regime in Idlib did not, however, lead to a change in government policy. Instead, Damascus appealed to its main two allies for more support, and Moscow made the political decision to intervene directly. The introduction of Russian troops and aircraft in September 2015 dramatically changed the war and made more complicated US policy deliberations because few in Washington were willing to risk escalation with Russia for the opposition in Syria. The Russian Federation had a malleable military strategy in Syria and, upon its intervention, quickly realized that the Syrian regime had crumbled and that it lacked combat power to launch the types of offensives needed to push back the opposition and to ensure regime victory. The Russian presence in Syria, throughout the intervention, has remained relatively small, but critical, to ensure that the regime did not collapse under the weight of the insurgency and had the equipment and training to retake the initiative in selected pockets. Moscow's strategy evolved into one of siege and coercion, using overwhelming firepower to isolate different fronts in the overarching war, cut them off from resupply, and then signal that the opposition needed to surrender and reconcile with the regime, or face near certain death.

To manage this strategy, Moscow and the regime engaged in a series of stop-and-start offensives, paired with diplomatic efforts with the United States and the other combatants involved in the conflict. Russia did, therefore, welcome engagement with the United States and was willing to work with Washington on what it perceived to be as a shard interest—counterterrorism—but was fundamentally unwilling to see nuance within the broader anti-Assad insurgency. For Moscow, the fight against the insurgency was viewed as a conventional fight against a relatively well-equipped force, which they viewed as dominated by extremists. As such, the foci for Kremlin were to prop up its regional partner, the Assad regime, and in so doing, push back on unilateral American military operations in the Middle East to change or pressure regimes the Kremlin backed. Russia's results were mixed, but the operational lessons from its own war in Syria have proved invaluable to the general staff, and there is little to no indication that the Russian forces will be withdrawn. Instead, Moscow has reestablished a foothold in the Middle East that it can use as a bridge for operations in North Africa and to enable more pronounced naval operations in the Mediterranean.

The broader American-Russian competition did not preclude efforts to find areas of overlap in Syria. The two sides were able to reach broad agreements that did not threaten each side's understanding of the conflict. The American push for UNSC 2254 gave Moscow enough wiggle room to ensure that its interpretation of the resolution could be used to its advantage in pushing for a modicum of changes, such as cursory changes to the constitution, could satisfy the language in the resolution and still then settle the conflict on terms Moscow could accept. For Washington, the resolution could be interpreted as a validation of its push for a Transitional Governing Body, which would then make the types of reforms that would enable Assad to step down from power.

The two sides did come close to cooperating more closely in Syria. First, the two sides seriously discussed setting up the JIG, but could never agree on key definitions and no-bomb zones linked to those definitions. The second, and perhaps most fruitful period of diplomacy, came amidst general policy dysfunction within the Trump administration and the early efforts to match American policy goals to Trump's nativist campaign rhetoric. This brief window allowed for Moscow and Washington, with support from Jordan, to reach an agreement on a southern ceasefire. The intent, of course, was to ignore the disagreement over the TGB, and instead focus on freezing violence in such a way as to try and minimize Syrian deaths. This approach recognized Russia as an equal and did not seek to use the forum as a means to pressure them to comply with the US vision of the conflict, and instead compromised on some core tenets to slow down an offensive. The agreement did break down, but the tensions stemmed from challenges within the United States and a shift in policy following the regime's use of chemical weapons, and a sharpening of US rhetoric around the need for a fundamental change in the regime's actions.

The American policy during the Trump administration was truly disorganized, vacillating from two extremes: the ending of US clandestine support for the anti-Assad opposition and overtures to Russia, while also doubling down on a hard-line policy against Iran and the Assad regime. This policy rested on the work of Secretary of State John Kerry, who delivered UNSC 2254, but who many in the Trump administration reviled as naive and overly sympathetic to the Islamic Republic of Iran. The American insistence on Tanf, however, was an afterthought and linked most closely to the broader bureaucratic dysfunction within the Trump organization.

The base was set up to assuage broader Jordanian concerns about border security and is linked closely with the Kingdom's effort to prevent refugees from crossing the border. The American training effort in Jordan was intended to build a small, mobile force to strike Islamic State positions in the desert east of the river. The program was, ultimately, leveraged into an ill-fated effort to try and wrest control of al Bukamal with forces never trained to take and hold territory. The small base grew in importance only after Donald Trump sought to remove all US troops, and it was given the nebulous role in challenging Iranian overland routes into the country and used as a means to justify retaining a ground presence indefinitely. The base's vulnerability, however, required that it receive near constant overhead protection from US jets to deter Iranian-linked and regime attempts to attack the base. This decision came only after a small base near Tanf, Bowling Green, was bombed by an Iranian-made drone and a Syrian Su-22, narrowly averting the first killing of US forces from air to ground attack since 1953.

The American-led war against the Islamic State was never truly a part of the broader political strategy that both the Obama administration and the Trump administration pursued in Syria. Instead, as the war progressed, the diplomatic efforts were lumped into two separate baskets. During the Obama administration, the United States was much more active in pursuing agreements with Moscow and the broader international community, although such efforts were often overlooked because they did not entail the threat of military force. However, to sustain the war against Islamic State, Washington found itself enmeshed in an open-ended series of negotiations with Ankara. The Turkish Republic's Syria policy vacillated from one of cautious engagement in 2011, designed to try and appease the protesters and to encourage the types of political changes that would lead to basic reforms. These efforts failed, culminating in Ankara's sharp turn from engagement to hostility—and the broader political decision to begin to sponsor and arm the anti-Assad opposition.

This effort included outreach to the United States to intervene in support of the Turkish decision to break with Assad and to seek to install a government in exile that Ankara had sought to support in a safe zone along its border. The Turkish and regional-led arming program also had the secondary effects of forcing the United States to intervene more aggressively, beginning with the empowerment of the CIA to help coordinate the arming program and to oversee a training program for the Arab-majority opposition. This effort never managed to harmonize the divergent efforts of the external actors giving lethal support. However, the American intervention came only after Islamic State carved out a protostate inside Iraq and Syria, and threatened the governing structures in Iraqi Kurdistan and in Baghdad. The means to intervene against Islamic State were grounded in the authorities available to the president at the time, and informed by Congressional resistance to military action inside the country. The reality is that neither Congress nor the executive were interested in a large-scale intervention in either Syria or Iraq, and domestic American politics played a role in shaping how Washington chose to intervene. This aversion to the large-scale use of force is critical to understanding how the war was eventually fought.

The Obama administration had a narrow set of authorities to wage war and was resistant to using the military to topple regional governments and sign up the United States for an open-ended nation-building effort. The authorities for such action, therefore, were narrowly built around a counter-terrorist effort, based upon decisions made to support the war against Al-Qaeda after the 9/11 attacks. These authorities shielded the administration from rigorous Congressional oversight and also created the parameters for how the war could be fought. As a result, the war in Syria was led by America's elite counterterrorism forces, working together with the Air Force. The geography of the fight was also a factor. These elite forces were tasked with defeating Islamic State, which was primarily based in the Euphrates River Valley and through northeastern Syria to Mosul in Iraq. Within these geographical confines, the SDF were the only such actor that could operate within the legal and strategic confines that the United States adopted.

In northwestern Syria, the United States and Turkey did seek to cooperate and create an alternative force, as part of the Train and Equip effort. This effort was an offshoot of the CIA-led program, incorporating the basic elements of the clandestine program into an overt military-led program. The program was based in Turkey and Jordan, with the standing up of training sites in each country and the assignment of a targeting officer to facilitate airstrikes in support of the trained groups. The training, particularly in Jordan, was designed to enable small groups of men to strike ISIS targets and to call in airstrikes, rather than launch assaults on urban areas. The Turkey-based program had support from Ankara, but the fighters selected for the program were unable to seize and hold territory. The United States, too, faced constraints and were unable to give the types of guarantees that the groups had demanded at the outset. Still, Washington did guarantee that they would protect the groups it trained from regime attack during their assaults on Islamic State, and did provide them with considerable weaponry and ammunition. However, the groups did not get as many air assets as were devoted to Iraq and northeastern Syria. The allocation of air assets was tied to the broader efforts against Islamic State, so the T/E struggles against ISIS all but ensured that high-demand assets would be assigned to other areas of the overall campaign against the group.

As the Train and Equip program faltered in northern Aleppo, the United States sent CIA-armed groups to the frontlines against the Islamic State. The authorities to launch air strikes only required that a Title 10, T/E group was in the area of the CIA-armed elements. This offensive, dubbed Agate Noble, did not fare any better. The catalyst for a change in strategy came only after the Islamic State attacks in Paris and the urgency to close the border, and to merge the effort to use the SDF to assault Raqqa with the clearing operations along the Turkish-Syrian border. The Agate Noble failures hastened planning for the SDF to be used to clear Manbij. The United States did seek to assuage Turkish concerns, offering Ankara increased targeting support for the PKK and allowing the Turkish military to use US targeting data for airstrikes, but this effort did not satisfy the Turkish government. The fall of Manbij heightened US–Turkish tensions and ultimately catalyzed three different Turkish invasions to push the SDF off the border and to challenge the American relationship with the Kurdish partners.

The diplomacy with Turkey eventually consumed US policymakers, requiring near constant management to try and stave off Turkish-led military action to prevent the war against Islamic State from being upended. Turkish security concerns eventually prompted Ankara to partner with Russia, a decision that enabled Moscow's diplomatic efforts to focus on changes to the constitution, and not a transitional governing body. Turkish efforts reflected Ankara's prioritization of the Kurdish threat and the reality that Assad would not be toppled and that the opposition Turkey had long sponsored would need to make concessions for peace. Ankara's final invasion, Operation Peace Spring, finally settled the debate within the Trump administration about the American role in the country.

President Trump had long sought to withdraw all American forces, but ran into resistance when tasking his bureaucracy with implementing his directive to drawdown US forces. The Turkish invasion forced a hasty US withdrawal from the border and, critically, allowed for Russian forces to cross the Euphrates Rivers and to ensconce itself in small bases along the Turkish-Syrian border. Russian forces also took control of Manbij, denying it to the Turks, but also using its position to politically pressure the SDF leadership to enter into negotiations with the regime. Moscow's goal is to stitch Syria back together, beginning with the subordination of the SDF into the Syrian armed forces. This outcome may not be ideal for Ankara, but it would push forward the Russian goal of settling the Syrian civil war on terms that ensure its core interests are satisfied. These interests preclude an overt US role in the country and are wedded to the removal of foreign forces, absent Syrian government support.

Winning a Limited War: The Chaos of Victory

The United States and its coalition partners defeated the Islamic State, winning its limited war to deny the group territory. The war demonstrated American technical prowess and the ability to fight a war through a trusted partner force, using precision airstrikes and battlefield intelligence to defeat an entrenched non-state actor. The war is certain to be viewed as a military success, but the use of the SDF had a series of secondary diplomatic effects that undermined US–Turkish relations. Further, the clandestine war had an unintended effect: the Russian Federation intervened directly in the conflict; a political decision that ensured that Assad would not be toppled by an external actor, and embedding Russian combat forces in the Middle East. Moscow's return to the Levant has allowed the Kremlin to use its airbase to support air operations in North Africa and to expand port facilities to bolster its naval presence in the Eastern Mediterranean.

For Ankara, the war has shaped a generation of officers, who in battles inside Turkey and in Syria and Iraq have lost scores of soldiers to the Kurdistan Workers' Party and its offshoots. The United States, long an overt supporter of Turkey's war against the PKK, chose to partner with the YPG and shaped the group into a capable force that it armed and trained to defeat the Islamic State. The American war in the country was truly a revolution in US combat operations, but it hinged on finding a capable partner willing to fight far from its villages, and in support of a nebulous operation focused only on dislodging a separate non-state actor that had carved out territory inside a war torn state, governed by an American adversary. The damage to the US–Turkish relationship may not be reversible, given the years of suspicion and hostility that now permeate the relationship, and Ankara's uneasy partnership with Moscow to drive US forces out of the country.

As one former Obama administration quipped, "We would always hear that 'By, with, and through' was messy. It is messy. But if you do it directly, the blob is still going to hate it, and then, inevitably, you are going to screw up post-conflict stabilization. All war is messy."[1] Looking back at the war, the legacy of the US involvement in Iraq featured prominently in the early thinking about Syria. The Obama administration was eager to avoid warnings from JSOC, pointing to the rise of Islamic State and the brittle Iraqi state. After the fall of Mosul, proponents of more robust action made the case that the best way to defeat Islamic State was to empower Sunni Arabs—a strategy lifted from the purported success of the "surge" in Iraq nearly a decade earlier. The SDF, too, were considered anathema to a "winning strategy" because their Kurdish cadres would undermine rapport with local Sunnis, creating the intra-ethnic tensions that Islamic State exploited to gain power.

As it would turn out, the war required a cohesive group with a clear command structure to be able to integrate with American advisors and air power. In retrospect, this need for a cohesive group is not at all surprising, given that the American way of war in both Syria and Iraq was to plug into the command elements that oversaw the ground fight against ISIS and then enable them to take territory. The SDF has also been able to hold territory and prevent Islamic State infiltration, using its internal security services to provide stability, even if they are Kurdish dominated.

This pattern repeated itself in Idlib: the key enabler of ground combat operations was a top-down, cohesive group to organize operations against the Syrian armed forces. The problem, of course, was that an Al-Qaeda affiliate and militants sympathetic to Al-Qaeda spearheaded the most successful operation in Idlib in 2015. The options available to the United States were not good, but the overriding push to pressure Bashar led Washington to ignore that the hardline groups were the dominant actors in the fight against the regime, even if on paper they had less fighters. The policymakers in charge of the war failed to grapple with the reality that the hard-line groups, like Nusra and its successors, had the most cohesive ideology and governing structures, so even though they may have had less fighters, they would still dictate political and security outcomes in areas taken from the regime. The Turkish-controlled areas, however, have served as a way station for dispersed Islamic State leaders, who fled from the Euphrates River Valley for relative safety in Idlib. The United States has continued to hunt for these leaders, using long-range weapons to strike, and then with unmanned aircraft after JSOC killed Abu Bakr al Baghdadi in Idlib.

The war has now settled into something that many Americans now treat as routine: the continued use of unmanned assets to find and kill high-value targets in territory with few Americans present. The war against the Islamic State's caliphate ended in victory. The tactics leveraged proved successful and are certain to serve as a template for future operations. The war against Islamic State and Al-Qaeda-linked individuals, however, remains active. In this sense, Syria has now shifted from a ground war to a counterterrorism operation, signaling that Washington will remain involved in the country for the foreseeable future and continue targeting Islamic State members. The war is not over, but the country is determined to move on. "The general mood is that the counter-ISIS war is in the rear view mirror," an official recalled.[2] The United States is committed to pivoting away from open-ended counteroperations in the Middle East, as it seeks to focus on potential combat with a large nation-state like Russia or China.

The American war in Syria may fade into the background, amidst now routine drone strikes in territory that Russia and Turkey now compete to control. The Syrian Kurds have a modicum of self-rule, but the gains are tenuous and the SDF remains wedged between a myriad of hostile actors. In Idlib, radical groups remain dominant, but have faced withering Russian airstrikes that have slowly eaten away at the territory they control, while Ankara's efforts to manage hard-line factions have failed to win significant Russian support. In response, these radicals have sought to soften their image, giving interviews to the press and speaking with Western analysts. Syria remains unstable, but Bashar remains ensconced in power. Russia and Turkey remain enmeshed in diplomatic talks that exclude the United States, which under President Biden is eager to focus on domestic issues and potential conflict in Asia. Meanwhile, the Task Force is still active, hunting for high-value targets as the war against extremists continues, even as the ground campaign fades from memory and the US war fades into the background, but never quite ends.

NOTES

Introduction

1   Brian Dodwell, Daniel Milton, and Don Rassler, "The Caliphate's Global Workforce: An Inside Look at the Islamic State's Foreign Fighter Paper Trail," Combatting Terrorism Center, West Point, April 2016, p. 25, https://www.ctc.usma.edu/posts/the-caliphates-global-workforce-an-inside-look-at-the-islamic-states-foreign-fighter-paper-trail.

2   Julian E. Barnes and Eric Schmitt, "Trump Orders Withdrawal of U.S. Troops from Northern Syria," *New York Times*, October 13, 2019, https://www.nytimes.com/2019/10/13/us/politics/mark-esper-syria-kurds-turkey.html.

3   Mark Mazzetti, Adam Goldman, and Michael S. Schmidt, "Behind the Sudden Death of a $1 Billion Secret C.I.A. War in Syria," *New York Times*, August 2, 2017, https://www.nytimes.com/2017/08/02/world/middleeast/cia-syria-rebel-arm-train-trump.html.

4   Author Interview, Coalition Pilot, Washington, DC, 2017.

5   See: Michael Kofman, "Syria and the Russian Armed Forces: An Evaluation of Moscow's Military Strategy and Operational Performance," in Russia's War in Syria: Assessing Russian Military Capabilities and Lessons Learned (Philadelphia: Foreign Policy Research Institute, 2020), pp. 35–66.

6   Aliza Marcus, *Blood and Belief: The PKK and the Kurdish Fight for Independence* (New York: New York University Press, 2007).

7   Miron Varouhakis, "Greek Intelligence and the Capture of PKK Leader Abdullah Ocalan," *Studies in Intelligence*, vol. 53, no. 1 (Extracts, March 2009).

8   Dan Bilefsky, "Turkish Border Businesses Miss the Syrian Neighbors," *New York Times*, December 12, 2011, https://www.nytimes.com/2011/12/13/world/europe/turkeys-sanctions-on-syria-hurt-business-for-border-city.html.

9   Dan Roberts and Tom McCarthy, "Obama Orders US Special Forces to 'Assist' Fight against Isis in Syria," *The Guardian*, October 30, 2015, https://www.theguardian.com/world/2015/oct/30/syria-us-deployment-troops-obama-special-operations.

10 Linda Robinson, *Masters of Chaos: The Secret History of the Special Forces* (New York: Public Affairs, 2009).

11 Simon Tisdall, "Syrian President Admits Military Setbacks, in First Public Speech for a Year," *The Guardian*, July 26, 2015, https://www.theguardian.com/world/2015/jul/26/syrian-president-public-speech-bashar-al-assad.

12 Sanu Kainikara, *In the Bear's Shadow: Russian Intervention in Syria* (Canberra: Air Power Development Centre, 2018).

13 Neil MacFarquhar and Steven Erlanger, "NATO-Russia Tensions Rise after Turkey Downs Jet," *New York Times*, November 24, 2015, https://www.nytimes.com/2015/11/25/world/europe/turkey-syria-russia-military-plane.html.

14 Author Interview, US Military Official, Washington, DC, 2018.

15 Martin Chulov, Julian Borger, Richard Norton Taylor, and Dan Roberts, "US Troops Land on Iraq's Mt Sinjar to Plan for Yazidi Evacuation," *The Guardian*, August 13, 2014, https://www.theguardian.com/world/2014/aug/13/us-ground-troops-direct-role-evacuate-yazidis-iraq.
16 Jennifer Hlad, "Breaking the Siege on Sinjar," *Air Force Magazine*, October 2015, http://www.airforcemag.com/MagazineArchive/Pages/2015/October%202015/Breaking-the-Siege-on-Sinjar.aspx.
17 David Ignatius, "The United States' Surprise Allies in Syria," *The Washington Post*, October 15, 2015, https://www.washingtonpost.com/opinions/the-us-hastily-reevaluates-its-syria-strategy/2015/10/15/92d62c54-735c-11e5-9cbb-790369643cf9_story.html
18 Author Interview, US Military Official, Washington, DC, 2018.

Chapter 1

1 "Remarks by the President at the National Defense University," Office of the Press Secretary, The White House, May 23, 2013, https://obamawhitehouse.archives.gov/the-press-office/2013/05/23/remarks-president-national-defense-university.
2 Helene Cooper and Eric Schmitt, "Airstrikes by U.S. and Allies Hit ISIS Targets in Syria," *New York Times*, September 22, 2014, https://www.nytimes.com/2014/09/23/world/middleeast/us-and-allies-hit-isis-targets-in-syria.html.
3 Neil MacFarquhar, "Hafez al-Assad, Who Turned Syria Into a Power in the Middle East, Dies at 69," *New York Times*, June 11, 2000, https://www.nytimes.com/2000/06/11/world/hafez-al-assad-who-turned-syria-into-a-power-in-the-middle-east-dies-at-69.html.
4 William E. Schmidt, "Assad's Son Killed in a Car Crash," *New York Times*, January 22, 1994, https://www.nytimes.com/1994/01/22/world/assad-s-son-killed-in-an-auto-crash.html.
5 Samer N. Abboud, *Syria* (Malden: Polity Press, 2016), pp. 32–40.
6 "Globalizing Torture: CIA Secret Detention and Extraordinary Rendition," Open Society Foundation, 2013, https://www.justiceinitiative.org/uploads/655bbd41-082b-4df3-940c-18a3bd9ed956/globalizing-torture-20120205.pdf, p. 111.
7 "Text of President Bush's 2002 State of the Union Address," *The Washington Post*, January 29, 2002, https://www.washingtonpost.com/wp-srv/onpolitics/transcripts/sou012902.htm.
8 Brian Fishman, *The Master Plan: ISIS, Al-Qaeda, and the Jihadi Strategy for Final Victory* (New Haven: Yale University Press, 2016), pp. 8–9.
9 Ibid., pp. 12–13.
10 Ibid., p. 19.
11 Bob Woodward, *Bush at War* (New York: Simon and Schuster, 2002); Benjamin Lambeth, *Airpower against Terror: America's Conduct of Operation Enduring Freedom* (Santa Monica: Rand Corp., 2005).
12 Mark Giaconia, Operation Viking Hammer: A Green Beret's Firsthand Account of Unconventional Warfare in Northern Iraq, 2003 (Self Published, 2003), pp. 43–5.
13 Author Interview, Electronic Communication, Philadelphia, PA, April 29, 2020.
14 Giaconia, *Operation Viking Hammer*, pp. 49–57.
15 Gordon W. Rudd, *Humanitarian Intervention: Assisting the Iraqi Kurds in Operation Provide Comfort, 1991* (Washington, DC: Department of the Army, 2004), pp. 122–5.

16   Richard Wayman, "Remembering the Kurdish uprising of 1991," *BBC News*, April 7, 2016, https://www.bbc.com/news/in-pictures-35967389.

17   Author Interview with Mike "Starbaby" Pietrucha, Philadelphia, PA, April 29, 2020.

18   Author Interview, Retired Special Operations Forces Officer, Washington, DC, June 9, 2017.

19   "Statement by the President in His Address to the Nation," The White House, September 12, 2001, https://georgewbush-whitehouse.archives.gov/news/releases/2001/09/20010911-16.html.

20   "Transcript of Powell's U.N. presentation," *CNN*, February 6, 2003, https://www.cnn.com/2003/US/02/05/sprj.irq.powell.transcript.09/index.html.

21   Aliza Marcus, *Blood and Belief: The PKK and the Kurdish Fight for Independence* (New York: Now York University Press, 2007).

22   Ibid., pp. 33–6.

23   Marcus, *Blood and Belief,* pp, 47–50.

24   "Weapons Transfers and Violations of the Laws of War in Turkey," Human Rights Watch, November 1, 1995, https://www.hrw.org/report/1995/11/01/weapons-transfers-and-violations-laws-war-turkey.

25   Mahmut Bali Aykan, "The Turkish-Syrian Crisis of October 1998: A Turkish View," Middle East Policy Council, 1999, https://mepc.org/journal/turkish-syrian-crisis-october-1998-turkish-view.

26   Ibid.

27   Tim Weiner, "U.S. Helped Turkey Find and Capture Kurd Rebel," *New York Times*, February 20, 1999, https://www.nytimes.com/1999/02/20/world/us-helped-turkey-find-and-capture-kurd-rebel.html; Miron Varouhakis, "Greek Intelligence and the Capture of PKK Leader Abdullah Ocalan in 1999," *Studies in Intelligence*, vol. 53, no. 1 (March 2009), pp. 1–8, available at: https://www.cia.gov/library/center-for-the-study-of-intelligence/csi-publications/csi-studies/studies/vol53no1/pdfs/U-%20Varouhakis-The%20Case%20of%20Ocalan.pdf.

28   "Statement Made By İsmail Cem, Foreign Minister, on the Special Security Meeting Held between Turkey And Syria October 20, 1998 (Unofficial Translation)," Republic of Turkey, Ministry of Foreign Affairs, October 20, 1998, http://www.mfa.gov.tr/_p_statement-made-by-ismail-cem_-foreign-minister_-on-the-special-security-meeting-held-between-turkey-and-syria_br_october-20_-1998_br__unofficial-translation___p_.en.mfa.

29   Foreign Terrorist Organizations, Bureau of Counter Terrorism, United States Department of State, accessed on May 5, 2020, https://www.state.gov/foreign-terrorist-organizations/.

30   Frank Antenori and Hans Halberstadt, *Roughneck Nine-One* (New York: St. Martin's Press, 2007), Kindle Edition, p. 1491.

31   Richard Boudreaux and Amberin Zaman, "Turkey Rejects U.S. Troop Deployment," *Los Angeles Times*, March 2, 2003, https://www.latimes.com/archives/la-xpm-2003-mar-02-fg-iraq2-story.html.

32   Giaconia, *Operation Viking Hammer,* p. 68.

33   Ibid.

34   James Dobbins, et. al., *Occupying Iraq: A History of the Coalition Provincial Authority* (Santa Monica: Rand Corp, 2009), pp. 91–2.

35   Jama'at al-Tawhid wal-Jihad, which was formed in Jordan in the late 1990s. For more information see: Patrick B. Johnston, et. al., *Foundations of the Islamic State: Management, Money, and Terror in Iraq, 2005–2010* (Santa Monica: Rand Corp,

2016), p. 14, available at: https://www.rand.org/content/dam/rand/pubs/research_reports/RR1100/RR1192/RAND_RR1192.pdf.

36 Haroro J. Ingram, Craig Whiteside, and Charlie Winter, *The ISIS Reader: Milestone Texts of the Islamic State Movement* (Oxford: Oxford University Press, 2020), pp. 37–54.

37 Joel D. Rayburn, et. al., *The U.S. Army in the Iraq War: Invasion, Insurgency, and Civil War, Volume 1* (Carlisle: U.S. Army War College Press, 2019), pp. 532–3, available at: https://publications.armywarcollege.edu/pubs/3667.pdf.

38 Ibid.

39 Carter Malkasian, *Illusions of Victory: The Anbar Awakening and the Rise of the Islamic State* (Oxford: Oxford University Press, 2017), pp. 41–72.

40 Author Interview, Electronic Communication, Philadelphia, PA, April 25, 2020.

41 "The Reflective Belt: An Icon of the Global War On Terror," *Task and Purpose*, October 26, 2015, https://taskandpurpose.com/mandatory-fun/the-reflective-belt-an-icon-of-the-global-war-on-terror.

42 Sean Naylor, *Relentless Strike: The Secret History of Joint Special Operations Command* (New York: Saint Martin's Press, 2015), pp. 279–90.

Chapter 2

1   Aron Lund, "The Politics of Memory: Ten Years of War in Syria," The Century Foundation, March 15, 2021, https://tcf.org/content/commentary/politics-memory-ten-years-war-syria/.

2   Author Interview with Michael Noonan, Philadelphia, PA, May 7, 2020.

3   Benjamin S. Lambeth, *Air Operations in Israel's War against Hezbollah: Learning from Lebanon and Getting It Right in Gaza* (Santa Monica: Rand Corp, 2011), available at: https://www.rand.org/pubs/monographs/MG835.html; Frederic C. Hof, "Mapping Peace between Syria and Israel," United States Institute of Peace, 2009, https://www.usip.org/sites/default/files/resources/mappingpeace.pdf.

4   "Syria's Assad Meets Erdogan as Turkey Mediates for Mideast Peace," *Hurriyet*, May 8, 2008, https://www.hurriyet.com.tr.

5   Stephen Kinzer, "Pro-Islamic Premier Steps Down in Turkey under Army Pressure," *New York Times*, June 19, 1997, https://www.nytimes.com/1997/06/19/world/pro-islamic-premier-steps-down-in-turkey-under-army-pressure.html.

6   "Istanbul Mayor, an Islamist, Is Given 10-Month Jail Term," *Reuters*, April 22, 1998, https://www.nytimes.com/1998/04/22/world/istanbul-mayor-an-islamist-is-given-10-month-jail-term.html.

7   Gareth Jenkins, "The Changing Objects of Fear: The Arrest of Ilker Basbug," Central Asia-Caucus Institute, Silk Road Studies Program, January 9, 2012, https://www.turkeyanalyst.org/publications/turkey-analyst-articles/item/290-the-changing-objects-of-fear-the-arrest-of-ilker-basbug.html.

8   Ryan Gingeras, "Last Rites for a 'Pure Bandit': Clandestine Service, Historiography and the Origins of the Turkish 'Deep State,'" *Past & Present*, no. 206 (February 2010), pp. 151–74.

9   "Turkey Agrees to Plans for Arab 'Free Trade Zone,'" *BBC News*, June 10, 2010, https://www.bbc.com/news/10290025.

10 Delphine Strauss, "Syrian Shoppers Bring Turkish Delight," *Financial Times*, May 11, 2020, https://www.ft.com/content/e2a589fc-5d44-11df-8373-00144feab49a; Dan

Bilefsky, "Syrians' New Ardor for a Turkey Looking Eastward," *New York Times*, July 24, 2010, https://www.nytimes.com/2010/07/25/world/middleeast/25turkey.html.

11 Rachel Donadio, "Libyan Immigrants Becoming Italian Immigrants," *New York Times*, May 13, 2011, https://www.nytimes.com/2011/05/14/world/europe/14refugees.html.

12 For a recounting of the debate inside the Obama administration, see: Robert M. Gates, *Duty: Memoirs of a Secretary at War* (New York: Alfred A. Knopf, 2014), pp. 510–23.

13 United Nations Security Council Resolution 1973, S/RES/1973, March 17, 2011, https://www.nato.int/nato_static_fl2014/assets/pdf/pdf_2011_03/20110927_110311-UNSCR-1973.pdf.

14 Charlie Savage and Mark Landler, "White House Defends Continuing U.S. Role in Libya Operation," *New York Times*, June 15, 2011, https://www.nytimes.com/2011/06/16/us/politics/16powers.html.

15 Tim Gaynor and Taha Zargoun, "Gaddafi Caught like 'Rat' in a Drain, Humiliated and Shot," *Reuters*, October 21, 2011, https://www.reuters.com/article/us-libya-gaddafi-finalhours-idUSTRE79K43S20111021.

16 Steve Gutterman, "No UN Mandate to Attack Gaddafi Forces: Russia," *Reuters*, March 28, 2011, https://af.reuters.com/article/topNews/idAFJOE72R0EL20110328.

17 As cited in Dexter Filkins, "The Moral Logic of Humanitarian Intervention," *New Yorker*, September 16, 2019, https://www.newyorker.com/magazine/2019/09/16/the-moral-logic-of-humanitarian-intervention.

18 As quoted in, Tom Blamforth, "For Russia, Qaddafi's Downfall Is No Cause for Celebration," Radio Free Europe Radio Liberty, October 25, 2011, https://www.rferl.org/a/moscow_not_celebrating_qaddafi_downfall/24370945.html.

19 Alexey Malashenko, "Russia and the Arab Spring," Carnegie Moscow Center, October 2013, p. 9, https://carnegieendowment.org/files/russia_arab_spring2013.pdf.

20 Dmitri Trenin, *What Is Russia up to in the Middle East* (Cambridge: Polity Press, 2018), Kindle Edition, p. 44.

21 Laura Rozen and Glenn Thrush, "Obama: Transition in Egypt 'Must Begin Now,'" *Politico*, February 1, 2011, https://www.politico.com/story/2011/02/obama-transition-in-egypt-must-begin-now-048613.

22 Trenin, *What Is Russia up to in the Middle East*, p. 44.

23 Abboud, *Syria*, p. 56.

24 Ibid., pp. 57–9.

25 Ibid.

26 Trenin, *What Is Russia up to in the Middle East*, p. 48.

27 As cited in, Aaron Stein, *Turkey's New Foreign Policy: Davutoglu, the AKP, and the Pursuit of Regional Order* (London: Routledge, 2014), p. 62.

28 Author Interview, Ambassador Robert Ford, Philadelphia, PA, May 22, 2020.

29 Macon Phillips, "President Obama: 'The Future of Syria Must Be Determined by Its People, but President Bashar al-Assad Is Standing in Their Way,'" The White House, August 18, 2011, https://obamawhitehouse.archives.gov/blog/2011/08/18/president-obama-future-syria-must-be-determined-its-people-president-bashar-al-assad.

30 Mark Mazzetti, "C.I.A. Study of Covert Aid Fueled Skepticism about Helping Syrian Rebels," *New York Times*, October 14, 2014.

31 Author Interview, Ambassador Robert Ford, Philadelphia, PA, May 22, 2020.

32 Author Interview, State Department Official, Philadelphia, PA, May 22, 2020.

33 Sebnem Arsu, "Turkish Premier Urges Assad to Quit in Syria," *New York Times*, November 22, 2011, https://www.nytimes.com/2011/11/23/world/middleeast/turkish-leader-says-syrian-president-should-quit.html.

34 Trenin, *What Is Russia up to in the Middle East,* p. 48.

35 Joe Vaccarello, "Iran Sending Banned Weapons to Syria, U.N. Report Says," *CNN,* May 12, 2011, https://www.cnn.com/2011/WORLD/meast/05/12/un.syria.iran.weapons/index.html.

36 Author Interview, Former NGO worker based in the area, Philadelphia, PA, May 14, 2020.

37 Author Interviews with Turkish experts and policymakers, Istanbul and Ankara, October–November 2012.

38 Author Interview, US Air Force Pilot, Philadelphia, PA, May 18, 2020.

39 Mark Mazzetti, C. J. Chivers, and Eric Schmitt, "Taking Outsize Role in Syria, Qatar Funnels Arms to Rebels," *New York Times,* June 29, 2013, https://www.nytimes.com/2013/06/30/world/middleeast/sending-missiles-to-syrian-rebels-qatar-muscles-in.html.

40 Taylor Luck, "Syria Pivot? Why Anti-Assad Rebels, Dropped by CIA, Could Land with Jihadists," *Christian Science Monitor,* July 26, 2017, https://www.csmonitor.com/World/Middle-East/2017/0726/Syria-pivot-Why-anti-Assad-rebels-dropped-by-CIA-could-land-with-jihadists.

41 Author Interview, Ambassador Robert Ford, Philadelphia, PA, May 22, 2020.

42 Vice President Biden, Harvard University Event, October 2, 2014, available at: https://www.youtube.com/watch?v=npd4OSPJrt0.

43 Author Interview, Senior Government Official, Philadelphia, PA, August 29, 2020.

44 Author Interview, Person Familiar with the CIA Program, Philadelphia, PA, August 20, 2020.

45 Michael E. DeVine, "Covert Action and Clandestine Activities of the Intelligence Community: Selected Definitions in Brief," Congressional Research Service, updated June 14, 2019, https://fas.org/sgp/crs/intel/R45175.pdf.

46 Author Interview, Former US Government Official, Philadelphia, PA, August 5, 2020.

47 Martin Chulov, "ISIS: The Inside Story," *The Guardian,* December 11, 2014, https://www.theguardian.com/world/2014/dec/11/-sp-isis-the-inside-story.

48 Johnston, et. al., *Foundations of the Islamic State,* p. 36.

49 Author Interview, Ambassador Robert Ford, Philadelphia, PA, May 22, 2020.

50 Saad Abedine and Laura Smith-Spark, "U.S. Blacklists al-Nusra Front Fighters in Syria," *CNN,* December 11, 2012, https://www.cnn.com/2012/12/11/world/meast/syria-civil-war/index.html.

51 "Remarks by the President to the White House Press Corps," The White House, August 20, 2012, https://obamawhitehouse.archives.gov/the-press-office/2012/08/20/remarks-president-white-house-press-corps.

52 "Government Assessment of the Syrian Government's Use of Chemical Weapons on August 21, 2013," The White House, August 30, 2013, https://obamawhitehouse.archives.gov/the-press-office/2013/08/30/government-assessment-syrian-government-s-use-chemical-weapons-august-21.

53 Ibid.

54 Nicholas Watt and Nick Hopkins, "Cameron Forced to Rule out British Attack on Syria after MPs Reject Motion," *The Guardian,* August 29, 2013, https://www.theguardian.com/world/2013/aug/29/cameron-british-attack-syria-mps.

55 Mark Murray, "NBC Poll: Nearly 80 Percent Want Congressional Approval on Syria," *NBC News,* August 30, 2013, https://www.nbcnews.com/news/world/nbc-poll-nearly-80-percent-want-congressional-approval-syria-flna8C11038428.

56 Paul Lewis and Spencer Ackerman, "US Set for Syria Strikes after Kerry Says Evidence of Chemical Attack Is 'Clear,'" *The Guardian*, August 31, 2013, https://www.theguardian.com/world/2013/aug/30/john-kerry-syria-attack-clear-evidence.

57 Chuck Todd, "The White House Walk-and-Talk That Changed Obama's Mind on Syria," *NBC News*, August 31, 2013, https://www.nbcnews.com/news/world/white-house-walk-talk-changed-obamas-mind-syria-flna8C11051182.

58 Patrick Homan and Jeffrey Lantis, *The Battle for U.S. Foreign Policy: Congress, Parties, and Factions in the 21st Century* (London: Palgrave Macmillan, 2020), p. 132.

59 Luis Martinez, "Gen. Martin Dempsey Lays Out US Military Options for Syria," *ABC News*, July 22, 2013, https://abcnews.go.com/blogs/politics/2013/07/gen-martin-dempsey-lays-out-us-military-options-for-syria.

60 Author US Army Officer, Interview, Philadelphia, PA, May 12, 2020.

61 Author Interview, Lt. General (Ret.) Michael Nagata, Philadelphia, PA, July 2, 2020.

62 Author Interview, Former US Official at the Department of Defense, Philadelphia, PA, May 14, 2020.

63 Ibid.

64 Linda Robinson, et. al., *Improving the Understanding of Special Operations: A Case History Analysis* (Santa Monica: Rand Corp, 2018) p. 112, available at: https://www.rand.org/pubs/research_reports/RR2026.html.

65 Nina M. Serafino, "Security Assistance Reform: 'Section 1206' Background and Issues for Congress," Congressional Research Service, December 8, 2014, https://fas.org/sgp/crs/natsec/RS22855.pdf.

66 "The Evolution of Cooperative Threat Reduction: Issues for Congress," Congressional Research Service, Updated November 23, 2015, https://fas.org/sgp/crs/nuke/R43143.pdf.

67 Author Interview, US Military Official, Philadelphia, PA, May 14, 2020.

68 Author Interview, US Army Officer, Electronic Communication, Philadelphia, PA, May 17, 2020.

69 Kirk Sowell, "Iraq's Second Sunni Insurgency," Hudson Institute, August 9, 2014, https://www.hudson.org/research/10505-iraq-s-second-sunni-insurgency.

70 Ibid.

71 "Iraq Protests Signal Growing Tension between Sunni and Shia Communities," *The Guardian*, December 26, 2012, https://www.theguardian.com/world/2012/dec/26/iraq-protests-tension-sunni-shia.

72 Author Interview, Patrick Osgood, Electronic Communication, May 20, 2020.

73 Ned Parker, Isabel Coles, and Raheem Salman, "Inside the Fall of Mosul," *Reuters*, October 14, 2014, https://www.pulitzer.org/files/2015/international-reporting/reutersisis/01reutersisis2015.pdf.

74 Author Interview, U.S. Military Member, Washington, DC, May 2017.

75 Author Interview, US Army Officer, Electronic Communication, May 9, 2020.

76 Amberin Zaman, "Turkey Ignored Direct Warnings of ISIS Attack on Mosul," *Al Monitor*, June 12, 2014, https://www.al-monitor.com/pulse/originals/2014/06/mosul-turkish-consulate-isis-ankara-syria-iraq-kidnappings.html#ixzz6N24MOVFW.

77 Naylor, *Relentless Strike*, p. 435.

78 Author Interview, US Air Force Pilot, Philadelphia, PA, April 29, 2020.

79 Naylor, *Relentless Strike*, pp. 435–6.

80 Barbara Starr, "Secret Heroes: Newly Revealed Silver Star Actions against ISIS," *CNN*, August 9, 2016, https://www.cnn.com/2016/08/09/politics/isis-battles-silver-stars-documented/index.html.

Chapter 3

1   Author Interview, Cathy Otten, Philadelphia, PA, May 20, 2020.
2   Author Interview, US Air Force Pilot, Philadelphia, PA, April 29, 2020.
3   Author Interview, Patrick Osgood, Philadelphia, PA, May 20, 2020.
4   Author Interview, US Army Officer, Philadelphia, PA, May 22, 2020.
5   Ibid.
6   Author Interview, US Army Officer, Philadelphia, PA, May 23, 2020.
7   Author Interview, Lt. General (Ret.) Michael Nagata, Philadelphia, PA, July 2, 2020.
8   Claudia Parsons, "Iraq Asks U.N. to Renew Mandate for U.S.-led Forces," *Reuters*, December 10, 2007, https://www.reuters.com/article/us-iraq-un/iraq-asks-u-n-to-renew-mandate-for-u-s-led-forces-idUSN1044951620071210.
9   R. Chuck Mason, "U.S.-Iraq Withdrawal/Status of Forces Agreement: Issues for Congressional Oversight," Congressional Research Service, July 13, 2009, https://fas.org/sgp/crs/natsec/R40011.pdf.
10 Author Interview, US Special Forces Soldier, Philadelphia, PA, May 22, 2020.
11 David Remnick, "Going the Distance: On and Off the Road with Barack Obama," *New Yorker*, January 27, 2014, https://www.newyorker.com/magazine/2014/01/27/going-the-distance-david-remnick.
12 Malkasian, *Illusions of Victory,* pp. 686–8.
13 Peter Baker, "Diplomatic Note Promises Immunity from Iraqi Law for U.S. Advisory Troops," *New York Times*, June 23, 2014, https://www.nytimes.com/2014/06/24/world/middleeast/us-advisory-troops-get-immunity-from-iraqi-law.html.
14 Author Interview, US State Department Official, May 11, 2020, Philadelphia, PA.
15 Ibid.
16 Author Interview, US State Department Official, May 11, 2020, Philadelphia, PA.
17 Author Interview, F-15E Weapons Systems Officer, Philadelphia, PA, April 29, 2020.
18 Helene Cooper, Mark Landler, and Alissa J. Rubin, "Obama Allows Limited Airstrikes on ISIS," *New York Times*, August 7, 2014.
19 Ibid.
20 Ibid.
21 Naylor, *Relentless Strike,* pp. 7–10.
22 Author Interview, JSOC Member, Philadelphia, PA.
23 Author Interview, Lt. General (Ret.) Michael Nagata, Philadelphia, PA, July 2, 2020.
24 Author Interview, Specialized US Soldier, Philadelphia, PA, May 9, 2020.
25 Author Interview, US Army Special Forces Officer Philadelphia, PA, June 6, 2020.
26 Author Interview, US Army Special Forces Officer Philadelphia, PA, June 8, 2020.
27 Author Interview, F-15E Weapons Systems Officer, Philadelphia, PA, April 29, 2020.
28 Author Interview, Lt. General (Ret.) Michael Nagata, Philadelphia, PA, July 2, 2020.
29 Author Interview, US Special Forces Soldier, Philadelphia, PA, May 29, 2020.
30 Author Interview, US Special Forces Officer, Philadelphia, PA, June 12, 2020.
31 Author Interview, US Special Forces Officer, Philadelphia, PA, June 6, 2020.
32 Author Interview, former Department of Defense Official, Philadelphia, PA, May 28, 2020.
33 Jennifer Hlad, "Breaking the Siege on Sinjar," *Air Force Magazine*, October 2015, https://www.airforcemag.com/PDF/MagazineArchive/Documents/2015/October%20 2015/1015sinjar.pdf.
34 Author Interview, F-15E Weapons Systems Officer, Philadelphia, PA, April 29, 2020.

35   Author Interview, Task Force Member, Philadelphia, PA, June 15, 2020.
36   Rebecca Collard, "This Fragile Iraqi Dam Could Pose a Bigger Threat than ISIS," *TIME*, March 26, 2016, https://time.com/4272242/mosul-dam-iraq-isis-collapse/.
37   Author Interview, US Special Forces Officer, Philadelphia, PA, May 22, 2020.
38   Author Interview, US Army Special Forces Officer, Philadelphia, PA, June 8, 2020.
39   Ibid.
40   Ibid.
41   Author Interview, Lt. General (Ret.) Michael Nagata, Philadelphia, PA, July 2, 2020.
42   Ibid.
43   Author Interview, F-15E Weapons Systems Officer, Philadelphia, PA, April 29, 2020.
44   Ibid.
45   Author Interview, US Special Forces Officer, Philadelphia, PA, June 6, 2020.
46   Author Interview, US Special Forces Officer, Philadelphia, PA, June 12, 2020.
47   Author Interview, US Air Force F-15E Pilot, Philadelphia, PA, June 6, 2020.
48   Oriana Pawlyk, "Air Force Acknowledges Clandestine Base in UAE," *military. com*, August 28, 2017, https://www.military.com/dodbuzz/2017/08/28/air-force-acknowledges-clandestine-base-in-uae.
49   Author Interview, F-15E Weapons Systems Officer, Philadelphia, PA, April 29, 2020.
50   Ibid.
51   Ibid.
52   Jim Miklaszewski and Cassandra Vinograd, "U.S. Bombs ISIS Sites in Syria and Targets Khorasan Group," *NBC News*, September 23, 2014, https://www.nbcnews.com/storyline/isis-terror/u-s-bombs-isis-sites-syria-targets-khorasan-goup-n209421.
53   Author Interview, F-15E Weapons Systems Officer, Philadelphia, PA, April 29, 2020.
54   Ibid.
55   Harriet Allsopp and Wladimir Van Wilgenburg, *The Kurds of Northern Syria: Governance, Diversity, and Conflicts* (London: I.B. Tauris, 2019), pp. 61–4.
56   Debbie Bookchin, "How My Father's Ideas Helped the Kurds Create a New Democracy," *New York Review of Books*, June 15, 2018, https://www.nybooks.com/daily/2018/06/15/how-my-fathers-ideas-helped-the-kurds-create-a-new-democracy/.
57   Murray Bookchin, "Libertarian Municipalism: An Overview," *The Anarchist Library*, October 1991, https://theanarchistlibrary.org/library/murray-bookchin-libertarian-municipalism-an-overview.
58   Harriet Allsopp and Wladimir Van Wilgenburg, *The Kurds of Northern Syria*, pp. 63–4.
59   "Syria Grants Citizenship to Kurds in Northeast," *Voice of America*, April 6, 2011, https://www.voanews.com/world-news/middle-east-dont-use/syria-grants-citizenship-kurds-northeast.
60   Author Interview, Former Senior US Government Official Philadelphia, PA, May 22, 2020.
61   Harriet Allsopp and Wladimir Van Wilgenburg, *The Kurds of Northern Syria*, pp. 64–5.
62   Liz Sly and Loveday Morris, "Kurds Open Escape Route for Some Trapped Yazidis," *Sydney Morning Herald*, August 10, 2014, https://www.smh.com.au/world/kurds-open-escape-route-for-some-trapped-yazidis-20140810-102e92.html.
63   Author Interview, US Government Official, May 6, 2020.
64   Ibid.
65   Bob Woodward, *Plan of Attack* (New York: Simon & Schuster, 2004).
66   Wladimir Van Wilgenburg, "Kurdish Counterterrorism Group Works to Prevent Terrorism in Kurdistan and Iraq," Jamestown Foundation, March 12, 2010.

https://jamestown.org/program/kurdish-counterterrorism-group-works-to-prevent-terrorism-in-kurdistan-and-iraq/.

67 Michael M. Gunter, "Kurdish Disunity in Historical Perspective," *Seton Hall Journal of Diplomacy and International Relations, Spring* 2018, pp. 33–7, http://blogs.shu.edu/journalofdiplomacy/files/2018/06/Kurdish-Disunity-In-Historical-Perspective.pdf.

68 Ben Brumfield, Josh Levs, and Gul Tuysuz, "200,000 Flee in Biggest Displacement of Syrian Conflict, Monitor Says," *CNN*, September 23, 2014, https://www.cnn.com/2014/09/22/world/meast/syria-civil-war/index.html.

69 Ersin Caksu, "Inside Kobane: Eyewitness Account in Besieged Kurdish City," *BBC News*, November 5, 2014, https://www.bbc.com/news/world-middle-east-29902405.

70 Cale Salih and Aaron Stein, "How Turkey Misread the Kurds," *Al Jazeera English*, January 20, 2015, https://www.aljazeera.com/indepth/opinion/2015/01/how-turkey-misread-kurds-201511910421859659.html.

71 Author Interview, Journalist who attended the BDP rallies, Geneva, Switzerland, May 2016.

72 Amberin Zaman, "Syrian Kurdish Commander Sparks Fresh US-Turkish Row," *Al Monitor*, October 25, 2019, https://www.al-monitor.com/pulse/originals/2019/10/mazloum-kobane-us-visit-uproar-turkey-erdogan.html.

73 Author Interview, F-15E Weapons Systems Officer, Philadelphia, PA, April 29, 2020; Author Interview, US Army Special Forces Officer, Philadelphia, PA, April 29, 2020.

74 Author Interview, Task Force Member, Philadelphia, PA June 15, 2020.

75 Rebecca Grant, "The Siege of Kobani," *Air Force Magazine*, August 29, 2018, https://www.airforcemag.com/article/the-siege-of-kobani/.

76 Author Interview US Army Special Forces Soldier, Philadelphia, PA, May 17, 2020.

77 As quoted in, Constanze Letsch, "US Drops Weapons and Ammunition to Help Kurdish Fighters in Kobani," *The Guardian*, October 20, 2014, https://www.theguardian.com/world/2014/oct/20/turkey-iraqi-kurds-kobani-isis-fighters-us-air-drops-arms.

78 Ceylan Yeginsu, "Turkish Leader Says U.S. Airdrop Aided ISIS Militants," *New York Times*, October 22, 2014, https://www.nytimes.com/2014/10/23/world/europe/isis-kobani-syria-turkey.html.

79 Former Obama Administration Official, Remarks at a Private Roundtable, Washington, DC, July 21, 2017.

80 Ibid.

81 Ibid.

82 Author Interview, A-10 Pilot, Philadelphia, PA, May 15, 2020.

83 Author Interview, F-15E Pilot, Philadelphia, PA, May 18, 2020.

84 Author Interview, DoD Official, Philadelphia, PA.

85 Author Interview, Specialized USSOF, Washington, DC, August 2016.

86 Author Interview, A-10 Pilot, Philadelphia, PA, May 5, 2020.

87 Author Interview, F-15E Weapons Systems Officer, Philadelphia, PA, April 29, 2020.

88 Author Interview, F-15E Pilot, Philadelphia, PA, April 27, 2020.

Chapter 4

1 Author Interview, Department of Defense Official, Philadelphia, PA, May 15, 2020.

2 "Statement by the President on ISIL," The White House, September 10, 2014, https://obamawhitehouse.archives.gov/the-press-office/2014/09/10/statement-president-isil-1.

3   Author Interview, Former DoD Official, Philadelphia, PA, May 29, 2020.
4   Author Interview, State Department Official, Philadelphia, PA, May 12, 2020.
5   Christopher M. Blanchard and Amy Belasco, "Train and Equip Program for Syria: Authorities, Funding, and Issues for Congress," Congressional Research Service, June 9, 2015, https://fas.org/sgp/crs/natsec/R43727.pdf; H.R.3979—Carl Levin and Howard P. "Buck," McKeon National Defense Authorization Act for Fiscal Year 2015, https://www.congress.gov/bill/113th-congress/house-bill/3979/text.
6   Author Interview, Former DoD Official, Philadelphia, PA, May 12, 2020.
7   Author Interview, Lt. General (Ret.) Michael Nagata, Philadelphia, PA, July 2, 2020.
8   Author Interview, Former Department of Defense Official, Philadelphia, PA, June 2, 2020.
9   Ibid.
10 Statement by the NATO Secretary General on Patriot Missile Deployment to Turkey, North Atlantic Treaty Organization, November 21, 2012, https://www.nato.int/cps/en/SID-C70E4803-817AEF2F/natolive/news_91426.htm.
11 Ivan Watson, "Turkey Strikes Targets in Syria in Retaliation for Shelling Deaths," *CNN*, October 4, 2012, https://www.cnn.com/2012/10/03/world/europe/turkey-syria-tension/index.html.
12 Author Interview, Ambassador Robert Ford, Philadelphia, PA, May 22, 2020.
13 Author Interview, Former Senior US Government Official, Philadelphia, PA, May 2020.
14 Ibid.
15 John Vandiver, "US Patriot Deployment in Turkey Mired in Bureaucratic Red Tape," *Stars and Stripes*, January 30, 2013, https://www.stripes.com/news/europe/us-patriot-deployment-in-turkey-mired-in-bureaucratic-red-tape-1.205778.
16 Thorsten Tanski, "The Competence Centre for Surface Based Air and Missile Defence," Joint Air Power Competence Center, 2017, https://www.japcc.org/the-competence-centre-for-surface-based-air-and-missile-defence/.
17 Author Interview, Former Senior US Government Official.
18 Adam Entous and Joe Parkinson, "Turkey's Spymaster Plots Own Course on Syria," *The Wall Street Journal*, October 10, 2013, https://www.wsj.com/articles/turkey8217s-spymaster-plots-own-course-on-syria-1381373295?tesla=y.
19 Karen DeYoung, "US Considers Opening a New Front against Islamic State to Create a Safe Zone in Syria," *The Washington Post*, December 1, 2014, https://www.washingtonpost.com/world/national-security/us-weighs-a-new-front-to-create-safe-zone-in-syria/2014/12/01/1aae1bb0-796b-11e4-9a27-6fdbc612bff8_story.html.
20 Author Interview, Senior US Government Official, Philadelphia, PA, June 29, 2020.
21 Author Interview, Department of Defense Official, Philadelphia, PA, June 9, 2020.
22 Ibid.
23 Tulay Karadeniz, "Turkey, U.S. Sign Deal to Train, Equip Syrian Opposition, Official Says," *Reuters*, February 19, 2015, https://www.reuters.com/article/us-mideast-crisis-training-turkey/turkey-u-s-sign-deal-to-train-equip-syrian-opposition-official-says-idUSKBN0LN1YY20150219.
24 Author Interview, US Special Forces Officer, Philadelphia, PA, June 9, 2020.
25 Author Interview, Former Marine Forces Special Operations Command Officer, Philadelphia, PA, April 14, 2020.
26 Author Interview, US Army Special Forces Soldier, Philadelphia, PA, May 17, 2020.
27 Author Interview, Former US Army Special Forces Officer, Washington, DC, June 9, 2017.

28 Author Interview, US Army Special Forces Officer, Philadelphia, PA, May 17, 2020.
29 Ibid.
30 Author Interview, Former DoD Official, Philadelphia, PA, June 10, 2020.
31 Author Interview, US Special Forces Officer, Philadelphia, PA, May 17, 2020.
32 Author Interview, Turkish MIT Official, Ankara, Turkey, March 2015.
33 Author Interview, A-10 Pilot, Philadelphia, PA, May 15, 2020.
34 Author Interview, Special Forces Officer, Philadelphia, PA, June 6, 2020.
35 "Kurdish Group Claims 'Revenge Murder' on Turkish Police," *Al Jazeera English*, July 22, 2015, https://www.aljazeera.com/news/2015/07/kurdish-group-claims-revenge-murder-turkish-police-150722132945249.html.
36 Author Interview, DoD Official, Philadelphia, PA, May 12, 2020.
37 Ibid.
38 Author Interview, State Department Official, Philadelphia, PA, June 10, 2020.
39 Author Interview, US Special Forces Officer, Philadelphia, PA, May 17, 2020.
40 Author Interview, DoD Official, Philadelphia, PA, June 11, 2020.
41 James Rosen, "In About-face, Pentagon Says U.S.-trained Syrians Gave Trucks, Weapons to al-Qaida," *The Miami Herald*, September 26, 2015, https://www.miamiherald.com/news/nation-world/world/article36639213.html.
42 Anton Lavrov, "The Russian Air Campaign in Syria: A Preliminary Analysis," Center for Naval Analysis, June 2018, https://www.cna.org/CNA_files/PDF/COP-2018-U-017903-Final.pdf.
43 Statement by Deputy National Security Advisor for Strategic Communications Ben Rhodes on Syrian Chemical Weapons Use, The White House, June 13, 2013, https://obamawhitehouse.archives.gov/the-press-office/2013/06/13/statement-deputy-national-security-advisor-strategic-communications-ben-.
44 Author Interview, Former National Security Council Staffer, Philadelphia, PA, July 17, 2020.
45 Author Interview, Former Senior Official, Philadelphia, PA, August 28, 2020.
46 Author Interview, Person Familiar with the Program, Philadelphia, PA, August 27, 2020.
47 Maher Samaan and Anne Barnard, "Assad, in Rare Admission, Says Syria's Army Lacks Manpower," *New York Times*, July 26, 2015, https://www.nytimes.com/2015/07/27/world/middleeast/assad-in-rare-admission-says-syrias-army-lacks-manpower.html.
48 Laila Bassam and Tom Perry, "How Iranian General Plotted Out Syrian Assault in Moscow," *Reuters*, October 6, 2015, https://www.reuters.com/article/us-mideast-crisis-syria-soleimani-insigh/how-iranian-general-plotted-out-syrian-assault-in-moscow-idUSKCN0S02BV20151006.
49 Author Interview, Former National Security Council Official, Philadelphia, PA, June 28, 2020.
50 Ibid.
51 Ibid.
52 Author Interview, DoD Official, Philadelphia, PA, June 9, 2020.
53 Author Interview, A-10 Pilot, Philadelphia, PA, May 29, 2020.
54 Ibid.
55 Author Interview, F-15E Pilot, Philadelphia, PA, April 27, 2020.
56 Author Interview, A-10 Pilot, Philadelphia, PA, May 25, 2020.
57 Ibid.
58 Author Interview, State Department Official, Philadelphia, PA, July 27, 2020.

59 Author Interview, Person Familiar with Agate Noble, Philadelphia, PA, June 20, 2020.
60 Ibid.
61 Author Interview, US Special Forces Officer, Philadelphia, PA, June 8, 2020.
62 Author Interview, US Special Forces Officer, Philadelphia, PA, June 14, 2020.
63 Author Interview, US Special Forces Officer, Philadelphia, PA, June 6, 2020.
64 Ibid.
65 Author Interview, US Special Forces Officer, Philadelphia, PA, June 8, 2020.
66 Ibid.
67 Ibid.
68 Author Interview, US Special Forces Officer, Philadelphia, PA May 29, 2020.
69 Author Interview, A-10 Pilot, Philadelphia, PA, May 25, 2020,
70 Author Interview, US Special Forces Officer, Philadelphia, PA May 29, 2020.
71 Ibid.
72 Author Interview, A-10 Pilot, Philadelphia, PA, May 25, 2020.
73 Author Interview, US Special Forces Officer, Philadelphia, PA May 29, 2020.
74 Author Interview, Special Forces Officer, Philadelphia, PA, May 29, 2020.
75 Author Interview, F-15E Pilot, Philadelphia, PA, April 27, 2020.
76 Author Interview, US Army Special Operations Officer, Washington, DC, December 30, 2016.
77 Author Interview, Task Force Member, Philadelphia, PA, June 15, 2020.
78 Author Interview, US Army Special Operations Officer, Washington, DC, December 30, 2016.
79 Author Interview, Specialized US Soldier Familiar with the Task Force in Syria, Philadelphia, PA, May 9, 2020.
80 Author Interview, DoD Official, Philadelphia, PA, May 22, 2020.
81 Brian Dodwell, Daniel Milton, and Don Rassler, "The Caliphate's Global Workforce: An inside Look at the Islamic State's Foreign Fighter Paper Trail," Combatting Terrorism Center, April 18, 2016, https://ctc.usma.edu/the-caliphates-global-workforce-an-inside-look-at-the-islamic-states-foreign-fighter-paper-trail/.
82 "Tracing the Supply of Components Used in Islamic State IEDs," Conflict Armament Research, February 2016, https://rinj.org/documents/war-crime/Tracing_The_Supply_of_Components_Used_in_Islamic_State_IEDs.pdf.
83 Author Interview, US Military Official, Philadelphia, PA, June 8, 2020.
84 Author Interview, Task Force Member, Philadelphia, PA, June 17, 2020.
85 Author Interview, DoD Official, Philadelphia, PA, May 22, 2020.
86 Author Interview, Person Familiar with the Islamic State War Plan, Philadelphia, PA, June 21, 2020.
87 Ibid.
88 Author Interview, DoD Official, Philadelphia, PA, May 22, 2020.
89 Author Interview, US Army Special Operations Officer, Philadelphia, PA, May 9, 2020.
90 Author Interview, US State Department Official, Philadelphia, PA, July 27, 2020.
91 Author Interview, US Special Operations Officer, Philadelphia, PA, June 8, 2020.
92 John Davidson and Phil Stewart, "U.S. Airdrops Ammunition to Syria Rebels," *Reuters*, October 12, 2015, https://www.reuters.com/article/us-mideast-crisis-syria-idUSKCN0S61LX20151013.
93 Author Interview, DoD Official, Philadelphia, PA, June 22, 2020.
94 Author Interview, State Department Official, Philadelphia, PA, July 27, 2020.

95   Clarissa Ward and Tim Lister, "Inside Syria: The Farm Airstrip That's Part of the U.S. Fight against ISIS," *CNN,* February 3, 2016, https://www.cnn.com/2016/02/02/middleeast/syria-isis-us-airstrip/index.html.

96   Author Interview, Former National Security Council Official, Philadelphia, PA, July 5, 2020.

97   Author Interview, A-10 Pilot, Philadelphia, PA, May 25, 2020.

98   Ibid.

99   Author Interview, State Department Official, Philadelphia, PA, June 23, 2020.

100 Author Interview, Coalition Pilot, Philadelphia, PA, May 10, 2020.

101 Author Interview, A-10 Pilot, Philadelphia, PA, May 19, 2020.

102 Author Interview, A-10 Pilot, Philadelphia, PA, May 29, 2020.

103 Author Interview, F-15E WSO, Philadelphia, PA, April 29, 2020.

104 Author Interview, F-15E WSO, Washington, DC, July 2017.

105 David Cenciotti, "Russian Su-30SM, Su-24 Violate Turkish Airspace. Flanker Locks on TuAF F-16 for +5 Minutes," *The Aviationist*, October 5, 2015, https://theaviationist.com/2015/10/05/russian-su-30sm-su-24-violate-turkish-airspace-flanker-locks-on-tuaf-f-16-for-5-minutes/.

106 Patrick tucker, "Did NATO Forces Just Down a Russian Drone over Turkey?" *Defense One*, October 16, 2015, https://www.defenseone.com/threats/2015/10/did-nato-forces-just-down-russian-drone-over-turkey/122882/.

107 Aaron Mehta and Jeff Schogol, "U.S. Pulls F-15 Fighter Jets from Turkey," *Defense News*, December 16, 2015, https://www.airforcetimes.com/news/your-air-force/2015/12/16/u-s-pulls-f-15-fighter-jets-from-turkey/.

108 Author Interview, A-10 Pilot, Philadelphia, PA, May 25, 2020.

109 Author Interview, US Air Force Weapons Systems Officer, Philadelphia, PA, May 25, 2020.

110 Author Interview, Person Familiar with the JOC at Incirlik, Philadelphia, PA, May18, 2020.

111 Author Interview, US Special Forces Officer, Philadelphia, PA, June 8, 2020.

112 Author Interview, A-10 Pilot, Philadelphia, PA, May 25, 2020.

113 Eliott C. McLaughlin, Don Melvin, and Jethro Mullen, "Turkey Won't Apologize for Downing Russian Warplane, Erdogan Says," *CNN*, November 26,2015, https://www.cnn.com/2015/11/26/middleeast/syria-turkey-russia-warplane-shot-down/index.html.

114 Judah Ari Gross, "Russia Deploys S-400 Missile Battery in Syria, State Media Says," *Times of Israel*, November 26, 2015, https://www.timesofisrael.com/russia-deploys-s-400-missile-battery-in-syria-state-media-says/.

115 Author Interview, US Special Forces Officer, Philadelphia, PA, May 8, 2020.

116 Author Interview, DoD Official, Philadelphia, PA, June 1, 2020.

117 Author Meeting with Turkish Representative for Syria at the Ministry of Foreign Affairs, Ankara, Turkey, March 2016.

118 Author Interview, A-10 Pilot, Philadelphia, PA, May 25, 2020.

119 Author Interview, F-15 WSO, Washington, DC, June 2018.

120 Author Interview, A-10 Pilot, Philadelphia, PA, May 29, 2020.

Chapter 5

1   Author Interview, State Department Official, Philadelphia, PA, May 11, 2020.

2   Author Interview, Trainer Located in Jordan, Philadelphia, PA, May 12, 2020.

3   Ibid.
4   Author Interview, State Department Official, Philadelphia, PA, May 11, 2020.
5   Author Interview, Special Operations Officer, Philadelphia, PA, May 17, 2020.
6   Ibid.
7   Author Interview, State Department Official, Washington, DC, May 2017.
8   Author Interview, Special Operations Officer, Philadelphia, PA, May June 12, 2020.
9   Ibid.
10   Author Interview, US Official Familiar with the ISIS War, Philadelphia, PA, May 24, 2020.
11   Author Interview, Task Force Member, Philadelphia, PA, June 19, 2020.
12   "Paris Attacks: What Happened on the Night," *BBC News,* December 9, 2015, https://www.bbc.com/news/world-europe-34818994.
13   "Brussels Explosions: What We Know about Airport and Metro Attacks," *BBC News*, April 9, 2016, https://www.bbc.com/news/world-europe-35869985.
14   "U.S. Envoy: 'We're Taking Out' About 1 ISIS Leader Every 3 Days," *National Public Radio*, June 30, 2016, https://www.publicradiotulsa.org/post/us-envoy-were-taking-out-about-1-isis-leader-every-3-days.
15   Author Interview, A-10 Pilot, Philadelphia, PA, May 29, 2020.
16   Author Interview, DoD Official, Philadelphia, PA, June 9, 2020.
17   Ibid.
18   Humeyra Pamuk, "Turkey Struck Kurdish Militia in Syria Twice: PM Davutoglu," *Reuters*, October 27, 2015, https://www.reuters.com/article/us-mideast-crisis-turkey-kurds/turkey-struck-kurdish-militia-in-syria-twice-pm-davutoglu-idUSKCN0SL0SP20151027.
19   Author Interview, A-10 Pilot, Philadelphia, PA, May 25, 2020.
20   Author Interview, US Special Forces Officer, Philadelphia, PA, June 27, 2020.
21   Author Interview, US Official Familiar with the Qara Qazak Crossing, Philadelphia, PA, October 4, 2020.
22   Ibid.
23   "Turkey Shells Kurdish Positions in Syria for 2nd Say," *The Chicago Tribune*, February 14, 2016, https://www.chicagotribune.com/nation-world/ct-turkey-syria-20160214-story.html.
24   Ayla Albayrak, "Urban Warfare Escalates in Turkey's Kurdish-Majority Southeast," *The Wall Street Journal*, August 19, 2015, https://www.wsj.com/articles/urban-warfare-escalates-in-turkeys-kurdish-majority-southeast-1440024103/.
25   Author Interview, Journalist who spent time with the YDG-H, Washington, DC, May 2018.
26   Cuma Cicek and Vahap Coskun, "The Peace Process from Dolmabahce to the Present Day: Understanding Failure and Finding New Paths," Peace Foundation, April 2016, https://tr.boell.org/sites/default/files/ingilizce.pdf.
27   Author Interview, Journalist who spent time with the YDG-H, Washington, DC, May 2018.
28   Author Interview, Person Familiar with Negotiations with Turkey, Philadelphia, PA, June 21, 2020.
29   Author Interview, Task Force Member, Philadelphia, PA, June 23, 2020.
30   Author Interview, DoD Official, Philadelphia, PA, June 9, 2020.
31   Author Interview, State Department Official, Philadelphia, PA, June 10, 2020.
32   Henry Austin, "Turkish Army Makes First Land Incursion into Syria to Evacuate Sacred Burial Site of Ottoman-Era King Besieged by Isis," *The Independent*, February

22, 2015, https://www.independent.co.uk/news/world/middle-east/turkish-army-makes-first-land-incursion-syria-evacuate-sacred-site-besieged-isis-10062269.html.
33 Author Interview, Person Familiar with Manbij planning, Philadelphia, PA, June 18, 2020.
34 Author Interview, Former National Security Council Official, Philadelphia, PA, June 28, 2020.
35 Author Interview, Former DoD Official, Philadelphia, PA, June 24, 2020.
36 Author Interview, Former National Security Council Official, Philadelphia, PA, June 28, 2020.
37 Author Interview, Special Forces Officer, Philadelphia, PA, May 20, 2020.
38 Author Interview, Person Familiar with the Manbij operation, Philadelphia, PA, June 20, 2020.
39 Ibid.
40 Author Interview, Weapons Systems Officer, Philadelphia, PA, May 15, 2020.
41 Author Interview, Person Familiar with the Targeting Process, Philadelphia, PA, May 30, 2020.
42 Author Interview, Senior US Government Official, Philadelphia, PA, June 29, 2020.
43 Author Interview, State Department Official, Washington, DC, February 16, 2018.
44 Author Interview, State Department Official, Philadelphia, PA, June 26, 2020.
45 Author Interview, US Special Forces Officer involved in the Manbij operation, Philadelphia, PA, June 27, 2020.
46 Author Interview, Former USAID Official, Philadelphia, PA, June 26, 2020.
47 Author Interview, State Department Official, Philadelphia, PA, June 26, 2020.
48 Author Interview, US Special Forces Soldier, Philadelphia, PA, June 28, 2020.
49 Author Interview, Task Force Member, Philadelphia, PA, July 2, 2020.
50 William McCants, *The ISIS Apocalypse: The History, Strategy, and Doomsday Vision of the Islamic State* (New York: St. Martin's Press, 2015), pp. 102–5.
51 Author Interview, Turkish Intelligence Official, Ankara, Turkey, March 2015.
52 Alec Luhn and Ian Black, "Erdoğan Has Apologised for Downing of Russian Jet, Kremlin Says," *The Guardian*, June 27, 2016, https://www.theguardian.com/world/2016/jun/27/kremlin-says-erdogan-apologises-russian-jet-turkish.
53 Author Interview, US Official present in Ankara, Philadelphia, PA, June 15, 2020.
54 Author Interview, Senior US Government Official, Philadelphia, PA, June 29, 2020.
55 Ibid.
56 Author Interview, NATO Official, March 2018.
57 "Hava Kuvvetleri'nde son durum: Bir koltuğa 0.8 pilot düşüyor," T24, August 16, 2016, https://t24.com.tr/haber/hava-kuvvetlerinde-son-durum-bir-koltuga-08-pilot-dusuyor,355200.
58 Shaun Walker and Jennifer Rankin, "Erdoğan and Putin Discuss Closer Ties in First Meeting since Jet Downing," *The Guardian*, August 9, 2016, https://www.theguardian.com/world/2016/aug/09/erdogan-meets-putin-leaders-seek-mend-ties-jet-downing-russia-turkey.
59 Karen DeYoung, "Biden Warns Kurds not to Seek Separate Enclave on Turkish-Syrian Border," *The Washington Post*, August 24, 2016.
60 Author Interview, Senior State Department Official, Philadelphia, PA, June 29, 2020.
61 "Turkey and Syrian Kurdish Forces 'Reach Ceasefire Deal'," *Al Jazeera*, August 31, 2016, https://www.aljazeera.com/news/2016/08/turkey-operations-continue-northern-syria-160830152146879.html.
62 Author Interview, DoD Official, Philadelphia, PA, July 1, 2020.

63   Author Interview, Special Forces Officer, Philadelphia, PA, July 2, 2020.
64   Author Interview, State Department Official, Washington, DC, October 2016.
65   Author Interview, DoD Official, Philadelphia, PA, July 1, 2020.
66   Author Interview, Special Operations Officer, Philadelphia, July 3, 2020.
67   Ibid.
68   Author Interview, Senior US Official, Philadelphia, PA, June 29, 2020.
69   Author Interview, DoD Official, Philadelphia, PA, June 21, 2020.
70   Author Interview, US State Department Official, Washington, DC, March 2017.
71   Anne Barnard, "Battle over Aleppo Is Over, Russia Says, as Evacuation Deal Reached," *New York Times*, December 13, 2016, https://www.nytimes.com/2016/12/13/world/middleeast/syria-aleppo-civilians.html.
72   Author Interview, US State Department Official, Washington, DC, March 2017.
73   Louisa Loveluck, "Aleppo Evacuation Efforts Falter as Islamist Fighters Burn Convoy of Rescue Buses," *The Washington Post*, December 18, 2016, https://www.washingtonpost.com/world/middle_east/cowardly-attack-in-syria-targets-buses-sent-to-evacuate-government-held-villages/2016/12/18/ba7671bc-c525-11e6-bf4b-2c064d32a4bf_story.html.
74   Christiaan Triebert, "The Battle for Al-Bab: Verifying Euphrates Shield Vehicle Losses," *Bellingcat*, February 12, 2017, https://www.bellingcat.com/news/mena/2017/02/12/battle-al-bab-verifying-turkish-military-vehicle-losses/.
75   Atakan Uslu, "El Bâb'da Bir Günde 16 Şehit," *One Dio*, December 21, 2016, https://onedio.com/haber/el-bab-da-bir-gunde-16-sehit-746320.
76   "Turkey Asks U.S.-led Coalition for Air Support at Syria's al-Bab," *Reuters*, December 26, 2016, https://www.reuters.com/article/us-mideast-crisis-syria-turkey-airforce-idUSKBN14F0KE
77   Michael R. Gordon and Eric Schmitt, "Airstrikes by Russia Buttress Turkey in Battle vs. ISIS," *New York Times*, January 8, 2017,https://www.nytimes.com/2017/01/08/us/politics/russia-turkey-syria-airstrikes-isis.html.
78   Author Interview, US Government Official, Philadelphia, PA, July 4, 2020.
79   Ibid.
80   Author Interview, US Official familiar with the Antalya Trilateral, Washington, DC, September 2018.
81   Author Interview, US Army Officer, Philadelphia, PA, April 17, 2020.

Chapter 6

1   Author Interview, Department of Defense Official, Philadelphia, PA, June 21, 2020.
2   Peter Baker and Neil MacFarquhar, "Obama Sees Russia Failing in Syria Effort," *New York Times*, October 2, 2015, https://www.nytimes.com/2015/10/03/world/middleeast/syria-russia-airstrikes.html.
3   Frederic Hof, "Syria: The G7+1 Communiqué," The Atlantic Council, June 19, 2013, https://www.atlanticcouncil.org/blogs/menasource/syria-the-g71-communique/.
4   Author Interview, State Department Official, Philadelphia, PA, July 7, 2020.
5   Author Interview, Ambassador Robert Ford, Philadelphia, PA, May 22, 2020.
6   Ibid.
7   "14 November 2015, Statement of the International Syria Support Group Vienna," United Nations, November 14, 2015, https://www.un.org/undpa/en/Speeches-statements/14112015/syria.

8   Author Interview, Person Familiar with the ISSG Talks, Philadelphia, PA, July 20, 2020.

9   Author Interview, Person Familiar with the ISSG Talks, Philadelphia, PA, July 27, 2020.

10   Author Interview, State Department Official, Philadelphia, Pa, July 27, 2020.

11   "Statement of the International Syria Support Group," United Nations, February 11, 2016, https://www.un.org/sg/en/content/sg/note-correspondents/2016-02-11/note-correspondents-statement-international-syria-support.

12   Author Interview, State Department Official, Philadelphia, PA, July 28, 2020.

13   Security Council Endorses Syria Cessation of Hostilities Accord, Unanimously Adopting Resolution 2268 (2016), United Nations, February 26, 2016, https://www.un.org/press/en/2016/sc12261.doc.htm.

14   Author Interview, State Department Official, Philadelphia, PA, July 8, 2020.

15   Author Interview, State Department Official, Philadelphia, PA, July 11, 2020.

16   Ibid.

17   Author Interview, State Department Official, Philadelphia, PA, July 10, 2020.

18   Author Interview, Former National Security Council Official, Philadelphia, PA, July 25, 2020.

19   Ibid.

20   Ibid.

21   Ibid.

22   Author Interview, DoD Official, Philadelphia, PA, June 15, 2020.

23   Author Interview, Official Familiar with the JIG Negotiations, July 11, 2020.

24   Author Interview, State Department Official, Philadelphia, PA, July 11, 2020.

25   Author Interview, US Official Involved in the Negotiations, Philadelphia, PA, April 4, 2020.

26   Author Interview, US Official familiar with the JIG discussions, Philadelphia, PA, April 10, 2020.

27   Ibid.

28   Author Interview, DoD Official, Philadelphia, PA, June 1, 2020.

29   Author Interview, Person Familiar with the JIG Discussions, Phildelphia, PA, April 10, 2020.

30   "Syria conflict: How Will the New Truce Work?" *BBC News*, September 13, 2016, https://www.bbc.com/news/world-middle-east-37340468.

31   Anne Barnard and Mark Mazzetti, "U.S. Admits Airstrike in Syria, Meant to Hit ISIS, Killed Syrian Troops," *New York Times*, September 17, 2016, https://www.nytimes.com/2016/09/18/world/middleeast/us-airstrike-syrian-troops-isis-russia.html.

32   "Russia, U.S. Tensions Spill Over At UN Security Council Meeting," Radio Free Europe/Radio Liberty, September 18, 2016, https://www.rferl.org/a/russia-us-syria-unsc-/27997902.html.

33   Ibid.

34   Julian Borger and Spencer Ackerman, "Russian Planes Dropped Bombs that Destroyed UN Aid Convoy, US Officials Say," *The Guardian*, September 21, 2016, https://www.theguardian.com/world/2016/sep/20/un-aid-convoy-attack-syria-us-russia.

35   Author Interview, US Government Official, July 7, 2020.

36   Borger and Ackerman, "Russian Planes Dropped Bombs That Destroyed UN Aid Convoy, US Officials Say," https://www.theguardian.com/world/2016/sep/20/un-aid-convoy-attack-syria-us-russia.

37 Author Interview, US Government Official, June 21, 2020.

38 Maggie Haberman and David Sanger, "Transcript: Donald Trump Expounds on His Foreign Policy Views," *New York Times*, March 26, 2016, https://www.nytimes.com/2016/03/27/us/politics/donald-trump-transcript.html.

39 Pamela Engel, "'I would bomb the s— out of' ISIS," *Business Insider*, November 13, 2015, https://www.businessinsider.com/donald-trump-bomb-isis-2015-11.

40 Haberman and Sanger, Donald Trump Expounds on His Foreign Policy Views," *New York Times*, March 26, 2016.

41 Author Interview, Former National Security Council Official, Philadelphia, PA, July 17, 2020.

42 Author Interview, Former National Security Council Official, Washington, DC, June 2017.

43 Author Interview, Former National Security Council Official, Washington, DC, August 2017.

44 Adam Entous, Gregg Jaffe, and Missy Ryan, "Obama's White House Worked for Months on a Plan to Seize Raqqa. Trump's Team Took a Brief Look and Decided not to Pull the Trigger," *The Washington Post*, February 2, 2017, https://www.washingtonpost.com/world/national-security/obamas-white-house-worked-for-months-on-a-plan-to-seize-raqqa-trumps-team-deemed-it-hopelessly-inadequate/2017/02/02/116310fa-e71a-11e6-80c2-30e57e57e05d_story.html.

45 Author Interview, US Special Forces Officer, Philadelphia, PA, July 2, 2020.

46 Author Interview, US Official Familiar with the Turkish planning efforts, Philadelphia, PA, July 5, 2020,

47 Ibid.

48 Ibid.

49 "Department of Defense Press Briefing by Secretary Mattis, General Dunford and Special Envoy McGurk on the Campaign to Defeat ISIS in the Pentagon Press Briefing Room," US Department of Defense, May 19, 2017, https://www.defense.gov/Newsroom/Transcripts/Transcript/Article/1188225/department-of-defense-press-briefing-by-secretary-mattis-general-dunford-and-sp/.

50 Author Interview, US Government Official, Philadelphia, PA, July 15, 2020.

51 Author Interview, Former National Security Council Member, Philadelphia, PA, June 15, 2020.

52 Author Interview, Former Department of Defense Official, Philadelphia, PA, July 18, 2020.

53 Harry Jaffe, "The Turkish Embassy Beat-Down," *The Washingtonian*, May 2, 2018, https://www.washingtonian.com/2018/05/02/turkish-embassy-riot-recep-tayyip-erdogan-washington-lawsuit/.

54 Author Interview, Official Familiar with Operation Nomad Shadow, Philadelphia, PA, July 19, 2020.

55 Author Interview, Official Familiar with Operation Nomad Shadow, Philadelphia, PA, July 20, 2020.

56 Ibid.

57 Author Interview, Official Familiar with Operation Nomad Shadow, Philadelphia, PA, July 22, 2020.

58 Author Interview, Official Familiar with Operation Nomad Shadow, Philadelphia, PA, July 20, 2020.

59 Ibid.

60 Author Interview, Person Familiar with Nomad Shadow, Philadelphia, PA, July 20, 2020.

61 Author Interview, US Official Familiar with the Distribution of Weapons to the YPG, Philadelphia, PA, July 22, 2020.
62 Author Interview, Former Department of Defense Official, Philadelphia, PA, July 21, 2020.
63 Ibid.
64 Maria Tsvetkova and Peter Hobson, "Russia, Iran, Turkey Say Ready to Broker Syria Deal," *Reuters*, December 20, 2016, https://www.reuters.com/article/mideast-crisis-syria-russia-iran-turkey-idINKBN1491ZQ.
65 Author Interview, State Department Official, Philadelphia, PA, July 17, 2020.
66 Ibid.
67 Ibid.
68 Author Interview, Former National Security Council Official, Philadelphia, PA, July 18, 2020.
69 Author Interview, Person Familiar with the Vienna Channel, Philadelphia, PA, July 10, 2020.
70 Julia Edwards Ainsley and Matt Spetalnick, "Trump Says He Will Order 'safe zones' for Syria," *Reuters*, January 25, 2017, https://www.reuters.com/article/us-usa-trump-syria-safezones/trump-says-he-will-order-safe-zones-for-syria-idUSKBN1592O8.
71 Ibid.
72 Author Interview, US Official Familiar with the Astana Process, Philadelphia, PA, July 20, 2020.
73 Michael D. Shear and Michael R. Gordon, "63 Hours: From Chemical Attack to Trump's Strike in Syria," *New York Times*, April 7, 2017, https://www.nytimes.com/2017/04/07/us/politics/syria-strike-trump-timeline.html.
74 Author Interview, Person Familiar with the Secretary's Thinking, Philadelphia, PA, July 22, 2020.
75 Author Interview, Person Familiar with the Vienna Channel, Philadelphia, PA, July 14, 2020.
76 Author Interview, State Department Official, Philadelphia, PA, July 18, 2020.
77 Author Interview, Person Familiar with the Southwest Ceasefire Negotiations, Philadelphia, PA, July 16, 2020.
78 Unpublished Principles to Govern the Formation of an Amman Monitoring Center.

Chapter 7

1   Author Interview, Task Force Member, Philadelphia, PA, September 29, 2020.
2   Shawn Snow, "Syrian Kurds are Now Armed with sensitive US Weaponry, and the Pentagon Denies Supplying It," *Military Times*, May 7, 2017, https://www.militarytimes.com/news/your-military/2017/05/07/syrian-kurds-are-now-armed-with-sensitive-us-weaponry-and-the-pentagon-denies-supplying-it/.
3   Author Interview, Person Familiar with Raqqa Planning, Philadelphia, PA, July 25, 2020.
4   Author Interview, Member of the Task Force, Philadelphia, PA, July 26, 2020.
5   Author Interview, United States Air Force Weapons Systems Officer, Philadelphia, PA, August 17, 2017.
6   Author Interview, A-10 Pilot, Philadelphia, PA, May 15, 2020.
7   Author Interview, F-15E Pilot, Philadelphia, PA, August 2017.
8   Author Interview, A-10 Pilot, Philadelphia, PA, May 15, 2020.
9   Author Interview, F-15E Pilot, Philadelphia, PA, May 18, 2020.
10 Author Interview, A-10 Pilot, Philadelphia, PA, May 15, 2020.

11 Author Interview, A-10 Pilot, Philadelphia, PA, May 19, 2020.
12 Author Interview, F-15E Weapons Systems Officer, Washington, DC, July 17, 2017.
13 Author Interview, F-15E Pilot, Washington DC, August 2017.
14 Author Interview, US Air Force Pilot, Philadelphia, PA, June 23, 2020.
15 Lara Seligman, "How U.S. Mission Creep in Syria and Iraq Could Trigger War With Iran," *Foreign Policy*, February 4, 2019, https://foreignpolicy.com/2019/02/04/how-u-s-mission-creep-in-syria-and-iraq-could-trigger-war-with-iran/.
16 Author Interview, Department of Defense Official, Washington, DC, June 2017.
17 Author Interview, State Department Official, Washington, DC, January 2019.
18 Ibid.
19 Author Interview, US Air Force Pilot, June 23, 2020, Philadelphia, PA.
20 Ibid.
21 Author Interview, US Air Force Pilot, Washington, DC, July 2017.
22 Author Interview, Pilot Familiar with the Battle over Tanf, Philadelphia, PA, May 18, 2020.
23 Author Interview, US Air Force Official Involved in Planning for the Defense of Tanf, Philadelphia, PA, May 17, 2020.
24 Author Interview, F-22 Pilot, Philadelphia, PA, June 23, 2002.
25 Author Interview, State Department Official, Washington, DC, October 2017.
26 Tyler Rogoway, "Here's The Definitive Account Of The Syrian Su-22 Shoot Down From The Pilots Themselves," The Drive, September 14, 2017, https://www.thedrive.com/the-war-zone/14344/heres-the-definitive-account-of-the-syrian-su-22-shoot-down-from-the-pilots-themselves.
27 Author Interview, F-15E WSO, Philadelphia, PA, June 2020.
28 Author Interview, Coalition Pilot, Washington, DC, September 3, 2017.
29 Author Interview, Retired US Military Official, Philadelphia, PA, April 14, 2020.
30 Ibid.
31 Author Interview State Department Official, Washington, DC, September 22, 2017.
32 Author Interview, United States Air Force Pilot, Washington, DC, September 30, 2017.
33 Author Interview, Former Department of Defense Official, Philadelphia, PA, April 4, 2020.
34 Ibid.
35 Author Interview, US Air Force Pilot, Philadelphia, PA, June 23, 2020.
36 Author Interview, F-15E Pilot, Philadelphia, PA, June 21, 2020.
37 Author Interview, A-10 Pilot, Philadelphia, PA, May 19, 2020.
38 Author Interview, State Department Official, Philadelphia, PA, July 28, 2020.
39 Author Interview, Senior State Department Official, Philadelphia, PA, May 22, 2020.
40 Author Interview, State Department Official, Philadelphia, PA, July 28, 2020.
41 Author Interview, State Department Official, Washington, DC, July 2017.
42 Ibid.
43 Author Interview, US Government Official Affiliated with the Task Force, Philadelphia, PA, August 5, 2020.

Chapter 8

1 Greg Jaffe and Ada Entous, "Trump Ends Covert CIA Program to Arm Anti-Assad Rebels in Syria, a Move Sought by Moscow," *The Washington Post*, July 19, 2017, https://www.washingtonpost.com/world/national-security/trump-ends-covert-cia-

program-to-arm-anti-assad-rebels-in-syria-a-move-sought-by-moscow/2017/07/19/
   b6821a62-6beb-11e7-96ab-5f38140b38cc_story.html.
2   Author Interview, US Government Official, Philadelphia, PA, August 26, 2020.
3   Author Interview, Senior US Government Official, Philadelphia, PA, July 31, 2020.
4   Carol Morello, "Tillerson Says Investment in Iraq is Critical to Avoid Islamic State's
   Return," *The Washington Post*, February 13, 2018, https://www.washingtonpost.com/
   world/national-security/tillerson-says-the-fight-against-the-islamic-state-is-far-from-
   over/2018/02/13/63876bfe-ea12-4cf9-83e2-ccde2dee07a4_story.html.
5   Author Interview, Senior US Government Official, Philadelphia, PA, August 9, 2020.
6   Author Interview, US Government Official, Philadelphia, PA, July 10, 2020.
7   Author Interview, Former US Government Official, Philadelphia, PA, May 8, 2020.
8   Paul Sonne and Karen DeYoung, "Trump Wants to Get the U.S. Out of Syria's War,
   so He Asked the Saudi King for $4 Billion," *The Washington Post*, March 16, 2018,
   https://www.washingtonpost.com/world/national-security/trump-wants-to-get-the-
   us-out-of-syrias-war-so-he-asked-the-saudi-king-for-4billion/2018/03/16/756bac90-
   2870-11e8-bc72-077aa4dab9ef_story.html.
9   Author Interview, US Government Official, Philadelphia, PA, August 11, 2020.
10 Author Interview, US State Department Official, Philadelphia, PA, October 5, 2017.
11 Author Interview, US Military Official, Philadelphia, PA, August 13, 2020.
12 Phil McCausland, "Tillerson Again Refuses to Answer Whether He Called Trump a
   'Moron'," *NBC News*, October 15, 2017, https://www.nbcnews.com/politics/politics-
   news/tillerson-again-refuses-answer-if-he-called-trump-moron-n810806.
13 Ryan Browne and Barbara Starr, "Trump says US will withdraw from Syria 'very
   soon'," *CNN*, March 29, 2018, https://www.cnn.com/2018/03/29/politics/trump-
   withdraw-syria-pentagon/index.html.
14 Author Interview, Former US Government Official, Philadelphia, PA, May 8, 2020.
15 Author Interview, US Official familiar with the NSC meeting, Philadelphia, PA,
   August 10, 2020.
16 Author Interview, US Official Familiar with the National Security Council Meeting,
   Philadelphia, PA, July 30, 2020.
17 Author Interview, State Department Official, Philadelphia, PA, August 10, 2020.
18 Author Interview, State Department Official, Philadelphia, PA, May 8, 2020.
19 Author Interview, Former US Government Official, Philadelphia, PA, May 8, 2020.
20 Author Interview, State Department Official, Philadelphia, PA, August 13, 2020.
21 Author Interview, State Department Official, Philadelphia, PA, August 11, 2020.
22 Michael R. Gordon, "U.S. Seeks Arab Force and Funding for Syria," *The Wall Street
   Journal*, April 16, 2018, https://www.wsj.com/articles/u-s-seeks-arab-force-and-
   funding-for-syria-1523927888.
23 Author Interview, State Department Official, Philadelphia, PA, August 11, 2020.
24 Joanne Stocker, "Coalition Retraining 15,000 veteran SDF Fighters to Serve as Syrian
   Border Force," *The Defense Post*, January 13, 2018, https://www.thedefensepost.
   com/2018/01/13/syria-border-security-force-sdf-coalition/.
25 Patrick Wintour, "Erdoğan Accuses US of planning to form 'terror army' in Syria,"
   The Guardian, January 15, 2018, https://www.theguardian.com/world/2018/jan/15/
   turkey-condemns-us-plan for-syrian-border-security-force.
26 Author Interview, State Department Official, Philadelphia, PA, August 13, 2020.
27 Can Kasapoglu and Sinan Ulgen, "Operation Olive Branch: A Political Military
   Assessment," Center for Economic and Foreign Policy Studies, January 30, 2018,
   https://edam.org.tr/en/operation-olive-branch-a-political-military-assessment/.

28 Author Interview, European Embassy Official, Washington, DC, January 20, 2018.

29 Ibid.

30 Author Interview, Senior US government Official, Philadelphia, PA, May 14, 2020.

31 Author Interview, US Military Official, Philadelphia, PA, May 17, 2020.

32 Author Interview, Senior US Official, Philadelphia, PA, February 25, 2018.

33 Author Interview, US Air Force Official, Philadelphia, PA, February 5, 2020.

34 Author Interview, Embassy Official in Ankara, February 21, 2018.

35 Author Interview, State Department Official, Washington, DC, April 1, 2018.

36 Author Interview, Former National Security Council Official, Philadelphia, PA, July 17, 2020.

37 Ece Toksabay and Mehmet Emin Caliskan, "Erdogan Says Turkey May Extend Afrin Campaign Along Whole Syrian Border," *Reuters*, March 19, 2018, https://www.reuters.com/article/us-mideast-crisis-syria-afrin-turkey/erdogan-says-turkey-may-extend-afrin-campaign-along-whole-syrian-border-idUSKBN1GV14U.

38 "Kazan Soda Elektrik Üretim Tesisi Açılış Töreni," *Milliyet*, January 15, 2018, https://www.milliyet.com.tr/yerel-haberler/ankara/kazan-soda-elektrik-uretim-tesisi-acilis-toreni-12532430.

39 Rod Nordland, "On Northern Syria Front Line, U.S. and Turkey Head Into Tense Face-off," *New York Times*, February 7, 2018, https://www.nytimes.com/2018/02/07/world/middleeast/us-turkey-manbij-kurds.html.

40 Author Interview, Task Force Member, Philadelphia, PA, August 19, 2020.

41 Ibid.

42 Author Interview, State Department Official, Washington, DC, February 15, 2018.

43 Author Interview, State Department Official, Washington, DC, February 18, 2018.

44 Author Interview, US Government Official, Philadelphia, PA, August 20, 2020.

45 Author Interview, US Government Official, Philadelphia, PA, August 21, 2020.

46 Author Interview, State Department Official, Philadelphia, PA, May 11, 2020.

47 Author Interview, US Government Official, Philadelphia, PA, August 20, 2020.

48 Author Interview, US Government Official, Philadelphia, PA, May 5, 2020.

49 Author Interview, US Government Official, Philadelphia, PA, August 22, 2020.

50 Author Interview, State Department Official, Washington, DC, July 2018.

51 Author Interview, State Department Official, Washington, DC, August 22, 2018.

52 Author Interview, State Department Official, Washington, DC, December 14, 2018.

53 Senior State Department Officials on the U.S.-Turkish Working Group on Syria, US Department of State, June 5, 2018, https://www.state.gov/senior-state-department-officials-on-the-u-s-turkish-working-group-on-syria/.

54 Author Interview, State Department Official, Washington, DC, June 8, 2018.

55 Author Interview, US Special Forces Officer, Philadelphia, PA, August 25, 2020.

56 Author Interview, US Special Forces Officer, Philadelphia, PA, August 26, 2020.

57 Author Interview, State Department Official, Washington, DC, November 2, 2018.

58 Author Interview, US Special Forces Officer, Washington, DC, November 3, 2018.

59 Author Interview, State Department Official, Washington, DC, December 4, 2018.

60 Author Interview, US Special Forces Officer, Washington, DC, December 4, 2018.

61 Author Interview, Senior US Official, Philadelphia, PA, May 22, 2020.

62 Nicholas Sakelaris, "Erdogan: Turkey Planning Military Operation to 'wipe out' Syria Terrorists," *United Press International*, December 12, 2018, https://www.upi.com/Top_News/World-News/2018/12/12/Erdogan-Turkey-planning-military-operation-to-wipe-out-Syria-terrorists/3411544637068/?rc_fifo=3&ur3=1.

63 Author Interview, State Department Official, Washington, DC, December 14, 2018.

64 Karen DeYoung, Missy Ryan, Josh Dawsey, and Gregg Jaffe, "A Tumultuous Week Began with a Phone Call between Trump and the Turkish president," *The Washington Post*, December 21, 2018, https://www.washingtonpost.com/world/national-security/ a-tumultuous-week-began-with-a-phone-call-between-trump-and-the-turkish-president/2018/12/21/8f49b562-0542-11e9-9122-82e98f91ee6f_story.html.

65 Author Interview, US Government Official, Washington, DC, December 16, 2018.

66 Author Interview, US Government Official, Philadelphia, PA, August 27, 2020.

67 Author Interview, US Government Official, Washington, DC, December 23, 2018.

68 Author Interview, US Government Official, Washington, DC, December 24, 2018.

69 Author Interview, US Government Official, Washington, DC, January 8, 2018.

70 Author Interview, US Army Officer, Philadelphia, PA, April 17, 2020.

71 Author, United States Air Force Official, Philadelphia, PA, August 16, 2020.

72 Author Interview, Person Familiar with the JASSM Strikes, Philadelphia, PA, August 15, 2020.

73 Author Interview, US Military Official, Philadelphia, PA, July 28, 2020.

74 Author Interview, Official Familiar with the Wagner Incident, Philadelphia, PA, August 12, 2020.

75 Author Interview, United States Air Force Official, Washington, DC, January 12, 2019.

76 Author Interview, Official Familiar with the Wagner Incident, Philadelphia, PA, August 12, 2020.

77 Thomas Gibbon-Neff, "How a 4-Hour Battle between Russian Mercenaries and U.S. Commandos Unfolded in Syria," *New York Times*, May 24, 2018, https://www.nytimes.com/2018/05/24/world/middleeast/american-commandos-russian-mercenaries-syria.html.

Chapter 9

1 Author Interview, US Official Familiar with the Baghouz Battle, Philadelphia, PA, September 1, 2020.

2 Author Interview, Person Involved in the Baghouz Operation, Philadelphia, PA, September 4, 2020.

3 Author Interview, Person Familiar with the Task Force role in prison management, Philadelphia, PA, September 1, 2020.

4 Author Interview, US Official Familiar with the Baghouz Operation, Philadelphia, PA, September 1, 2020.

5 Author Interview, Person Involved in the Baghouz Operation, Philadelphia, PA, September 4, 2020.

6 Author Interview, Official Involved in the Baghouz Battle, Philadelphia, PA, September 5, 2020.

7 Author Interview, Person Familiar with the Task Force Role in Prison Management, Philadelphia, PA, September 1, 2020.

8 *Ibid.*

9 Author Interview, Former US Government Official, Philadelphia, PA, September 4, 2020.

10 Author Interview, Official Familiar with Prison Management, Philadelphia, PA, August 30, 2020.

11 Author Interview, US Government Official, Philadelphia, PA, September 7, 2020.

12 Author Interview, US Government Official, Washington, DC, January 2019.
13 Author Interview, US Government Official, Washington, DC, February 7, 2019.
14 Author Interview, Senior US Government Official, Philadelphia, PA, May 22, 2020.
15 Author Interview, Official Familiar with the Safe Zone Task Force, Philadelphia, PA, September 7, 2020.
16 Author Interview, Person Familiar with the Safe Zone Task Force Meetings, Washington, DC, February 15, 2019.
17 "Turkey Will Enter Area East of Euphrates, Notified US, Russia, Erdoğan Says," *Daily Sabah*, August 4, 2019, https://www.dailysabah.com/war-on-terror/2019/08/04/turkey-will-enter-area-east-of-euphrates-notified-us-russia-erdogan-says
18 Author Interview, Person Familiar with the Safe Zone Task Force Meetings, Philadelphia, PA, September 7, 2020.
19 Ibid.
20 Author Interview, Person Involved in the Negotiations with Turkey, Washington, DC, August 10, 2019.
21 Author Interview, Senior US government Official, Washington, DC, September 22, 2019.
22 Author Interview, Person Involved in the Negotiations with Turkey, Washington, DC, September 10, 2019.
23 Author Interview, Official Involved in Planning the Joint Patrols, Washington, DC, September 8, 2019.
24 Author Interview, US Military Official, Washington, DC, September 23, 2019.
25 Author Interview, US Military Official, Washington, DC, September 15, 2019.
26 Author Interview, US Military Official, Washington, DC, September 24, 2019.
27 Ibid.
28 Author Interview, Department of Defense Official, Washington, DC, October 5, 2019.
29 Author Interview, Person Familiar with Trump's Phone Call with Erdogan, Washington, DC, December 2018.
30 Author Interview, US Air Force Pilot, Philadelphia, PA, April 27, 2020.
31 Author Interview, US Military Official, Familiar with Operation Peace Spring, Philadelphia, PA, September 12, 2020.
32 Ibid.
33 Aron Lund, "The Factory: A Glimpse into Syria's War Economy," The Century Foundation, February 21, 2019, https://tcf.org/content/report/factory-glimpse-syrias-war-economy/?session=1.
34 Author Interview, Former US Development Official, Philadelphia, PA, May 9, 2020.
35 Author Interview, US Government Official, Philadelphia, PA, May 10, 2020.
36 Author Interview, Person Familiar with the Task Force, Philadelphia, PA, September 12, 2020.
37 Author Interview, US Military Official, Philadelphia, PA, September 28, 2020.
38 Author Interview, State Department Official, Philadelphia, PA, September 13, 2020.
39 Sarah Dadouch, "Grief, Accusations Surround Killing of Kurdish Politician in Northeastern Syria," *The Washington Post*, October 16, 2019, https://www.washingtonpost.com/world/middle_east/grief-accusations-surround-killing-of-kurdish-politician-in-northeastern-syria/2019/10/15/1c21437c-ef55-11e9-bb7e-d2026ee0c199_story.html.
40 Author Interview, US Government Official, Philadelphia, PA, August 31, 2020.
41 Jen Kirby, "The US and Turkey Reached a Syrian Ceasefire. But What Does That Mean?" *Vox*, October 17, 2019, https://www.vox.com/2019/10/17/20919566/turkey-syria-us-ceasefire-erdogan-pence-kurds.

42   Author Interview, State Department Official, Washington, DC, October 28, 2019.
43   "Russia and Turkey Begin Joint Patrols in Northeast Syria," *Al Jazeera*, November 1, 2019, https://www.aljazeera.com/news/2019/11/russia-turkey-joint-patrols-northeast-syria-191101105341261.html.
44   Author Interview, US Government Official, Washington, DC, November 11, 2019.
45   Author Interview, Senior Government Official, Philadelphia, PA, May 22, 2020.
46   Ibid.
47   Maggie Haberman and David E. Sanger, "Transcript: Donald Trump Expounds on His Foreign Policy Views," *The New York Times*, March 26, 2016, https://www.nytimes.com/2016/03/27/us/politics/donald-trump-transcript.html.
48   Author Interview, US Government Official, Philadelphia, PA, September 17, 2020.
49   Author Interview, Special Forces Officer, Washington, DC, October 26, 2019.
50   Allison McCann, Anjali Singhvi, and Weiyi Cai, "See Where the Raid on al-Baghdadi Took Place in Syria," *The New York Times*, October 27, 2019, https://www.nytimes.com/interactive/2019/10/27/world/middleeast/baghdadi-isis-leader-maps.html.
51   Author Interview, Person Familiar with the Task Force, Philadelphia, PA, August 31, 2020.
52   Author Interview, US Government Official, Philadelphia, PA, September 12, 2020.
53   "Remarks by President Trump on the Death of ISIS Leader Abu Bakr al-Baghdadi," The White House, October 27, 2019, https://www.whitehouse.gov/briefings-statements/remarks-president-trump-death-isis-leader-abu-bakr-al-baghdadi/.
54   Author Interview, US Government Official, Washington, DC, February 11, 2020.
55   Author Interview, US Government Official, Philadelphia, PA, September 15, 2020.
56   Ibid.
57   Selcan Hacaoglu, "Turkey Seeks U.S. Patriot Missiles to Deter Russia in Syria," *Bloomberg*, February 20, 2020, https://www.bloomberg.com/news/articles/2020-02-20/turkey-asks-u-s-for-patriot-missiles-to-deter-russia-in-idlib.
58   Author Interview, US Military Official, Washington, DC, February 24, 2020.
59   Author Interview, US Government Official, Philadelphia, PA, November 9, 2020.

Conclusion

1   Author Interview, Senior Obama Administration Official, Washington, DC, June 2016.
2   Author Interview, US Government Official, Philadelphia, PA, March 1, 2018.

BIBLIOGRAPHY

Aaron Stein, Turkey's New Foreign Policy: Davutoglu, the AKP, and the Pursuit of Regional Order (London: Routledge, 2014).

Aliza Marcus, *Blood and Belief: The PKK and the Kurdish Fight for Independence* (New York: New York University Press, 2007).

Becca Wasser, et al., *The Air War against the Islamic State: The Role of Airpower in Operation Inherent Resolve* (Santa Monica: Rand, 2021).

Benjamin Lambeth, *Airpower Against Terror: America's Conduct of Operation Enduring Freedom* (Santa Monica: Rand Corp., 2005).

Benjamin S. Lambeth, *Air Operations in Israel's War Against Hezbollah: Learning from Lebanon and Getting It Right in Gaza* (Santa Monica: Rand Corp, 2011).

Benjamin S. Lambeth, *Airpower against ISIS* (Annapolis: Naval Institute Press, 2021).

Bob Woodward, *Bush at War* (New York: Simon and Schuster, 2002).

Brian Fishman, *The Master Plan: ISIS, Al-Qaeda, and the Jihadi Strategy for Final Victory* (New Haven: Yale University Press, 2016).

Carter Malkasian, *Illusions of Victory: The Anbar Awakening and the Rise of the Islamic State* (Oxford: Oxford University Press, 2017).

Dmitri Trenin, *What Is Russia up to in the Middle East* (Cambridge: Polity Press, 2018).

Haroro J. Ingram, Craig Whiteside, and Charlie Winter, *The ISIS Reader: Milestone Texts of the Islamic State Movement* (Oxford: Oxford University Press, 2020).

Harriet Allsopp and Wladimir Van Wilgenburg, *The Kurds of Northern Syria: Governance, Diversity, and Conflicts* (London: I.B. Tauris, 2019).

James Dobbins, et al., *Occupying Iraq: A History of the Coalition Provincial Authority* (Santa Monica: Rand Corp, 2009)

Joel D. Rayburn, et al., *The U.S. Army in the Iraq War: Invasion, Insurgency, and Civil War*, Volume 1 (Carlisle: U.S. Army War College Press, 2019).

Linda Robinson, *Masters of Chaos: The Secret History of the Special Forces* (New York: Public Affairs, 2009).

Patrick B. Johnston, et al., *Foundations of the Islamic State: Management, Money, and Terror in Iraq, 2005–2010* (Santa Monica: Rand Corp, 2016).

Samer N. Abboud, *Syria* (Malden: Polity Press, 2016).

Sanu Kainikara, *In the Bear's Shadow: Russian Intervention in Syria* (Canberra: Air Power Development Centre, 2018).

Sean Naylor, *Relentless Strike: The Secret History of Joint Special Operations Command* (New York: Saint Martin's Press, 2015).

William McCants, *The ISIS Apocalypse: The History, Strategy, and Doomsday vision of the Islamic State* (New York: St. Martin's Press, 2015).

INDEX